SOCIAL WORK IN CANADA

An Introduction

SECOND EDITION

Education either functions as an instrument which is used to facilitate the integration of generations into the logic of the present system and bring about conformity to it, or it becomes "the practice of freedom," the means by which men and women deal critically and creatively with reality and discover how to participate in the transformation of their world.

— Paulo Freire, *Pedagogy of the Oppressed*

About the Author

Steven Hick is an associate professor in the School of Social Work at Carleton University. His published works include *Social Work: A Critical Turn* (2005), *Social Welfare in Canada: Understanding Income Security* (2004), *Advocacy and Activism on the Internet: Community Organization and Social Policy* (2002, lead author), *Human Rights and the Internet* (2000), *Land Our Life: A Study of the Struggle for Agrarian Reform in the Philippines* (1987), and numerous journal articles and studies on social work, social policy and human rights. He is a co-founder of War Child Canada, which seeks to aid children affected by war. He has practised social work in Canada and abroad as a human rights worker, social service worker and social policy analyst. His teaching of introductory social work on the instructional television (ITV) and on the Internet has won him a teaching award and numerous accolades.

SOCIAL WORK IN CANADA

An Introduction

SECOND EDITION

STEVEN HICK

Carleton University

THOMPSON EDUCATIONAL PUBLISHING, INC.

TORONTO

Information on how to obtain copies of this book may be obtained from:

Website:	http://www.thompsonbooks.com
E-mail:	publisher@thompsonbooks.com
Telephone:	(416) 766–2763
Fax:	(416) 766–0398

Library and Archives Canada Cataloguing in Publication

Hick, Steven F.
  Social work in Canada : an introduction / Steven Hick. — 2nd ed.

Includes bibliographical references and index.
ISBN-10   1–55077–157–4
ISBN-13   978–1–55077–157–2

  1. Social service — Canada — Textbooks. I. Title.

HV105.H525 2005   361.3'0971   C2005–902251–5

Credits:

Cover illustration:	Courtesy of Esme Nichola Shilletto, Nelson, British Columbia. Adapted with permission of the Canadian Association of Social Workers.
Copy Editing:	Elizabeth Phinney.
Cover Design:	Elan Designs.
Page Asembly:	Peter M.Thompson
Photo Research:	Jane Affleck.
Photo Credits:	Credits are provided with each photograph. Health Canada photos are provided courtesy of the Health Canada website and Media Photo Gallery, Health Canada: http://www.hc-sc.gc.ca. Reproduced with the permission of the Minister of Public Works and Government Services Canada, 2005.
Permissions:	Jane Affleck.
Proofreading:	Colborne Communications, Toronto.

We acknowledge the support of the Government of Canada through the Book Publishing Industry Development Program for our publishing activities.

Printed in Canada.
1 2 3 4 5   09 08 07 06 05

Contents

Preface to the Second Edition

Since the publication of this first edition of this textbook, there have been several excellent books that have advanced the teaching of social work in Canada . However, I still believe that this book fills a need for an introductory-level book written from a truly Canadian perspective. It is especially addressed to students who are new to social work and may be considering a career in the field. Unlike many foreign texts, which tend to emphasize techniques, this book emphasizes the importance of being clear about one's values and world view before practising social work.

Important developments have occurred since the first edition of this book was published and new data has also come to light. Accordingly, the chapters have been updated with this new data and the new information relevant to each chapter. In addition, this second edition contains a completely new chapter that deals with social work with the elderly (Chapter 11). Also, two of the original chapters (Chapter 12 on sexual diversity and Chapter 13 on disabilities) have been completely rewritten for this second edition.

We are grateful for several anonymous reviewers who took the time to go though the first edition carefully and offer suggestions for improvement. And, of course, we are particularly grateful for the many faculty members across the country, and their students, who have used the book in their courses and have thereby encouraged us to pursue this new edition. Further suggestions for improvement are always welcome and will be incorporated in future editions.

Social work is a complex field and this book does not pretend to provide an easy "ten-step" recipe that students can simply apply to any particular problem. Instead, the book presents a variety of viewpoints and approaches, all of which have something useful to offer when determining an appropriate course of action to rectify a problem. Throughout the text, there is emphasis on the need for students to think deeply about issues, particularly controversial ones, before arriving at a course of action. The author feels, above all, that practitioners should possess a broad knowledge and a multifaceted outlook, and always be open to new ideas.

Steven Hick
Carleton University

The Raging Grannies protest during a rally to mark National Medicare Day (May 15, 2002) at a park in Peterborough, Ontario, to demonstrate that senior citizens feel the pressure of living on a fixed income while experiencing increased health problems.

Acknowledgments

This book began with discussions between myself and Allan Moscovitch while teaching an introductory social work course at Carleton University. Allan, in particular, played an important role in initiating the work on this book and provided invaluable guidance in its preparation. The book went through several stops and was re-started when Keith Thompson at Thompson Educational Publishing encouraged its completion.

From the beginning, the intention was to give a voice to people from the communities or groups in society who are directly in the field. A special thanks to Gordon Bruyere for his contribution to the history section of the chapter on Aboriginal peoples; to Shirley Judge for her guidance on the examples in the chapter on social work with women; to Bernice Moreau for the advice on the section dealing with the history of Black Canadians; and for the hard work of Emily Cronin, Kate Belcher, Andrea Johnson, and Andria Samis, graduate students who made the instructor's manual a possibility. Special thanks also to Roy Hanes for his chapter on disability, to Sarah Todd for the chapter on sexual diversity, and to Reva Gutnick for her work on Chapter 2 in the first edition.

Once again, I must express my deep-felt thanks to my family — Vaida, my partner, Justin, my son, and Kristina, my daughter — not only for bearing with me but also for encouraging my work on the book through their support and lively dinner conversations.

Finally, and once again, a special thanks to Allan Moscovitch, who initiated the project with me and laid much of the groundwork, and to Keith Thompson, for his tireless support.

CP PHOTO/Maclean's–Gerard Kwiatkowski.

Social work student Jodi Arnold volunteered twelve hours a week with the Winnipeg Police Victim Service Unit and counselled at-risk youths. The previous spring, she won the Manitoba Premier's volunteer service award for her dedication to social work.

I

The Canadian Welfare State Today

Introduction

One hundred years ago private charity was the main recourse for persons in distress (and even then for only a small part of the population). Today, however, public (government-run or government-funded) social programs and services are widespread and affect nearly every Canadian at some point in his or her life. Nevertheless, while the social services are commonplace, Canadians in general are not well aware of the history of social work in their country or the role it plays in our daily lives.

This book is an effort to redress that imbalance. We hope that you, with the aid of this textbook, will become familiar with the key concepts and issues in social work practice in Canada.

The work that social workers do is not always valued and respected by Canadians, nor even sometimes by the people social workers work with. Yet, every Canadian is eventually touched by a social worker at some point in their life, whether while in hospital or through a child welfare agency, community centre or income security agency.

What Is Welfare?

While this book focuses on social work and the provision of social services, it is important to understand that social services are part of a range of activities that fall more generally under the term **social welfare**. Social welfare includes not only the **social services** proper (the provision of personal or community services to help people improve their well-being — including child care, child protection services, women's shelters, counselling and so forth) but also a range of **income security** provisions — Employment Insurance, Social Assistance, Old Age Security, Workers' Compensation — that provide monetary or other material benefits to supplement income or maintain minimum income levels. Taken together, social services and income security comprise what is known, loosely, as social welfare.

The distinction between social services and income security is an important one, but, in real life, it is difficult to maintain. This is often a source of confusion for beginning social workers because, frequently, difficulties come in pairs or in even more complex combinations. For example, a man who becomes ill or has an accident may also lose his job and, as a result, his home. A woman who is subjected to violence may be forced to leave her home and may need assistance in obtaining child support as well as personal income support. A man with an addiction

Social worker Joe Hooper works with BC teens.

**TWO COMPONENTS OF
SOCIAL WELFARE**

• Social services — personal or
  community services provided
  to help individuals and families
  improve their social well-being.
• Income security — financial or
  material assistance provided to
  increase the income or other
  resources of individuals and
  families.

Chapter 2 provides an overview
of the income security system.
The remainder of the chapters
focus on social work and the
social services proper.

may lose his employment and is at risk of becoming homeless, or ending up in the prison system and/or the mental health system. Thus, social services are often needed to deal with problems that have their roots in economic insecurity and vice versa.

This book deals primarily with the social services and the practice of social work; it does not cover in any depth the complex income security programs in Canada that provide monetary assistance to individuals and families. However, because a basic understanding of the income security system is necessary for effective social work practice, the second chapter in this book provides a quick overview of this vast field. A companion volume to this one (*Social Welfare in Canada: Understanding Income Security*) more fully examines the income security field.

The Welfare State

The range of programs and services available to Canadian citizens is commonly referred to as the welfare state. The **welfare state** could be defined as a system whereby the state undertakes to protect the health and well-being of its citizens, especially those in social and financial need. The key elements of the welfare state are the use of state power (government, bureaucracy, the judiciary, political parties) to achieve the desired ends; altering the normal operation of the private marketplace; and the use of grants, taxes, pensions, social services and minimum-income programs, such as welfare and social insurance.

The basic goal of our social welfare system is simple: to help people through difficult times until they can rebuild their lives. This involvement may sometimes be over the long term, as, for example, when a person has a physical or psychiatric disability or a continuing illness or lacks the skills required by the labour market and requires ongoing help. The kinds of difficulties that may arise for individuals and their families are varied. Retirement, unemployment, decreasing income and rising prices are examples of contingencies that affect *economic survival*. Disability, illness, violence, homelessness, addiction, racism, warfare and death are examples of contingencies that affect *the integrity of the person*. Separation, divorce, the ageing of family members and additional children are events that threaten the *survival of the family*.

In Canada today, the state's involvement in the welfare of individuals and families can be quite extensive, particularly if an individual or family is in a period of difficulty. Yet, the role of the state in such situations is still quite controversial — some people reject the idea that the state has any role to play and others want to see the state take a bigger role in redressing social imbalances and improving the lives of those who are experiencing difficult times. As we will see over the course of this text, these debates over the proper role of social welfare are far-reaching and can be heated at times. In sorting through all this for oneself, as a newcomer to the field, a cool head is a useful asset.

• Social Policies and Social Programs

As mentioned, welfare services are very extensive throughout Canada. They are provided to citizens through social policies developed by the various levels of government and they are delivered by means of specific social programs that are designed to carry out these social policies.

- **Social policies** are the overall rules and regulations, laws and other administrative directives that set the framework for state social welfare activity. For example, universal medicare is a social policy to which the Government of Canada is committed.

- **Social programs** are specific initiatives that follow on from and implement social welfare policies. Continuing with the medicare example, there are special incentives (programs) to encourage newly accredited physicians to move to outlying areas, thus ensuring greater equality of access to medical services (in line with the commitment to universal medicare for Canadians).

The network of laws, policies and programs currently in place around the country is vast. It is through such devices that the Canadian state creates opportunities for individuals experiencing difficulties in their lives and helps them get back on their feet. This **social safety net** gives Canadians a greater sense of security — and, many would say, a greater sense of belonging. In countries where the social safety net is weak or non-existent, there is little or no protection of this kind and individuals are often left to fend for themselves.

Ontario Archives, 10005419.

Homeless men sleep outside in Toronto during the late 1930s. The Great Depression was a global economic slump that began in 1929 and "bottomed out" in 1933. The remainder of the 1930s was spent recovering from the severity of the economic contraction.

HOMELESS WOMEN IN TORONTO

Homeless people are at a higher risk of illness and have higher death rates than the general population, according to a 2004 study by Angela Cheung and Stephen Hwang released in the *Canadian Medical Association Journal*.

The research followed 1,981 Toronto women not accompanied by dependent children who used homeless shelters in Toronto in 1995. They found that homeless women 18–44 years of age were 10 times more likely to die than women in the general population of Toronto. HIV/AIDS and drug overdose are the most common causes of death in these women.

———

Source: Canadian Medical Association Journal (April 13, 2004). Available on-line at: http://www.cmaj.ca

The Provision of Social Welfare

There are several types of welfare services available to Canadians. An important distinction is between public programs on the one hand and private programs on the other.

Because Canada is a federal state, **public welfare** occurs at the three levels of government: the federal or national government, the provincial and territorial governments and the regional and municipal governments. As well, there are public non-government agencies, such as advisory and appeal boards, which are the creations of government (whether federal, provincial or municipal) but which consist of members who are appointed from the public by government. The government is ultimately responsible for their activities, but they are either completely independent or semi-independent.

There is also **private welfare**. Here we should distinguish between two types of organizations: private non-profit and private for-profit.

- *Non-profit organizations* are mandated to provide a service or an activity but not to create a profit. In Canada, such organizations are often registered by law, and rules and regulations govern what steps must be taken if a profit is generated. Many of these agencies are incorporated as non-profit corporations; they receive funds from one or more levels of government and from private sources. At the same time, they can earn money by providing services for other organizations. Take the example of the Children's Aid Societies in Ontario. They receive their principal funding from the provincial government of Ontario, they are registered as non-profit organizations, they have boards of directors composed of private citizens who are elected annually, and they also receive funds from private organizations or individuals.

- *For-profit organizations*, on the other hand, are prevalent in certain social service areas, such as nursing homes, home care and child care. These organizations provide services that are often purchased by government on behalf of individuals, but their purpose is to generate a profit for the owner of the organization. With government cutbacks in recent years, more and more welfare services are being provided by non-profit and for-profit private agencies.

All three organizations — public, private non-profit and commercial — are part of the structure of social services in the Canadian welfare state. (Another important source of funding for income security and social services in Canada, not covered in this text, is industrial welfare. Industrial welfare is available through employment and provides everything from dental and optical plans to legal aid services and pension plans. Only people employed by companies offering these services can access these benefits.)

• Disputes about Social Welfare

For most people, the idea of providing social services to citizens in need is no longer a controversial one in Canada. Major disputes do arise, however, in determining which groups are genuinely in need and to what extent they need state assistance.

Generally, there are two such approaches. These are sometimes referred to as the "residual view" and the "institutional view."

- In the **residual view**, social welfare is a limited and temporary response to human need, implemented only when all else fails. It is based on the premise that there are two natural ways through which an individual's needs are met — the family and the market economy. The residual model is based on the idea that government should play only a limited role in the distribution of social welfare. The state should only step in when these normal sources of support fail, and the individual is unable to help him or herself. Residual social welfare is, therefore, highly targeted to those most in need. Additionally, residual social welfare tends to provide benefits at a low level in order to discourage use and not make social welfare appear desirable. Canadian public social welfare programs, from early history to the Depression of the 1930s, can be characterized as largely residual in nature. Many argue that, with the severe cutbacks to our welfare system and social services, the general drift of government policy over recent years has been towards an even more residual view of the role of social welfare in our lives.

- In the **institutional view**, on the other hand, social welfare is a necessary public response in helping people attain a reasonable standard of life and health. Within this view, it is accepted that people cannot always meet all of their needs through family and work. Therefore it is both proper and legitimate in a complex industrial society for society to help people through a set of publicly funded and organized systems of programs and institutions. The institutional model promotes the principle that all citizens are entitled, as a matter of right and unconditionally, to a decent standard of living, and it is the role of the state to ensure this. The institutional model, then, seeks to even out, rather than promote, stratification or status differences that arise in the market. Advocates of this viewpoint have been in the forefront of campaigns to reverse recent cutbacks to our welfare system.

These views represent different overall approaches to social welfare and capture the political controversy surrounding welfare today. It is useful to think about and understand this distinction, since each gives a different sense of what social welfare is all about and how extensive it should be — and, more particularly, how much government funding social welfare programs should receive.

SOCIAL WORK

The term *social work* has been credited to Jeffery Brackett, who was a Charity Organization Society volunteer in the early 1900s. He argued for the adoption of the term to differentiate between professionals doing social work and the volunteers who helped at various societies as a recreational or volunteer activity. The inclusion of the word "work" was meant to emphasize this distinction.

Government cutbacks have seriously eroded social services.

EMPLOYMENT SETTINGS

"93% of all [social workers] are employed either in the health and social services or government industries, with 74% in the former and 19% in the latter. There is increasing participation ... in health and social services and a corresponding decrease in their presence in government services. This is at least in part a reflection of government withdrawal from the direct provision of social services.

"Relatively few social workers are employed in private practice offices, but the number almost doubled between 1991 and 1996."

Source: CASSW. 2001. *In Critical Demand: Social Work in Canada: Final Report*. Ottawa.
To find out more about this important study, go to:
http://www.socialworkincanada.org

What Do Social Workers Do?

People are often confronted with unforeseen events, such as accidents, illness, incidents of violence and death. People are also faced with economic contingencies, such as unemployment, retirement and homelessness. A whole range of welfare services are available to Canadians to help them deal with such circumstances, and it is within this complex web of social welfare institutions (income security programs and social services) that social workers work or practice.

Those who choose social work as their profession do so for a variety of reasons. In general, they appear to be motivated by a combination of humanitarian and egalitarian values, and by a desire to understand how society works and how to make it better for everyone. Frequently, a person is motivated to become a social worker following exposure to injustice and oppression. Whatever the combination of factors that leads a person into the profession, social work demands more than just the desire to "do good." It requires that the practitioner possess the necessary analytical and hands-on skills that can allow him or her to bring about effective change.

The Canadian Association of Social Workers' *Code of Ethics* (1994; see Appendix A) defines social work practice as including the assessment, remediation and prevention of social problems, and the enhancement of social functioning of individuals, families and communities by means of:

- the provision of direct counselling services within an established relationship between a social worker and client;
- the development, promotion and delivery of human service programs, including that done in collaboration with other professionals; and
- the development and promotion of social policies aimed at improving social conditions and equality.

• Direct and Indirect Social Work

The *Code of Ethics* distinguishes between two types of social work. **Direct social work** involves providing services (such as individual counselling, group work and community development). Most often, social workers who are doing direct social work will be working for public or publicly funded but privately administered social service agencies and institutions. Some social workers also work on their own or in groups in a private practice. The second type, **indirect social work**, also benefits those in need, but usually those who do this type of social work will work directly with governments and non-governmental agencies — formulating, analyzing, developing and evaluating social policies and programs. Others will be involved with social service agencies, advocacy or research groups and organizations whose purpose is to advocate for

Websites

http://www.policyalternatives.ca
http://www.ccsd.ca
http://www.caledoninst.org
http://www.napo-onap.ca

people in need and to conduct research. Examples of such organizations are the Canadian Centre for Policy Alternatives, the Canadian Council on Social Development, the Caledon Institute of Social Policy and the National Anti-Poverty Organization (NAPO).

Using different terminology (but with the similar meaning), the different kinds of practice can also be described as being either "micro," "mezzo" or "macro" social work. "Micro social work" refers to direct practice with individuals. "Mezzo social work" is social work with groups and communities. Finally, "macro social work" involves working with organizations or communities to improve or change laws or policies in general society.

Whether involved directly with citizens or indirectly in research, social workers are above all committed to serving people in need. They are there when circumstances go wrong and people need help. As professionals, social workers approach difficult situations with compassion and a skill set that can help people overcome obstacles and get people back on track with their lives. The traditional notion of the social worker has been that of a caseworker — a practitioner doing one-on-one counselling with individuals, usually working as part of a social service agency. However, the idea of social work has now broadened somewhat as practising social workers have come to realize that their roles are more complex. Today, social work involves not only attending to individual problems but also changing the social environment and empowering people to improve their situations.

• Approaches to Practice

In this book, the criterion used for distinguishing the different approaches to social work practice is where, primarily, the social worker locates the cause of the particular problem at hand. At one end are approaches that emphasize the personal (or internal) factors. At the other are theories and approaches that view structural (or external) factors as being dominant. Of course, few problems are organized by either internal or external factors alone.

- *Approaches that locate the problem in the individual.* There are a wide variety of approaches within this category. Some locate the problem in the body (such as in traditional medical practice), while others locate the problem in the mind (for example, psychoanalytic approaches such as Gestalt and Transactional Analysis, cognitive-based theories and behaviour-based theories). These approaches say very little about how to address issues outside of the individual concerned. On the other hand, other theories within this school of thought — such as developmental-based theories, task-centred and problem-solving approaches, and generalist approaches — do take into account the environmental demands and the changes in social systems involved in the problem. In these

SOCIAL WORK VALUES

- Humanitarianism
- Egalitarian ideals
- Self-determination
- Mutual respect and dignity of every person
- Privacy
- Human rights
- Fairness and non-judgmental
- Cooperation

CP PHOTO/Ryan Remiorz.

Mohawk drummers take part in a National Day of Action.

approaches, the purpose is to enhance the coping and problem-solving abilities of the client, link such people to resources, promote access to services and contribute to better social policy.

- *Approaches that locate the problem in social structures.* Approaches within this category give emphasis to the wider social factors influencing a particular problem. These factors may include, for example, social class, poverty, racial discrimination and patriarchal relations. Approaches within this category include structural or critical social work practice, radical casework, and feminist, anti-racist and Aboriginal social work. These approaches vary according to their particular emphasis and clientele, but they are all based on the belief that structural factors have major significance for many types of social work problems.

The two dominant approaches in Canadian social work are discussed at the end of Chapter 5 — "ecological /systems theory" and the "structural" approaches. Other viewpoints (such as "anti-oppressive" and "critical" social work) are variations on the structural approach, often with theoretical influences from postmodern, feminist, Aboriginal and anti-racist approaches to practice.

What is important for the beginning social worker to understand is that there is no single approach that works in every situation. To be effective, the practitioner must be prepared to approach daily practice from all angles and to find the one that works in particular situations. With that overall flexibility, he or she will be able to help clients overcome the particular difficulties they are facing and get their lives back on course. They may also help to bring about wider changes in society.

Health Canada.

Social work professionals work closely with people of different ages, races and genders in order to improve the lives of individuals and families and bring about social change.

Defining Social Work

A new definition of social work was adopted at the General Meeting of the International Federation of Social Workers (IFSW) in Montreal in July 2000 (available on-line at http://www.ifsw.org):

> The social work profession promotes social change, problem solving in human relationships and the empowerment and liberation of people to enhance well-being. Utilizing theories of human behaviour and social systems, social work intervenes at the points where people interact with their environments. Principles of human rights and social justice are fundamental to social work.

This definition is important as it represents a broad-based, international consensus as to what social work is all about. It emphasizes four key concepts: social change, problem solving, person-in-the-environment and empowerment. To begin to understand this complex work it is necessary to explore these four key concepts.

• Social Change Mandate

A **social change mandate** means working in solidarity with those who are disadvantaged or excluded from society so as to eliminate the barriers, inequities and injustices that exist. Social workers should be at the forefront of promoting policies and legislation that redistribute wealth in favour of those who are less well-off — that is, promoting equal opportunity for women, gays, lesbians, bisexuals, transgender persons, people with disabilities, Aboriginal peoples and racial and other minorities, and defending past gains made in these areas.

• Problem Solving

Social workers respond to crises and emergencies as well as everyday personal and social problems. Within this process, social workers use **problem-solving techniques** to identify the problem and formulate possible plans of action. A problem is not usually clearly defined when someone comes to a social service agency. It is therefore crucial for the social worker to explore the person's concerns, to identify the need(s) involved, to identify barriers to meeting need(s) and to carefully determine the goals and possible plans of action. A key characteristic of the problem-solving process is the inclusion of the client at each stage. The process should also teach clients problem-solving skills so that they can better deal with future problems on their own.

• Person-in-the-Environment

A key aspect of effective social work practice is to go beyond the "internal" (psychological) factors and examine the relationship between individuals and their environments. In the context of modern social work, it is this **person-in-the-environment** approach that largely

EMPOWERMENT

Jan Fook, a well-known Australian author and social work practitioner, notes that the notion of empowerment involves analyzing power relationships and recreating situations that correct these power imbalances.

First, she believes that workers should examine how power is exercised and experienced in and around the client's life. Both the controlling aspects and the potential imbalances of power need to be examined.

Armed with this knowledge, Fook maintains that clients can, with the aid of the social worker, then begin to look at ways that might help to eliminate the problems at hand and improve the client's life.

Source: Steven Hick, Jan Fook, Richard Pozzuto. 2005. *Social Work: A Critical Turn*. Toronto: Thompson Educational Publishing.

distinguishes social work practice from other helping professions. These "environments" extend beyond the immediate family and include interactions with friends, neighbourhoods, schools, religious groups, laws and legislation, other agencies or organizations, places of employment and the economic system. Based on this understanding, intervention may focus on the individual, interactions between people and any given system or structure, or on the system or structure itself.

• "Empowerment" and Social Work

In order for the interventions of social workers to be successful, the clients must believe that the efforts of the social worker will make a difference. This leads to the important concept of empowerment. Being empowered means feeling that you have power and control over the course of your life.

Empowerment is the process of increasing personal, interpersonal or political power so that one can improve one's particular situation. Power can be a personal state of mind, in the sense that one feels that one can make a difference and have control and influence over one's own life. It can also be empowerment within an organization in the sense that one has tangible influence and legal rights. Empowerment, then, involves both a personal perception of being in control and tangible elements of power within the various social structures of society. Social workers seek to empower their clients as a way of helping them to focus on, among other things, access to resources and the structures of power.

"Empowerment-based social work," therefore, has three aspects:

- making power explicit in the client-worker relationship (in order thereby to help equalize the relationship between the client and the worker);

- giving clients experiences in which they themselves are in control (to allow them to see the potential for controlling their lives); and

- always supporting the client's own efforts to gain greater control over their lives as a way of promoting change.

Empowerment-based social work involves fostering personal control.

Putting an empowerment perspective into practice can involve techniques that make power relations between the workers and their clients explicit, thereby equalizing the client-worker relationship. Additionally, it may entail giving clients powerful experiences or experiences that put them in a position to exercise power. Offering voluntary work experiences that allow clients to use their skills to help others can often be an empowering experience. Another approach may be to support clients' efforts to change policies or practices that impinge on their lives and the lives of others. Such experiences can help people see the potential for power in their lives.

In other instances, an empowering perspective may involve simply focusing on the strengths of the person, rather than on the "pathology" side (or with what is "wrong" with that person). In all relationships, it is generally acknowledged that constructive feedback and positive reinforcement are conducive to helping people make positive changes in their lives. Clearly, it is more helpful for social workers to guide their clients' focus towards the success they have achieved in the past rather than dwelling on points where they have been less successful.

An empowerment perspective is the key to good social work practice. And like other aspects of good practice, it involves not a specific set of skills, but a general orientation on the part of the worker. This orientation is based on helping clients identify their own needs and then helping them to deal with the exigencies of their own particular situation.

Of all the fundamental techniques available to the social work practitioner, the ability to empower the client is perhaps the most critical and the most useful. The key to getting a person, family or community back on track with their lives is to have them gain some sense that they have control over the difficult situation at hand and that what they do themselves will lead to positive results. Having the skills and know-how to be able to foster such a sense of empowerment in difficult situations is an important part of the social worker's toolkit.

Community empowerment is evident in this march by the Peterborough Coalition Against Poverty in 2004. The marchers were protesting low welfare and disability rates, part of the province-wide "Raise the Rates" campaign.

CP PHOTO/Peterborough Examiner–Clifford Skarstedt.

Conclusion

The complex field known as social welfare includes two major components: income security (or programs that provide financial or material assistance) and social services (which provide personal and community services to help people improve their well-being). This book deals with social services. A companion volume by the same author entitled *Social Welfare in Canada: Understanding Income Security* provides an overview of the income security field.

The social services are provided by a large number of public and private agencies and employ social workers in both direct and indirect social work. Key to comprehending the nature of social work practice are four concepts: social change, problem solving, person-in-the-environment and empowerment. Using these basic concepts, professional social workers carry out their work at the individual, group, community and societal levels.

Politicians, and even the general public, do not agree on the extent to which the state should provide income security or social services to people in need. Yet it is within this uncertainty that social work practitioners face real people with real problems, and increasingly with fewer and fewer resources to do so. To be effective, social workers are more and more using an empowerment process to develop the personal, interpersonal and political power of the people they are helping so that they may gain greater control over their lives and thereby promote change.

Chapter I Review
The Canadian Welfare State Today

Questions for Discussion

1. What are the main components of the social welfare system today in Canada?

2. Define and compare the following terms: (1) social policy and social program, and (2) public welfare and private welfare.

3. Define the different types or levels of social work practice. What is meant by the "residual" and "institutional" approaches to welfare?

4. List and describe the four key concepts contained in the International Federation's definition of social work practice.

5. Define "empowerment" and outline what a social worker could do to put an empowerment perspective into practice.

Websites

• Social Work Glossary
http://www.socialpolicy.ca

This site contains Steven Hick's personal collection of over 600 definitions of social welfare terms. It also includes links to publications and on-line course materials.

• Canadian Council on Social Development (CCSD)
http://www.ccsd.ca

CCSD is one of Canada's most authoritative voices promoting better social and economic security for all Canadians. A national, self-supporting, non-profit organization, the CCSD's main product is information and its main activity is research, focusing on concerns such as income security, employment, poverty, child welfare, pensions and government social policies. Check out the Internet launch pad for a variety of excellent links.

• Canadian Social Research Links
http://www.canadiansocialresearch.net

This is Gilles Séguin's virtual resource centre for Canadian social program information. His purpose in creating and maintaining this site is to provide a comprehensive, current and balanced collection of links to Canadian social program information for those who formulate Canadian social policies and for those who study and critique them.

• Critical Social Work
http://www.criticalsocialwork.com

An on-line journal with articles on how social work can contribute to social justice. In part the goal of Critical Social Work is to assist in collectively recognizing the current potentials for social justice as well as the future possibilities. Theorists propose that through dialogue there exists the possibility of refining our ideas about the individual and community, clarifying the relationship between interpersonal relations and institutional structures, and identifying actions that promote both individual and community well-being.

Key Terms

• **Social welfare**

• **Social services**

• **Income security**

• **Welfare state**

• **Social policies**

• **Social programs**

• **Social safety net**

• **Public welfare**

• **Private welfare**

• **Residual view of social welfare**

• **Institutional view of social welfare**

• **Direct social work**

• **Indirect social work**

• **"Micro," "mezzo" and "macro" social work practice**

• **Caseworker**

• **Social change mandate**

• **Problem-solving techniques**

• **Person-in-the-environment**

• **Empowerment**

A forestry worker during a Newfoundland and Labrador Federation of Labour demonstration at the Revenue Canada Taxation Centre in St. John's. The labour rally was protesting the massive cuts to Unemployment Insurance programs.

2

Income Security and Social Welfare

—

Weighing up the Benefits

There is no question that income security programs are at the core of the welfare state in Canada. However, two myths need to be dispelled. The first is that income security programs are used only by the poor. The reality is that every Canadian over the course of his or her life is a beneficiary of Canada's income security infrastructure, whether it be in the form of a retirement pension, Employment Insurance, Death Benefits, Social Assistance or Family Benefits. The second myth is that income programs serve only to keep the poor from destitution. While it is true that they accomplish this, more or less, they also provide the government with key levers over the economy. In the post-World War II period, social welfare spending played a vital role in the macro management of the Canadian economy and labour force.

The level of commitment to social welfare, in Canada or any other country, is derived from what the members of the society in question value as a society, and what they believe the role of government is in their lives. For example, should the risk of unemployment be shared or should those who fall on bad times be left to fend for themselves? What are the long-term costs to society of letting people spiral into hopelessness? Should we as a society be concerned about the social and personal welfare of others? These are a few of the underlying questions that need to be considered as this chapter attempts to sort through some of these issues.

This chapter focuses on income security in Canada. In addition to detailing the many government programs currently in place, the chapter surveys some of the ideas and debates surrounding income security provisions. It also draws attention to some of the major social issues that the welfare state attempts to address, such as unemployment, poverty and globalization.

Income Security and Social Services

In this text, we try to maintain a distinction between income security and social services. Social services, in our sense of the term, essentially involve providing non-monetary help to persons in need; that is, the work done largely by social workers as outlined in the other chapters of this book. Examples are child welfare (e.g., Children's Aid Societies, which include adoption services and foster care), probation services, addiction treatment services, youth drop-in centres, parent-child resource centres and shelters for abused women.

Seniors protest de-indexing of old age pensions, Ottawa.

By contrast, the income security system has income redistribution or income supplementation as its primary aim. Unlike social services, these programs provide monetary or financial assistance to individuals and families. If all members of a society were able to consistently meet their income needs (through wages from employment, investment income or inheritance), the need for income security programs would be drastically reduced or eliminated. Unfortunately, most people do not have a secure income throughout their lifetime. Without income security programs, all Canadians would be much more vulnerable.

• The Emergence of Income Security

The immediate relief of poverty and of severe destitution sparked the earliest government involvement in social welfare. However, early social welfare was of a residual nature or meant to serve those in need only when all else had failed. Following World War II and the Great Depression of the 1930s and 1940s, a new consensus developed. Citizens of Canada began to recognize that hard times could strike anyone through no personal fault. This new consensus led to the development of a comprehensive set of income security programs.

Income security programs provide monetary support to individuals or families. They are often called transfers because they "transfer" cash and other benefits from government-funded or government-administered programs to individuals or families. Public income security programs fall into the following four broad categories:

- **Social insurance.** These are programs that follow the insurance principle of shared risk. People contribute to insurance plans with the understanding that not everyone will need to access the benefits. Insurance-based programs are generally linked to employment. All workers contribute, and only those who contribute become eligible for benefits, should the need arise. Employment Insurance, Workers' Compensation and the Canada/Quebec Pension Plan are social insurance programs.

- **Minimum income.** These are programs that provide monetary assistance to those with no other source of income. They are primarily geared towards those deemed to be living in poverty, and the quantity of assistance tends to be determined by the minimum amount necessary to meet basic needs. Social Assistance, also called welfare or workfare, is a minimum income program.

- **Demogrants.** These are universal flat-rate payments made to individuals or households on the sole basis of demographic characteristics, such as number of children or age, rather than on the basis of proven need (as in minimum income programs) or contributions (as in social insurance programs). The Old Age Security (OAS) paid to all persons aged 65 and over was a universal program before a clawback was implemented. Now it is considered an income

National Archives of Canada, PA125093.

Unemployment insurance dates back to 1940 in Canada.

supplementation program. The former 1944 Family Allowance program, benefitting all families with children under the age of 18, was Canada's first widespread universal program.

- **Income supplementation.** These are programs that, as the name suggests, supplement income that is obtained elsewhere, whether through paid employment or through other income security programs. They are not intended to be the primary source of income. These programs may have a broad entitlement, in that they may be available to everyone within a very broad category, or they may be targeted to those most in need. The National Child Benefit Supplement (NCBS) and the Guaranteed Income Supplement (GIS) are income supplementation programs.

Government participation in income security covers a broad range: cash benefits for people with disabilities and those recovering from occupational injuries and illness, the elderly, the unemployed, families and survivors. However, the above list of direct government cash benefits does not reflect the entire spectrum of income security expenditure.

First, income security is provided through the tax system when governments provide tax breaks, forego the collection of taxes or when income or benefits are taxed differently. While this is not often thought of as income security, it can dramatically affect the income of Canadians. By not collecting taxes from those who have a taxable income, an individual's income is effectively increased. A personal tax exemption for a single parent with income high enough to be taxed provides income for the parent and a foregoing of tax revenue (a tax expenditure) for the state. When the government provides a tax deduction for Registered Retirement Saving Plans (RRSP), it foregoes collecting taxes, which effectively allows a tax break to those with enough money to put some away towards retirement.

Second, income security can be provided by the private sector — both private employers and the voluntary sector. Some countries, such as Norway, the Netherlands and Denmark, have substantial mandatory employer-paid income security programs. Canada does not. Conversely, Canada has comparatively high amounts (3.5 percent of Gross Domestic Product [GDP]) of voluntary sector income security benefits, outstripping all other developed countries except the United States and the United Kingdom (Adema 1999, 15).

Employment-related policies and legislation can also affect the income of Canadians and therefore should be considered a part of our income security framework. These policies and legislation include labour standards and minimum wage legislation, as well as policies that affect the quantity and distribution of employment and employment equity programs. Employment equity and pay equity legislation attempted to address wage discrimination based on gender, ethnicity and disability.

A Family Allowance Office in Charlottetown, PEI (1940s).

National Archives of Canada, C45315.

Public Income Security Programs

Canada's income security programs are in the newspaper headlines on a daily basis, and the effectiveness and affordability of such programs are frequent topics of discussion. The emphasis is often on the need to cut spending and to reduce the deficit, but the host of benefits that these programs bring to families, society and the economy are rarely mentioned. Nevertheless, many Canadians rely on the following income security programs to bring some economic stability to their lives, without which they would not be able to regroup and again be able to participate fully in society.

- **Employment Insurance (EI).** This federally administered program, originally called Unemployment Insurance (UI), dates back to 1940. Since then, UI has undergone numerous changes, including its name change to Employment Insurance. EI provides a level of income replacement to workers who are temporarily unemployed and meet strict eligibility conditions. Sickness, maternity and parental benefits are included in this program. Also included in EI are benefits for those whose livelihood depends on the fishing industry. Claimants are eligible for a range of re-skills development programs. EI is paid for through employer and employee contributions. Recently, the program has become restricted, providing coverage for fewer and fewer workers.

- **Workers' Compensation.** Workers' Compensation programs provide provincially administered benefits and are designed to protect individuals against income loss due to workplace injury or disease. Employers fund the programs. In return for participation in the provincial programs, workers waive their rights to sue their employers in the case of a work-related injury or disease. The first Workers' Compensation program was instituted in Ontario in 1914. This was the first social insurance program in Canada.

- **Social Assistance or Welfare.** Social Assistance programs have their roots in early municipal and provincial relief programs that were designed to provide minimal support to the deserving poor or those deemed unable to work because of age or infirmity. Gradually expanded to include those in need but without resources, Social Assistance has remained a residual program of last resort for those with no other source of income or savings. Social Assistance programs, also called welfare or workfare, have remained a provincial responsibility with some funding coming from the federal government. The provinces are free to design their own programs and set the level of benefits. In some provinces, "employable" recipients must participate in work placements. This is known as workfare.

CP PHOTO/Winnipeg Free Press-Phil Hossack (2003).

Winnipeg family with a disabled child wins UI discrimination case.

- **Canada Child Tax Benefit (CCTB)/National Child Benefit Supplement (NCBS).** There is a long history in Canada of providing benefits to families with children. Some of these have been and continue to be delivered through the tax system in the form of tax credits and exemptions, and others have been direct cash transfers. In 1944, a universal benefit called the Family Allowance was instituted, and this went to all families with children, regardless of income. Over time, this benefit became targeted towards middle- and low-income families. In 1993, this benefit was eliminated completely. The Canada Child Tax Benefit includes two aspects: the CCTB basic benefit and the National Child Benefit Supplement. The CCTB provides a tax credit to those who qualify, based on an income test, as low- and middle-income families with children. Currently, up to 80 percent of families receive some portion of the CCTB. Some low-income families are eligible for an additional benefit — the NCBS. An interesting aspect of this federal benefit is that provinces are allowed to claw back the benefit from families on Social Assistance. All provinces take all or part of the benefit away from Social Assistance families, except for Newfoundland and New Brunswick.

- **Canada/Quebec Pension Plan (C/QPP).** The Canada/Quebec Pension Plan is a national contributory and earnings-related pension program introduced in 1966. It provides benefits in the case of retirement, death and long-term disability. Employees and employers jointly finance the CPP and QPP, with current contributions supporting current beneficiaries. In this sense, the plan is a pay-as-you-go system. Any funds not paid out are invested for the purpose of creating a larger reserve fund. The plan consists of Retirement, Disability, Survivor's and Orphan's Death Benefits. Eligibility for this benefit begins at 60 years of age, with maximum benefits paid out after age 65. The pension is earnings-related, so there is a maximum amount for which claimants are eligible. It should also be noted that periods of low earnings, because of caring for young children, illness, unemployment or retraining, are considered exempt from the calculation. This provision is particularly significant for women, who often take time out of the labour force to provide caregiving. People with disabilities who qualify for C/QPP may be eligible to receive benefits through provincial Social Assistance programs, Workers' Compensation, the Canada/Quebec Pension Plan, and, in some cases, through the Veterans Disability Pension.

- **Disability.** Severe and prolonged disability resulting in the inability to participate in the labour force qualifies one for a disability pension. This consists of both an earnings-related portion and a basic flat-rate portion, which is unrelated to the earnings one had

COMPASSIONATE CARE BENEFITS (2004)

Bill C-28 amends the *EI Act* to provide up to six weeks of compassionate care benefits for workers with 600 hours of insurable earnings.

Workers can leave work to care for:

- spouse or common-law partner,
- child or the child of their spouse/partner,
- parent or the spouse/partner of their parent, or
- any other person who may be defined as a "family member" in subsequent regulations.

The person requiring care must have a serious medical condition with significant risk of death within 26 weeks and must require care.

FEDERAL LEGISLATION ON-LINE

The federal Department of Justice keeps up-to-date and historical copies of all of Canada's laws and legislation. The *Employment Insurance Act* and the old *Unemployment Insurance Act* can be obtained at this site: http://laws.justice.gc.ca

while employed. Recipients may also qualify for supplemental child benefits if there are dependants. Tax credits and exemptions play an important income security role for people with disabilities.

- **Survivor and Death Benefits.** In the case of a contributor's death, surviving family members may be eligible for benefits. These benefits are intended to provide support to both the surviving spouse and children.

- **Old Age Security (OAS); Guaranteed Income Supplement (GIS); Spouse's Allowance (SPA).** Between 1952 and 1989, all elderly Canadians received a universal monthly benefit called Old Age Security — an income security program financed and administered by the federal government. Prior to 1952, this benefit was targeted to the very low-income elderly population. Since 1989, the benefit has again become targeted, with only those who qualify because of low or modest income being eligible for benefits. OAS benefits are quite low in relation to the cost of living. Without another source of income upon retirement, such as C/QPP or Registered Retirement Savings Plans (RRSPs), many seniors would still live in poverty. To further assist those who do not have access to these programs, there are two related programs: the Guaranteed Income Supplement (GIS) and the Spouse's Allowance (SPA). The SPA is now called the Allowance. These benefits supplement the OAS for the low-income elderly. From 1966 until today, the GIS has provided a politically popular add-on to the OAS for those pensioners with little or no other income.

- **Veterans Disability Pension.** A Veterans Disability Pension is available to those who apply to Veterans Affairs Canada, provided they have a service-related permanent disability resulting from an injury or disease. Income and assets are not considered as eligibility criteria; the benefit is based solely on the extent of the disability and the fact that it is military service-related. As is the case with disability benefits, what constitutes a disability and its extent are not always easily determined or agreed upon by all interested parties.

- **Occupational Benefits.** In addition to publicly administered benefits, private occupational benefit plans also exist. These plans may be directly tied to one's workplace and include both retirement plans and other insurance-based benefits such as dental and drug plans, or they may be savings plans with tax-supported provisions, such as Registered Retirement Savings Plans (RRSPs). While individuals save and invest this money for future use, the government foregoes the collection of tax on this saved money. The lost revenue not collected by government amounts to billions of dollars per year.

National Archives of Canada, C13233.

Dominion-Provincial Agreement on Old Age Pensions (signed 1928).

Selective and Universal Programs

When designing income security programs, a key distinction is made as to whether they are universal or selective.

- **Universal programs** are available to everyone in a specific category (such as people aged 65 and over and children), on the same terms and as a right of citizenship. The idea is that all persons are equally eligible to receive program benefits, regardless of income and financial situation.

- **Selective programs** target those who are found to be in need or eligible, based on a means test (or income test) or a needs test. A means test determines eligibility based on the income of the prospective recipient. The benefit is reduced according to income level, and there is always a level at which no benefit is granted. A needs test determines eligibility based on the income and the need of the prospective recipient. Eligibility criteria define need, which is then compared to the prospective recipient's life situation.

In the post-war era, universal programs were seen as a way to build national solidarity. More recently, they have been viewed as too expensive and have all but disappeared. The foremost objection to universal programs is their cost. Giving a benefit to everyone, regardless of income, means that even the wealthy get a benefit. On the other side of the issue, universal programs are less expensive to administer, as government workers are not required to scrutinize each person's situation. Selective programs are often viewed as more efficient and less costly, as the government provides benefits only to those most in need. However, identifying eligible recipients using means or needs tests can be administratively complex and costly and take money out of the system that could be directed towards benefits. In some cases, the higher administrative costs are being partially avoided by using the tax system as a method of determining eligibility and dispensing benefits. Increasingly, social policy experts are seeing that some selective programs are necessary for tackling poverty and inequality.

Universal program supporters argue that universal income security promotes a sense of citizenship, solidarity and nationhood. They claim that selective programs for the needy tend to be punitive and stigmatizing, are more susceptible to cutbacks and lack necessary mass public support. If services are only for the poor, then they are likely to be poor services. Finally, many believe that universal income security programs can fulfill various economic functions, such as economic stabilization, investment in human resources and development of the labour force.

Over the years, Canada has had a mix of selective and universal programs. Governments have moved away from a focus on citizenship rights and inclusion, to an anti-poverty strategy geared towards promoting attachment to the labour force.

National Archives of Canada. C145001.

Cartoon lampoons clawbacks in pensions and family allowances.

**TOTAL GOVERNMENT
EXPENDITURES**

Federal, Provincial/Territorial and
Local Government Expenditure,
2001– 02
(Total, $430 billion).

● Social Welfare, $113 billion

● Education, 64.1 billion

● Health, $76.9 billion

———

Source: Statistics Canada. 2002.
Cansim Matrices.

While some programs include aspects of universality, there are no income security programs remaining that can be exactly defined as universal. Health care and education are examples of universal service programs, but they are not income security programs. In the past, there were a number of universal income security programs available to Canadians. Family Allowance, which was available from 1944 to 1993, is the most commonly cited example. All families with a child under the age of 18 were entitled to a financial benefit. Because of the progressive tax system, wealthier people paid much of that back through taxation, but it was nevertheless an acknowledgment of citizenship entitlement and the importance and cost of raising children. In 1993, the Family Allowance was redesigned to become a targeted program, the National Child Benefit, now available to low- and middle-income families.

All of Canada's other income security programs offer selective entitlements. Most have complex selection criteria based on income, work history or the willingness to find a job. Employment Insurance is based on an insurance principle with eligibility tied to employment and income levels. Everyone within the broad category of "employee" pays into the program, and in this sense it is comprehensive, but a strict set of criteria determines who is eligible to receive benefits. The level of benefits depends on the earnings and contributions one has made. In recent years, eligibility for EI has become more restrictive. Other programs are based solely on how much money one has and whether this meets one's needs. To be eligible for Social Assistance (or Ontario Works, as it is referred to in Ontario), one must prove that income and assets fall below a certain specified maximum level. In provinces with workfare, such as Ontario and Alberta, applicants must also comply with an employment or training placement. The National Child Benefit is another example of selective programming. If family income falls below a specified level, benefits are paid through the tax system.

Table 2.1: Distribution of After-tax Income of Economic Families with Two Persons or More Canada, 2002; and Shares, 1996 and 2002

	Quintile value in 2002 dollars	Share of total income in 1984	Share of total income in 2002
Lowest Quintile	32,000	7.4	7.4
Second Quintile	45,500	13.1	12.9
Third Quintile	60,800	18.1	17.7
Fourth Quintile	81,900	23.8	23.5
Highest Quintile	-	37.6	38.5

Source: Statistics Canada, *Income After Tax, Distributions by Size in Canada,* Catalogue No. 13–210–XPB. Quintiles and percentiles for distribution of after-tax income of economic families with two persons or more Canada, 2002; and shares, 1996 and 2002.

Poverty and Inequality

Poverty is usually brought on by an unexpected turn of events, such as loss of employment, death or disability of a family breadwinner, family breakup or increased costs from a major illness or mishap. Of course, changes in the economy can also result in limited employment opportunities, not enough hours of work, a decline in the real value of minimum wages or wages so low that people cannot earn enough to live on. Furthermore, some groups in our society face a greater risk of poverty than others due to such things as discrimination, unequal opportunities, lack of recognition for their work (paid or unpaid) and inadequate income support for those unable to work.

• Measuring Poverty

Canada is one of only a few countries without an official poverty line. For the past 30 years, however, Statistics Canada has produced **Low Income Cut-offs** for different household sizes in different regions. A family is considered to have a low income when it falls below the LICO for its family size and community population. LICOs are set by taking what the average household spends on food, clothing and shelter and adding 20 percent. Today, the average Canadian household spends 35 percent of its income on food, clothing and shelter. Twenty percentage points are added to this to obtain a 55 percent threshold. This 55 percent threshold is then converted into a set of LICOs that vary with family and community size. The process is carried out for seven family sizes and five community sizes, providing a matrix of 35 cut-offs. For example, the 2003 LICO for a family of four in a medium-sized city of 100,000-500,000 people is $31,952. A family of four living in a very large Canadian city with a before-tax income of less than $37,253 in 2003 would have been living below the poverty line.

Statistics Canada has another measure of poverty called the **Low Income Measure (LIM)**, which is widely used for international comparisons of child poverty. The LIM measures the relative low-income rates as one-half of the median income of the country. Because it is a straightforward calculation and can be collected in all nations, it allows for simple comparisons between countries.

Human Resources Development Canada (HRDC) has proposed yet another poverty measure called the **Market Basket Measure (MBM)**. This index calculates the amount of income needed by a given household to meet its needs based on "credible" community norms. The calculation reflects changes in the cost of consumption rather than changes in income. By defining income needs rather than bare subsistence terms, it goes beyond an absolute measure of poverty. The basic issue raised by the MBM is what to include and what not to include. A limited market basket would result in a low poverty line, thus creating the assumption that fewer people are living in poverty.

WHAT IS THE "PERSONAL SECURITY INDEX"?

Developed by Canadian Council on Social Development, the PSI is a five-year-old tool to measure annual changes in the security of Canadians according to three key elements:

• economic security in the broad sense of job and financial security;

• health security in the sense of protection against the threats of disease and injury;

• physical safety in the sense of feeling safe from violent crime and theft.

The PSI measures changes in both empirical data and in people's perceptions of their personal security. The 2003 PSI results are available at: http://www.ccsd.ca/pubs/2003/psi/

POVERTY
LINE ▽

DONATO
TORONTO SUN

National Archives of Canada. C144988.

Cartoon makes fun of government efforts to redefine the poverty line.

Child and Family Poverty

As mentioned elsewhere, in 1989 the Canadian federal government declared its commitment to "seek to achieve the goal of eliminating poverty among Canadian children by the year 2000." On the fifteenth anniversary of this commitment, **Campaign 2000**, a national anti-poverty coalition, recently released a report on child poverty in Canada, appropriately entitled *One Million too Many: 2004 Report on Child Poverty in Canada*.

According to the report, nearly one in six of Canada's children lives below the Statistics Canada LICO. The report also summarizes the deteriorating economic situation of Canada's children since 1989. It reveals a 43 percent increase in the population of poor children to 402,000; an increase of 27 percent in the number of families living with less than $20,000 per year; and an increase of 49 percent of poor children in single-parent families.

Table 2.2: How is Canada Doing in Addressing Child and Family Poverty?

Focus Area	Assessment	What's Happening?
Child and Family Poverty	Worsening	• More than one million children live in poverty — an increase since 1989. • Child poverty rate up for the first time in six years to 15.6% — higher than in 1989. • One third of all children in Canada exposed to poverty for at least one year since 1996.
Couples with Children	No Progress	• Low income couples with children still $9,000, on average, below poverty line. • Poverty rate virtually unchanged from previous year — 10%.
Lone Mother Families	Worsening	• Child poverty rate for female lone parent families rose above 50% for the first time in three years. • Low income lone mother families would need, on average, $8,800 to reach poverty line.
Gap Between Rich and Poor	No Progress	• Deep inequality entrenched through economic boom. Canada's top 10% richest families with children had average incomes that were more than 11 times higher than the bottom 10%.
Food Bank Use	Worsening	• 2003 was record year for food bank use — 317,242 food bank users were children.
Social Exclusion	Worsening	• Child poverty rates for Aboriginal children, immigrant children and children in visible minority groups are more than double the average for all children; the poverty rate among children with disabilities is 27.7%.

Source: Campaign 2000. 2004. *One Million Too Many: Implementing Solutions to Child Poverty in Canada. A 2004 Report Card on Child Poverty in Canada*. Ottawa.

Food Security and Insecurity

With cutbacks in many income security programs, Canadians are having to rely on **food banks and feeding programs** in order to survive. In 2003, there were over 639 food banks in Canada, and 777,869 people received emergency food at one of these food banks (Canadian Association of Food Banks, 2003). This is a 1.2 percent drop from March 2000, when the number stood at 726,902 (Wilson and Steinman 2000, 1). The number of people who utilized food banks had doubled since March 1989. Over 40 percent of those being helped were under the age of 18, representing an estimated 294,516 children.

Of those Canadians using food banks, 81.2 percent relied on income security programs as their income source (65 percent on Social Assistance, 12 percent on Employment Insurance (EI) and nine percent on Disability Benefits). Only 12 percent were employed, and four percent reported no income (Wilson and Tsoa 2001, 3).

Feeding programs often operate out of shelters or church basements and provide two meals per day. Such programs are operated by volunteers and by those who use the service. For example, The Well in Ottawa does not start providing meals until enough people volunteer to help. Many programs are run in conjunction with emergency shelters and provide additional free services, such as laundry facilities, telephone access, newspapers and clothing. In certain instances, access to computers is also available. At most times, social workers are available and may even work directly from within the feeding program.

There is difficulty in keeping pace with demand. Almost half, or 49 percent, of food banks report that they often run out of food and must turn people away. Many believe that the steady unravelling of the social safety net means that access to basic food is in jeopardy.

Table 2.3: Pre-tax Low Income Cut-offs (LICOs), 2003

Family size	Population of Community of Residence				
	500,000 +	100,000– 499,999	30,000– 99,999	Less than 30,000	Rural
1	$19,795	$16,979	$16,862	$15,690	$13,680
2	$24,745	$21,224	$21,077	$19,612	$17,100
3	$30,744	$26,396	$26,213	$24,390	$21,268
4	$37,253	$31,952	$31,731	$29,526	$25,744
5	$41,642	$35,718	$35,469	$33,004	$28,778
6	$46,031	$39,483	$39,208	$36,482	$31,813
7+	$50,421	$43,249	$42,947	$39,960	$34,847

Source: Prepared by the Canadian Council on Social Development using Statistics Canada's Low Income Cut-offs, from low income cut-offs from 1994–2003 and low income measures from 1992–2001, Catalogue No. 75F0002MIE No. 002, March 2004. See: http://www.ccsd.ca/facts.html

CHT AND CST

On April 1, 2004, federal contributions to health, post-secondary education, early childhood education, child care and social services were divided into two separate transfers: the Canada Health Transfer (CHT) and the Canada Social Transfer (CST). This funding was formerly delivered through the Canada Health and Social Transfer (CHST).

Canadian Federalism and Social Welfare

Federalism is a system of government in which a number of smaller states (in Canada's case, provinces and territories) join to form a larger political entity while still retaining a measure of political power. When Canada was formed in 1867, social welfare was largely a private responsibility of the individual, family and church. Not surprisingly, the *British North America Act* (1867) said little about jurisdiction over income security or social services. The terms, in fact, did not even exist at the time. Political wrangling, informal side-deals between the federal government and the provinces, and constitutional amendments therefore formed the basis for our social security system.

Through this process, income security emerged as an area of federal jurisdiction and the provinces largely prevailed in the delivery of social services. An important point to note, however, is that while the provinces were given this responsibility, the federal government retained its responsibilities for Aboriginal people, as defined by the *Indian Act*. "Lands and lands reserved for Indians" remained within the jurisdiction of the federal government. The provision of social welfare to Aboriginal people is, therefore, different than for the rest of the population.

• Reforms to the Social Welfare System

One of the most significant changes to Canada's social welfare system arose with the introduction of the **Canada Health and Social Transfer (CHST)** in 1996. Previous to CHST, federal government contributions to social assistance and social services had been funded through the **Canada Assistance Plan (CAP)**, established in 1966. Federal government contributions to health care services and post-secondary education had been funded through Established Programs Financing (EPF) since 1977. Both of these programs were replaced with the CHST. In its first two years, CHST paid the provinces $7 billion less than they would have received under CAP/EPF.

In 2004, the CHST was split into the **Canada Social Transfer (CST)** and the **Canada Health Transfer (CHT)**. Like the CHST, the CST and CHT are federal block transfers to provinces and territories with the CST in support of post-secondary education, social assistance and social services, including early childhood development, early learning and child care. The CHT is dedicated to funding health care. The portion of the existing CHST legislated cash amounts and tax transfers apportioned to the CST is 38 percent. Some social policy analysts maintain that this amount is too low and may relegate higher education and social services to a secondary priority. CST cash and tax transfers were $14.9 billion in 2004–05, of which $8.3 billion was cash transfers and $6.6 billion tax transfers. The CHT transferred $25.1 billion in 2004–05 for health care, of which $14.3 billion was cash transfers and $10.9 billion was tax transfers.

CP PHOTO/Adrian Wyld.

PM Paul Martin visits an early childhood education class (2004).

CAP was a 50/50 cost-shared program — the federal government shared 50 percent of the cost of eligible Social Assistance and social services expenditure with the provinces. With CAP, federal transfers rose as provincial social welfare expenditures increased. CAP therefore provided a kind of economic stabilizing function; as federal transfers increased in economic recessions, it helped stimulate the economy through social spending. The CST and CHT, on the other hand, are fixed per-capita or per-person amounts (also called "block transfers") based on the population of the province. Hence, federal transfers are not connected to either the needs of the people or the state of the economy. Many believe that it is the economic stabilizing effect of social spending that has prevented a depression-style drop-off in the Canadian economy since the Great Depression of 1930. With the CST and CHT, this stabilizing effect is greatly reduced.

The national standards as set out in CAP are also largely gone under the CHST. CAP stipulated that the provinces should establish eligibility for Social Assistance based on need as determined by a means test, make services available for all those eligible regardless of when they established residency in the province, establish an appeal procedure and require no community or other work (also known as "workfare") in return for social benefits. Under the CHST, the regulations associated with CAP were removed except for the ban on residency requirements, and funding regulations associated with medicare were retained. Many analysts fear that, with the removal of the national standards, provinces will establish very different benefit levels and eligibility criteria.

Another recent welfare reform is the **Social Union Agreement of 1999** between the Government of Canada and the provinces and territories (see sidebar). According to the federal government, the objective of the Social Union Agreement is to reform and renew Canada's system of social services and to reassure Canadians that their pan-Canadian social programs are strong and secure. So far, several social welfare initiatives have been established under this framework, such as the National Child Benefit, the National Children's Agenda for child care, and services for persons with disabilities.

The Social Union Agreement was largely a response to the disapproval on the part of provincial governments of the unilateral cancellation of CAP and its replacement with CHST. The provinces wanted to be notified of and participate in formulating any changes in federal-provincial arrangements. They wanted the federal government to agree that, if it initiated new social programs, even ones for which it paid the total costs, a province could opt out and take the cash instead with virtually no strings attached. In that case, the province would only be required to spend the money in the same general area as the national plan. The provinces also made it clear that they wanted more say about how the federal government acted when stepping into provincial jurisdictions.

THE SOCIAL UNION AGREEMENT

The Social Union Agreement of 1999 between all the provinces (except Quebec) and the federal government established the procedures for changing social policy.

It was agreed that the first priorities should be children in poverty and persons with disabilities. In addition, the provinces and the federal government agreed that they would give one another advance notice prior to the implementation of a major change in a social policy or program that would likely substantially affect another government.

The federal government also agreed that it would consult with the provincial and territorial governments at least one year prior to renewal or significant funding changes in the existing social transfers to the provinces and territories, unless otherwise agreed, and will build due-notice provisions into any new social transfers.

The "official" Government of Canada Social Union website provides a good overview of this important social welfare agreement. It can be found at: http://www.socialunion.gc.ca

Ideology: Or, Why People Differ on What to Do

Canadians differ in their perception and explanation of social issues or problems and on how they believe these issues or problems should be solved. Opposing views are also held of the role of government in solving or alleviating such problems. As discussed in Chapter 1, the two political approaches to social welfare — the residual and institutional — capture the controversy surrounding social welfare today. Indeed, the history of the welfare state is a perpetual controversy over what the boundaries or extent of the welfare state should be.

The residual and institutional views of social welfare are informed by ideas and values that can be lumped together under broad categories of thought called ideologies. The term ideology refers to a set of ideas, values, beliefs and attitudes held by a particular person or group that shapes our way of thinking. Political ideologies can be categorized along a spectrum, with communism on the far left and fascism on the extreme right. The more left-wing views of the democratic socialists and social democrats hold that social welfare is part of our collective responsibility to our fellow citizens and should be publicly provided within an institutional framework. The more right-wing approach of the neo-conservatives and liberals (although liberals move around from the centre to the right) includes the belief that welfare should be an individual responsibility within a residual model and that private-sector provision should be encouraged.

• Workfare

Some provincial welfare programs require applicants to work as a term of eligibility. This is commonly known as workfare, and it has drawn criticism. Refusal to participate in the program results in some sort of penalty. For example, workfare could require people to work at specific jobs in order to get a government cheque, or it could mean that people receive a smaller cheque if they refuse to accept work through a government program. It might also require applicants to select retraining or pursue self-employment programs. Workfare placements could involve working in a community or social service agency. Applicants may also choose community work placements as a workfare option for the purposes of increasing skills, knowledge and networks in the labour market.

Critics equate workfare as a return to the "work test" of the Elizabethan Poor Laws. Others cite research to show its failure in other countries — particularly the United States. It has also been criticized for being expensive to administer, and for taking away jobs from the paid labour force. Others see workfare as a blame-oriented approach that ignores job creation, arguing that people want to work, but that there are not enough good jobs.

Workfare worker is unsure library job will lead to lasting employment.

CP PHOTO/Corinna Schuler (1996).

• Social Welfare Economics

Some of these ideological debates have become part of public discourse. This is the case, for example, with the debates among professional economists over the causes of unemployment. In very broad terms, the **Keynesians** (named after the famous British economist John Maynard Keynes, 1883–1946) believe that governments should emphasize policies that combat unemployment in order to maintain the income of consumers. **Monetarists**, on the other hand, believe that governments should keep inflation in check and not worry so much about unemployment. Those adhering to the more radical **political economy** perspective believe that private ownership creates two classes that are antagonistic, and unemployment results when unions are weakened and cannot protect the jobs of the working people.

The Keynesians and monetarists also have contrasting views on social spending in general. The monetarists believe that social spending stimulates inflation, undermines labour market flexibility and productivity and distorts the work/leisure trade-off. Keynesians believe that economic efficiency and social equity are compatible; that social spending helps economic recovery, enhances productivity and keeps the labour market flexible. The political economy perspective holds that the operation of economic markets is tied to private ownership and is essentially exploitative; that social spending is a right fought for by the working class. Canadian government policy has alternated between the Keynesian and monetarist views.

Needless to say, the political economy perspective has never figured prominently in the social policy of Canadian governments — but it has certainly shaped its many critiques.

GUARANTEED ANNUAL INCOME

Canadian governments have examined the feasibility of a lifetime guaranteed annual income (GAI) program.

Modern proposals have taken two basic forms. The form favoured by people who place a high value on simplification and work incentives is the **negative income tax** (NIT). This is a selective payment to persons or households below a certain income level.

The second form is the **universal demogrant** (UD), a payment to all persons regardless of income and usually favoured by those who see the GAI as a right of citizenship whose purpose is to eliminate poverty and lead to more equal sharing of the economic benefits of society.

Currently, the federal government is reviewing the creation of a lifetime guaranteed annual income program to combat poverty. Whether any GAI plan adopted by the government will work to lessen income inequality in Canada will depend on the form it takes.

Globalization and Social Welfare

Canada does not exist apart from the rest of the world. This is especially true as the era of "globalization" increasingly takes hold.

Economic globalization is the growing integration of international markets for goods, services and finance. It is the latest expression of market liberalism and the latest stage in the development of advanced capitalist economies. It includes the expansion of free trade and investment, the expansion of trade in goods and services between countries, the geographical expansion and increase in power of transnational corporations (TNCs) and the use of agreements between nations and international bodies such as the World Trade Organization (WTO) to protect the rights of TNCs.

Globalization reflects, perhaps above all, the global expansion of large corporations. Of the 40,000 corporations operating in the world today, 200 control a quarter of the world's economic activity. These top 200 have combined revenues ($7.1 trillion) larger than all the economies of the world minus the largest nine. In other words, these corporations are more powerful than most countries in the world (Rice and Prince 2000).

CP PHOTO/AP-John Moore.

The Raging Grannies, a political awareness group from Ottawa, sing anti-globalization songs before a march at the "People's Summit" in Quebec City during the Summit of the Americas (2001).

• Less Power to the People

Globalization also means that national and local governments increasingly have less freedom to act on behalf of their citizens, especially on the big economic and social questions of the day. In view of this, in the future, income security provisions aimed at creating greater equality of income and opportunity among individuals will likely become intertwined with the issue of global human rights. Indeed, what might be called global social welfare (a concern with justice, social regulation, social provision and redistribution between nations) is already a part of the activities of various supranational organizations or international governmental organizations, such as the United Nations. The fight to gain and maintain global human rights in the face of economic globalization is, in many respects, today's epic struggle. Advocacy for equality within and between nations is an integral part of social welfare.

The economic pressures of globalization will continue to have a direct effect on income security policy and practice in this country. In many nations, especially poorer ones, economic restructuring and cutbacks to social programs have been imposed by international agencies, such as the World Bank and the International Monetary Fund, in the form of so-called "structural adjustments." The Canadian government is not immune to these pressures and adjusts its own income security programs to meet the new economic order and battle with other nations to be the most "investor friendly."

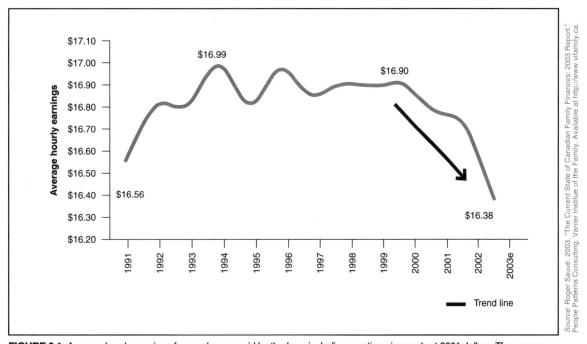

Source: Roger Sauvé. 2003. "The Current State of Canadian Family Finances: 2003 Report." People Patterns Consulting. Vanier Institue of the Family. Available at http://www.vifamily.ca.

FIGURE 2.1: Average hourly earnings for employees paid by the hour including overtime, in constant 2001 dollars. The reason family incomes have risen is that more family members are now working.

Unfortunately, the impact of globalization on Canada's income security programs at this point is being felt mainly by the most disadvantaged in our society, and they are also the ones who are least able to fight back. Cutbacks and strict eligibility criteria mean that many are often left without even the bare necessities. The rise in the number of people who are homeless, the growing number of food banks and the persistence of child poverty are signs of this. But, it is not only the very poor that suffer. The middle class is increasingly finding that high-paying jobs are moving offshore to corporate tax havens or export processing zones. Income security increasingly affects them as well, insofar as welfare cutbacks will mean that ordinary working Canadians may not be able to depend on the traditional social protection offered by such programs as Employment Insurance and Old Age Security.

Conclusion

Social welfare is about helping the citizens of Canada face difficulties in their lives — whether they be social or economic. It is a way of sharing the risk of events such as poverty, unemployment, disability and old age among all citizens. Social welfare is also about regulating and stabilizing our economic and social system. A healthy, well-trained and educated workforce is required for our economy to grow. Social welfare programs also help to relieve some of the distress of economic downturns, thereby preventing social unrest and stimulating the economy, by putting money into the hands of those who will spend it. For example, the Baby Bonus or Family Allowance program introduced following World War II gave a $20 monthly amount to every mother with the belief that the mother would spend the money on her children and stimulate the post-war economy.

Canadians do not always agree on whether social welfare programs should be expanded and strengthened or whether they should be reduced. Politicians agree even less. What is clear is that in recent years the welfare state in Canada has been reformed in ways that weaken overall social equality and social justice. Moreover, the economic forces of globalization seem to be leading to a harmonization of our social welfare system with that of the United States, our largest trading partner, and this will mean a serious deterioration in our welfare system.

Emulating the United States is not the only path open to us. Other countries in Europe, notably Denmark and the Netherlands, have continued to support and even expand their social welfare commitments and continue to have good productivity and economic growth. What is certain is that the debate over the future of the welfare system in Canada will be at the forefront of public discourse in the coming years.

Chapter 2 Review
Income Security and Social Welfare

Discussion Questions

1. What are the four categories of income security programs?

2. What is the main difference between a social insurance program and a minimum income program?

3. List five income security programs and describe the level of government responsible for them and who is eligible.

4. Who benefits from income security programs?

5. What are the two primary differences between universal and selective programs? Does Canada currently have any universal programs?

6. How did the discontinuation of the Canada Assistance Plan (CAP) affect social welfare programs?

7. What is the Social Union Agreement and has it changed social policy in Canada?

Websites

Policy.ca
http://www.policy.ca

Check out the social policy issue area. Policy.ca is a non-partisan resource for the public analysis of Canadian policy issues. It consists of a constantly growing database of on-line public policy resources in 16 different issue areas. These resources are selected to provide users with a balanced review of both documents and organizations in key Canadian public policy issue areas.

Canadian Centre for Policy Alternatives
http://www.policyalternatives.ca

The CCPA is a non-profit research organization, funded primarily through organizational and individual membership. It was founded in 1980 to promote research on economic and social policy issues from a progressive point of view. Check out the "Behind the Numbers" section.

Caledon Institute of Social Policy
http://www.caledoninst.org

The Caledon Institute of Social Policy does rigorous, high-quality research and analysis; seeks to inform and influence public opinion and to foster public discussion on poverty and social policy; and develops and promotes concrete, practicable proposals for the reform of social programs at all levels of government.

Key Terms

- **Social insurance**
- **Minimum Income**
- **Demogrants**
- **Income supplementation**
- **Universal programs**
- **Selective programs**
- **Low Income Cut-offs (LICOs)**
- **Low Income Measure (LIM)**
- **Market Basket Measure (MBM)**
- **Campaign 2000**
- **Food banks and feeding programs**
- **Federalism**
- **Canada Health and Social Transfer (CHST)**
- **Canada Assistance Plan (CAP)**
- **Canada Social Transfer (CST)**
- **Canada Health Transfer (CHT)**
- **Social Union Agreement of 1999**
- **Ideology**
- **Workfare**
- **Keynesians**
- **Monetarists**
- **Political economy**
- **Economic globalization**
- **Global social welfare**

Soup kitchens were the only recourse for the poor in Montreal, Quebec, 1931. For people across Canada, the Depression brought great uncertainty and hardship. The effects of the severe economic crash (1929–33) lasted through the 1930s and beyond.

3

The History of Social Work

The Development of a Profession

The systematic giving of charity to the poor coincides, more or less, with the upheaval of the Industrial Revolution and, in particular, with the consolidation of the wage-labour system (at the time, capitalism was quickly becoming the dominant economic system). The immediate antecedents of Anglo-Canadian social work can be found in such socioeconomic changes in Britain and the United States in the eighteenth and nineteenth centuries.

Broadly speaking, relief in the nineteenth century was based on the poorhouse or house of industry. In the twentieth century, it shifted to the provision of food and other necessities to people in need in their homes, and later to the provision of cash. From the mid-twentieth century onwards, the state came to play an increasingly important role. Following World War II, Canada's economic surplus grew, as did the expectation that the state would ensure the economic and social security of its citizens. As state provision of social welfare has expanded, so has the social work profession. Most members of this profession are now employed in government-financed social welfare agencies.

We can thus divide the history of social work practice into three more or less distinct phases. These coincide roughly with major social and economic changes taking place at the time. In each phase, certain characteristics predominate.

- The era of moral reform: the pre-industrial phase from the formation of Canada until 1890;

- The era of social reform: the transition from a commercial to an industrial society from 1891 to 1940; and

- The era of applied social science: the post-war transformation period of rapid economic growth and mass consumption from 1940 to the present.

This chapter looks at each phase so as to provide a quick overview of the evolution of social work practice in Canada. For a more detailed survey of the history, readers are referred to the various reference sources listed at the end of this chapter.

In the early twentieth century, social work established itself as a vocation committed to major social reform, social change and the eradication of poverty. Over time, it shifted from a religious and charitable practice to a more systematic, professional one. Along with this, social service shifted from a privately funded and volunteer activity to a publicly funded, paid occupation.

National Archives of Canada. PA93921.

Lining up to get into the Scott Mission, Toronto, 1953.

SOCIAL WORK HISTORY

The author's website provides an overview of the history of social work and income security. The site can be found at: http://www.socialpolicy.ca/cush

PHASE 1: The Era of Moral Reform — to 1890

The pre-industrial phase of the development of social work includes the period from the formation of Canada up to the 1890s. **Private charities** developed during this time, offering material relief and lessons in moral ethics. Many were explicitly associated with religious organizations, and it was religiously motivated individuals working through these organizations who became the early social workers. This period saw the rise of the charity movement, epitomized by the Charity Organization Society (COS; see below). The roots of casework and the notion of helping people adjust to their environment can be traced to the COS.

The response to urban poverty in Canada during this phase was the result of two types of religious motivation. The explanation by James Leiby of the development of charitable activity in the United States provides some insight into similar development in English Canada as well:

> The early institutional responses to urban poverty came from people who had religious interests and motives. There were two broad types. One was native, Protestant, and missionary. It expressed a concern of pious and rather well established people for those whom they perceived as strangers and outsiders (and of course unchurched). The other type developed among the immigrant groups as forms of mutual aid and solidarity in a threatening environment (Leiby 1978, 75).

These two religious thrusts underlie the subsequent history of divergent views of social work. The missionary motive led to the COS and, ultimately, to social casework. The solidarity motive led to initiatives such as the settlement house movement and, later, community work and social justice.

• Early Charity Organization: The Roots of Social Work

In the nineteenth century, public assistance in English Canada was guided largely by the example of England. The early English legislation, the Poor Law, required local parishes to provide relief to the deserving poor (those who were elderly, ill or disabled). Parishes were administrative districts organized by the Church of England. Each had a local council that was responsible for assistance to the poor, known as **poor relief**. The Poor Law of 1601 and its reform in 1832 carefully distinguished two types of indoor relief: one for the elderly and sick who could receive relief in almshouses or poorhouses, and one for the able-bodied poor who were made to work for relief in workhouses, the purpose of which was to make public assistance cruel and demeaning.

Early in the nineteenth century, "relief," where it was available, was provided primarily by private philanthropic societies founded in the territories that would become Canada. Organizations such as the

Canadian family living in one-room accommodation, 1912.

Society for Improving the Condition of the Poor of St. John's (1808), the Society for Promoting Education and Industry among the Indians and Destitute Settlers in Canada (1827), the Kingston Benevolent Society (1821), the Halifax Poor Man's Friend Society and the Montreal Ladies Benevolent Society (1832) were preoccupied with the termination of begging and the value of labour. Relief, rarely given in cash, was usually in return for work. These same organizations, however, resisted the introduction of scientific methods of charity that were advocated from the 1830s onwards (Rooke and Schnell 1983, 46–56).

Following a request for assistance, a charity visitor would be designated to visit and interview the applicant in his or her home. Their role was to promote industry, thrift and virtue among the poor. The visitors were volunteers, generally elite men and women from the upper classes and people from the ranks of the emerging professional and business classes. Their first task was to classify the applicant as either deserving poor or undeserving poor.

People designated as **deserving poor** were seen as being of good moral character and only temporarily out of luck due to no fault of their own. The deserving did not ask directly for help and were clean and tidy. The **undeserving poor** were deemed to be lazy and/or morally degenerate. Once an applicant was judged to be deserving, he or she had to appear before a committee of trustees who made the final decision to grant aid. The board granted aid in only about half of the cases determined to be circumstances of destitution. While the work required experience and skill, the early boards resisted proposals to hire full-time visitors.

The early relief provided by these volunteers in numerous charities and church parishes was soon deemed disorganized and inefficient, as there was very little regulation or coordination. In Toronto alone there were 43 different charity organizations by 1894. Over time, the agencies developed their own training programs for volunteers, which, when a shift to a more scientific approach surfaced, formed the basis for the University of Toronto Social Services Program in 1914.

Proponents of better organization of charitable assistance in England formed the London-based **Charity Organization Society** (COS) in 1869 to coordinate the efforts of the various charities. The voluntary charity work conducted under the auspices of the COS was possibly the most widespread attempt to help the poor. COS brought some order to the chaos created by the overlapping activity of 640 charitable institutions. Workers in this organization were expected to cooperate with other charities and with the agents of the Poor Law so as to give aid to the deserving poor. The popularity of this voluntary organization partly stemmed from the relief it accorded to local taxpayers. Money could be saved if private charities used unpaid volunteers and members of religious orders (Blyth 1972, 21).

Early charity organizations were active in eradicating child labour.

National Archives of Canada. C4239.

The Protestant Charity Organization Society arrived in Montreal in 1901, following a similar and earlier effort to organize in Toronto. It was primarily directed by businessmen and upper-class women who believed that poverty was the fault of the individual. The COS, which differentiated between the deserving and undeserving poor, believed that indiscriminate material relief would cause pauperism; relief could lure a person from thrift and hard work into a life of dependency and reliance on handouts. The COS tried to control relief provision and, therefore, the poor. They believed that the existence of so many charities was more likely to create poverty than eliminate it. They also believed that neighbourhood-organized charities would promote a sense of community among the poor.

The Charity Organization Society believed that the charity visitors in the homes of the poor could serve as models of the value of hard work and thrift. However, the visitors encountered many difficulties and soon sought out specific training and "scientific methods" to cope with their problems. As these visitors became more familiar with standardized techniques, they formed the base of what came to be called social "casework" (Copp 1974, 108–120).

The COS goals were as follows:

1. *Restore people to a life of self-sufficiency, moral rectitude and Christian values.* Visitors were often rigidly moralistic; the COS was notorious for its rigid moralistic stand. Relief was a matter of Christian uplifting.

2. *Restore the bonds of obligation and understanding between the classes.* This was similar to the relationship between feudal lord and serf out of which could come a social and moral contract.

3. *Organize and control charity work, aiming for efficiency and communal relations.*

• The Settlement House Movement

That aspect of social work concerned with community work has its roots in the **settlement house movement**. The first social settlement house was established in the east end of London in 1884. It was named Toynbee Hall, after an Oxford University historian who had settled in London's East End (Arnold Toynbee had died in 1883).

The purpose of the settlement house was to bring the youth of the educated middle class and the charitable gentry to live among the urban natives — a kind of mission to the poor. The term derived from the notion of "settling in," whereby a worker would live in the homes of the poor. As its founder Canon Barnett explained, the idea was simple: "to bridge the gap that industrialism had created between rich and poor, to reduce the mutual suspicion and ignorance of one class for the other, and to do something more than give charity…. They would make their settlement an outpost of education and culture." (Davis 1967, 6).

TEP Photo Archives.

Arnold Toynbee, an advocate and supporter of workers' education.

From the 1880s through to the 1930s, the settlement house movement was a major factor in the emergence of social work as a profession. Young men and women, largely from the middle-classes, volunteered to live and work in converted residential buildings in poor, urban neighborhoods. With the best of intentions, they hoped to bring about an improvement the lives of less-well-to-do families. By such means, they provided amenities and services that were not, at that point, widely available to the poor through government agencies — clubs, educational classes and recreational gatherings, as well as more practical help. The hard-working, committed individuals involved in the settlement house movement saw their mission as sweeping social reform at the community level. These experimental settlements became, in a sense, social work "laboratories" and an arena for training those involved in the emerging field of social work.

The settlement house workers were more inclined to engage in social reform activities than were those involved with the COS. They tended to advocate for better working conditions, housing, health and education. Many early workers came to the settlement house movement with radical political ideas, but this radicalism faded out after World War I. It is worth noting that during this period, women began to be involved more actively in work on social and political issues outside the home (Allen 1971). The settlement house movement's influence on the development of social work continued for years to come.

Jane Addams was the most prominent of Americans who transported the idea of social settlements to the United States, founding Hull House in Chicago in 1889. The young Mackenzie King, later to become prime minister of Canada, worked at Hull House in the 1890s to learn about the charitable work of Addams and others (Addams 1961, viii; Ferns and Ostry 1976, 37). Evanglia, the first settlement house in Toronto, was founded in 1902 by Libby Carson and Mary Bell with the support of the Toronto YWCA. Carson had founded several other settlement houses, including Christadora House in New York in 1897.

Several other settlement houses were established in Canada. In Winnipeg, J.S. Woodsworth (who would later would become the independent labour Member of Parliament for Winnipeg, and the first leader of the Co-operative Commonwealth Federation, the forerunner of the present-day New Democratic Party) directed the All People's Mission, which was founded in 1907; in Montreal, the University Settlement House was established in 1909; and in Toronto, the St. Christopher House was founded in 1912, the University Settlement in 1910, and the Central Neighbourhood House in 1911. Most large Canadian cities had at least one settlement house by World War I. During the war, the radical activist aspects of the movement declined, however. The first schools of social work in Canada were connected to, or often started by, settlement workers (Davis 1967, 3–25).

Children wait while their mother enquires about housing, 1940.

National Archives of Canada, C28353.

PHASE 2: The Era of Social Reform — 1891 to 1940

During this period, the notion of helping the needy shifted from private philanthropy or charity provided by volunteers to public welfare funded by government bodies and provided by trained and paid workers. This shift in emphasis provided the foundation for the birth of social work as an occupation. The perception that a publicly funded response to poverty was needed arose from fears among the middle class that increased poverty might result in mob violence and the spread of illness.

In the late nineteenth century, church members in charities were motivated by a desire for a more socially oriented church, based on a scientific rather than a moral worldview. Recognition grew that skilled and trained workers were required, rather than volunteer, untrained charity visitors.

The notion of **scientific philanthropy** emerged from the early ideals of reform and social progress. These ideals were increasingly influenced by scientific approaches at the time. James Leiby summarizes the interaction of ideas of science and philanthropy:

> Faults might lie in a particular line of argument or judgment, but in theory at least, the scientific spirit pointed toward self-correction and consensus. Of course in thinking about philanthropy and social justice there would be partisans of religious and political causes, and they would disagree; probably all of them had some insight into the situation, most likely all of them were to some degree fallible. On what better ground could they meet and agree than that of a "scientific philanthropy"? (Leiby 1978, 91).

According to this new scientific approach to social work, the purpose of this more scientific approach was to depart from moral judgments of deservingness; the client was seen as having an objective problem and the role of the social worker was to help him or her deal with it. To be effective in this role, it was necessary for the worker to have a scientific understanding of human behaviour and social processes. It was assumed that a thorough gathering of information would lead to an understanding of the causes of the person's problem. Further, it was assumed that once the problem was identified a solution would be objectively found and then applied.

As large urban areas grew, and the number of people in need grew with them, the large number of poor could no longer be evaluated by a system of charity visitors alone. Charity organization and the founding of children's aid societies led to the replacement of voluntary organization with paid and trained staff. Organizations were forced to hire paid workers to efficiently handle the growing demands. This transformation was common to many cities and districts in Canada, as well as to other parts of the world, during the early part of the twentieth century.

National Archives of Canada, C85881.

Early welfare activist John Joseph Kelso with his family.

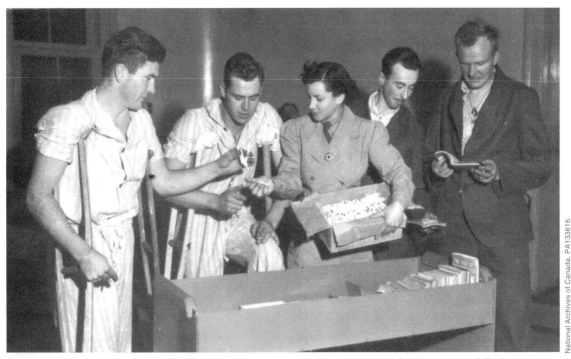

National Archives of Canada, PA133616.

Social worker Mary Wright hands out Red Cross supplies to wounded soldiers in 1944. Helping to organize and distribute charitable aid has long been an important activity of Canadian social workers throughout the world.

There was a moral as well as a pragmatic concern that poverty might lead to social instability. In the latter third of the nineteenth century, people of the middle and upper classes in England became concerned, either for moral or political reasons, with the unequal distribution of wealth and the poor conditions of the working class. They also feared that, with an increase in poverty, the working classes might rise up in mob violence, or that the poor might become diseased and therefore spread illness to all members of society.

These concerns also emerged in Canada as **social survey research** was used to highlight the extent of poverty and inequality in Canadian cities. One of the first social survey research studies was carried out by H.B. Ames in Montreal. Published in 1897 under the title *The City Below the Hill*, it illuminated the conditions of the poorest of Montreal residents. Early studies by other social researcher/reformers, such as J.J. Kelso in Toronto and J.S. Woodsworth in Winnipeg, contributed to the Canadian middle and upper classes' understanding of poverty and what to do about it. Royal Commissions, such as the Dominion Commission on the Relations of Labour and Capital (1889), the Ontario Royal Commission on the Prisons (1890) and the Dominion Board of Inquiry into the Cost of Living (1915), also contributed to increased awareness and a growing interest in social service and social work.

CHARLOTTE WHITTON

Between 1922 and 1941, Charlotte Whitton led the Canadian Welfare Council, a forerunner to the Canadian Council on Social Development, and followed that by lecturing across North America on social programs. She was Canada's most influential voice on social welfare matters at the time.

She was elected mayor of Ottawa in 1952, 1954, 1960 and 1964 and later served as an alderman until 1972. She was not a believer in the role of the state in providing welfare and social services; today she would be regarded as neo-conservative in her outlook on such matters.

Feisty to the end, she is also attributed with the wry remark: "Whatever women do, they must do twice as well as men to be thought half as good. Luckily, this is not difficult."

National Archives of Canada, PA137535.

Charlotte Whitton, Canadian Council on Child Welfare.

The transition from friendly visitors to paid social workers was not a smooth one. The fact that many workers accepted payment often incurred the criticism of the rich and the opprobrium of the unthinking. A willingness to work for nothing, it was considered, was the hallmark of a sincere charity worker (Woodroofe 1962, 97).

• The Rise of Trained Social Workers

The training of social workers gradually shifted from agency-based volunteer training to a university-based professional education as the more scientific view of human services emerged. This shift occurred simultaneously in countries such as Britain and the United States.

In 1914, the University of Toronto established a Department of Social Services for the scientific study of society. This program was the first in Canada to undertake the task of training social workers. In 1918, McGill University opened up the second English-language social work training program, the School of Social Study and Training. Carl Dawson, its director, was convinced that study and action did not fraternize well in the university. According to Dawson, the study of social phenomena should proceed separately from its application, which should be left to others. A similar program was begun in 1928 at the University of British Columbia. Several other schools developed after World War II. Training was based on the idea that social work had already evolved a base of knowledge that could be passed on to potential participants.

Originally based on the concept of charity, social work had evolved from a set of rules to guide volunteers in their work as friendly visitors of the poor into a philosophy that embodied many of the principles of modern casework and a technique that could be transmitted by education and training from one generation of social workers to another (Woodroofe 1962, 54). Social work in Canada gained a professional prominence in 1927 when the Canadian Association of Social Workers (CASW) was established.

In 1947, the first professional social work degree (Master of Social Work) was offered by the University of Toronto. In 1966, they awarded the first Bachelor of Social Work degree (Armitage 1970).

• Social Casework

The development of modern casework — systematic methods of investigation, assessment and decision-making — was strongly influenced by Mary Richmond, who worked for the Charity Organization Societies of Baltimore and Philadelphia and for the Russell Sage Foundation. Her 1917 text, *Social Diagnosis*, was used in the training of workers, and its contents reflect "the strong influence played by medicine in Miss Richmond's conception of social casework" (Coll 1973, 85–86). Richmond felt that the casework technique could approach a "scientific understanding of social dynamics and human behaviour"

(Pitsula 1979, 39). In *Social Diagnosis,* she described the social work process as follows:

1. Collection of social evidence, data on family history and data pertaining to the problem at hand;

2. Critical examination of the material leading to diagnosis; and,

3. Development of a case plan with the involvement of the client.

Richmond originally used the term *diagnosis* for the construct of assessment, borrowing the term from medicine. Her work became the source of what would later be known as the medical model.

The Social Service Commission in Toronto first introduced the practice of professional casework in Canada. The Commission was appointed by the city in 1911, and employed staff who were paid for their work. It requested that the House of Industry in Toronto hire paid staff to operate their relief program. The distribution of out-of-door relief was coordinated according to modern social work principles.

> Distress is relieved with care and sympathy, but the emphasis is not placed on mere relief giving. With each family helped the work includes co-operation with other agencies, diagnosis of need, decision as to remedy, application of remedy, subsequent care and tabulation of results. This is not haphazard "tinkering" with human beings but a real effort to render constructive and progressive service (Social Service Commission Annual Report 1916).

After World War I, the emergent social work profession was called upon to assist with the resettlement of war veterans and with others who were not poor but in need of assistance. In 1918, Charlotte Whitton was chosen as assistant to the Reverend J.G. Shearer at the Social Service Commission and began a period of 25 years of intense involvement in social work and in the development of the social services. She subsequently became a successful municipal politician, becoming a local councillor and then mayor of Ottawa. By 1921, the Social Service Commission had become the social welfare division of the Department of Public Health, illustrating the shift from the premise of moral to social reform. In fact, social work gradually became a secular and scientific alternative to moral and religious work. As this replacement occurred over time, religious faith continued to be central to the practice of social work.

The story of the founding of the Canadian Council on Child Welfare, which became the Canadian Welfare Council and is currently the Canadian Council on Social Development, is told in the work of Rooke and Schnell. A group of social reformers who met at the end of World War I encouraged the founding of a children's bureau in Canada, based on the American model. What resulted was a child welfare bureau in the federal Department of Health, and the founding of a private organization of which Charlotte Whitton became secretary. She did this work

Many child welfare programs were founded in the early 20th century.

J.S. WOODSWORTH

James Shaver Woodsworth was born in Etobicoke, Ontario, in 1874 and moved to Brandon, Manitoba, in 1885. Woodsworth was ordained in 1896 and spent two years as a Methodist circuit preacher.

Having observed industrial capitalism in Canada and Britain and its failure to meet the needs of working people, Woodsworth came to the view that personal salvation could not right social and economic wrongs. While working with immigrant slum dwellers in Winnipeg between 1904 and 1913, he wrote extensively, expounding the "social gospel" in which he called for the Kingdom of God "here and now."

Woodsworth was elected to Parliament in the federal election of 1921 as the member for Winnipeg North Centre. His first resolution was one on unemployment insurance.

J.S. Woodsworth, an ardent democratic socialist.

until the late 1920s while she supported herself by working for a Conservative Member of Parliament. She then became a full-time staff member supported by memberships and funds from contracts.

As secretary, she initiated the social survey as a method of modernizing and professionalizing the provision of charity, a task she saw as her mission. She believed that the use of scientific methods had to replace the dated methods of charity visiting. At the same time, Whitton disagreed strongly with the new breed of social worker/reformer as espoused by Harry Cassidy and Leonard Marsh. She believed in containing and not expanding the role of the welfare state. In *The Dawn of Ampler Life*, a book she wrote at the behest of the leader of the Conservative Party for whom she worked, she explained how charity was a sensitive task requiring the involvement of private organizations and not the involvement of the state. Writing in 1943, she opposed the development of state social programs in Canada, criticizing the work of Leonard Marsh, who wrote what many consider to be the blueprint for the welfare state in his *Report on Social Security for Canada* earlier the same year (Whitton 1943, 205–221).

• Psychology and Social Work

Freudian thought played an increasingly important role in social work in the 1920s, in tandem with Richmond's text, *Social Diagnosis*. While the latter provided guidance on procedure, Freud provided insight into the inner workings of the individual. Social work shifted from a concern with the societal context to a concern with a person's psychological make-up as the source of problems. Goldstein's comments on the American situation apply since the American influence was still very strong in Canada: "Freudian theory overshadowed all other approaches to social problems and orientations about behaviour. By the mid-1920s casework teaching staffs at universities taught psychoanalytic principles as a basis for casework practice." (Goldstein 1973, 31).

Freudian ideas led to a change in social work, in a sense, supporting a move from a more active to a more passive role for the worker. This was designed to permit social work clients to express themselves. Casework remained the dominant form of social work practice, but social workers began to specialize in such areas as family welfare, hospitals and psychiatry. In the 1930s, what became known as functional social work, in which the casework relationship itself would aid the client, began to emerge. Also during this time, group work and community work emerged as different forms of social work (Goldstein 1973, 31–38).

• Social Gospel, Social Work and Social Action

In this period, the **social gospel movement** had a particular influence on Canadian social work. Movements for a more socially oriented church began to appear within the major Protestant churches in the latter part of the nineteenth century. Within each of the Methodist, Presbyterian, Anglican and Congregationalist churches, there were movements for a more socially oriented message, or social gospel, concerning justice and social action. The social gospel wings of the churches eventually started many of the settlement houses in Canada. The movement had strong roots in the prairies.

In 1907, these main Protestant churches established the Moral and Social Reform League. This was the first organization in the country to advocate for social reform. The League was the forerunner of the Social Service Council of Canada, founded in 1914, with the Rev. J.G. Shearer serving as its first director. The Council remained the main social service advocacy organization in Canada for the next 20 years. The name change indicated the shift from a religious and moral perspective to a more scientific one. Not carried out casually, this move was indicative of larger changes in Canadian society, promoting a reform movement that sought to distance itself from a moral base. Several leading members of Canada's trade union movement were active in the Council. After 1925, the Social Service Council declined in significance and was replaced by the Canadian Association of Social Workers in 1927.

Another noted Canadian figure, J.S. Woodsworth, applied social gospel ideas to his work in social services and later to his political life. He helped develop the work of social workers in Winnipeg, which then spread to other parts of Canada. For example, he created the All People's Mission, which provided a variety of direct social services. Woodsworth also served as secretary of the Social Welfare League. Social gospel reformers such as Woodsworth were greatly influenced by the labour movement, particularly by ideas concerning worker control of enterprises and workers' direct participation in decision-making. For these reformers, service to other human beings was considered a form of service to God. In the churches, this spirit manifested itself as the social gospel, implying the achievement of justice in this world rather than in the next. Woodsworth and other social gospellers were also at the forefront in the western agrarian populist movements and political parties. Many Canadian historians, such as Ramsey Cook (1985), view social work as the secular replacement of the social gospel movement.

• Social Work and the Depression

The **Great Depression** of the 1930s was a time of mass unemployment and seriously reduced living standards. In 1933, nearly one-quarter of the labour force was unemployed. This period left an indelible mark on Canadian society. For many Canadians, the Depression shattered the idea that market forces should be left unregulated. They came to see unemployment as a socioeconomic problem requiring a national response, rather than as a personal problem to be solved by local charity.

Unemployed men demand greater respect during the 1930s.

Table 3.1: Key Events of the Post-War Period and the Implications for Social Work

Canada and World Events	Social Welfare	Social Work
1940s		
• War-related state controls • Crown corporations • End of World War II • High labour unrest • International revolutions • Keynesian economics	• Universal Social Legislation • Family Allowance, 1944 • Veterans benefits, 1944 • CMHC, 1945 • White paper on employment, 1945 • Hospital construction • Organization of provincial departments of social services • End of federal grants for relief	• First social work degree (M.S.W.) awarded • Well-paid social work jobs • State regulation • Men in SW administration • Modest growth in employment • First social work unionization • National Committee of Schools of Social Work established
1950s		
• Prosperity • High employment • Cold War purges of left • Low level of unrest • Liberal government	• Expanded social programs • Old Age Pension for all at 70 (1952) • Means-tested pension at 65 (1952) • *Disabled Persons Act* (1955) • *Unemployment Assistance Act* (1956) • Allowances for blind disabled • Hospital care coverage (1957)	• Professionalism (CASW expansion) • Private agencies dominant • Volunteerism • *Child Welfare Act* (Ont) (1954)
1960s		
• Grassroots unrest-growth of anti-poverty, Aboriginal peoples, labour, student, peace organizations • Founding of NDP • Quebec separatism • Economic growth & employment	• *General Welfare Assistance Act* (Ont) (1960) • *National Housing Act* (1964) • Canada Pension Plan (1965) • Canada Assistance Plan (1966) • *Medicare Act* (1968)	• State becomes main employer • Grassroots advocacy & social action programs • Radical social work • Unionization of public sector • First Bachelor of Social Work awarded in 1966 • CASSW established (1967)
1970s		
• Fiscal crisis of state • Conservative business strike • US influence rises in Canada • Rise of women's movement • Rise in women's employment	• Cutbacks begin in health, education, welfare programs • More law and order • Rise of contracting out • NGO funding of militant groups	• Community college SSW programs • Contracting out • Co-optation of militancy • Large growth in schools of social work • CASSW begins accreditation of social work degree programs
1980s		
• Monetarist economics • Conservative policies • US dominance in Canada • Decline in US empire • Cold War tensions • Third World unrest • Waves of refugees • Rise in militancy & popular coalitions	• Major contracting out, cutbacks, workfare • Increases in punitive programs • Women's issues (day care, reproductive choice, pay equity, violence) discussed — little concrete progress • Rise of food banks, charities • Rise of free trade (NAFTA) • *Young Offenders Act* (1984)	• Restraint, burnout • Cuts of advocacy programs • Privatization • Short-term training • Unionization of NGO workers
1990s		
• Economic stabilization • Rising militancy of Aboriginal peoples, women, visible minorities, persons with disability, etc. • Environmental movement strong • Polarization of rich and poor • Popular demands for real social justice • Rising labour militancy at grassroots • Rise of information and communications technology (ICT)	• Attempts to dismantle welfare state, and transfer costs to provinces, cities • Regressive taxes • Cuts in corporate taxes • Free trade • Privatization of universal programs • Cuts to women's, immigrant, Aboriginal peoples rights and programs • Move to workfare and privatization (residual model)	• Split between professional vs. union and coalition strategies in SW • Defensive era • Potential for linkages with client groups • Continued erosion of social services • Rapid expansion of health care spending • Concern over the future of public health care

One important outcome was a change in the nature of politics in Canada, a change that endures to this day. In the 1920s, J.S. Woodsworth began working with a group called the Ginger Group. When the Depression struck, they joined with various labour and socialist groups in 1933 to found the Co-operative Commonwealth Federation (CCF). The CCF is the precursor of the current New Democratic Party of Canada, a party formed in 1961 when the CCF came together with the union movement to forge a new party committed to advocating on behalf of farmers and working people.

This period saw remarkable growth in the number of social workers. During the Depression of the 1930s, new staff had to be hired to run the expanding social service agencies called on to administer relief to a large percentage of the population. In the year 1941, the census recorded 1,805 social workers in Canada, a 65 percent increase over 1931.

PHASE 3: The Era of Applied Social Science — 1941 to Present

During the war, the federal and provincial governments began to realize that social services were not a luxury but a vital part of a smoothly functioning economy. They were required to assist the many returning war veterans and their families. The war ended a period of massive unemployment, sped up industrialization and urbanization, doubled the number of women in the labour force and increased and legitimized government intervention in the economy. In the post-World War II period, a period of rapid economic growth and mass consumption, the career opportunities for social workers began to open up. Education and training programs for prospective social workers increased as well.

Following World War II, the federal Liberal government legislated a series of social welfare measures that were, in retrospect, seemingly intended to forestall the election of the Co-operative Commonwealth Federation. The CCF had achieved considerable popularity during the war with a social reform platform. The Liberals were also concerned with the possibility of a recession, which could cause considerable social unrest. The federal government therefore introduced the Family Allowance, which put more funds into the hands of families, helping to spur more economic growth. In 1951, through constitutional amendment, the federal government introduced a federally financed and administered universal Old Age Pension. Several years later, they introduced benefit programs for persons with disabilities.

A man finds warmth in a manhole shelter, 1955.

National Archives of Canada, PA93920.

Many of these programs led to the expansion of employment in the administration of these new services and programs, precipitating a fundamental change in the nature of Canadian social work. Social work opportunities were now shifting from mainly private, voluntary agencies to government departments or government-financed agencies.

The ideas of Freud continued to have a impact on how social workers practised during this period. Debate occurred between the adherents of the Freudian or diagnostic approach and the newer functional approach. In the **diagnostic approach**, the emphasis was on understanding the condition of the individual by reference to causal events in his or her early life. This approach required a skilled worker who could diagnose the problem and establish and carry out a plan for treatment. The **functional approach** was based on the belief in the potential of clients to determine their own direction with the assistance of a skilled worker. The role of the worker was to establish a structured relationship with the client and facilitate a process of change (Goldstein 1973, 38–39).

In the 1960s, the profession renewed its interest in poverty as a result of anti-poverty measures instituted by the federal government. Community organizing initiatives sprang up in major cities across the country. In Ontario, a second generation of more radical social workers unionized, forming the Federation of Children's Aid Staff in the early 1970s. Several years later, this group of unions joined the Canadian Union of Public Employees, which today represents a large number of social workers who are employed by municipalities across the country.

A range of new models of social work practice also appeared in the 1960s and 1970s, such as the generic or integrated approach, the problem-solving approach, the behaviour modification approach and the structural approach. The latter was based, in part, on a critique of approaches to individual and family social work that tended to seek explanations for and solutions to problems within the individual alone and not within the institutions or structures of society.

Table 3.2: Numbers of Post-Secondary Institutions Offering Social Services Education, Levels of Accreditation, and Number of Graduates

	College/CEGEP (Quebec)	University (34 total)	Number of Graduates
Bachelors	Not Applicable	31	2,085 (1997)
Masters	Not Applicable	23	705 (1997)
Ph.D.	Not Applicable	8	9 (1996)
Certificate/ Diploma	46	Not Applicable	4,540 (1996)

Source: CASSW. 2001. "In Critical Demand: Social Work in Canada, Final Report." Ottawa.

• The Expansion of Social Services and Social Work

Despite the economic expansion of the post-war years, demands on private organizations for relief grew. The few church and private charities could not keep up. Pressure was brought to bear on the federal government by these organizations and by the Canadian Welfare Council, which presented the case for a national program of support for those who were unemployed but not eligible for Unemployment Insurance. The 1956 *Unemployment Insurance Act* provided federal assistance to the provinces for the so-called unemployed but employable person who did not have access to other income security programs or employment income. A condition of this assistance was that the province could not impose a residency requirement on an applicant.

This federal legislation marked the beginning of the process of modernization of relief administration, which led to the passage of the Canada Assistance Plan in 1966. By offering to share 50 percent of the provincial costs of welfare and social services, the federal government effected key changes in social assistance, transforming it into a publicly financed and administered program. This was accompanied by a rapid expansion of social services in child welfare, child care and other services for people in need.

The period from 1963 to 1973 saw the expansion of income security and social service programs. By the end of this period, Canada had become a welfare state with a public system of health and hospital care, and expanded or new income security programs for children, the unemployed, single parents and persons with disabilities. Public or publicly financed social services, including child welfare and child care, were also expanded, many of which were extended for the first time to meet the needs of Canada's Aboriginal population, including those on reserves. Social workers were required to fill a wide range of new positions created by the need to administer these new programs and deliver the expanded social services. The number of persons who identified themselves in the census as social workers rose from 3,495 in 1951 to 30,535 in 1971, with most of that increase occurring in the decade following 1961. The current number is 85,955.

With the increased demand for trained social work staff to administer and deliver the wide range of new social service and income security programs, there was also an increase in college and university social work enrollment. The Canadian Association of Schools of Social Work was established in 1967 to oversee professional university-based education programs in Canada, replacing the American Council on Social Work Education. Currently, there are 34 universities and 46 colleges providing social work and social service education. Social workers now earn wages that are comparable to others in nursing and teaching, with hospitals and child welfare agencies currently employing the largest numbers of social workers.

National Archives of Canada. P141529.

The new clinic at the Montreal Children's Hospital in 1976.

Conclusion

Social work is a profession with a largely twentieth-century history. In the nineteenth century, charities and settlement houses expanded to provide assistance to the large number of people in need. This later led to the desire to put charity on a more systematic footing. Subsequently, in the late nineteenth and early twentieth centuries, charities received public funds to carry out their work. It was this sequence of events that ultimately lead to the formation of the profession of social work — a profession dedicated to helping those in need. The Canadian Association of Social Workers was formed in the 1920s.

The two World Wars (1914–17 and 1939–45) and the Great Depression of the 1930s contributed to the need for an expansion of social services and income security programs and an increased demand for social workers. Later, in the 1960s, federal and provincial funding for social assistance and social services increased substantially as a result of a national funding program (the Canada Assistance Plan). Consequently, the demand for training also increased, resulting in many new social work programs in the community colleges and universities.

Social work practice itself has undergone considerable change. At its inception, casework was the predominant form of social work practice, but since that time both group work and community work have been added. Further, some universities have recognized social administration and policy as an additional arena of practice, rather than simply as a useful background to practice. From the 1920s onwards, social work was strongly affected by the development of the social sciences. Freud's influential ideas about individual psychology tended to lead social work to focus initially on the individual, but later the area of focus was broadened to include a wider range of factors. In the 1930s, a minority in the profession were attracted by radical political ideas and saw social work as a way of address the social ills of society. They supported a broad alliance with the trade union movement and the unionization of social work practitioners. From the 1940s, functionalism in social work began to replace the Freudian approach. By the 1970s, there was a proliferation of approaches that included both Freudian and functional but also the generalist, the problem-solving, the behavioural and the structural approaches, all testifying to the importance of the field to society and the economy.

Chapter 3 Review
The History of Social Work

Discussion Questions

1. What are the historical roots of social work?

2. What are the three phases of the evolution of social work in Canada, and what are the defining characteristics of each phase?

3. What has been the influence of charity organization, the settlement house movement and social reformers on social work in Canada?

4. Describe the influence of the social gospel movement on social work in Canada.

5. What was the effect of the Depression of the 1930s on the development of social work in Canada?

6. How has casework changed since the days of Mary Richmond?

7. What was the influence of Freudian psychology on the way social work was understood and practised? Why has this influence lessened since the 1960s?

8. What is the scientific approach to social work and how did it change the nature of social work practice?

Websites

• **A History of Social Work — On-line Materials**
  http://www.socialpolicy.ca/cush

  This website contains text, audio lectures, videos and photographs. By going through the site, students will become more familiar with the major concepts and issues in social welfare — what they are, where they come from, how they work and why they work the way they do.

• **History of Toynbee Hall**
  http://www.toynbeehall.org.uk/history.htm

  Toynbee Hall has been working to combat poverty in London's East End for 120 years, and the organization started an international movement that focused attention on tackling social problems. Toynbee inspired many well-known national organizations and involved eminent people from all walks of life. Toynbee Hall today strives to help the people who live in the impoverished area of Tower Hamlets — an area on the City of London's doorstep.

• **World Wide Web Resources for Social Workers**
  http://www.nyu.edu/socialwork/wwwrsw

  This vast resource for social workers, produced by Dr. Gary Holden at New York University, offers an eclectic collection of material on social welfare with a useful search engine, covering many of the topics in these pages. It is particularly helpful for researching a particular topic or locating an international association. Try clicking on "social work," then "general" and finally "history" for a few interesting history links.

Key Terms

• **Private charities**

• **Poor relief**

• **Deserving poor**

• **Undeserving poor**

• **Charity Organization Society (COS)**

• **Settlement houses**

• **Scientific philanthropy**

• **Social survey research**

• **Casework**

• **Freudian thought**

• **Social gospel movement**

• **Great Depression**

• **Diagnostic approach**

• **Functional approach**

Social service workers in New Brunswick celebrate in October 2002 after hearing that a tentative deal was reached between the provincial government and the Canadian Union of Public Employees (CUPE) that could end a month-old strike.

4

Social Work as a Profession

People Making a Difference

According to available census data, there were 1,056 self-described social workers in 1931, the first year for which data is available. Thirty years later, in 1961, there were 10,854 social workers. As a result of the funding made available after the passage of the Canada Assistance Plan in 1966, there was enormous growth in the number of social workers in the following years. The 1971 census recorded 30,535 social workers. By 1991, the number of workers had doubled to 61,135. In 2004, the combined total number of social workers and community and social service workers was 121,800 (43,000 social workers and 78,800 community and social service workers). Of this total, approximately 80 percent of social workers and 75 percent of community and social service workers were women (http://www.jobfutures.ca).

It was not until the end of World War I that social work began to be recognized as a distinct profession in Canada. Since that time, there has been rapid growth in the number of professional social workers. All levels of government, federal, provincial and municipal, now fund and deliver social services and income security programs.

Of course, this growth in the number of social workers reflects the expansion of social services and income security programs over this period, particularly in the 1960s when significant new money was put into child welfare and income security. As the importance of social welfare programs increased, and as more and more people were involved in providing these services, a higher level of organization and a greater degree of professionalization was required. Also, important legislation was passed by provincial legislatures to meet the increasing demands for social services, and provincial associations were created to help train and organize social workers at the local level. Training and professional programs were introduced to accommodate this expansion, and codes of practice were elaborated to ensure quality service.

The social work profession in Canada faces many challenges and it will face many more in the coming years. Foremost among these are demographic changes that are affecting the client base served by practitioners and widespread cutbacks and "efficiencies" that will affect how well practitioners can serve individuals and families. This chapter describes the contexts in which social workers function, the associations that represent them, the training they undergo and the difficulties they face. The picture that emerges is one of hard-working and dedicated professionals who would be able to do much more if they were given the necessary resources to carry out their work effectively.

Canadian Association of Schools of Social Work (2005).

Canadian Association of Schools of Social Work homepage

CASW, CASSW AND IFSW
WEBSITES

**The Canadian Association of
Social Workers (CASW)**

• The CASW website contains
useful information about how
the CASW represents
Canadian social workers,
information about the
profession and the status of
professional legislation in each
province. The site is located at:
http://www.casw-acts.ca

**The Canadian Association of
Schools of Social Work
(CASSW)**

• The CASSW website lists
many useful reports, some of
which are available for
downloading. Information
about university programs in
social work is also available.
The site is located at:
http://www.cassw-acess.ca

**The International Federation of
Social Workers**

• The IFSW website is worth a
visit. Once you are there, you
will find general information
about the IFSW, its history and
aims, as well as several of their
publications. All 13 policy
papers and the IFSW *Code of
Ethics* are also on-line. The
site is located at:
http://www.ifsw.org

**The International Association
of Schools of Social Work
(IASSW)**

• The main mission of the
IASSW is to develop and
promote excellence in social
work education, research and
scholarship. Information on its
activities can be found at:
http://www.iassw-aiets.org

Social Work Associations

The profession of social work in Canada is regulated by 10 provincial associations and one territorial organization, each with its own name, policy and regulations. Each association is mandated by provincial legislation to regulate and monitor professional social workers and social work practice in their jurisdiction. Each province has established regulatory bodies (sometimes referred to as "colleges") to govern the profession in accordance with the legislation. Individual social workers become registered or licensed by becoming a member of the regulatory body in the province where they work.

The associations come together under the umbrella of the Canadian Association of Social Workers (CASW), which provides national leadership in strengthening and advancing the social work profession. The education of social workers is monitored by the national Canadian Association of Schools of Social Work (CASSW).

• The Canadian Association of Social Workers (CASW)

The Canadian Association of Social Workers (CASW) was "founded" at the 1924 American National Conference of Social Work, which was held in Toronto. At this meeting, several Canadian social workers discussed the need for a professional association that addressed the specific needs of Canadians. The Association was formally established in 1927, and the first edition of its professional journal, *The Social Worker*, appeared in 1932. Initially, social workers joined the Association individually. Today, CASW is a federation of 10 provincial associations and one territorial organization. The Association has jurisdiction over some issues, while the provincial associations maintain jurisdiction over others. Because social services are a provincial responsibility in Canada, the provincial associations assume great importance in the development and administration of social work.

Data on the membership of the Canadian Association of Social Workers is an indication of the rapid growth of the profession: By 1939, CASW had 600 members; by 1966, it had 3,000; and by 1986, there were 9,000 members. Today, there are about 14,000 CASW members across the country, all with some formal credentials in social work.

CASW supplies members with relevant professional documents, a national journal, activities and events, access to benefits, representation nationally and internationally, and an opportunity to participate in professional development panels and organizations. CASW also influences governments through consultations, position statements and the presentation of briefs. The main benefit of belonging to the CASW is being part of a like-minded group of people who share the same goals and who work together to improve their profession.

All provinces have introduced legislation that will give more control over the title and practice of social workers. Employers frequently ask that their employees be members of CASW or their provincial association. Social workers, in turn, have supported this move as a way to protect the public and to guarantee a level of professionalism. Like the provinces themselves, the associations vary in terms of their level of organization, their activities and their priorities. The box at the end of this chapter describes the provincial associations and the legal framework within which they operate.

• The Canadian Association of Schools of Social Work (CASSW)

The **Canadian Association of Schools of Social Work (CASSW)** was established in 1967, replacing the National Committee of Schools of Social Work, which, since 1948, had been the forum for programs offering professional education in social work. The CASSW is a national association of university faculties, schools and departments offering professional education in social work at the undergraduate, graduate and post-graduate levels.

The purpose of CASSW is to advance the standards, effectiveness and relevance of social work education and scholarship in Canada and, through participation in international associations, in other countries. CASSW is responsible for reviewing and approving social work educational programs. It also publishes a quarterly journal entitled the *Canadian Social Work Review* and undertakes research studies of relevance to the profession, such as research on women and HIV and anti-racism.

• The International Federation of Social Workers (IFSW) and the International Association of Schools of Social Work (IASSW)

The **International Federation of Social Workers (IFSW)** is a successor to the International Permanent Secretariat of Social Workers, which was founded in Paris in 1928. In 1950, the IFSW was created, with the goal of becoming an international organization of professional social workers. Today the IFSW represents over half a million social workers in 55 different counties. The IFSW promotes social work as a profession, links social workers from around the world and promotes the participation of social workers in social policy and planning.

The **International Association of Schools of Social Work (IASSW)** is an association of educators and institutions involved in social work education worldwide. It helps to promote social work education, facilitate mutual exchanges and represent social work educators at the international level. The IASSW adheres to all UN Declarations and Conventions on human rights, recognising that respect for the inalienable rights of the individual is the foundation of freedom, justice and peace.

IFSW WORKING PAPERS

The titles of these papers are:

- Health
- HIV-AIDS
- Human Rights
- Migration
- Older Persons
- The Protection of Personal Information
- Refugees
- Conditions in Rural Communities
- Women
- Youth
- Peace and Social Justice
- Displaced Persons
- Globalization and the Environment
- Indigenous People

War Child Canada provided aid in the aftermath of the Kosovo war.

Steven Hick.

Regulating the Social Work Profession

Each Canadian province or territory has extensive legislation governing the practice of social work, most of which has come into effect over the last 30 years. Manitoba was the first to enact legislation, in 1966, and Ontario was the last, having only recently (1998) passed social work legislation.

In general, each Act governs who can call themselves a social worker, the qualifications required to use the title and penalties for contravening the regulatory Act or for unethical behaviour. For example, in British Columbia, the *Social Workers Act* of 1979 provides for the control of the use of the title Registered Social Worker and stipulates that whoever contravenes these provisions commits an offence and is liable to a fine of not more than $1,000. It also specifies that a Board of Registration be appointed by the Lieutenant Governor in Council to enforce the Act. Similarly, the early Manitoba legislation, the *Manitoba Institute of Registered Social Workers Incorporation Act* (1966), provides for voluntary registration and control of the designation Registered Social Worker. The Board of the Manitoba Institute of Registered Social Workers requires either a B.S.W. or an M.S.W. from an accredited university or college or the equivalent as they determine.

In 1998, the Ontario government enacted the *Social Work and the Social Service Work Act*, which stipulates that any practitioner wishing to use the title Social Worker/Registered Social Worker or Social Service Worker/ Registered Social Service Worker must be a member of the College of Social Workers and Social Service Workers of Ontario. The College's regulatory functions include a complaints and disciplinary process that can result in suspension or revocation of a license to practice.

CASSW report on the social work profession in Canada

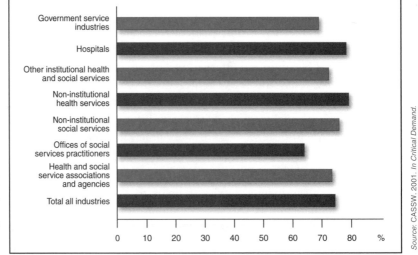

Source: CASSW. 2001. In Critical Demand.

Figure 4.1: Proportion of female social workers in selected sectors.

Integrated Service Delivery (ISD)

Increasingly, social and health services are being provided to Canadians using **Integrated Service Delivery (ISD)**. The ISD model recognizes that individuals or families coming to an agency for help often have a variety of needs. It is therefore important that programs coordinate effectively so that those needs are met without systems getting in the way.

Integrated Service Delivery is a team-based and client-focused model that enables people to access services in one location, but from a variety of service providers. In Manitoba, for example, a long list of services — including child and family services, child day care, children's special services, mental health, employment and income assistance, home care, housing and supported living — can be accessed in a Community Access Centre. A **Community Access Centre** is a place to get program information and services, fill out applications and ask questions. In such centres, citizens can access more than one service, which is then delivered by a service delivery team following a service plan.

Social workers are playing a key role in these integrated service delivery systems. With their multi-disciplinary and collaborative skills, they act as case managers and service planners and provide direct services to those members of the community who are in need.

Trefann Court community centre (1973). Modern versions of this early community centre in Toronto are increasingly used as a way of effectively delivering coordinated services to entire communities.

DEFINING "SOCIAL WORK"

A new international definition of social work was adopted at the IFSW General Meeting in Montreal in July 2000. The new definition replaces the IFSW definition of 1982, and recognizes that social work in the twenty-first century is dynamic and evolving and therefore no definition should be regarded as exhaustive. (There is a further discussion of this new definition of social work on page 19.)

The Roles of the Social Worker

A practitioner may assume a number of social worker roles, depending on the nature of their job and the approach to practice that they use. The role that is selected and applied should ideally be the role that is most effective with a particular client in the particular circumstances.

- The role of *enabler* involves the worker in helping people to organize to help themselves; for example, helping a community identify problems, explore and select strategies, organize and mobilize to address the problems.

- A *broker* links individuals and groups who need help; for example, linking a woman who is abused by her spouse to a shelter for battered women.

- In the role of *advocate,* the worker provides leadership in advocating on behalf of a person or in challenging an institution's decision not to provide services.

- The *initiator* calls attention to problems or the problems a particular policy or program may cause.

- The role of *mediator* involves participating as a neutral party in a dispute between parties to help them reconcile differences or achieve mutually beneficial agreements.

- As a *negotiator*, the social worker is allied with one side in a dispute and tries to achieve agreement by bargaining on his or her client's behalf.

- The *activist* seeks to change institutions and structures in society, helping to organize people to shift power and resources to oppressed or disadvantaged groups.

- As an *educator*, the social worker is providing information and awareness of problem and solutions.

- The social worker is frequently a *coordinator*, bringing all the pieces together in an organized manner to accomplish a task.

- As a *researcher*, the social worker provides resources for clients and stays abreast of his or her field.

- The *group facilitator* may lead a group activity as part of group therapy, a self-help group or any other type of group.

- The social worker may be engaged as a *public speaker* at schools, service organizations, with police or within related agencies.

Whatever the particular context that social workers find themselves in, they must apply themselves at all times in a professional manner, using all the knowledge and skills they have at their disposal and taking into account the specific needs of the client and the range of remedies currently available.

Some of the roles social workers find themselves in.

Table 4.1: A Comparison of Three Helping Professions: Social Work, Psychology and Psychiatry

	Social Work	Psychology	Psychiatry
Focus of attention	Dual focus on individual and environment and interaction between the two	Individual behaviour, which includes internal thoughts, feelings and emotional responses	Mental illness; wide range of disturbed behaviour and emotional reactions
Assessment/diagnostic tools	Social history; client interviews; observation	Diagnostic tests (IQ, personality, etc.); interviews; observation	Medical exam; use of International Classification of Disease; interviews; observation; tests
Intervention methods	Casework; family and/or group therapy; education/information; referral to community resources	Behaviour modification; psychotherapy; environmental modification	Prescribe psychotropic medication; psychotherapy; biological treatments
Aim of intervention	To help individuals, families and communities understand and solve personal and social problems	To solve or prevent behavioural, cognitive and affective problems	To reduce symptoms, change behaviour or promote personality growth
Specializations	Counselling, group work, social administration, research and evaluation, community organization, teaching	Clinical, experimental, neurological, developmental, social, counselling, educational, industrial, personality	Child, geriatric, forensic, liaison, behaviour, family, sexual, psychoanalysis, research
Education	B.S.W., M.S.W., D.S.W., Ph.D.	B.A. or B.Sc., M.A., Ph.D.	Medical doctor and at least five years' psychiatric training
Professional association (national)	Canadian Association of Social Workers	Canadian Psychological Association	Canadian Psychiatric Association

Source: R. Chappell. 2001. *Social Welfare in Canadian Society*, 2nd Edition. Toronto: Thomson Nelson Learning, 152.

SOCIAL WORK VALUES

The CASW *Code of Ethics* encompasses the values and principles of human worth, dignity, self-determination and justice upon which social work is based. Its key principles deal with confidentiality, respect for the individual and his or her opinion and conflicts of interest.

The CASW *Code* summarizes these values as follows:

- The profession of social work is founded on humanitarian and egalitarian ideals. Social workers believe in the intrinsic worth and dignity of every human being and are committed to the values of acceptance and self-determination.

- Social workers are dedicated to the welfare and self-realization of human beings; to the development and disciplined use of scientific knowledge regarding human and societal behaviours; to the development of resources to meet individual, group, national and international needs and aspirations; and to the achievement of social justice for all.

- Social workers are pledged to serve [their clients] without discrimination on any grounds of race, ethnicity, language, religion, marital status, gender, sexual orientation, age, abilities, economic status, political affiliation or national ancestry (CASW 1994).

CASW's Code of Ethics

The CASW has a **Code of Ethics** to help guide social workers in the course of their work. The code, a set of guiding principles that can lead to the formulation of more specific standards of practice, is reprinted in Appendix B of this book. It is a key document and should be studied carefully by those entering the profession.

Above all, the *Code of Ethics* demands that a social worker take the best interests of the client as the primary consideration in any intervention. The best interests of client means:

- that the wishes, desires, motivation and plans of the client are taken by the social worker as the primary consideration in any intervention plan developed by the social worker (subject to change only when the client's plans are documented to be unrealistic, unreasonable or potentially harmful to self or others or otherwise determined inappropriate).

- that all actions and interventions of the social worker are taken subject to the reasonable belief that the client will benefit from the action, and

- that the social worker will consider the client as an individual, a member of a family unit, a member of a community, a person with a distinct ancestry or culture and will consider those factors in any decision affecting the client (CASW 1994).

Whether dealing with **voluntary clients** (people who have chosen to seek the services of a social worker) or **involuntary clients** (those who are legally obligated to accept services, such as prisoners on parole or children in care), social workers have a responsibility to their clients to address their needs while respecting their dignity and self-worth.

According to C.S. Levy (1993), codes of ethics focus typically on three broad types of principles. Identifying these three dimensions can help one gain a better understanding of the various aspects of professional ethics.

- *Normative standards* identify what the expected standard should be.

- *Aspirational ethics* identify the principles that social workers should attempt to reach.

- *Prescriptive ethics* refer to behaviours to which professionals are held accountable to uphold.

The second part of the CASW code (referring to ethical responsibilities) is concerned with the first two aspects of ethics (normative and aspirational). The IFSW code refers predominantly to aspirational ethics. Prescriptive ethics are contained in the first seven statements in the code — a breach of these form the basis for disciplinary action. These correspond to what are referred to as "ethical duties" in the CASW *Code of Ethics*.

As with other professionals, and arguably more so given the nature of their work, social workers regularly face situations that demand a clear understanding of ethical obligations and responsibilities. For this reason, social workers must have a comprehensive and solid understanding of the CASW *Code of Ethics* and any provincial code, if they are different. But, this is not enough. Practitioners also need to know workplace and legislated guidelines and obligations and how these apply in any given context.

Ethical codes of conduct try to define acceptable behaviour, but they can only provide very broad guidelines for resolving dilemmas and not specific answers to localized problems. Ethical dilemmas exist when there are conflicts between different values. An often-cited example of this is the potential conflict that arises if a client voices an intention to hurt someone. This presents a clash between a client's right to confidentiality and the rights of society to protection from harm.

● The Ambiguity of Social Work

The **ambiguity of social work** refers to the fact that the social worker frequently has to balance urgent and practical intervention measures with more difficult ethical and sometimes "political" questions. In the course of their work, for example, social workers are inevitably confronted with situations in which the policy and regulations of the agency conflict with what they, as experienced social workers, see as being in the best interests of their client. As well, the standards and ethics of the profession may be inconsistent with the established procedures and practices of a particular agency. Balancing one's beliefs, professional standards and agency rules can be difficult. In this context, the social worker's place of employment can be either a source of empowerment or a source of distress.

Ethical dilemmas often arise, for example, in income support and child custody cases. Welfare workers interview clients and, based on their assessment, often refer them to particular services for which they qualify. However, part of the mandate of welfare organizations is to spend public money wisely. Therefore, welfare workers must ensure that the client is genuinely in need and eligible for assistance, while representing the client's interests as fairly as possible. Striking a balance is often more easily said than done.

Similarly, in child custody cases (where a child welfare worker is expected to act in the best interest of the child), the social worker may be criticized for leaving a child in the home or for taking the child away from its family prematurely. Such dilemmas are obviously aggravated when there are large caseloads or tight budgets that make it difficult for social workers to provide services in a way that is consistent with their professional and personal beliefs.

A HELPING HAND

One social worker working in child welfare describes the job as follows:

"I would like to change people's perceptions that I as a social worker can come in and fix the problem. I'm not the fixer.

"I'm simply someone with an objective point of view who comes in and says, 'Have you tried this or have you thought about this option?'

"It's not up to me to fix your problems. It's up to you to identify what they are and to say 'yes, I want to change it' or 'no, I don't.'

"If you don't want to change it, that's fine, that's your business. But if you do want to change it, great, I'll be in there like Flynn to help you. But I can't do it for you."

"I think that's the biggest misconception people have about what social workers do."

Child welfare workers attend to the child's best interests above all else.

SIX-STEP PROCESS FOR ETHICAL DECISION-MAKING

The Canadian Counselling Association (CCA) provides a six-step process for ethical decision-making.

- **Step One. What are the key ethical issues in this situation?** This first step consists of the counsellor identifying the ethical issues and/or behaviours which are of concern in the particular situation.

- **Step Two. What ethical guidelines are relevant to this situation?** The second important step consists of referring to the CCA Code of Ethics to see if the situation is dealt with under one or more of the articles in the Code. If there are appropriate articles (for example, on confidentiality or informed consent), following it may be sufficient to address the ethical issue. If the ethical problem is more complex, however, the following further steps will be needed.

- **Step Three. What ethical principles are of major importance in this situation?** The third step consists of examining the ethical principles that are important in the situation including those that may be in conflict. This would include a review of the six ethical principles as stated in this Code of Ethics: (a) respect for the dignity of persons; (b) not wilfully harming others; (c) integrity in relationships; (d) responsible caring; (e) responsibility to society; (f) respect for self-determination.

- **Step Four. What are the most important principles, and what are the risks and benefits if these principles are acted upon?** The fourth step consists of choosing the most important principles and relevant ethical articles and beginning to

implement some possible action by: (a) generating alternatives and examining the risks and benefits of each; (b) securing additional information, including possible discussion with the client; (c) consulting with knowledgeable colleagues, with provincial or CCA ethics committees, or with other appropriate sources; and (d) examining the probable outcomes of various courses of action.

- **Step Five. Will I feel the same about this situation if I think about it a little longer?** Until this point, this decision-making process has concentrated on fairly cognitive, rational steps, so at the fifth step counsellors should acknowledge and include in their decision-making process the feelings and intuitions evoked by the ethical challenge. In so doing, they could use such techniques as: (a) Quest - a solitary walk in the woods or park where your emotions evoked by the ethical challenge are brought into full awareness; (b) Incubation — "sleep on it"; and (c) Time projection — projecting the ethical situation into the future and thinking about the various probable scenarios.

- **Step Six - What plan of action will be most helpful in this situation?** The sixth step consists of taking some action. Counsellors should follow a concrete action plan, evaluate the plan and be prepared to correct any negative consequences that might occur from the action taken.

Many introductory texts present the delivery of social services in an idealized form, assuming that the professional's relationship with the client will always be governed by an exclusive concern for the client's well-being. Unfortunately, this is sometimes not the reality. While staffed with the most dedicated and hard-working people, many social work agencies may enforce rigid rules and regulations, engage in excessive paperwork and enforce computerized control over the client-social worker relationship. And too often such rigid controls are at direct odds with the needs of the client.

The working life of a social worker, then, is very much a mix of the "ideal" and the "practical." They have a *Code of Ethics* with high ideals, but the reality is that they must practice within a context of institutions and laws that in many ways limits the capacity of an individual to deliver on such ideals. In the face of many difficulties, individual social workers make judgments based on their knowledge and experience and, in the end, that is all they can be expected to do. Then again, those entering the profession normally do so hoping the journey will, on the whole, be mostly satisfying while knowing full well that it will not always be simple or easy.

SOCIAL WORK KNOWLEDGE

- human growth and behaviour
- family dynamics
- communication theory
- community development theory
- organizational theory
- theories of the state
- theories of oppression and empowerment
- social treatment interventions
- social action methods
- social research methods and policy analysis

A reception held for members of the Canadian Association of Schools of Social Workers at the CASSW's Annual Conference, held at the University of Manitoba in Winnipeg, June 2004.

The Education of Social Workers

Whatever type of work is pursued, some post-secondary education is required in order to practice in the field of social work. In general, a university-trained person is referred to as a "social worker," whereas a community college-trained individual is called a "social service worker." In some provinces, and in everyday contexts, this distinction is often ignored, though obviously university-trained individuals will have more years of training behind them.

The first trained Canadian social workers graduated from the University of Toronto's Department of Social Services in 1914. Until the early 1970s, social work schools in Canada were accredited by the American Council of Social Work Education. There are now 34 universities offering social work degrees and 46 community colleges offering diplomas. Nearly 5,000 students enroll annually in social work degree programs, and about 370 faculty are employed to teach them.

A Bachelor of Social Work (B.S.W.) normally requires four years of university study. At least one additional year of graduate study is required for the Master of Social Work (M.S.W.) degree. A Diploma in Social Service Work from a community college also requires several years of training. Those holding a non-social work undergraduate degree normally must complete two years of study for a Master of Social Work degree. There are currently seven M.S.W. programs offered in Canada. Post-graduate study leading to a doctoral degree in social work is normally pursued by those who wish to teach at a university or those involved in high-level research, social policy or large-scale administration.

Table 4.2: Values, Beliefs and Attitudes

Values that Hinder	Values that Help
I know what is best for my clients.	People are capable of finding their own answers and making decisions.
People don't want to change.	People can and do change.
My religion/culture/viewpoint is the best.	I can accept a wide variety of cultures, religions and viewpoints.
It is essential that my clients like me.	The purpose of social work is to help people exercise choice, not make clients like me.
Some people are not deserving of our respect and caring.	Every person has intrinsic worth and deserves respect.

Adapted from: B. Shebib. 2004. *Choices: Interviewing and Counselling Skills for Canadians.* Toronto: Prentice Hall, 60.

Employment Opportunities in Social Work

The career opportunities for qualified social workers today are quite diverse:

- *Health and social services.* Job settings include family and child welfare agencies, hospitals and other health care facilities, group homes and hostels, addiction treatment facilities and social assistance offices.

- *Government services.* A large number of social workers work directly for some level of government, although this setting is declining as more and more services are devolved to community agencies. These services include planning and administration of programs, correctional facilities and the justice system.

- *Communities.* Community organizers work out of community health centres, resource centres and other grassroots organizations and counselling and support to local communities.

- *Research.* The federal, provincial and local governments frequently call upon researchers to conduct surveys and carry out pertinent research that impacts on social work practice in various settings.

- *Self-employment.* A small but growing number of social workers are self-employed, offering services directly to the public for fees or contracting their services to large organizations.

WHERE ARE THE JOBS?

- Managers, 11.4%
- Social workers, 30.2%
- Family, marriage and related counsellors, 23.7%
- Probation officers, 3.6%
- Community and social service workers, 39.1%

Source: CASSW. 2001. *In Critical Demand.*

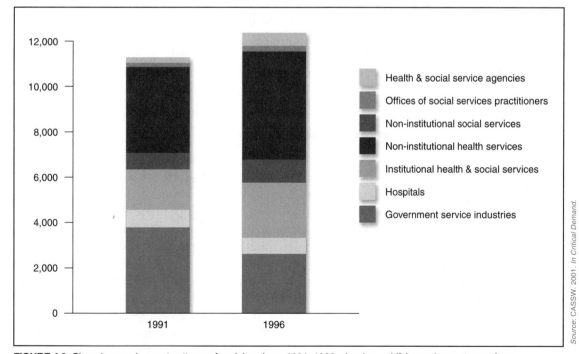

Source: CASSW. 2001. *In Critical Demand.*

FIGURE 4.2: Changing employment patterns of social workers, 1991–1996, showing a shift in employment away from government services and into the non-institutional and not-for-profit agency sectors.

Unionization and Salaries

Today, most Canadian social workers are members of **public sector unions**. Indeed, they were part of the wider unionization of the public sector during the 1960s and 1970s, when, for the first time, public sector employees were permitted to join a union.

Of course, there was some debate over whether social workers should join trade unions. Did they not, after all, have their own **professional associations** and were trade unions not traditionally more associated with industrial workers than with people who were professionally trained? This matter was resolved, in the end, by a division of labour. The associations represent social workers in issues pertaining to the development of the profession, the education of their members and in discussions of social issues and social policy. The unions represent them in the areas of pay or working conditions. The professional association and the union in effect complement each other and both have mandates to act as voices for those they represent.

According to 2004 Job Futures data (http://www.jobfutures.ca), 64 percent of social workers belong to unions, compared with 32 percent for all occupations. Forty-seven percent of community and social service workers are unionized. The largest unions representing social workers in Canada are the Canadian Union of Public Employees (CUPE) and the Public Sector Alliance of Canada (PSAC). CUPE members are represented by provincial level divisions and sectors. For example, the membership of CUPE Ontario is broken down into five principal sectors: municipal, health care, school boards, university and social services. social workers in children's aid societies, associations for community living, children's care centres, municipal social services, community agencies (such as women's shelters) and municipal and charitable homes for the aged are all unionized.

Newfoundland social workers protest low wages.

• Salaries of Social Workers

Social workers have benefitted from unions in ways similar to other workers. Unions have helped to raise salaries, improve working conditions and enhance job security. Pressure from female social workers and from the broader women's movement has encouraged the unions to address issues important to women, such as equal pay for work of equal value, child care, maternity leave, better pensions and sexual harassment. Unions in social work agencies have also played another important role that is less well recognized. Labour unions have, throughout history, advocated for improved social programs, income security and social services. Programs such as Employment Insurance and medicare would not exist today without pressure from the union sector. As these programs come under increasing pressure from funding cuts, the unions are again playing a key role in opposing cutbacks.

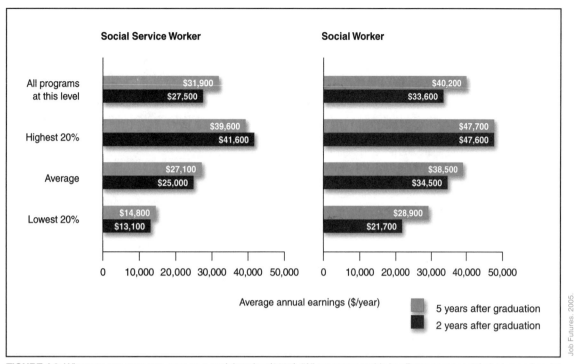

FIGURE 4.3: What you can expect to earn as a social worker (2005). "All programs at this level" compares social service and social workers' earnings with the earnings of those employed in related fields with similar qualifications.

It is probably safe to say that people enter social work more for the selfless rewards of helping people in need than for earning high incomes from such work. However, having said that, and taking into account the importance of their work for other human beings, one might expect a somewhat higher level of remuneration in the field. Social workers are generally among the lowest-paid service workers.

Two main reasons have been advanced to explain why this is so. First, social workers are paid less because they work with underprivileged people who are themselves not highly respected and have little power. Second, the profession has always been seen as female-dominated (and since women in general are paid less than men, social work tends to pay less than male-dominated professions). Unfair as this may be, both explanations are undoubtedly a large part of the reason for the low wages (and, of course, beg even larger questions).

Recent cutbacks have directly affected the income of social workers. As well, all levels of government are moving towards "contracting out" the delivery of social services to the private sector (arguing that it will save money). Accordingly, social workers increasingly find themselves working for non-unionized, underfunded private agencies, and the wages of social workers are squeezed. With the likelihood of even deeper funding cutbacks in the near future, there will be an ever greater need for social workers, their associations and their unions to be more forceful in demanding just compensation for their efforts.

SOCIAL WORK LEGISLATION IN CANADA: A SUMMARY

Alberta College of Social Workers

Title of Act/Regulation: The *Health Professions Act* (1999) replaces the *Social Work Professions Act* (1995)

Mission and Goals: The mission and goals of the College are to promote, regulate and govern the profession of social work in the Province of Alberta; to advocate for skilled and ethical social work practices; and, to advocate for policies, programs and services that promote the profession and protect the best interests of the public.

Membership: The ACSW now receives its mandate from the *Health Professions Act*. In 1999, the Provincial Legislature passed an amendment to the *Social Work Profession Act* making it mandatory for people who have a social work education, who work within the scope of social work practice and who work with the public, to be registered. To be considered for Registration you must be actively engaged in social work practice, meet the character and reputation requirements, provide two references from Registered Social Workers who can attest to your social work practice, and complete additional training in social work ethics and standards of practice.

Governing Body: The Alberta College of Social Workers (ACSW) is both the designated regulatory body for the practice of social work in Alberta and the professional association representing the interests of social workers.

Website: http://www.acsw.ab.ca

British Columbia Association of Social Workers and the Board of Registration for Social Workers

Title of Act/Regulation: *Social Workers Act*, R.S.B.C., c.389, (1979)

Mission and Goals: The mandate of the British Columbia Association of Social Workers (BCASW) is to advocate for the interests and concerns of professional social workers. The Association does not carry a disciplinary role, which is the mandate of the profession's regulatory body, the Board of Registration for Social Workers (BRSW), which provides for the control of the use of the title Registered Social Worker. The Association is currently advocating for new legislation to govern the profession. See regulation update on their website for the most up-to-date information.

Membership: You are eligible to join BCASW if you hold a graduate degree in social work or are a student currently enrolled in a social work degree program. To become a Registered Social Worker with the BRSW you require a bachelor's or master's degree in social work; or a degree or certificate deemed by the Board to be equivalent to a master's degree in social work or postgraduate degree in social work; or to be a "Registered Social Worker" or "Professional Social Worker" in another province where the standards are not less than the minimum standards prescribed under this Act and regulations.

Governing Body: A board of directors of the BCASW comprises seven members and nine regional representatives. The Board of Registration for social workers is composed of not more than 12 or less than 10 members appointed by the Lieutenant Governor in Council including two persons who are not social workers and the remainder are R.S.W.s.

Website: http://www.bcasw.org

Manitoba Association of Social Workers/ Manitoba Institute of Registered Social Workers

Title of Act/Regulation: *The Manitoba Institute of Registered Social Workers Incorporation Act* (1966)

Mission and Goals: The Manitoba Association of Social Workers (MASW) is the voice of the social work profession, providing peer support and connecting people with social workers across Canada. The Manitoba Institute of Registered Social Workers (MIRSW) is the regulatory arm of the profession, and is responsible for certifying members and protecting the public through recognized, ethical standards of practice. It requires registrants to maintain current knowledge through education. It is a disciplinary body that investigates public complaints.

Membership: Membership in the MASW requires a B.S.W., M.S.W., or D.S.W. degree or a Welfare Worker's Certificate from a Manitoba Community College, or its equivalent, and two consecutive years of employment and letters of recommendation.

Individuals are eligible for registration with the MIRSW if they are employed by an agency or are in private practice, possess a B.S.W., M.S.W. or D.S.W. degree from an accredited school of social work and have practiced social work for a minimum of one year.

Governing Body: The Board of the Manitoba Institute of Registered Social Workers.

Website: http://www.geocities.com/masw_mirsw

New Brunswick Association of Social Workers

Title of Act/Regulation: The *Act to Incorporate the New Brunswick Association of Social Workers* (1988)

Mission and Goals: The New Brunswick Association of Social Workers ensures quality social work services to the population of New Brunswick. It accomplishes its mission by ensuring all persons practising and/or using the title social worker are registered; establishing and enforcing standards of qualification, knowledge, skill and efficiency of practice; investigating complaints against its members; promoting public awareness of the role of social work; and assisting members in the pursuit of social justice and social change.

Membership: To become a regular member, you require a bachelor's, master's or doctoral degree in social work or the equivalent from a School of Social Work approved by the Committee; a person who has passed the examination prescribed by the Committee and has sufficient experience; or a person who is a member of an association of social workers approved by the Committee.

Governing Body: The Board of Directors is comprised of an elected executive, one director from each local chapter, the NB Director to the CASW board and one public member appointed by the Minister of Health and Community Services. The Board serves as the governing body of the general membership and administers the affairs of the Association.

Website: http://www.nbasw-atsnb.ca

Newfoundland and Labrador Association of Social Workers

Title of Act/Regulation: *Social Workers Association Act* (1993)

Mission and Goals: The Act provides for the control of practice of social work and the use of the title social worker or registered social work, or abbreviations of such titles. The NLASW enforces the Act and works to promote excellence in the social work profession.

Membership: A bachelor's, master's or doctoral degree or equivalent education in social work from an educational institution approved by the committee of examiners and completion of the examination prescribed.

Governing Body: The Board of the Newfoundland and Labrador Association of Social Workers is composed of the president, a president-elect, an at-large executive member, a member who is a member of the Board of CASW, other members as provided by the bylaws and a member appointed by the Minister. The Board of Directors is empowered to be the regulatory body and the professional association for social workers.

Website: http://www3.nf.sympatico.ca/nlasw

Nova Scotia Association of Social Workers

Title of Act/Regulation: *Social Workers Act* (1993)

Mission and Goals: The Nova Scotia Association of Social Workers promotes and regulates the practice of social work so its members can provide a high standard of service that respects diversity, promotes social justice, and enhances the worth, self-determination and potential of individuals, families and communities.

Membership: To become a member everyone must pass an examination. Other requirements include a doctoral or master's degree or a graduate-level diploma in social work from an approved faculty of social work and two years of experience, or a bachelor's degree in social work from an approved faculty of social work and three years of experience, subsequent to the degree.

Governing Body: The Council of the NSASW consists of the president, vice-president, secretary, treasurer, immediate past president, the chair of the Board of Examiners and other members as provided by the bylaws.

The Board of Examiners consists of seven social workers appointed by the Council who represent the diversity of various fields of social work practice and who reflect the sex, racial, and ethnic composition of the Association, one of whom is teaching at an approved school of social work and three persons appointed by the Governor in Council who are not social workers.

Website: http://www.nsasw.org

Ontario College of Social Workers and Social Service Workers

Title of Act/Regulation: *Social Work and Social Service Work Act* (1998)

Mission and Goals: The *Social Work and Social Service Work Act*, 1998, was proclaimed in law with Bill 76 in 2000. Anyone wishing to call him or herself a "social worker" or "social service worker" must belong to the Ontario College of Social Workers and Social Service Workers. The Ontario Association of Social Workers is not the regulatory body. It promotes the profession and advocates with other levels of government.

Membership: A person who has a combination of academic qualifications and practical experience that the Registrar determines is equivalent to the qualifications required for *either* a degree in social work from a social work program accredited by the Canadian Association of Schools of Social Work *or* a diploma in social service work from a social service work program offered in Ontario at a College of Applied Arts and Technology may apply for membership.

Governing Body: A 21–member Council comprised of seven elected social workers and seven elected social service workers representing five electoral districts across the province, and seven public members appointed by the Lieutenant Governor, govern the OCSWSSW.

Website: http://www.oasw.org

Ordre professionnel des travailleurs sociaux du Québec

Title of Act/Regulation: *Code des professions* (1973, Amended 1974, 1975, 1994)

Mission and Goals: The Act provides for control of the use of the title social worker or other title which suggests this designation or an equivalent one, or the use of the initials P.S.W., T.S.P., S.W., T.S.

Membership: To become a member and to use the titles above a person must have a B.S.W. or M.S.W. or equivalent diploma if obtained outside the province.

Governing Body: The governing body consists of a Board of 20 directors elected on a regional basis, and four directors appointed by the Office des professions du Québec.

Website (French only): http://www.optsq.org

Prince Edward Island Association of Social Workers

Title of Act/Regulation: *Social Work Act* (1988)

Mission and Goals: The Act provides for the control of the practice of social work and the use of the title social worker or Registered Social Worker, or abbreviations of such titles.

Membership: To become a member you require a degree from a School of Social Work recognized by the Board; practical training as prescribed; professional competency demonstrated by examination; good standing under any existing legislation; and currency of professional knowledge and skills.

Governing Body: The PEI Social Work Registration Board is composed of five members nominated by the PEI Association of Social Workers and appointed by the Minister, including four Registered Social Workers and members of the Association, and one person to represent the perspective of the general public.

The Prince Edward Island Association of Social Workers executive of the Association consists of a president, vice-president, secretary, treasurer and other members as prescribed by their bylaws.

E-mail: panmure.island@pei.sympatico.ca

Saskatchewan Association of Social Workers

Title of Act/Regulation: *An Act Respecting Social Workers* (1993) a.k.a. *The Social Workers Act*.

Mission and Goals: The Act provides for the control of title. Sec. 24 states that no person other than a member shall engage in the practice of social work by using the title "social worker." The Saskatchewan Association of Social Workers (SASW) administers the Act.

The association maintains the standards for the profession, promotes the profession, provides a means by which the association through its members may take action on issues of social welfare, disseminates publications and information and encourages studies in field.

Membership: Membership requires a certificate or bachelor's or master's or doctoral degree in social work from a university approved in the bylaws.

Governing Body: The Council of the SASW consists of seven members elected by the members and a person appointed by the Lieutenant Governor in Council. The officers are Past President, President, President-elect, Secretary, Treasurer and two members-at-large.

E-mail: sasw@cableregina.com

The above information is for general interest only and it should not be relied upon as being either comprehensive or current. It was compiled from information found in large part on the CASW website (http://www.casw-acts.ca) and from provincial association websites. For up-to-date information, check with the appropriate provincial association.

For information on the Association of Social Workers of Northern Canada (ASWNC), contact the Association, c/o Aurora College Box 1008, Inuvik, NT X0E 0T0) or through the web at: http://www.socialworknorth.com.

The Future of the Profession

The profession of social work will face significant challenges in the future. Four main factors contribute to these challenges.

- **Demographics.** Demographics and, therefore, service demands are rapidly shifting. The overall population is growing older, common-law and lone-parent families are increasing, as is the proportion of children living in poverty, and immigration is creating cultural shifts.

- **Privatization.** There is a devolution of services from direct government delivery at the federal, provincial and local levels to third-party community or private provision.

- **Funding cutbacks.** There is decreasing financial support and a weakening of public support for the work social workers do and for those they serve.

- **Technology.** There is intensification of the use of technology in the workplace.

Nevertheless, employment opportunities for social workers will continue to be good, according to the recent CASSW report *In Critical Demand*. Employment in the social work and social service sector is expected to grow by two percent per year, in line with Canadian population growth projections. The types of jobs will change as the need for services for the elderly, children in dire straits and recent immigrants becomes more urgent.

• The Paradox

The profession of social work currently finds itself facing a dilemma: there is an unprecedented demand for the skills and knowledge of social workers, but at the same time there is a devaluation of social services and of those providing them.

Services are rapidly being devolved from direct government delivery to third-parties, community or private provision. This is causing shifts in the types of jobs and earnings of social workers. Social workers are increasingly finding jobs in community-based and non-institutional social services where they earn less, have fewer benefits and have less security than government and hospital social workers.

As a result, it seems likely that social service workers in the next period will be expected to do more with less funding, resulting in increased caseloads and a higher level of work-related stress. Moreover, as the use of computer and communications technology for case management and file recording intensifies, workers will need to be aware of the implications of this for judgments about client needs as well as client privacy.

WHAT SOCIAL WORK GRADUATES SAY ...

- 85% say they would make the same educational choice again
- 95% say they are satisfied with their work
- 85% say that their work directly matches with their training

Source: Job Futures at: http://www.jobfutures.ca

Conclusion

There has been a tremendous increase in the number of practising social workers and social service workers over the past 50 years. This reflects not only the need for their services but the complex nature of Western societies today. Certainly, without the efforts of committed social work practitioners, the day-to-day lives of a great many Canadian individuals and families would be much worse.

Increasingly, the task of the social work practitioner is legally defined or mandated, and their work is guided by professional standards — that is, there are laws, practices and precedents that provide a structure for their work. More often than not, however, situations arise in daily practice for which there are no clear laws or precedents. This is ultimately why values, training and approach are so important and why there has been a significant expansion in the accreditation of social workers at colleges and universities.

The task of the social worker is to simultaneously act in the best interests of their clients and adhere to agency policy and procedures. These basic objectives sometimes are at odds with each other, and the social worker is left using all of his or her knowledge, experience and skill to resolve the conflict. While ethical codes of practice are in place, none can address every particular complex situation as it arises. Inevitably, a great deal of discretion resides with the practitioner.

Social work is a noble profession, and social workers require a dedication no less than those in the other "helping professions." Above all, social work requires an overriding commitment to the welfare of people, to the development of resources to meet individual, group, national and international needs and aspirations, and to the achievement of social justice for all.

The opportunity to make a difference is the defining characteristic of social work, whether with individuals and small groups or on a larger scale. And, whatever the employment setting, the opportunities to make a difference are plentiful. To meet the challenges of the future, social workers will need a clear sense of purpose and strong professional identity.

Chapter 4 Review
Social Work as a Profession

Discussion Questions

1. What are the main associations to which Canadian social workers belong?

2. Define the ambiguity of social work, and discuss its implication for direct practice.

3. Social work has its own code of ethics. What is the purpose of the code, and what are three of the key elements contained in the code?

4. Define and describe the various roles that social workers may take on in the course of their work.

5. Does the composition of the profession (women, Aboriginal peoples and visible minorities) reflect the diversity of Canadian society? Why is this important?

6. How are the employment patterns of social workers changing and what are the implications for social workers?

7. What four challenges does the profession of social work in Canada face, and how will they affect the social workers and social work practice?

Websites

* **Canadian Association of Social Workers**
  http://www.casw-acts.ca
  The CASW website contains useful information about how the CASW represents Canadian social workers, information about the profession and the status of professional legislation in each province.

* **The Canadian Association of Schools of Social Work (CASSW)**
  http://www.cassw-acess.ca
  CASSW-ACESS is a voluntary, national charitable association of university faculties, schools and departments offering professional education in social work at the undergraduate, graduate and post-graduate levels. Check out their research reports, news and school information.

* **International Federation of Social Workers and International Association of Schools of Social Work — Code of Ethics**
  http://www.ifsw.org
  "The Ethics of Social Work: Statement of Principles" was approved at the General Meetings of the IFSW and the IASSW in Adelaide, Australia, in October 2004. It is reproduced in Appendix C.

* **In Critical Demand: Social Work in Canada**
  http://www.socialworkincanada.org
  A major review and analysis of the profession of social work. The study examined human resource issues such as wages and benefits, working conditions, qualifications and experience, turnover rates, opportunities for advancement, job satisfaction, career and educational paths, portability of credentials, licensing and regulation, training and human resource development programs and unionization.

Key Terms

* **Canadian Association of Social Workers (CASW)**
* **Canadian Association of Schools of Social Work (CASSW)**
* **International Federation of Social Workers (IFSW)**
* **International Association of Schools of Social Work (IASSW)**
* **Integrated Service Delivery (ISD)**
* **Community Access Centre**
* **Social worker roles**
* **Code of Ethics**
* **Voluntary clients**
* **Involuntary clients**
* **Ambiguity of social work**
* **Ethical dilemmas**
* **Public sector unions**
* **Professional associations**

Social and personal assistance to homeless individuals will require community-wide involvement if effective and lasting solutions are to be found to this widespread social problem.

5
Individuals, Groups and Communities

Direct Social Work Practice

I t is important for all social workers to have a basic understanding of the processes and activities for the three fields of social work commonly defined under the category of direct practice or direct intervention. They are (1) social work with individuals, (2) group work and (3) community work. The purpose of this chapter is to introduce each of these fields and to discuss the main kinds of activities a social worker is likely to encounter in each field. (Direct practice is not the only type of social work — social workers may also find themselves working in social policy and administration settings.)

These three specializations or fields of direct intervention emerged in the 1940s. Today, many schools of social work use this breakdown for purposes of social work training. **Social work with individuals** is directed at helping individuals, using counselling and other one-on-one methods. **Group work** aims to assist a group of people in a variety of ways — the group could be a therapy group, a peer group or a family. Assisting a local community to plan, implement and evaluate efforts at health and social welfare can be fostered through **community work**.

Most social workers will find themselves involved in one or another of these three forms of direct practice at different times in their careers, and more likely they will be involved in all three. This diversity of fields requires that social workers have multiple skills and a broad-based perspective on social work practice. Although one may specialize in one of these areas, all social workers will require a range of basic skills with which to carry out their work effectively, whether it is with individuals, groups or communities.

Three Fields of Direct Practice

Social work practice essentially consists of a series or process of interventionist actions. The worker calls upon his or her repertoire of helping knowledge, skills and values and applies them in particular ways in specific situations to achieve planned and purposeful change. While each situation will require a different pattern of interventions, the process or steps are essentially the same.

Social work practice is the use of social work knowledge and skills to implement society's mandated policies and services in ways that are consistent with social work values. It is the values and principles that social workers work and live by that are at the core of this work. It is what motivates social workers to do what they do.

Social worker comforts distraught relative of Swissair Flight 111.

CP PHTOT/AP-Fabrice Coffrini.

SOCIAL WORK PRACTICE THEORIES

An individual's background knowledge and beliefs about social work (practice theories) obviously affect how that person intervenes in a particular situation.

Social work draws from a wide variety of such practice theories:

- Anti-racist theory
- Aboriginal theory
- Behaviour therapy
- Cognitive therapy
- Communication theory (Communicative-Interactive)
- Crisis intervention theory
- Developmental theory
- Ecological (life model) theory
- Ego-state therapy
- Existential therapy
- Feminist therapy
- Functional theory
- Generalist theory
- Gestalt therapy
- Integrative theory
- Locality development theory
- Mediation theory
- Narrative therapy
- Organizational theory (remedial-group)
- Person-centered therapy
- Play therapy
- Psychosocial theory
- Problem-solving theory
- Rational-emotive therapy
- Social action theory
- Social planning theory
- Socialization theory
- Structural theory
- Task approach theory

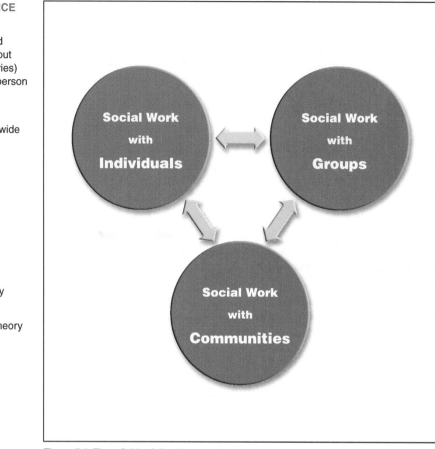

Figure 5.1: Three fields of direct intervention.

Social work practice is not a mechanical process to be executed in a rigid, step-like manner. Rather, each case or person must be viewed as being unique. To do otherwise would not be effective social work, as one would miss many of the intricacies and nuances of each new situation. Social work, therefore, involves more than technical knowledge and skills applied in a set series of steps. It is an interplay of action, reflection and more action. A useful analogy is that of a dancer who has the technical skills to dance, who knows the steps and moves involved in a particular dance, but to be truly excellent, must combine and re-combine the moves into new patterns. Social work needs this kind of artful improvising, or the ability to "think on one's feet." It is art as much as it is science.

Regardless of the approach taken to social work, it is important to have a basic understanding of all three fields of direct practice. The above diagram indicates how each field influences the other and reveals that a primary intervention in one field may involve some level of intervention in the others.

Social Work with Individuals

The process of helping individuals is sometimes called "social case-work," although this term is used infrequently nowadays. A majority of social workers spend their time working with individuals in private or public agencies or in private practice. Even though other types of social work are increasing, the practice of social work with individuals still predominates.

Individual social work is aimed at helping people resolve their problems or situations on a one-to-one basis, that is, helping unemployed people obtain work or training, providing protective services for abused children, providing counselling for mental health, providing parole or probation services, supplying services to the homeless and poor, coordinating services for people with AIDS and coordinating discharge services for a person being released from hospital. All of us on occasion find ourselves with problems that we cannot resolve alone. At times the help of a friend or family member may be enough, but at other times the skilled help of a social worker is necessary. Social work with individuals can take different forms depending on the philosophy and perspective of the social worker. While some workers may address personal problems, others may emphasize the social relations underlying the problems. Still others may address both dimensions simultaneously.

ACTION-REFLECTION-ACTION

The notion of "action-reflection-action" originates with Paulo Freire in his book *Pedagogy of the Oppressed* (1970). For Freire, becoming conscious of how social, political and economic relations affect one's life and the lives of others, and taking action to challenge those structures, involves the practice of "praxis" — the synthesis of "reflection and action upon the world in order to transform it."

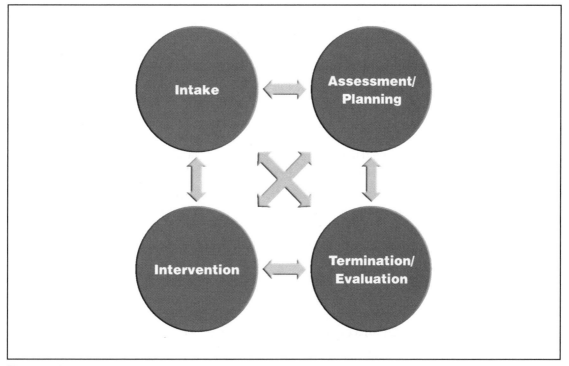

Figure 5.2: The social work process.

THE TERM "CLIENT"

Throughout this text the term *client* is used to denote the person or persons with whom the social worker is working. However, some social work practitioners view the term as a somewhat derogatory one, since it seems to imply that the person is a powerless object of practice. This text certainly does not intend to give this negative connotation to the term, but rather sees the client as being involved in a partnership with the social worker in a relation of empowerment. For a further discussion of empowerment, see Chapter 1, page 20.

In general, social work practice with individuals involves the following steps. These steps are common to most social work interventions with individuals and families. Although assessment precedes intervention, and intervention precedes termination, the process can be cyclical. For example, during intervention the client and worker may discover new information that in turn raises the need for more planning. In fact, each process is taking place throughout the intervention, but at each step one or more is emphasized. As mentioned previously, the steps are mere guideposts for a process that involves combining and re-combining actions into new ways of looking at things — that is, a praxis or a process of "action-reflection-action."

Social work scholars such as Bob Mullaly (2002), emphasize the importance of what is sometimes called "critical self-reflection" or "knowledge about oneself." This self-reflection helps social workers understand how their own identities, beliefs and their professional and personal lives are shaped by forces in society such as the media, parental influence, educational institutions and social structures. Many beginning social workers find it useful to write a short description of themselves and then reflect on where they think these views come from and how these views might influence their perceptions of the people with whom they may eventually be working.

• Intake

Intake is usually the first step taken by a worker when a client seeks help. Intake is a process whereby a request for service is made by or for a person, and it is then determined whether and what kind of service is to be provided. The social worker attempts to gather initial information from the client in order to determine what assistance is needed, and whether the agency and worker is the appropriate provider. If it is mutually determined by both the worker and client that the agency can be of service, then some sort of agreement or contract is made. When it is determined that the person's needs cannot be met by the agency, then a referral to a different service is made or a decision is made that no social work service is required.

During the intake phase, the client makes a personal request for help or someone from the community directs the client to a particular social work agency. The social work relationship can be either voluntary or involuntary. The intake step is voluntary when a client willingly seeks help from a social work agency. For example, a parent who recognizes the difficulties of caring for a child may approach a child welfare agency for assistance. By contrast, an involuntary client is ordered to see a social worker or is required to do so by law. For example, a social worker is required by law to assist a child in danger when, for example, the child's situation has been reported as unsafe by a physician, hospital worker, police officer or schoolteacher. In such cases, families are often uncooperative, especially if allegations of child abuse are reported.

In the intake step, the social worker acknowledges the client's need for help, collects information from the client, assesses the client's problem or situation and, based on the agency's resources, determines if the social work agency can help the client. In essence, when they first meet, both the worker and client want answers to specific questions. The applicant or potential client wants to know: Can I get the help I need here? Can this person help me? How can I get the help I need at this agency or with this person? The worker will ask: Can I help this person or would it be more appropriate for someone else to help? How can I help this person?

• Assessment and Planning

The **assessment and planning** step includes two processes. In the assessment process, the social worker and the client analyze what help is needed based on the client's ideas, thoughts and feelings about the particular problem. Once the assessment is complete, the social worker formulates a plan in collaboration with the client that is designed to help the client with the particular problem. The plan is not set in stone but provides an initial course of action.

Many social work textbooks describe a process that involves problem definition, data collection and objective setting. This type of model flows more from a management or bureaucratic approach to social work that stresses technical rationality. In this model, the worker knows best and can rationally plan the optimal course of action. In this section, we are emphasizing a social work process that stresses reflection-action-reflection in which the social worker continually thinks things through while acting on the problem at hand, and always in consultation with the client. He or she adapts the intervention based on dialogue and reflection on experiences of and feelings about past actions. Assessment is both a process and a product of understanding on which action is based (Siporin 1975, 219). It involves gathering relevant information and developing an understanding. How a social worker selects information and how he or she analyzes it is accomplished with reference to the assumptions that underlie a particular social work model, and by one's own experience of the world. In order to form a plan in the assessment phase, the social worker also relies on other people who know the client personally. For example, in cases in which a client is provided with social services as a result of an involuntary intervention, the social worker may initially rely on information provided by a teacher, doctor or police officer (or, for example, an elder in a First Nations community).

• Direct Practice Skills

During assessment and planning, the worker and client identify problems and a set of actions needed to reach the desired goals. The skill set for direct intervention would include the following items:

CHARACTERISTICS OF EFFECTIVE ASSESSMENT

Regardless of the model or approach one takes, social work assessment has several important characteristics:

- It is ongoing and not a static stage in a linear process.
- It provides the basis for subsequent action.
- It involves mutual dialogue between client and worker.
- It provides an understanding that is developed through an analysis related to both the worker's and client's assumptions, as well as technical knowledge.
- It is related to the specific situation of clients.

Health Canada.

Listening to stories and reflections is crucial to effective assessment.

INTERVENTIONS WITH THE ELDERLY

The number of elderly persons in Canada is growing rapidly and this will be a major area for social programming in the future.

The age-group 65 and older grew by 11% between 1991 and 1996 (the 75 and older age-group grew by 15%). This is expected to further accelerate as the baby boom generation ages.

Of course, social workers have always been the primary service providers for the elderly. The types of interventions commonly include:

- enhancing health and continuing care;
- helping access resources and housing;
- addressing isolation by connecting individuals with larger groups;
- working with family members to facilitate intervention planning; and
- analyzing and confronting gaps in service delivery systems.

- *Listening.* Some say this is the first and most important skill, since it underlies many of the other skills. Without genuinely listening, the social worker cannot fully appreciate the message and feelings of the client.

- *Validating feelings.* The social worker validates the client's feelings by conveying an understanding of them. This builds a rapport and helps the client to identify and sort out a variety of feelings. The social worker must also consider non-verbal emotional responses in developing this understanding.

- *Interviewing.* Open-ended and closed-ended questions are used in an interview to elaborate information. Open-ended questions give the client the opportunity to discuss aspects of the problem that they see as important in more depth. The questions often begin with "how" or "what." Closed-ended questions give the social worker the opportunity to clarify details of the client's narrative. They are often used late in a session to check for accuracy.

- *Paraphrasing.* Paraphrasing is a basic social work communication skill. With paraphrasing the social worker re-states what the client has said in her or his own words. Social workers use paraphrasing to confirm that the meaning the worker has attached to a client's message is indeed the meaning intended by the client. It also provides feedback to the client. Beginning social workers need to be aware that overuse of paraphrasing can give the client the impression of being mimicked.

- *Clarifying.* This skill is used to determine if the worker and client are on the same "wavelength." You may, for example, pull together the essence of a situation in the form of a mini-summary, which can be used to compare your understanding of the particular situation with that of the client. It is often used to probe an issue that is not understood by the social worker. It involves asking for specific details about an event. Clarification often becomes a reciprocal process between the social worker and client as each tries to understand the true meaning of what the other is saying.

- *Summarizing.* This skill is used in attempts to capture or pull together the most important aspects of the problem or situation. It provides focus for the next interview and can assist in planning. Both the feelings and content of the client's message should be used. It is also useful when the social worker believes that it is time to move on to another topic.

- *Giving Information.* Without overwhelming people with too much information at one time, the social worker often shares information about resources in the community (e.g., women's shelters) or information that shows that the client is not alone in experiencing the problem. Be sure the client realizes that they can refuse the information, and provide pamphlets or brochures where possible.

- *Interpreting.* This skill enables the social worker to delve into the presented problem and "read between the lines." By using this method, you may be able to "re-frame" the issue, giving it your own unique angle. The worker's insights may help the client develop a deeper understanding of what is really going on, and not just what appears to be happening. It may provide an alternative way of looking at the problem or a new frame of reference. Always check both verbal and non-verbal responses of the client to your interpretation.

- *Building consensus.* Consensus building attempts to work out an agreement on what should be done to address a problem. It may be easily attained or there may be discrepancies between what a client says they want and their behaviour, or between separate messages given by a client. Confrontation may be used to challenge a client to examine discrepancies. It should be non-adversarial, respectful and used only when a safe and trusting relationship exists.

Planning is based on sets of decisions made by the worker and the client that are shaped by the worker's analysis of the information collected in the assessment phase. The planned actions may be at a wide variety of levels: individual, environmental, multi-person, systemic or structural. For example, they might involve therapeutic, educational and social action-oriented approaches. What frequently varies between

RECORD KEEPING

In general, social workers should ensure that the client is aware that records are kept and what kind of information sharing may be required of the worker, so that the client can make informed decisions. Also, social workers must use information in such a way as to protect a client's privacy and confidentiality.

Health Canada.

Open-ended interview techniques are vital to an effective assessment of the problem at hand, insofar as they can help the worker capture nuances that might otherwise be missed in a more formalized interview.

practice models is the focus of attention. A behaviour therapy approach would tend to focus on changing individual behaviours, whereas a social action or structural approach may focus on changing systems or structures in society in order to shift power relations. In any event, the social worker assesses the client's problem with the client and negotiates a plan with the client that includes:

- the type of actions or interventions;
- the length of the intervention;
- the frequency of their meetings;
- the desired effects; and
- the intervention plan (where a contract is made with the client).

The next step, following assessment and planning, is intervention.

• Intervention

The worker, the client or both may undertake the intervention stage. The actions taken may be directed at the client, other individuals, groups, communities, institutions, social policies or political and social structures or systems. In other words, intervention can include a wide variety of actions, tactics and techniques that are not always directed at the treatment of the individual alone. For example, where the social worker is using a structural or feminist approach to practice, the intervention will usually include some kind of organizational, community or social action measures.

It is through the process of intervention that the worker and client implement the assessment and plans. The intervention undertaken is directed at meeting the client's needs as determined by the worker and client. In the intervention stage of social work with individuals, the client shares with the social worker any information regarding what progress has been made in resolving the problem or situation. During this step, the social worker:

- establishes a rapport with the client;
- accompanies the client in the intervention;
- provides advice and support to the client;
- adjusts the intervention based on the client's information; and
- helps the client to resolve the problem or situation by providing new knowledge and skills that assist in solving the problem.

Establishing a rapport and creating dialogue with the client is crucial.

The intervention phase should focus on creating a dialogue between the client and worker and perhaps others who are implicated in the situation being addressed. There will always be jumps, hesitations, uncertainties and half-formed ideas. In situations where the uncertainties are large or numerous, it would be advisable to take small, cautious steps and then reflect on the experience. This opens up the possibility of enhancing an understanding of the important elements in the situation and altering the course of action.

● Evaluation and Termination

In this final step, evaluation and termination, the client and the social worker work together to assist the client to achieve a resolution to the original problem or situation, and to prevent the situation from occurring again. In this step, the social worker evaluates the following items with the client and the social work supervisor:

- the choice of the intervention;
- the length of the intervention;
- the frequency of their meetings;
- the outcomes;
- the need for any follow-up; and
- when to terminate the intervention — in most cases, the decision is mutually agreed upon by the client and the social worker.

Evaluation is an ongoing part of the social work process, aimed at determining whether the goals and needs of the client are being met. Evaluation should identify the rationale for the actions chosen, whether or not needs were met, the expected and unexpected effects and alternative courses of action that may need to be taken.

Clients are usually not involved in the evaluation process because it is believed that specific skills are required and evaluation is focused primarily on issues of accountability. Increasingly, however, there is a recognition of the benefits of client participation: clients can have an insider's perspective on agency functioning, information can be validated, issues of confidentiality can be discussed, plans and contracts can be adjusted, knowledge and skills can be gained, the client-worker relationship may be strengthened and clients can be empowered.

Termination, or the ending of the client-worker relationship, occurs ideally when the action plan is completed and the client's goals have been met. In the termination stage, essential records are organized and stored. The use of records raises concerns about the confidentiality of sensitive information: What constitutes the ethical disclosure of information about a client? In addressing this question, social workers are obligated to follow the guidelines of the agency or organization employing them. They must also obey legislation and association policy. The CASW *Code of Ethics* stipulates, at length, the requirements for collecting, recording, storing and accessibility of client records.

Social workers must ensure that appropriate supports are in place before the intervention is ended. A client who has become reliant on assistance and interaction with the social worker may have difficulties with termination, and this potential hazard needs to be kept in mind throughout the social work process. Helping clients build their own support network is crucial. Such support may come from family and friends, informal helpers, self-help groups or through community or voluntary activities. If an empowerment perspective is taken, termination is often smoother.

SELF-HELP GROUPS

The number and significance of self-help groups in Canada is increasing. Self-help groups are voluntary groupings of people who come together for mutual assistance in addressing a common need or problem, or to bring about personal or social change. Self-help groups are voluntary mutual aid groups, which may or may not involve a social worker.

Self-help groups are also emerging on the World Wide Web at a rapid rate. Go to your favourite web search engine and type in "self-help groups" — you will find many sites available. Besides providing emotional support, these sites offer practical, valuable insights gained through first-hand experience of the same situation. Many self-help groups advocate to bring about policy changes for the benefit of all who share the group's concern. National self-help organizations offer support through newsletters, hotlines, and assistance in starting groups.

TALKING STICK

The "talking stick" is often used by First Nations to ensure that everyone's message and opinion is heard by the group, but it can be used in a variety of social work groups.

One stick or feather (or almost any object) is required, and the group usually positions itself in a circle without obstructions in the middle. Each group member can speak only when he or she has the stick. The speaker passes the stick to the next person who wants to speak.

The method ensures that everyone can contribute without interruption, and encourages shy members to participate.

Social Work with Groups

Social work with groups has its historical roots in informal, recreational groups such as those organized by the YWCA, the YMCA, settlement houses, scouting organizations, and more recently, in self-help groups. Today, most social agencies do some kind of group work, including recreation, education, socialization and therapy.

When deciding between individual or group intervention, a social worker must consider which method would be most effective. In some cases, group work may be the most appropriate and least costly mode of intervention. Group work may be more appropriate in cases where the problem lies within group systems, such as families or peer groups. In other cases, a problem may be dealt with by a group of people experiencing a similar problem. For example, a group of abused women may be able to relate to one another and share a common experience, thereby overcoming feelings that the abuse was somehow their own fault. Group work may also be appropriate when addressing the problems involved in the development of relationships between people.

It can be more economical to work with people in a group. For example, it may be a more efficient forum for sharing information, delivering education and providing support. A group may also be more effective in working to change the policy of an agency or advocating for particular benefits, as a group generally has a stronger voice than any one individual. The choice of group work or individual work depends largely on the particular situation being addressed. Neither is necessarily more effective than the other.

Social work practice with groups occurs in hospitals, mental health settings, institutions for persons with disabilities (which led to the popularity of self-help groups), prisons, halfway houses for former prisoners (to prepare them for reintegration into the community), residential treatment centres, residential centres for adolescents in trouble with the law, education groups dealing with issues such as child rearing and violence, self-help groups such as Alcoholics Anonymous, abused women's groups, and therapy groups dealing with emotional or personal problems and other settings. Today, almost every social service agency has one or more such groups for their clients.

• Ingredients of Group Work

Group social work involves several key elements: an agency, a group with membership, a group consensus and a contract. An agency has social workers that have an interest in particular issues and the expertise to deal with them in a group situation. The group work experience also requires individuals who need each other in order to work towards the goals they have set for themselves. These members must hold a degree of consensus on the issues with which they will deal. Finally, a contract must exist that outlines an understanding between the potential group members and the social worker (agency) and the terms and frames of reference for the group work experience.

For the purposes of social group work, groups can be classified in a variety of ways. Generally, groups are classified according to the purpose that brings the group together. For example, Mesber (Turner 1999, 213) describes two types of groups based on the main purpose of the group: **treatment groups** and **task groups**. She also quotes Toseland and Rivas (1995, 14) as they differentiate between the two types:

> The term treatment group is used to signify a group whose major purpose is to meet members' socio-emotional needs… In contrast, the term task group is used to signify any group in which the major purpose is neither intrinsically nor immediately linked to the needs of the members of the group. In task groups, the overriding purpose is to accomplish a mandate and complete the work for which the group was convened.

Treatment groups gather for the purpose of meeting the therapeutic objectives of the group members. Individuals work as a group to address problems that they experience personally.

The three types of treatment groups are (1) family or household groups, (2) therapy groups and (3) self-help or peer groups.

During group work, the social worker will be involved in facilitation, coordination, therapy or conflict resolution. Frequently, he or she will be involved in all these activities.

- **Family or household groups** consist of family or household members. They may be members of the opposite or same sex, with or without children. Family group work or counselling is most effective when the issues that need to be addressed require interaction between family members.

- **Therapy groups** consist of individuals who do not share a household together or have any kind of relationship with one another outside the group setting. They are people seeking individual assistance. Interaction in a group environment is merely part of the therapy for the individual members. The group has no purpose outside of its therapeutic objectives.

- **Self-help or peer groups** consist of people who have similar problems or interests and believe that working and interacting together will provide opportunities for all the group members to grow and change. A social worker may or may not guide the group.

• Group Work Intervention: Tasks and Group Phases

Successful group work intervention involves an understanding of group intervention tasks and the stages of group development. Group workers need to be aware of the group intervention tasks necessary to help maintain and guide a group. In a group, the tasks take place in a group context and therefore generally pass through identifiable stages of development. Often the specific social work interventions or tasks are most effective at particular group development stages.

For successful group work intervention, it is also important to know how to identify the **stages of group development**. The intervention tasks for group work will be quite different depending on the type of group (e.g., self-help or treatment), but the stages of group development will often be the same for each type of group. By identifying the group's stage of development, workers can better help the group meet its needs and goals.

The stages of group development are:

1. *Orientation stage.* Group members commit to the group and task roles begin to emerge.

2. *Authority stage.* Members challenge each other and there is often conflict over power and control issues. Although conflicts are usually resolved through the sharing of feelings, members frequently drop out at this stage.

3. *Negotiation stage.* Group norms and task roles are designated and accepted and group cohesion and sharing increases.

4. *Functional stage.* Integration enables the group to implement plans and accomplish tasks. Few groups reach the end of this stage.

5. *Disintegration stage.* Groups may fall apart during any of the stages, but once the group feels that its goals have been accomplished, it will often disband. Social workers may also bring a treatment group to an end to enable the members to move on.

Throughout these stages, social workers will undertake specific tasks. Depending on the type of group, social workers will take on any or all of the following tasks:

- *Facilitation.* This is the most frequent role for social workers in non-treatment groups. The goal is to enable the group to function smoothly by asking questions, helping the group stay on topic, summarizing decisions and being supportive of members.

- *Coordination.* This more administrative task involves monitoring the task completion by group members, and helping the group plan future activities.

- *Therapy.* This is a broad task category and can include any of the skills discussed previously in the discussion of intervention with individuals. Often, social workers are working with "the multi-person client," such as a family. The focus is often on issues around group interaction and communication.

- *Conflict resolution.* While not always identified as a group work task, conflict resolution is increasingly a task of social workers (especially in child welfare, family therapy and international human rights work). The core elements include defining it as a group (rather than an individual) problem, listening to the different points of view and seeking to draw out common ground. The aim is to create a "win-win" situation and encourage cooperation.

• Group Work Intervention Steps

The steps for social work with groups are similar to those for work with individuals, except that they involve groups of people.

- *Intake.* During intake, the social worker acknowledges the client's need, collects information from the client (for example, self-referral or referral by someone in the community), assesses the client's situation and his or her capacity and motivation to change, and determines the agency's capacity to help the client by using any type of group that it has available.

- *Assessment and planning.* The worker completes a preliminary assessment of the client's situation or problem, provides a potential group process intervention plan and proposes a potential group to the client or adds the client's name to a waiting list.

- *Group intervention.* In working with groups, the social worker may do any of the following:

Peer groups play an especially important role for young people.

- help the group to find common ground in terms of the issues they wish to deal with;
- anticipate obstacles to the group work experience and bring them to the group's attention;
- educate the group, providing information and support thought to be useful to the group;
- contribute thoughts, feelings, ideas and concerns regarding the group work experience (drawing upon insights derived from similar group work experience);
- define the needs and limitations of the group-social worker relationship; and
- monitor the group's progress and provide ongoing evaluation of the group experience.

- *Evaluation and termination.* The final stage deals with issues that arise from terminating the group experience, such as evaluating the group process with the group and the social work supervisor. The worker may terminate the relationship with the group or mutually agree with the group members to end the group process.

More than 4,000 demonstrators representing community groups march to the Quebec legislature in October 2002, requesting more money from the government.

Social Work with Communities

Social work with a community (or community work, as it is usually called) is often either not addressed in social work texts or is limited to a few pages at the back. Students are left with little knowledge of what community work is and often feel that it is too complex or too abstract for them to learn. They end up deciding that they would rather work directly with people or that community work is for social activists only. In this book, community work is given equal treatment.

Community work can be thought of in different ways. A community may be a **geographic community** as defined by a specific neighbourhood, city district or local ward, with specific geographical boundaries. It might also consist of a **membership community** as defined by a sense of belonging to a specific group; for example, the gay and lesbian community, the Black community, the Native community and so on. Or, it may be a **self-help community** consisting of persons with similar problems or difficulties; for example, those living with addiction, disability or unemployment, or those coping with illness or the death of a loved one. Community work is frequently a central part of international social work or social work in developing countries. (This type of community work is discussed in more detail in Chapter 14, which deals with international social work.)

• Four Models of Community Work

The nature of community work differs depending on the perspective informing one's practice. A useful approach is **Rothman's model of community development**, which allows one to see the differences between the various forms of community development discussed and debated in Canada today. Rothman's typology regards community work as a continuous process and one that includes the staff who sustain and plan the process (Rothman 1970, 474). To this model, we would add a fourth component, "participatory action research" (PAR).

Community social work can therefore be seen as consisting of the following four types:

- *Locality development.* Community action for change involves the participation of a broad range of people in the community who focus on goal determination and action. This model emphasizes community building to enable people to solve their own problems. It is closely associated with adult education and self-help. Within this model, the primary problems are identified as anomie (disorganization), lack of communication and lack of problem-solving capacities. The basic strategy is to involve a broad cross-section of people in determining and solving their own problems, with the aim of achieving consensus and increasing communication among the various groups. Members of the local power structure are

Mohawk leaders protest transport of plutonium through their territory.

TEN RULES OF COMMUNITY ORGANIZING

1. Nobody's going to come to the meeting unless they've got a reason to come to the meeting.

2. Nobody's going to come to a meeting unless they know about it.

3. If an organization doesn't grow, it will die.

4. Anyone can be a leader.

5. The most important victory is the group itself.

6. Sometimes winning is losing.

7. Sometimes winning is winning.

8. If you're not fighting for what you want, you don't want enough.

9. Celebrate!

10. Have fun!

Source: Dave Beckwith, (with Cristina Lopez). 1997. Community Organizing: People Power from the Grassroots. Center for Community Change, Washington DC.

encouraged to become involved as well and are seen as potential collaborators in a mutual venture. The definition of community in locality development is geographic; that is, the community is composed of people in a specific geographic area who share common interests or reconcilable differences. Organizations involved in locality development may include overseas development programs, neighbourhood workers and consultants to community development teams. Historically, settlement houses were of this type.

- *Social planning.* When individuals plan and gather data about problems in order to choose the most rational course of action, they are engaged in social planning. The focus is on rational, deliberately planned and controlled change. Social planning involves people in the community to varying degrees, depending on the nature of the problem. The approach focuses on gathering information about problems and making rational decisions for change. The change strategy may seek consensus or may acknowledge conflict. Social planning focuses more heavily on gathering information than on changing the system. This model's definition of community is functional and may include a segment of a community in which the people are clients of a particular service or face a particular problem. The client population are considered to be consumers or recipients. Typical organizations may include social planning councils, welfare groups or government-sponsored organizations.

- *Social action.* Social action organizes disadvantaged groups in the community to redistribute power, resources or decision making. It involves the disadvantaged segments of a community, those in need of more resources or improved facilities, in accord with social justice or democracy. The change strategy is to work with a community to investigate and identify issues and to organize people to take action against groups who are exploiting or oppressing the disadvantaged groups. It can involve conflict, confrontation, direct action or negotiation. Social action is concerned with the shifting of power relationships and resources and sees issues as revolving around conflicting interests, which may not easily be reconciled. Typical social action initiatives include anti-poverty groups, peace groups, civil rights groups, welfare rights groups, trade unions, partisan groups and liberation movements.

- *Participatory action research.* Research that is directed towards changing the structures that promote inequality is called participatory research. Participatory research is similar to the social action model, but emphasizes the direct participation of the disadvantaged segment of the community in the entire research and action process. This emphasis is based on the belief that people must produce their own body of knowledge, representing their own history and lived experiences, in order to redress social inequality. The basic change strategy for social workers is to help identify local social problems, to design action research in collaboration with local people, to collect information and to use that information to confront power structures with the need for structural change. Participatory researchers are critical of the standard social planning model. They argue that, when doing "social planning," researchers more often than not work for the existing power structure — outsiders design the studies, and the results of their studies primarily benefit people in power. The plan, therefore, ignores the capability of local residents to form their own questions, design their own studies, collect their own information and, most importantly, use the knowledge gained for their own benefit. The results are then subject to market forces and tend to benefit the powerful over the powerless. (PAR is discussed further in Chapter 13, page 340.)

Every practising social worker will at some point become involved in community work of some kind or other. This is particularly true for those who emphasize changing social structures or changing the client's immediate social environment. Like individual work and group work, social work with communities is a challenging area. It involves working with individuals and groups in tandem, and therefore it requires a unique set of skills. Students sometimes see community work as an optional field of knowledge, one in which they are unlikely to be involved. In fact, community work can be immensely satisfying as a main area of work, and a working knowledge of it is essential for anyone who wishes to become a well-rounded and effective social work practitioner.

• Virtual Community Work

Today, the Internet makes it possible for community workers and activists to expand their networks by identifying and contacting people in other communities who have similar interests and concerns. This could be loosely referred to as a kind of **virtual community work**. Its importance should not be minimized.

By joining the appropriate Internet-based discussion lists and news groups, social workers can identify and communicate with people in other communities who are working on similar issues. By sharing information, strategies and advice, the effectiveness of efforts may be enhanced. For example, human rights workers have dramatically improved the effectiveness of Urgent Action work to call attention to human rights violations by spreading the news via the Internet. As well, Jubilee 2000, a global movement for Third World debt relief, was organized primarily using Internet communication. A social worker in the community work field can be certain that there is a group on the Internet with similar interests. And, as globalization increasingly affects

CP PHOTO/Edmonton Sun-Darryl Dyck.

Sudanese-Canadian attends rally protesting massacres in Darfur.

VIRTUAL COMMUNITIES

Several websites provide community workers, individuals and groups with a place on the Internet to learn, meet and organize.

For example, IGC Internet (http://www.icg.net) offers a portal into a range of communities. Their vision is to actively promote change towards a society founded on the principals of social justice, shared economic opportunity, a democratic process and sustainable environmental practices.

They offer on-line access to a variety of groups including PeaceNet, EcoNet, WomensNet, and AntiracismNet as well as daily headlines, advocacy tips, calendars of events and work opportunities.

our economy and the nature of social issues, there is growing importance in connecting with other groups and individuals.

Social workers worldwide are beginning to use the Internet to organize and mobilize on behalf of disadvantaged groups in society. These individuals are turning to the Internet as a way to connect with each other, learn from each other and challenge what they see as injustices in society. Grassroots activists are finding that they can interact on the Internet without the restrictions normally associated with official social services agencies. Social workers are using the Internet to connect not only with those in distant areas of Canada but with like-minded people in other countries. The new communications technology has opened up possibilities for conducting social work more effectively, and knowledge of this technology will be increasingly important to social workers in the future.

• Community Work Intervention Steps

The worker will take the following steps for social work with a community.

• Entry

The entry step is comparable to the intake step of the social work relationship with individuals. In this step, the community usually consults a community worker about its particular problem. The social worker acknowledges and responds to the community's need or is hired by someone to help the community. For example, the Canadian International Development Agency (CIDA) might hire a social worker to go to Kenya to assist a community in organizing to meet their health needs.

The worker needs to start slowly by getting to know the local contacts and developing an understanding of the power relations in the community. The community leaders need to be informed about what the worker intends to do. If the community feels that what is being proposed is not valuable, then it is best to know this at the outset — and perhaps leave, rather than wasting the time of the worker and the community.

Bill Lee, an accomplished community organizer in Canada, believes three primary principles must be adhered to at this stage: (1) The organizer must begin where the people are and respect their value system; (2) his or her contacts must be broad (and include not only the elite or powerful); and (3) he or she should attempt to find out who in that particular context has the power and credibility to mobilize and organize others into action (Lee 1999, 60).

• Data Collection and Analysis

It is important that the social worker work with key members of the community to determine what information and efforts are required.

One of the common goals of community work is to increase self-reliance within the community. This goal will be hampered if the social worker enters the community as an expert and undertakes top-down social action. Development goals can also be negatively affected when only the elite, or people with high social status, are participating. It is critical that power be equally distributed in decision making.

The social worker and members of the community:

- collect information from interviews, questionnaires and observations (individuals and groups);
- document and analyze the community in order to determine who the stakeholders are or what the distribution of power is (major/minor stakeholders/powerholders);
- determine how community needs can be met;
- ask how the community will evaluate the intervention; and
- propose a plan and ask how the community will react to the proposed intervention plan.

In recent years, community social workers have become somewhat concerned with research itself as a social process and have begun to question the role of the "independent" researcher. In this context, some social workers have found the idea of participatory research to be useful (see the discussion on participatory action research on page 100–101). Here, research is conducted not only by the social worker but includes the direct participation of the community members. Certainly this can be an effective way to do research in communities, and it may, in some cases, be the only way.

As with other aspects of community work, the type of research that would work best in any particular situation needs to be evaluated and discussed with the community. In some cases, the best arrangement might be a conventional study; in others, a participatory model; and in still others, some combination of the two.

• Goal Setting

The social worker brainstorms with the community to establish goals, evaluates the goals in terms of their feasibility, sets priorities with the community and provides education to community members. Again, the maximum participation of community members from all social levels is critical.

• Action Planning

The social worker, working with members of the community, creates an action plan. The plan will include action steps, implementation steps, monitoring and evaluation steps, and re-planning steps. Generally the plan should be a participatory process and may include:

A COMMUNITY TOOL BOX

This website contains 46 chapters of information and tools to help social workers be more effective community organizers.

For instance, there are sections on leadership, strategic planning, community assessment, advocacy, grant writing and evaluation. Each section includes a description of the task, advantages of doing it, step-by-step guidelines, examples, checklists of points to review and training materials.

The website is at: http://ctb.ku.edu/

Community education programs are effective for reaching youth at risk.

- what action or change will occur;
- who will carry it out;
- when it will take place, and for how long;
- what resources (i.e., money, staff) are needed to carry out the change; and
- communication (who should know what).

• Action Taking

In its simplest terms, this step involves the implementation of the action plan on the part of the social worker and the community. However, "action taking" is not a separate activity; the worker and people in the community have been taking action throughout the entire process.

What most clearly distinguishes this stage is that action is being taken more by the members of the community than by the social worker. Seeing a self-reliant community begin to improve its situation is one of the most rewarding aspects of being a community social worker.

• Evaluation and Termination/Re-planning

In the evaluation stage, the social worker and the community evaluate the intervention and re-plan in light of its effectiveness. Evaluations in community work increasingly involve the direct and active participation of the community's members.

Evaluating the success of the intervention and planned activities is a critical part of any organizing effort, and it is important not to wait until the completion of the organizing effort to evaluate its effectiveness. The following questions provide a basic framework for a more extensive evaluation. Try discussing these questions at an early stage.

1. Are we moving closer to achieving our intended objectives?
2. What other unintended impacts and effects have resulted?
3. What activities in particular are contributing to the achievement of our objectives?
4. Are there better ways to achieve the desired results?
5. Are our actions and work helping us to gain support in the community?

An evaluation of results might reveal that the reason objectives have not been met is that the strategy was correct but not implemented effectively. For example, the actions may have been timed inappropriately or the actions were too infrequent or not carried through thoroughly. Revisions to strategy are frequently necessary. Action-evaluation-action is a cycle that allows the worker and the community to change tactics. The central indicator for evaluating success is, of course, whether your efforts have created the change you desired.

TEP Photo Archives.

Evaluation is a time to take stock and prepare future actions.

SOCIAL WORKERS' GENERALIST SKILLS

Generalist social workers are influenced by different assumptions and viewpoints along a continuum. Part of that continuum ranges from ecological to anti-oppression perspectives. Using a sample of general social work skills, this chart suggests how workers apply these skills, reflecting different themes, such as adaptation or emancipation.

Social Workers Applying …	Ecological/Systems Theory Perspectives	Structural/Critical/Anti-Oppression Perspectives
Assessment Skills	Use systems theory and ecological concepts: (1) to explain dysfunctional interactions among different systems (e.g. individual, familial, communal, and formal systems); (2) to explore imbalances between individuals and their environments; (3) to identify areas for reciprocal adaptation by individuals and other systems, to optimize human well-being.	Use structural theory and liberation concepts: (1) to learn how experiences of oppression (e.g., colonialism, patriarchal capitalism, racism, heterosexism, ableism, ageism) are harming the service user's well-being; (2) to identify immediate survival needs; (3) to explore longer-term goals for emancipation.
Empathy Skills	Communicate an understanding of the client's feelings and of the situation (as part of developing trust within a professional relationship). Use this skill in working directly with individuals, as well as with individuals in families, groups and communities. Develop anticipatory empathy by tuning in, as part of preparing to work with specific client systems.	Communicate efforts to learn about and appreciate the service user's feelings and meanings (as part of trust evolving within a non-elitist professional relationship). Widen focus to include emancipatory empathy: i.e., dialogue about systemic barriers faced by others similarly oppressed, and about ways to overcome such barriers.
Reframing Skills	Aim to reduce clients' sense of hopelessness by suggesting new, more hopeful ways of viewing the situation. Congratulate clients for achievements that are ignored or devalued by others. Invite clients to identify unrecognized strengths within themselves and in their interactions with other systems, to help empower alternative, positive and more hopeful client responses.	Aim to reduce self-blame by co-investigating with service users: (1) external and internalized oppression and (2) external and internalized privilege, due to unjustified power over others. Explore new, more hopeful ways of understanding/acting, in light of social justice inspirations and initiatives and solidarities.
Communication Skills	Listen. Explore ways that clients and their environments can better adapt to each other. Focus on services/resources, while affirming client strengths. Explore stress reduction among clients, families and other systems. Support client self-determination. Mediate/guide client systems in their problem-solving and solutions-finding.	Listen. Explore ways that clients may be victims and survivors of oppression. Focus on services/resources, while affirming people's strengths. Work at power-sharing with service users. Unmask oppressive structures. Support personal/political change to dismantle multiple oppressive practices, while creating equitable alternatives.
Spiritual Sensitivity Skills	Validate religious pluralism. Support spirituality by clients as a strength to cope with stress (e.g. life transitions, crises caused by painful losses). Honour/appeal to spiritual values of compassion and charity within/across diverse communities to encourage more generous help for people in need	Validate religious pluralism. Oppose religious practices that are oppressive. Learn about/honour spirituality from diverse cultures, including its role in indigenous people's helping and healing. Find spiritual support for progressive personal and social change within/across diverse communities.
Advocacy Skills	Work at convincing formal and informal systems to better meet clients' needs, by mediating between clients and their environments. Act with others in lobbying larger systems for better policies, coordination, integration and delivery of social services. Seek support from private, public and charitable sectors, for additional resources to alleviate social problems.	Act with others, including service users, to defend human rights (e.g., to decent incomes, jobs, social services) by organizing grassroots power upward to challenge harmful policies/decisions/processes/structures. Contribute to social movement mobilization (local and global) for personal, political, economic and spiritual emancipation.

Source: Chart developed by Ben Carniol, Ryerson School of Social Work (Work-in-progress, 2005).

"KNOWLEDGE" AND "THEORY" IN SOCIAL WORK PRACTICE

The knowledge used by social workers includes foundation knowledge and social work practice knowledge. **Foundation knowledge** comprises general theories about individual behaviour and interactions and society. **Social work practice knowledge**, by contrast, is specific to social work practice. It draws from the foundation theory and is concerned with how planned social work intervention will occur.

For example, the foundation knowledge could be drawn from psychology, sociology, economics, political science, and the allied health professions, to name a few. This knowledge base consists of theories about individual personality and behaviour, people in society, and social, political and economic relations. From this base of theory, social work theorists have developed distinct social work knowledge in the form of social work practice theory that is more directly concerned with how to intervene in planned and helpful ways.

Social Work Practice Theory

As outlined above, different knowledge and theory bases significantly affect the worker's explanation of social problems and individual behaviour. Theories about social work practice are important for social workers as a guide to research, as a framework to interpret research results and as a framework for explaining why certain things happen the way they do.

Social work practice theory can be classified into two categories: individual level and structural level.

Individual-level theory focuses on individuals and their interactions. This body of theory concentrates on aspects such as interactions between people or the effect of negative attitudes on people. Some researchers criticize these theories because they focus on what people do rather than on the social structures and policies that cause or influence what they do.

Structural-level theory emphasizes social structure, social processes and systems, and their interrelationships and influence on the experience of people. For example, this body of theory would examine the effects of the Canadian economy on people's status or how gender relations impact the income of Canadians. This approach is criticized for minimizing people's ability to act and overcome the limits of social structures.

The area of individual-level theories is varied and complex. Social workers tend to draw from a range of such theories (cognitive, developmental or narrative, among others) depending on the population with whom they work and their field of practice, and combine these with systems theory (generalist approach) or critical social theory (structural approach).

For example, a social worker providing social support to children may draw upon developmentally based theories and incorporate play therapy into their practice. Social workers in the addictions field may use cognitively based theory. Finally, social workers working with the homeless may use crisis intervention theory and social action theory.

While the structural-level and individual-level distinction is popular in the social work literature, this book takes the view that both are important. We cannot understand one without the other as individuals and the societies in which they live are intimately interrelated. There is a tendency in social work literature, generally, to focus on the characteristics of individuals and neglect the structural level.

Two Approaches

In Canada, two social work practice approaches predominate: the ecological/systems theory approach and the structural approach. The ecological/systems approach predominates in undergraduate and introductory training in Canada.

This ecological/systems approach evolved from attempts by social workers to address issues in a way that goes beyond diagnosing individual problems by looking only at the individual factors. Practitioners recognized that it is also important to examine elements such as the family, community and institutions in society. Whereas those formulating a structural approach looked to critical theory, power theory and political economy theory, those developing the ecological/systems approach adopted "systems theory." Systems theory focuses on the systems in the person's immediate environment that may be causing the individual's problem.

With the ecological/systems approach, the worker is trained to use the problem-solving process in combination with systems theory to assess and intervene to establish the social functioning of individuals, families, groups, communities or organizations. Social systems theory provides a framework for understanding how systems such as the individual, the family, the small group, the school, the church, the social agency, the community and societies interact and relate, causing both private problems and public issues. When assessing the situation with the client, the social worker decides which system is the appropriate unit of attention or focus.

This approach integrates knowledge about human behaviour and knowledge about the influence of social environment on behaviour. It is, therefore, the job of the ecological/systems theory practitioner to understand both the personal reasons for the client's behaviour and also the environmental factors influencing this behaviour.

For example, when presented with a case of child abuse, the social worker would look at each of the separate factors. First, the parent may have alcohol abuse problems, may have a low income or problems with anger control. The family may be one where the parents are separated and hostile towards one another. The community may include support groups that would be appropriate for the child and the parent. In the institutional area, the child welfare worker may have such a large caseload that individual attention is non-existent and resources for family education are limited.

The **structural approach** to social work is largely a Canadian development (originating at Carleton University). As with the ecological/systems theory approach, there is no unanimous agreement as to the meaning of structural social work practice.

Social workers taking a "structural approach" frequently arrive at this approach from a critical analysis of the outcomes of their own interventions. Workers who previously concentrated only on personal factors or interpersonal Interactions between individuals find that, by ignoring the broader social structures that shape the individual's problem, they are minimizing the very changes required to alleviate their client's difficulty (as well as those of many others experiencing the problem). They find that it is more effective to focus on the root causes of the problems at hand and deal with the client's personal issues or behaviour at the same time.

The skills involved in structural social work are, of course, similar to the ecological/systems theory approach and draw on the same sense of humanism, empathy and reflection. It is the way in which the social worker analyzes problems and the type of actions that result from this analysis that distinguishes the structural approach. The structural social worker is concerned with helping the individual deal with a difficult problem, but he or she is also concerned with changing the overall situation that is causing the problem, whenever that is possible.

Structural social work, then, can be defined as practice that focuses on the impact of wider social structures on personal problems. It involves a critical analysis of these structures, whether they are based on class, race, age, gender, ability or sexuality. These include primary structures — such as patriarchy, racism, capitalism, heterosexism, ageism and ableism (discrimination against persons with disabilities) — as well as secondary structures such as personality, family, community, and bureaucracy. In this respect, it draws heavily from "critical social theory," which also seeks to provides a way to connect everyday life with large-scale social structures.

Advocates of structural social work emphasize the links between a person's feelings and behaviour, and the larger society. Client empowerment and social worker activism are emphasized. The structural approach works simultaneously at liberating people and transforming social structures. Individual and social changes are seen as inextricably related.

Like the ecological/systems theory approach, the structural approach requires that the social worker be skilled in casework, family counselling, group work and community organizing, as well as have a deep knowledge of social policy and social welfare. Structural social work differs in that it goes beyond an analysis of the immediate family and community as external factors and looks to the broader analysis of socio-economic factors such as class, gender and race.

Critical Social Work

More recently, social work academics have been discussing and writing about "critical social work" and "anti-oppressive social work." In many cases, these variations draw heavily from the structural approach to social work and incorporate ideas from other social theories (for example, feminism, postmodernism and critical social theory).

Conclusion

To be successful in the three fields of social work (social work with individuals, group work and community work), a social worker requires knowledge and a variety of skills as well as a commitment to certain basic social work values.

Social work with individuals, or one-on-one practice, moves from intake, assessment and planning to intervention. The intervention is the action stage in which the issues and concerns of the client are addressed. These interventions will not only be directed at the individual client, but will often include actions at the group, community, institutional, policy or political level. The evaluation and termination phase terminates the intervention and determines whether or not it was effective. It also includes a review of clients' records. Keeping accurate client records according to agency policy and the *Code of Ethics* is critical to ensuring effective continued care and protecting the client should his or her records be subpoenaed for a court case.

Social work with groups is increasingly being used as a practice technique due to its proven success with particular groups of people, including abused women, homeless people, youth, and people with various mental illnesses, to name a few. For the group worker, it is crucial to understand both effective practice techniques and the stages of group development.

Community work, another growing field, can take many forms including developing the capacity of a locality, planning services for a group or community, or challenging power structures to advocate for rights or access to resources. In community work, the participation of community members in decision making and the actions undertaken is critical. Virtual community organizing or on-line social activism is another rapidly growing social work field as citizens use new communications technology to challenge the globalization of power. In a sense, it is a kind of "globalization from below."

All types of social work and approaches share a body of knowledge, skills and values that involve a commitment to humanitarianism and egalitarianism aimed at empowering people and building on their strengths, whether as individuals, groups or communities.

Chapter 5 Review
Individuals, Groups and Communities

Discussion Questions

1. What are the three fields of social work practice and how do they differ?

2. What steps does a social worker usually follow in providing help to: (a) an individual; (b) a group; (c) a community?

3. Social work practice involves continually reflecting with the client on past actions. Explain this process.

4. What is a community and what different types of communities exist?

5. What are the main features of community-based social work?

6. What is the key feature of participatory action research and what is the role of the social worker?

7. What is the significance of the new information technology for community organizing?

8. Explain what is meant by the "ecological/systems theory" and the "structuralist" approaches to social work practice.

Websites

● **A Community Toolbox**
http://ctb.lsi.ukans.edu

This website contains information and tools to help social workers be more effective community organizers. The core of the Tool Box is the "how-to tools." These sections explain how to do the different tasks necessary for community development.

● **Charity Village**
http://www.charityvillage.com

Defines itself as Canada's supersite for the non-profit sector. It has 3,000 pages of news, jobs, information and resources. The resources section of the site should connect you with a cause or group that interests you. You can even volunteer or donate on-line.

● **Canadian Social Work Discussion Group**
http://groups.yahoo.com/group/csocwork

This is a listserv that enables social workers in Canada to discuss general practice issues as they arise. Go to the website to subscribe.

● **Anti-oppressive Social Work Electronic Resource Center**
http://www.dal.ca/~aosw/

Designed to be of use to social work students, educators, and practitioners, the Center: provides a general introduction to anti-oppressive social work; explores the key theoretical concepts underpinning anti-oppressive social work; discusses pedagogical issues related to teaching anti-oppressive social work; offers a bibliography of selected readings related to anti-oppressive social work; provides links to relevant resources and organization; provides a forum for debate and discussion concerning anti-oppressive social work.

Key Terms

● **Social work with individuals**

● **Group work**

● **Community work**

● **Social work practice**

● **Intake**

● **Assessment and planning**

● **Intervention**

● **Evaluation and termination**

● **Confidentiality**

● **Treatment groups**

● **Task groups**

● **Family or household groups**

● **Therapy groups**

● **Self-help or peer groups**

● **Stages of group development**

● **Geographic community**

● **Membership community**

● **Self-help community**

● **Rothman's model of community development**

● **Virtual community work**

● **Foundation knowledge**

● **Social work practice knowledge**

● **Structural approach**

● **Ecological/systems theory perspectives**

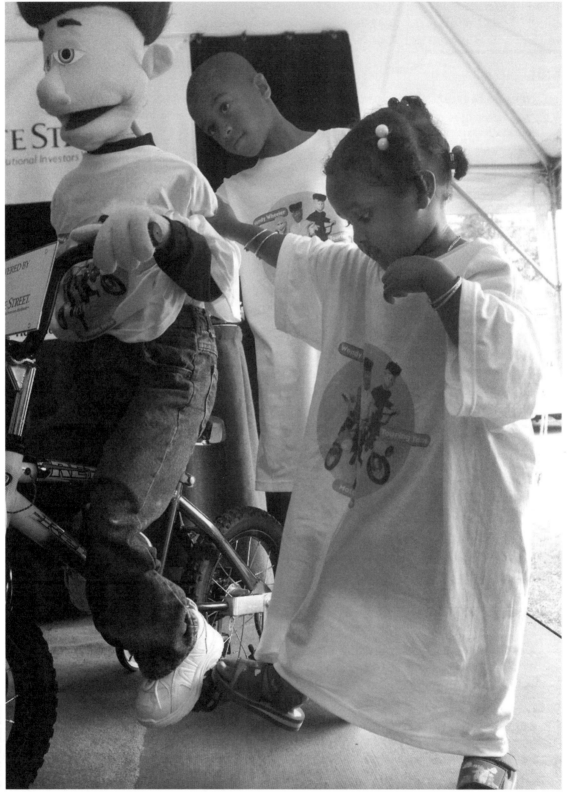

A three-year-old volunteer checks out "Motoring Mike" at a Children's Aid Foundation news conference (2000). "Motoring Mike" is an animatronic robot with video/audio capabilities used by the Foundation to help abused and neglected children communicate.

6
Social Work with Children and Youth

—

Child Protection and Family Support

The 1995 federal budget marked a turning point for social services across Canada. Thenceforth, social funding was substantially cut in an all-out effort to reduce the federal government's deficit. Over the ensuring decade, the cutbacks were relentless, causing a great deal of hardship for service agencies and their clients. Those involved in the sensitive area of family and child services perhaps felt it most of all.

Across the country, state and non-profit welfare agencies are responsible for providing a range of indispensable service to children and families. These services include child protection, foster care coordination, group homes and a variety of family support services. Collectively, they are what as known as the child welfare system, and social workers play a major role in it. For example, in Ontario, child protection and family support, over 7,000 social workers provide services through fifty-two Children's Aid Societies (CASs) with an annual budget of over $1 billion. Despite determination and hard work, however, the lesson of the past decade is that child welfare practitioners across the country cannot make good on their commitment to provide families and children unless there is adequate government funding to back them up. The sweeping funding cutbacks following 1995 made it impossible for child welfare practitioners to perform their tasks professionally and meet their responsibilities to their clients.

However, a decade later, the federal government has now been "in the black" for seven years in a row, with an accumulated surplus of more than $60 billion over that time. There is every reason, therefore, to think that things should improve. And indeed there some are positive signs. For example, the Liberal minority government recently announced a commitment to funding a nationwide child care program similar to the one that has been operating in Quebec. The details are still unclear, but this is certainly a step in the right direction.

Child welfare is a major area of employment for social workers today. It is also one of the most difficult areas of work for practitioners in terms of the heart-wrenching cases that can arise and the often complex ethical issues involved. This chapter provides an overview of child welfare policy and practice in Canada.

Social workers have always been at the forefront in advocating for improvements in policy and services for children and youth. Child welfare work is one of the most common fields for graduating social workers today — and perhaps the most challenging.

Health Canada.

Our most vulnerable citizens and our hope for the future.

KEY ISSUES IN CHILD
WELFARE WORK

- Too many children and families live in poverty.
- There are not enough inexpensive, quality child care spaces for working parents.
- There are not enough places for children in care to live.
- Across Canada children in care receive different levels of service.
- Child protection workers are extremely overloaded.
- Child welfare policy must consider children's rights as well as family preservation.
- Foster and adoptive families must be seen as part of a team.
- Adoption needs to be broadened to include plans that would improve adoption rates for older children.

The Organization of Child Welfare

Child welfare work in Canada is largely the domain of social worker practitioners. Much of the social worker's typical daily activity involves complex and sensitive issues and decisions surrounding children and their families. Over 76,000 Canadian children are currently under the protection of the various provincial child and family service agencies.

The work of child welfare across the country involves much more than simply removing children from unsafe home environments. Child welfare is highly regulated through provincial laws and regulations and involves five key activities:

- *Family support.* Providing a range of family programs and services in order to maintain healthy families, support families at risk and protect children.
- *Child protection.* Protecting children at risk by removing them from their families and finding substitute care.
- *Child placement.* Finding temporary substitute care, such as foster and group homes, for children who cannot continue to live with their parent(s) or guardian(s).
- *Adoption.* Finding permanent homes for children who cannot live with either of their parents.
- *Foster care.* Recruiting foster homes and providing training and support as well as monitoring foster homes.

Acting in these many ways through state agencies and non-profit centres, social workers intervene on behalf of children and their families — without them, the lives of a great many Canadian families and children would be much more tenuous.

In-home and Out-of-home Services

Canadian social workers also provide a wide variety of related services for children and youth, in the form of in-home services and out-of-home services.

- **In-home services** are provided to help a household or family members live together harmoniously in a secure and safe environment. The main categories of in-home services include family counselling services, parenting supports, child protection, in-home child care, homemaker services and family educational services.
- **Out-of-home services** are implemented when the home situation becomes unsuitable for the child. These services include foster care, adoption, day care centres, community supports (e.g., the Community Action Program for Children and Aboriginal Head Start), group homes, institutional care, parenting self-help and empowerment groups and family housing assistance.

Provincial Agencies and Legislation

Each of the 10 Canadian provinces and three territories has different organizations and legislation governing child welfare. Provincial services for children and youth may be provided by a branch of the provincial government or by a private or non-profit agency. In each jurisdiction, a wide variety of child and family services are provided.

Besides the child protection agencies, there are a variety of youth and children agencies across the country. The Ottawa-based Youth Services Bureau (YSB), for example, is representative of many such child and youth programs. It provides community programs that work with families in the home as well as individual counselling. It also has a residential program for girls under 16 years of age to help build their self-esteem, as well as a six-month transitional residence program for youth 16 years of age and older who are not quite ready to live on their own and require skills development.

Another innovative program for children, but in this case for children up to age six, is the Aboriginal Head Start (AHS) program. Funded by Health Canada, AHS funds early childhood development programs for First Nations, Inuit and Métis children and their families. There are over 120 AHS sites in urban and northern communities across Canada. AHS emphasizes a holistic approach by fostering the spiritual, emotional, intellectual and physical growth of the child. Many attribute the success of the program to its focus on Aboriginal self-determination. Aboriginal communities designed the program and continue to control its operation and evaluation. Programs are controlled locally and are based on traditional community beliefs and cultural practices. AHS illustrates how an approach that uses self-determination and participation can succeed, especialy for Aboriginal people.

• Provincial Legislation

Provincial legislation and policy in this area obviously changes frequently. An overview is provided below.

- First Nations child welfare services are provided by either the provincial agency on behalf of the federal government or directly by First Nations agencies as negotiated under the federal government's policy on Aboriginal self-government. Arrangements must be negotiated individually with each First Nation, and generally involve federal and provincial representatives.

- In British Columbia, child protection services are provided by the Ministry for Children and Families, a branch of the provincial government under the terms of the 1996 *Child, Family and Community Service Act*. The Ministry states that its role is to ensure a child-centred, integrated approach that promotes and protects the healthy development of children and youth while recognizing their

CENTRE OF EXCELLENCE FOR CHILD WELFARE

The Centre of Excellence for Child Welfare encourages collaborative projects that integrate child maltreatment prevention and interventions across a variety of sectors, including health care, education, justice and recreation.

The Centre's four main functions are fostering research, disseminating information, developing policy and forging networks.

A summary of legislation and policy across the country can be found on their website: http://www.cecw-cepb.ca

Health Canada.

For an overview of provincial child welfare, visit CECW's website.

ONTARIO ASSOCIATION OF CHILDREN'S AID SOCIETIES

The OACAS today represents 51 Children's Aid Societies in Ontario and has served its members, the community, the public and the government in a variety of ways since 1912.

Sixty children's aid societies came together on January 25, 1912, to form the Associated Children's Aid Societies of Ontario, which later became the OACAS.

Visit them on-line at http://www.oacas.org and explore their "About Child Welfare" section. It provides an overview of the history of child welfare in Ontario, what the CAS does, and a variety of facts and statistics about child welfare.

lifelong attachment to family and community (British Columbia Ministry for Children and Families 1999). The 2002 *Child, Family and Community Service Amendment Act* expands the options available for placing children once they have been taken into custody. Now children can be placed in the custody of extended family, friends of the family and other community members shortly after removal from the home.

- Alberta child protection services are provided by Alberta Family and Social Services, which is run by the provincial government and is governed by the *Child Welfare Act* of 2000 and the *Child Welfare Amendment Act* of 2002.

- In Manitoba, child protection services are provided through the non-governmental "Child and Family Services Agencies," which are mandated under the *Child and Family Services Act* of 1985. These are overseen by the provincial Ministry of Family Services.

- In Ontario, child protection services are delivered through 51 separate Children's Aid Societies (CAS). These organizations are legislated under the *Child and Family Services Act* (1990), the *Children's Law Reform Act* (2002) and the *Family Law Act* (2002) to investigate allegations of abuse and neglect, provide services to families for protecting children and to prevent circumstances requiring the protection of children, and provide care or supervision for children and provide adoption services. As of 1998, the provincial Ministry of Community and Social Services assumed 100 percent funding of Children's Aid Societies.

- The New Brunswick provincial government provides child protection services through its Family and Community Social Services (a department of the Ministry of Health and Community Services) under the *Family Services Act* of 1983.

- The Children's Aid Society of Halifax provides services in Nova Scotia. Under the *Children and Family Services Act* of 1990 (amended 2002), child protection workers and designated social workers in child welfare agencies investigate all reports of alleged child abuse and neglect. There are 20 child welfare offices throughout the province. Six are district offices of the government and 14 are privately run societies and/or family and children's services agencies. The Mi'kmaq Family and Children's Services Agency provides services for families living on reserves. Adoptions are regulated by the *Adoption Information Act*, 1996.

- In Newfoundland, the *Child, Youth and Family Services Act of 2000* replaces the *Child Welfare Act*. The new Act represents a shift in the way child welfare services will be provided in the province. The legislation supports a move away from remedial approaches towards prevention and early intervention strategies, with services delivered by community-based agencies.

National Archives of Canada, PA123686.

Children's aid societies in Ontario are non-profit, transfer payment agencies that advocate for children and families. OACAS is one of five children's associations in Ontario that provide specialized children's services in the province.

- In Prince Edward Island, the 2003 *Child Protection Act* makes major changes in child welfare practice, including lowering the age for defining a child (from 18 to 16 years), progressive and preventive approaches, and tightening time frames, particularly for younger children.

- The government of the Northwest Territories provides child protection services through its Department of Health and Social Services. The 1997 *Child and Family Services Act* and the *Adoptions Act* define "best interests of the child" with the recognition that differing cultural values and practices must be respected. Under the legislation, applicable Aboriginal organizations must be informed whenever someone who is eligible to become a member of the organization has a child protection case proceeding to court. This creates an opportunity for the organization to provide input, particularly with respect to any unique customs and traditions that may be important in the development of a case plan for the child and family.

- Saskatchewan has the *Child and Family Services Act* (1990). Bilateral agreements continue to be negotiated between Saskatchewan Social Services and First Nations bands for the control and delivery of child and family services on reserves.

History of Child Welfare

Over the years, each of the provinces accumulated its own imposing array of child welfare legislation. Nevertheless, certain patterns can be discerned in the history of child welfare legislation and practice in Canada.

• Pre-industrial Child Welfare: Pre-1890

The problems of child abuse and neglect did not suddenly appear in the twentieth century. The children of "traditional" rural settler families typically worked at farming along with other family members and household employees. Often the work was difficult and a strict division of labour was enforced. The mother was responsible for family care needs, such as cooking, cleaning and nursing. The father was responsible for the economic survival needs of the family. The wife and children existed as economic dependants of the family patriarch, the husband and father. Patriarchal authority was reinforced by the state through a variety of laws and practices.

By contrast, Aboriginal communities had rather more inclusive ideas concerning the raising of children. First Nations believed that a child belonged to his or her people, and that a child was a gift from the Creator. They believed that this connection of child to community was non-discretionary — he or she simply belonged to the nation and it was the responsibility of all to meet the child's needs.

In 1792, The Province of Upper Canada proclaimed that the Common Law of England would be in force for the new province. This body of law was exceedingly harsh towards children. For example, Upper Canada introduced the first Act concerning children in 1799. It was called the *Orphans Act*, and it gave town wardens the power to bind a child under 14 to an employer as an apprentice. In 1827, this Act was replaced with the *Guardianship Act*, which allowed guardians to be appointed by the court. The guardian then had the right to bind the child as an apprentice. The role of the family in the early laws in Canada did not extend beyond its value as an economic unit. Therefore, families that were poor were viewed as moral and economic threats, and their children were to be "bound out" to proper self-supporting families who would not taint the children with their parental failure.

The period from 1867 to 1890 saw the introduction of new laws that changed the exalted position of husbands and fathers. The legislative right of men to inflict arbitrary and severe punishment on their wives and children was beginning to be challenged. These new laws also affected the treatment and rights of children. The period began with amendments to Ontario's *Apprentices and Minors Act* (1874) and saw the introduction of compulsory education, regulation of work hours, the right of women to hold property and the rise of new and improved social agencies. For the first time, courts would decide whether a child's

Aboriginal grandfather with his grandson, BC, c. 1920.

National Archives of Canada, PA30581.

best interests would be better served with his or her family, one parent or an employer. Until this time, children generally were not seen as needing special care or nurturing; their needs were ignored and severe punishment was meted out to enforce rules.

It should also be noted that, in relation to Aboriginal peoples, the system of child welfare became part of an orchestrated campaign to dismantle communities and assimilate Aboriginal children into mainstream Canadian society. The *Indian Act* of 1876 exemplified the colonizer's views towards First Nations and their children. Beyond outlawing traditional ceremonies, such as the potlatch, the laws of the day attempted to eradicate Aboriginal culture by taking children out of First Nations homes and communities and placing them in residential schools administered by a number of Christian churches in association with the government. (For more on the residential schools, see Chapter 9, page 202.)

• A New Era in Child Welfare Legislation: 1890–1940

There was a marked increase in government involvement in children's issues in the late nineteenth and early twentieth centuries. In particular, legislation was enacted that allowed the state to remove children from the care of their parents or guardians. The federal *Juvenile Delinquent Act* of 1908 and the Ontario *Act for the Prevention of Cruelty to Children* of 1893 were both aimed at the protection of children. The legal mandate for promoting the "best interests" of children was given to the state, and the state could decide whether parents were good or bad. It had the authority (through legislation and the courts) to remove children from homes and put them into care.

In the 1890s, Canadian provinces also began to establish commissions to inspect the working conditions for children in factories. Many children as young as eight and nine years of age were employed, and inspections often revealed a callous disregard for the welfare of these children by factory owners. For example, there were repeated reports of poor ventilation and a lack of sanitary equipment. As well, the children were receiving no education while working in the factories, which contributed to the large number of illiterate adults across the country. As a result, new legislation was passed to regulate working conditions and hours of work. For example, Ontario passed the *Factory Act* and the *Regulation of Shops Act*. Eventually, the age of those considered to be children was raised to 16 years.

Several important women's organizations emerged in the late nineteenth century that affected the rights of children. The Women's Missionary Societies, which originally had an evangelical approach, began addressing the needs of women and children. The Women's Christian Temperance Union, founded in 1874, emphasized the prohibition of the sale of alcohol. Their broader social goals were helping children and

The late 1800s saw a marked increase in child welfare laws.

National Archives of Canada.

J.J. KELSO

Irish immigrant, journalist and child welfare pioneer, J.J. Kelso helped found the Toronto Humane Society in 1887, which concerned itself with the prevention of cruelty to children and animals. He became superintendent of neglected and dependent children until his retirement in 1934. During this time, he was instrumental in helping to establish Children's Aid Societies throughout Ontario — sixty by 1912 — and in British Columbia, Manitoba, Prince Edward Island and Nova Scotia during the first two decades of the 1900s.

His influence led to the Ontario *Children's Protection Act*, the first in Canada. He was a skilled organizer and a tireless promoter of children's rights who firmly believed that wide community mobilization is required for social change. His fresh and new ideas on children are exemplified in his presentation to the Social Service Congress in 1914 in which he said, "The child is the central figure in all social reform."

J.J. Kelso, first president of the Children's Aid Society in 1891.

included ensuring child protection, establishing reformatories for juveniles and building cottage-style homes to replace institutional care. The Young Women's Christian Association (YWCA) addressed the needs of urban working women, including assisting them with their children. The National Council of Women, formed in 1893, was an alliance of women's organizations aimed at coordinating policies at a national level. They considered many women's issues to be "mothering" issues, and their goal was to bring private mothering practices to public and national attention.

In Toronto, John Joseph Kelso, a journalist who had himself been raised in a single-parent family, began organizing meetings to address the problem of street children and their abuse. He was critical of the care provided by many of the private charities and orphanages, such as Maria Rye's Our Western Home for Girls at Niagara-on-the-Lake. He believed the children suffered from careless policies, lack of supervision and a lack of inspection or visitation.

Kelso's work resulted in numerous changes to child welfare services in Ontario and in Canada. The Toronto Children's Aid Society was incorporated in 1891, with Kelso serving as its first president. In 1892, the name was changed to the Children's Aid Society of Toronto, and a charter was granted to carry out the administration of the *Act for the Prevention of Cruelty and Better Protection of Children*. Kelso also played a pivotal role in the formation in Ontario of a Royal Commission on Prisons and Asylums in 1890, the creation of an office for the protection of children, and the *Children's Protection Act* of 1888, which is the forerunner of the current *Child and Family Services Act*.

The passing of the 1893 *Children's Protection Act* in Ontario ushered in a new era of modern child welfare legislation protecting children from abuse and neglect. The notion of neglect, which is still controversial today, stated that a child found sleeping in the open air was considered to be neglected. Those found guilty of mistreating a child were sentenced to three months of hard labour. The idea of foster homes, supervised by Children's Aid Societies, also originated with this Act. In 1908, the *Child Welfare Act* repealed some of the more draconian aspects of the previous Act and provided for procedures to rehabilitate mistreated children. Between 1891 and 1912, 60 Children's Aid Societies sprang up in Ontario. In 1912, they joined together as the Associated Children's Aid Societies of Ontario, now known as the Ontario Association of Children's Aid Societies (OACAS).

The obligation on the part of society to protect children began to crystallize during this period and a new notion of "childhood" emerged. Prior to this, children had been regarded essentially as adults. Now children were beginning to be seen in a different light and the period of childhood itself was viewed as having great bearing on the later development of the person. This was a fundamental shift in thinking.

FIGHTING CHILD AND FAMILY POVERTY — A PROGRESS REPORT

Child Poverty Rises: More than One Million Children Still in Poverty

Economic growth and social investments have combined to drive down the child poverty rate each year since 1996. By 2001, the child poverty rate of 14.9 percent matched the level in 1989, at the peak of the last economic recovery (Figure 6.1).

One-third of Canada's Children Experience Poverty in Good Times

Looking at one year of child poverty in Canada does not give us a full picture of the extent and nature of the problem. In fact, during the economic boom years of 1996 to 2001, 2.1 million children were exposed to poverty for at least one year; that is, one-third of all children in Canada (Figure 6.2).

Low-income Families Still Deep in Poverty

Although low-income couples with children saw some improvement in their situation in 2002, they remained, on average, $9000 below the poverty line. The circumstances for low-income female lone-parent families actually deteriorated compared to the previous year. Irrespective of whether or not low-income female lone-parents were employed, the distance between their family's incomes and the poverty line increased.

No Progress in Narrowing Gap Between Rich and Poor Families

Deep inequality between rich and poor families was entrenched throughout the economic boom. In 2002, Canada's top 10 percent richest families with children had incomes that were more than 11 times higher than the bottom 10 percent. In real dollars, between 1996 and 2002, the gap between the richest and poorest families actually widened. By 2002, the gap in the average incomes of the top and bottom 10 percent of families with children was $171,500.

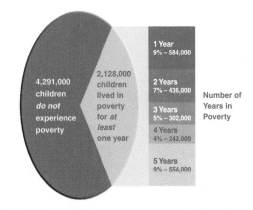

Figure 6.1. Children's exposure to poverty in Canada, 1996-2001.

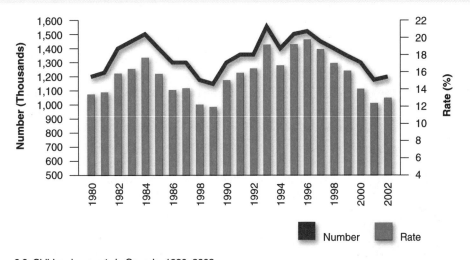

Figure 6.2: Children in poverty in Canada, 1980–2002.

Sources: Statistics Canada. 2002. *Income Trends in Canada.* No. 13F0022XCB. Canadian Centre for Policy Alternatives, Ottawa.

- In 1998, the Government of Canada increased the Canada Child Tax Benefit (CCTB) for low-income families by adding the new National Child Benefit Supplement (NCB).

- Over the years, the basic CCTB and NCB benefits have increased. People with an income below $23,000 who are not on Social Assistance receive up to $2,719 per year (2004).

- The federal government is planning to increase the CCTB to a maximum of $3,243 for the first child by 2007.

- Increasing investments in the CCTB combined with an end to the "clawback" of the NCB from families on Social Assistance would vastly improve family income security in Canada.

Modern Child Welfare Policy: 1940–Present

Since 1940, literally hundreds of provincial laws have been passed that affect child welfare. Across the country, while each province has distinct and separate legislation, several trends have emerged:

- a shift from a volunteer to a professional service system;

- the development and implementation of risk-assessment models and standardized record-keeping;

- provincial governments' acceptance of direct responsibility for the delivery of child welfare services through public financing, agency reporting and provincial supervision;

- a shift from institutional and protection-oriented services to non-institutional and prevention-oriented services;

- a shift towards legislation that emphasizes the "best interests" of the child over a model that stresses keeping children in their families; and

- an improvement in the capacity of Aboriginal agencies to provide services under Aboriginal leadership.

Within this broad framework, a number of new developments and shifts of emphasis occurred over this period. During the mid-1950s and 1960s, the near total reliance on foster homes and large-scale institutions such as orphanages and training schools came under scrutiny. Increasingly, child welfare agencies dealt with older children. These older children had emotional problems and exhibited more troublesome behaviour. Social workers were spending a lot more time with foster parents, families and the children themselves. By the end of the 1960s, the number of foster homes was declining.

In response, two alternatives to foster homes and large-scale institutions emerged. First, treatment regimes were emphasized. This involved many different kinds of treatment, ranging from strict discipline to a more permissive approach that concentrated on free expression and creativity. Second, group homes were launched. Reformers noted that children were being shuffled from foster home to foster home. One out of every three permanent wards of the court could expect to be placed five or more times in the care of various foster parents. The children were simply not able to adjust. Both the government and social workers believed that group homes would be less stigmatizing and impersonal than the large institutions of the past and more able to meet the adjustment needs of the children. They hoped that group homes would provide the children with the remedial help they needed.

In the 1970s, there was increased concern about the damaging effects of child welfare agencies on children in their care. A new generation of reformers argued that children were coming out of the child welfare system more damaged than when they went into it. Some of this

CP PHOTO/Frank Gunn.

A researcher with some children at OISE's Institute for Child Studies.

concern was reflected in a new 1978 *Child Welfare Act* in Ontario, which defined child abuse for the first time. However, it wasn't until Ontario's *Child and Family Services Act* of 1984 that this concern was expressed in legal language. The 1984 Act begins with a statement of principles that includes: "The least restrictive or disruptive course of action should be followed keeping the child in the home, if possible. Social workers can no longer 'apprehend' a child unless imminent risk can be shown."

In 1990, new legislation in Ontario shifted to stating that the paramount purpose was "to promote the best interests, protection and well-being of children." Many similar sentiments can be noted in provincial child welfare legislation across the country around this time. The provincial Acts of the 1970s and early 1980s had stressed the least disruptive course of action in addressing the abuse and neglect of children — the child was to remain in the home if at all possible. The more recent provincial Acts have swung back somewhat to the notion of acting in the best interests of the child. Several widely publicized deaths of children who were left in the home caused a reaction on the part of some provincial governments. The legislation now allows for the quicker removal of children who may be in danger. As well, the expansion of the notion of neglect has increased the likelihood that social workers will determine that a child needs to be removed and placed in care.

Table 6.1: Child Poverty in Canada and the Provinces, 2002

	Child Poverty	**Average Amount Required to Reach Poverty Line**		
	Rate (%)	**Number**	**Low-Income Couples with Children**	**Low-Income Lone Female Parents**
Canada	15.6	1,065,000	$9,000	$8,000
Newfoundland and Labrador	21.9	24,000	$6,300	$7,100
Prince Edward Island	11.4	4,000	-	-
Nova Scotia	18.1	36,000	$6,900	$7,300
New Brunswick	14.3	23,000	$7,700	$6,200
Quebec	16	245,000	$8,500	$9,700
Ontario	13.6	373,000	$9,700	$9,100
Manitoba	20.8	53,000	$9,900	$10,300
Saskatchewan	18.7	44,000	$5,700	$7,400
Alberta	13.3	98,000	$8,800	$8,900
British Columbia	19.6	167,000	$10,000	$10,400

Source: Statistics Canada. 2002. *Income Trends in Canada*. Catalogue No. 13F0022XCB.

A NEED TO PROMOTE SOCIAL INCLUSION

While poverty and disadvantage are too common throughout society, some social groups are disproportionately affected. Persistent social inequality based on gender, race, ethnicity and ability demonstrates the impact of eroded social protections and exposes the limitations of relying primarily on economic growth to achieve social inclusion. Specific policies and investments are needed to address the systemic sources of disadvantage and promote greater equity in our communities.

The level of child poverty among female lone-parent families showed a marked deterioration compared to the previous two years. While 2000 and 2001 marked the first time that the rate of child poverty in lone mother families fell below 50 percent, the trend was reversed in 2002. That year, the child poverty rate for female lone-parent families jumped by almost seven percentage points — from 45 percent in 2001 to 51.6 percent in 2002. Meanwhile, the level of child poverty remained virtually unchanged among couple families. In fact, the increase in child poverty between 2001 and 2002 can be attributed almost exclusively to worsening circumstances among female lone-parent families.

The contributions of immigrants will continue to be absolutely central to the prosperity of Canada. It is projected that immigration will account for virtually all of Canada's labour force growth by 2011. Yet, a precarious labour market has led to high levels of poverty and exclusion among recent immigrants. Many recent immigrant workers are clustered in low-wage work with few, if any, benefits.

Despite having the highest ever educational credentials, today's immigrants have undergone a sharp decline in living standards compared with immigrants from previous decades. Canadian employers often do not recognize internationally attained credentials and job experience. While the child poverty rate among all immigrants in Canada is quite high at 40.4 percent, it climbs to almost 50 percent for recent immigrants who arrived since 1996.

Among racialized groups, barriers to employment are compounded by discrimination. Workers belonging to a visible minority group averaged $27,149 in employment earnings in 2001 — $4,600 less than the average for all other workers. The poverty rate for children in racialized families stood at 33.6 percent in 2001.

It is significant that more and more recent immigrants are in racialized groups who are more likely to face discrimination than previous generations of immigrants. Almost three-quarters of the immigrants who

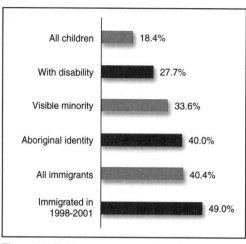

Figure 6.3: Child poverty among selected social groups, 2001.

Source: Statistics Canada. Canadian Census 2001.

arrived during the 1990s were members of visible minority groups, up from 68 percent in the 1980s, and 52 percent in the 1970s. As the vast majority of recent immigrants settle in urban centres, the racialization of poverty is becoming a harsh reality in Canada's largest cities.

Aboriginal people still have one of the highest rates of poverty. The child poverty rate among off-reserve children was 40 percent, more than double the average for all children in Canada. While Aboriginal people represent a large and growing share of Canada's urban population, particularly in cities from Winnipeg to Vancouver, there are few supports to assist Aboriginal families who live in urban areas.

Despite some progress in educational attainment and participation in the labour market, Aboriginal people are still less likely to be employed than the general population and Aboriginal workers still had the lowest average employment earnings of all workers. In 2001, Aboriginal workers earned only two-thirds of an average worker's wages.

Children with disabilities face barriers to full inclusion and their families encounter immense financial, social and emotional stresses. Children with a disability were more likely than children without a disability to live in low-income families, both because of the financial costs related to disability and the earnings lost when primarily mothers leave the workforce to care for their children. In 2001, the child poverty rate of children with disabilities was 27.7 percent.

Source: Campaign 2000. 2004. One Million Too Many: Implementing Solutions to Child Poverty in Canada. A 2004 Report Card on Child Poverty in Canada. Ottawa.

The Dilemma of Child Protection

The primary response to child abuse and neglect in Canada is through the provincial child protection systems. The provincial child welfare laws require that all cases of suspected child abuse and neglect be reported and investigated. Various actions or interventions occur if an investigation indicates that a child is in need of protection. Responses range from the provision of counselling and support services to the family, to the temporary or permanent removal of the child from the home, to the removal of the abuser or abusers from the home. In the most serious cases, abusers may be convicted of a crime if the abuse can be proven under the Criminal Code of Canada.

Child protection agencies have long grappled with the dilemma of deciding when children should be brought into the care of the state and when they should be left in the home. The social worker operates with the knowledge that she or he must obtain and assess as much background information as possible and use the information to make judgments regarding the parents' and the child's best interests, all the while knowing that the process is not an exact science. As one CAS administrator put it, "The work is not for the faint of heart. It is not a vocation for those who are just 'well-meaning.'" The work requires knowledge, stamina, exceptional versatility and an ability to find common ground with parents in order to secure safety for children. It is sometimes stated that social workers must "desensitize" themselves when they work in the child welfare field. Of course, in practice this is nearly impossible since, in order to do their jobs effectively, social workers must be very sensitive to the needs and feelings of the children and families they are involved with.

• The "Best Interests" of the Child

Throughout the history of modern child protection legislation in Canada, the terms *best interests of the child* and *least restrictive* intervention have been debated, and Acts have been passed that move between the two approaches. The **"best interests" approach** emphasizes the protection and well-being of the child, whereas the **"least restrictive" approach** emphasizes the course of action that will cause the least change for the child, leaving him or her with the family if at all possible.

Deciding what is in the best interests of a child can be difficult. The social worker makes the initial decision to remove a child from the home, but the case must go before a judge for a final decision. There is no easy solution for either the social worker or the court. When provinces have had "best interest" legislation, the number of children taken from their families generally increased, in some cases quite dramatically. A few high-profile cases in which children have been harmed as a result of being left in a dangerous situation have led several provinces to change their "least restrictive" legislation. The state, however, must

> "Being a social worker is probably one of the toughest jobs on the face of the earth because not only do you have to take into consideration how the family operates, and you can go back generations to see how things have developed, but you also have to take into consideration who you are and how you react to things. So, there are a lot of variables going on at all times and so what I try to do is make sure that I ask all the questions that I need to ask."

Source: Anonymous social worker.

Health Canada.

Who will catch a child if he or she should fall?

CHILDREN IN CARE

The latest evidence suggests that there has been a resurgence in the number of children in care. Currently 30–40% of children in care are Aboriginal children.

consider the damage that may be caused by removing many more children from their families and placing them in group homes.

In Nova Scotia, for example, the following factors are considered in deciding which criteria are to be used by social workers and the courts when trying to decide on the best interests of the child:

1. the child's physical, mental and emotional needs and the appropriate care or treatment to meet those needs;

2. the child's cultural background and religious faith;

3. the importance for the child's development of a positive relationship with a parent and a secure place as a member of a family;

4. the child's relationships by blood or through an adoption order;

5. the importance of continuity of care; whether it is likely that the child will be moved from one agency or home to another;

6. the child's views and wishes, which must be respected;

7. the risk that the child may suffer harm through being removed from or kept away from the care of a parent; and

8. the degree of risk, if any, that justifies the finding that the child is in need of protection (Nova Scotia Department of Community Services 1990).

For example, section 22 (j) of the *Children and Family Services Act* of 1990 (amended 2002) states that, in the case of neglect, a child is in need of protective services when he or she "has suffered physical harm caused by chronic and serious neglect by a parent or guardian of the child, the parent or guardian does not provide, or refuses, or is unavailable or unable to consent to services or treatment to remedy, or alleviate the harm" (Nova Scotia Department of Community Services 1993, 17). In the same province, a child is considered in need of protective services when "the child has suffered physical harm, inflicted by a parent or guardian of the child or caused by the failure of a parent or guardian to supervise and protect the child adequately." However, the Act does not provide clear and specific directions as to what a social worker must do. Rather, it provides only general guidance on what a social worker or judge must consider when deciding what to do.

More recent Ontario legislation, on the other hand, is directive in declaring what a social worker must do to protect the best interests of the child. In 2000, the Ontario government stiffened its previous legislation with the *Family Services Amendment Act.* The words "least restrictive" were removed to ensure that the "best interests" clauses were clearly paramount. It also expanded the reasons for finding a child in need of protection. For instance, the word "neglect" was specifically included, and the threshold for risk of harm and emotional harm to children was lowered.

CP PHOTO/Toronto Sun-Michael Peake (2001).

Renee Heikamp fields questions following death of "Baby Jordan."

Children in Care

The numbers of children in care tell most of the story. Consistent with the hopes of the 1978 and 1984 Ontario legislation, there was a decline of children "in care" between 1971 and 1988. In this period, the CAS reported an increase of 160 percent in the number of families served, but the number of children in care decreased by 45 percent (Trocmé 1991, 63). However, the trend subsequently changed. The 1994 and 2000 changes in legislation emphasized the best interests of the child, and the number of children in care has again increased. The latest total of 19,105 children in care in Ontario represents an increase of nearly 34 percent from January 1995 (OACAS 2004).

A similar trend exists in other provinces as well, although the increases are not as dramatic. Alberta Children's Services (1999–2000, 38) reports that the number of children under permanent state guardianship increased from 3,862 to 4,318 during 1999–2000. This represents an increase of 12 percent. British Columbia reports (Ministry for Children and Families 1998–99) that 9,813 children were under state care in 1999, an increase of 4.8 percent over the previous year. The British Columbia Ministry emphasizes court order supervision in the home, rather than state custody of children at risk. They report 1,355 children under ordered supervision — an increase of 39 percent over 1998. In all of Canada (other than Quebec), the number of children in care increased by 20 percent between 1990 and 1997 (CASSW 2001).

• Economic Strains on Parents and Families

The increase in the number of families involved with child welfare agencies can be partly explained by population growth, but the increased economic stress families are experiencing is certainly an important factor. Poverty rates have increased, the number of families living below the poverty line has gone up, as has the number of children living in poverty. In particular, there has been an increase in the number of lone-parent families living in poverty, with the attendant stress this entails. Moreover, a large and growing proportion of the low-income population consists of lone-parent families headed by women (Ross, Shillington, and Lochhead 1994, 61, 122–23).

Social workers are presented with a persistent dilemma in their daily practice; namely, to what extent they and their agency should take into account the broader social context of individuals, families and communities. Before taking a child from a home, for example, should the social worker consider such things as economic stress caused by family poverty (say, in the case of a single-parent family)? Should the social worker first seek ways to address and rectify obvious economic problems? These are judgments individual social workers currently make largely on their own, without clear direction from child welfare or other legislation.

NATIONAL YOUTH IN CARE NETWORK

The National Youth in Care Network is a "by youth, for youth" organization. This national charitable organization was started by a small group of young people in care from across Canada in 1985. The group shared a feeling of powerlessness — they felt strongly that the child welfare system had taken away their control over their own lives.

The Network exists to help members find their voice and regain control over their lives through support, skill building and healing opportunities. Young people in and from care can support, educate and advocate for each other.

Visit their website at:
http://www.youthincare.ca

Criticisms of Policies

Child welfare agencies in Canada are not mandated to protect a child from the abuses of poverty or other social problems — since these are not considered to be protection issues. Strong arguments have been made for having children's agencies do more work as child advocates on prevention programs and on combatting widespread child poverty. In fact, critics argue, when government finances are strained, as they are now, prevention programs are the first to be cut. Consequently, child welfare and protection programs are increasingly reactive and crisis-oriented.

However, others argue that child welfare agencies should be involved only in straightforward protection issues, such as neglect or abuse. Only when there is an immediate danger should the state intervene. This viewpoint rests on the belief that child welfare agencies are already sufficiently intrusive and that they should not be concerned with broader social issues as well.

While the outcome of such policy debates has important consequences, both sides firmly maintain that what they are advocating will be in the best long-term interests of Canadian children and their families. By and large, governments have pursued a short-term perspective, dealing with emergencies at hand, and overall the trend seems to be away from proactive intervention that seeks lasting solutions to underlying causes.

Table 6.2: Children in Care

Province/Territory	Children in Care	Children in Care who are Aboriginal	Children in Care in Family-Based Care
Newfoundland-Labrador (1999)	703	Unknown	93%
Prince Edward Island (Mar 2002)	329	Unknown	70%
New Brunswick (Mar 1999)	1,193	Unknown	81%
Nova Scotia (Mar 1999)	1,906	Unknown	58%
Quebec (Feb 2003)	20,506	Unknown	Unknown
Manitoba (Mar 1999)	5,358	68%	72%
Saskatchewan (Mar 1999)	2,710	67%	75%
Alberta (Mar 2001)	15,032	38%	77%
British Columbia (Mar 2002)	10,450	40%	59%
Yukon (1999)	182	Unknown	Unknown
Northwest Territories (Mar 2001)	825	Unknown	77%
Nunavut	NA	Unknown	Unknown
Total	**76,183**		

Source: Child Welfare League of Canada. 2003. *Children in Care in Canada: A Summary of Current Issues and Trends with Recommendations for Future Research.*

The Incidence of Child Abuse

Child abuse entails the betrayal of a caregiver's position of trust and authority over a child. It involves the physical, psychological, social, emotional and sexual maltreatment of a child, whereby the survival, safety, self-esteem, growth and development of the person are threatened. It can take many forms:

- **Neglect** — sustained deprivation of food, clothing, hygiene, shelter and other needed care so as to cause, or potentially cause, physical, emotional, developmental or psychological harm.

- **Physical abuse** — physical assaults, such as hitting, kicking, biting, throwing, burning or poisoning, that cause, or could cause, physical injury as well as behaviours or omissions that cause, or could cause, physical injury to a child.

- **Sexual abuse** — any sexual exploitation of a child whether consented to or not. It includes touching of a sexual nature or any behaviour of a sexual nature towards a child.

- **Emotional abuse** — emotional attacks or omissions that cause, or could cause, serious emotional injury, including the behaviour of parents or guardians who do not take an interest in their child; for example, not talking with or hugging their child, or being emotionally unavailable to their child. This could also include repeated threats, confinement, exposure to violence, ongoing humiliation and ridicule and attacks on a child's fundamental sense of self.

A recent national survey, the Canadian Incidence Study of Reported Child Abuse and Neglect (CIS), provided national estimates on the incidence of child abuse and neglect (Trocmé et al. 2001). Prior to this study, there was no central source of comprehensive, Canada-wide statistics on children and families investigated because of suspected child abuse and neglect. The CIS helps to fill a nation-wide need for accurate data on child maltreatment. Among the most thorough of its kind in the world, this study provides detailed estimates of the scope and characteristics of child abuse and neglect across Canada.

The CIS had the full participation of all provincial and territorial governments. Four provinces (British Columbia, Ontario, Quebec, Newfoundland) provided additional funds to increase the sample size in their jurisdiction. The study's aims were as follows:

- to examine the rates of investigated physical abuse, sexual abuse, neglect and emotional maltreatment, as well as multiple forms of maltreatment;

- to examine the severity of maltreatment as indicated by duration and physical and emotional harm;

CP PHOTO/The Kitchener Waterloo Record-Robert Wilson.

Art counselling for abuse victims at Family and Children's Services.

CHILD ABUSE

The Investigation and Protection Services branch of the Ontario Association of Children's Aid Societies reports the following statistics:

- CAS responded to 65,542 inquiries in the 12 months from April 1, 1999, to March 31, 2000.
- CAS received 55,572 referrals that were assessed as requiring no investigation.
- CAS completed 63,712 investigations in 1999–2000.
- There were 18,136 open protection cases on April 1, 2000.
- There were 6,518 other child welfare cases open on April 1, 2000.
- There were 204,487 inquiries, referrals, investigations and assessments, protection and prevention services provided to children and families in 1999–2000.

———
Source: OACAS 2000.

- to examine selected determinants of health for investigated children and their families; and
- to monitor short-term investigation outcomes, including substantiation rates, out-of-home placement, use of child welfare court and criminal prosecution.

The CIS provided a snapshot of children who were reported to, and investigated by, child welfare services during a three-month period, from October to December 1998. The highlights below on physical abuse, sexual abuse, neglect and emotional maltreatment are based on 7,672 investigations from 51 sites in all provinces and territories.

- In 1998, there were an estimated 21.52 investigations of child maltreatment per 1,000 children in Canada. Forty-five percent of these investigations were substantiated, 22 percent remained suspected, and 33 percent were found to be unsubstantiated.
- Child maltreatment investigations were divided into four primary categories: physical abuse (31% of all investigations), sexual abuse (10% of all investigations), neglect (40% of all investigations) and emotional maltreatment (19% of all investigations).
- Thirty-four percent of the physical abuse investigations were found to be substantiated. This compares with 38 percent for sexual abuse, 43 percent for neglect and 54 percent for emotional maltreatment.
- Substantiated cases of physical abuse consisted of:
  - inappropriate punishment (69% of physical abuse cases),
  - shaken Baby Syndrome (1%),
  - other forms of physical abuse (31%).
- The most common forms of substantiated sexual abuse included:
  - touching and fondling of the genitals (68% of sexual abuse cases),
  - attempted and completed sexual activity (35%),
  - adults exposing their genitals (12%).
- The most common forms of substantiated neglect included:
  - failure to supervise leading to physical harm (48% of neglect cases),
  - physical neglect (19%),
  - permitting criminal behaviour (14%),
  - abandonment (12%),
  - educational neglect (11%).
- Substantiated cases of emotional maltreatment included:
  - exposure to family violence (58% of emotional maltreatment cases),
  - emotional abuse (34%),
  - emotional neglect (16%).

The Ontario Association of Children's Aid Societies also provides the following statistics on child maltreatment and neglect on their website (http://www.oacas.org):

- The incidence of child maltreatment is estimated to be one in five children;

- Thirty-three percent of sex offenders experienced some form of sexual trauma as children;

- Eighty percent of female prisoners were victims of child physical or sexual abuse;

- Eighty percent of people with eating disorders experienced some form of abuse and/or witnessed violence between their parents as a child;

- Children with a history of sexual abuse are seven times more likely to become alcohol and/or drug dependent;

- Suicide prevention programs find that children with a history of sexual abuse are 10 times more likely to attempt suicide;

- Child prostitution prevention programs for ages nine and up find that 99 percent have a history of child abuse;

- Eigthy-five percent of runaways served by Covenant House in Toronto have been sexually abused;

- Children with a history of child abuse are more likely to have psychiatric and other health problems, commit crimes, drop out of school or be unemployed.

• The Problem of Under-Reporting

Over the past two decades, there has been a dramatic increase in both reports of suspected abuse and neglect and in the number of children found to be in need of protection. Even with these increased numbers, many cases of child abuse are still not reported. People working with children, including professional social workers, may not report child abuse because they do not recognize its signs and symptoms. They may also resist admitting that it is really happening or convince themselves that it is not serious enough to report. Other factors inhibiting voluntary reporting are the nature of family problems related to child abuse and neglect, the sense of secrecy and shame surrounding child maltreatment, the possible consequences of intervention by child protection authorities or police and the fact that many of the victims are young and relatively dependent.

Children may want to disclose their abuse, so it can be stopped, but they are often afraid that no one will believe or help them. They may be afraid of what will happen. Abusive parents frequently warn their children not to tell anyone about their actions. They may convince the child that the abuse is the child's fault and that telling someone will only get them into more trouble.

CHILD ABUSE

The 1998/99 National Longitudinal Survey of Children and Youth (NLSCY) indicates that an estimated 8 percent, or one in 12 children, between the ages of four and seven had witnessed some type of physical violence in the home. Of the children who had witnessed violence, the majority had "seldom" witnessed violence (64%), one-third (30%) had witnessed violence "sometimes," and 5 percent, "often."

According to a 2002 analysis of 94 police department reports of violence in the home, children and youth under the age of 18 represented 23 percent of victims and 61 percent of victims of sexual assault and 20 percent of all victims of physical assault.

Source: Statistics Canada and Canadian Centre for Justice Statistics. 2004. *Family Violence in Canada: A Statistical Profile.* Available on-line at: http://www.statcan.ca Catalogue no. 85–224–XIE.

Hockey star Sheldon Kennedy raising money to fight child abuse.

PARENTING IN CANADA

The Canadian Resource Centre on Children and Youth (CRCCY) has published a pamphlet called "Parenting in Canada." The pamphlet provides general information and answers questions frequently asked by parents.

It is available on-line at:
http://ia1.carleton.ca/52100/m18/pam.html

Risk Assessment

A key component of child protection services is risk assessment. A discussion paper on best practice in child welfare assessments issued by the Children's Aid Society of Metropolitan Toronto gives a fairly complete overview of the process of assessment and the principles for service. **Risk assessment** is used to estimate the likelihood that a child will be maltreated, based on a careful examination of pertinent data, so that action can be taken to prevent it.

Research has identified the risk assessment factors that correlate with the abuse of children. Of course, such risk assessments are not foolproof and must be used in conjunction with worker judgment. Such research helps in supporting casework judgment, standardizing decision making, providing a teaching tool, focusing service plans on risk and demonstrating accountability. Workers therefore require a sound knowledge of the risk factors to enable them make judgments that are supported by credible information.

• A Duty to Report

It is important to note that it is not only child protection workers who have a responsibility to report suspected instances of child abuse or neglect. Every member of society has a responsibility to report child abuse or neglect when there are reasonable grounds for believing a child may be in need of protection. People in professions that bring them into contact with children have a particular responsibility to ensure that young people are safe. In the course of their duties, they have a professional **duty to report** if they have reasonable grounds to suspect that a child is or may be in need of protection. If professionals do not report their suspicions of child abuse or neglect, they can be convicted for such and fined up to $1,000. This professional duty to report affects the following persons:

- health care professionals, including physicians, nurses, dentists, pharmacists and psychologists;
- teachers and school principals;
- social workers and family counsellors;
- priests, rabbis and other members of the clergy;
- operators or employees of day nurseries;
- youth and recreation workers (but not volunteers);
- police officers and coroners;
- solicitors;
- service providers and employees of service providers; and
- any other person who performs professional or official duties with respect to children.

Steps in Providing Child Welfare Services

Child welfare service procedures are outlined in detail in the various provincial standards manuals. Specific criteria for determining whether or not a child is in need of protection are found in provincial child welfare Acts. These Acts outline the conditions under which children are considered to be in need of protection. In general, the steps for providing child welfare services in Canada are as follows:

• 1. Initial Response to Reports of Abuse and Neglect

The person receiving the report of child abuse and neglect must exercise careful judgment. Workers should collect accurate information from various sources, such as the child, other family members, anonymous neighbours and other callers, and from persons with well-meaning intentions as well as persons intending to make malicious accusations. Even though decision-making may be difficult and emotional, workers must make decisions in the best interests of the child.

The Response Steps are as follows:
- receiving the report;
- obtaining complete information from the informant;
- assessing the motivation and credibility of the informant;
- checking records;
- determining if investigation is necessary;
- developing initial investigation plan; and
- documenting the reported abuse.

• 2. Investigation

The social worker should obtain detailed and complete information using interviews, observations, assessment and service reports from professionals, and by checking available records. All decisions must be based on detailed, accurate and documented evidence. Crucial decisions must be made at this juncture in response to the following questions:
- Has the child been abused?
- What are the immediate safety needs of the child?
- Is there a risk of future harm?
- What is the capacity of the family to protect the child?
- What services are required by the child and family?

All provincial child welfare Acts empower child protection workers to enter premises to remove children whom they deem to be in need of protection. Workers will frequently interview children at school, as this is considered a safe and familiar environment. Interviewing children requires considerable skill.

As mentioned, the assessment of risk to the child is increasingly seen as the key component of child welfare practice (see above, page 130).

REASONABLE DISCIPLINE

Attitudes towards discipline and punishment of children are changing in Canada. Parents have a lot of discretion but some forms of punishment are clearly abusive and against the law. Many Canadians believe that physical force is an unacceptable means of disciplining children.

The law currently allows parents to use "reasonable force" to discipline children. What is reasonable depends on the situation, but judges have indicated that forms of physical punishment that were acceptable in the past may no longer be permitted.

Clearly, any injury that requires medical attention is not reasonable discipline. Physical discipline that results in bruising, welts or broken skin would also almost certainly be considered abuse.

CP PHOTO/London Free Press-Dave Chidley.

Usually, the removal of children from families is highly controversial.

DIFFERENTIAL RESPONSE MODELS

Due to the growth in child protection cases, many child welfare policy experts are interested in developing alternative response models or "differential response models" within communities.

These would involve tailoring responses to the needs of the particular maltreated children. For example, lower-risk cases could be shifted to an alternative community track where the focus of intervention is on brokering and coordinating services rather than on custody.

While each province and, indeed, each local agency has its own policies and procedures, general investigative guidelines are common. An investigation includes the following steps:

1. Conduct a telephone interview with the person who reported the alleged abuse and any others who have information.

2. Search existing Society records for any present or past contact with the family, the alleged abuser or the child.

3. Contact the Child Abuse Register to ascertain if the alleged abuser was registered in the past and, if so, what the details were of that registration. Contact any child welfare authority that previously registered the alleged abuser.

4. See the child who is alleged to have been abused and conduct an interview using methods appropriate to the child's developmental stage and ability to communicate.

5. Ensure that the alleged abuser is interviewed by the police and/or a Society worker pursuant to the protocol established between the Society and the police.

6. Interview the parent or person having charge of the child, if they are not the alleged abuser.

7. Interview other potential victims (for example, siblings, other children in the home, classmates).

8. Gather evidence from other professionals involved in the investigation (for example, medical, law enforcement, educational).

9. Gather information from other witnesses.

Assessing the urgency of a response is critical. The child who is the subject of a report of abuse must be seen as soon as possible, but generally not later than 12 hours after receipt of the report. To assess urgency, the social worker should consider the child's age, the nature of the alleged abuse, the known injury to the child, the potential for the child to suffer physical harm, the availability of possible evidence (for example, visible marks) and the immediate need for counselling or support. The worker should ensure that a medical examination by a qualified medical practitioner is performed when there is a need to document the child's condition.

A medical examination may also be necessary in certain situations to ascertain whether the child has been harmed. This can be arranged by obtaining the cooperation of the parent. However, if the parent's cooperation cannot be obtained, the social worker may need to apprehend the child and authorize the medical examination without parental consent.

CP PHOTO/Red Deer Advocate-Randy Fiedler.

Neighbours protest the release of known sex offender in Red Deer.

• 3. Verification

Agencies generally have established policies and procedures outlining the process and factors to be considered when a protection verification decision is made. The verification decision must be made at a formal meeting in consultation with the social worker's supervisor and/or higher authorities. The worker should record the process of verification and the standards of proof for making the decision in the case file.

There are generally four possible investigative outcomes:

- The complaint is not verified, and the child protection concern does not appear to exist.

- A protection concern is verified, but the child remains in the home. This outcome occurs when the abuse has been perpetrated by a non-family member.

- A protection concern is verified, and the child remains in the home but may be in need of protection. With this option, a plan must be developed to ensure the child's safety, including a schedule of visits and restricted access by some family members. This approach is consistent with the philosophy of taking the "least restrictive" course of action necessary to protect the child.

- A protection concern is verified, and the child is removed from the home. The child welfare agency must decide on and seek from the court a report order that it believes to be the least restrictive or disruptive. Court order options include the placement of the child with some other person subject to the agency's provision, child welfare agency wardship, Crown wardship, or consecutive child welfare agency wardship and supervision order.

• 4. Assessment Report and Service Plan

If abuse is verified, the law requires a complete assessment and plan of service for the child and family. The assessment report should address numerous issues, including the nature of the abuse, precipitating factors, the nature of the dispute, family dysfunction, family background, parental capacity, family relationships, family strengths, service needs, child development and the risk of further abuse. The service plan should include the specific risk factors, service needs, strategies and service providers, ongoing care responsibility and coordination, expectations, review dates and client involvement in the the service plan.

• 5. Case Management

Careful record-keeping is mandatory in child welfare agencies. If called upon, a worker must be able to substantiate the decisions made. Supervision, consultation, review and decision-making occur frequently during the management of all child abuse cases. All agencies have strict documentation requirements.

CHILD POVERTY, 2004

On the fifteenth anniversary of the Canadian Parliament's vow to end child poverty, 1,065,000 children (or nearly one in six of Canada's children), still remain in poverty.

Not only is Canada's record on child poverty actually worse than it was in 1989, but Canada's rate of poverty jumped for the first time in 2002, following five straight years of decline.

——

Source: Campaign 2000. 2004. O*ne Million Too Many: Implementing Solutions to Child Poverty in Canada. A 2004 Report Card on Child Poverty in Canada.* Ottawa.

Campaign 2000's Report Card on Child Poverty in Canada (2004).

Social Services for Children and Youth

Many families and individuals experience stress due to problems that are not restricted to the poor, the uneducated or the unmotivated. These difficulties may take a number of forms, such as addiction or substance abuse, wife assault, eating disorders and so forth. Some of these problems involve children and youth. There are a number of programs, agencies and organizations that exist to assist these families and are, in the broad sense of the word, concerned with child "well-fare." These include youth services agencies, crisis intervention and residential treatment centres, youth addiction centres, shelters for homeless youth and income support programs.

• Services for Young Offenders

Prior to the *Juvenile Delinquents Act* in 1908, young offenders were treated like "little adults." They were sentenced as adults, and were incarcerated with adult prisoners. In 1892, Canada's Criminal Code contained measures to supposedly protect children in the justice system. It established a minimum age of seven for charging a child, and a child under the age of fourteen could not be charged unless he or she was competent to understand the nature of the crime "and to appreciate that it was wrong."

In 1894, the *Youthful Offenders Act* legislated the separation of youth from adults both in trials and in prison facilities. Alternatives to imprisonment were also enacted and encouraged in this Act, including placing young offenders in foster care or sending them to reformatories. The reforms had little impact, and young offenders were still given sentences equivalent to those of adults and incarcerated in adult facilities. In practice, however, the 1908 *Juvenile Delinquents Act* (JDA) provided a separate justice system for youth. For the first time youth were treated within a different system and in youth-specific facilities.

In 1984 the JDA was replaced with the *Young Offenders Act* (YOA). Due to outcries from the public regarding youth crime, the YOA was amended three times. It was criticized on many counts: for being too soft on the offender; for lacking a clear philosophy on youth justice in Canada; for inconsistent and unfair sentences; for not properly addressing serious and violent offences; for an overuse of the court system; and for not giving enough recognition to the victims. Agencies such as the John Howard Society were highly critical of the YOA. The more punitive approach of the YOA resulted in the increasing use of custody sentences for juvenile offenders. Under the YOA, youth were more likely than adults to be sentenced to custody for all offences and, in particular, for minor offences. Youth were serving longer sentences than adults for the same crimes and were being incarcerated at a much higher rate than in other western nations (John Howard Society of Alberta 1999).

Child welfare can involve teenagers as well as children.

Dick Hemingway.

• The Youth Criminal Justice Act

In 2002, Parliament replaced the YOA with the **Youth Criminal Justice Act (YCJA)**. The Act was implemented in 2003. The YCJA sought to emphasize the rehabilitation and re-entry of a young offender into society. It also addressed the criticism that the youth justice system lacked a clear philosophy by laying out a Declaration of Principles:

> The youth criminal justice system is to prevent crime by addressing the circumstances underlying a young person's offending behaviour, rehabilitate young persons who commit offences and reintegrate them back into society, and ensure that a young person is subject to meaningful consequences for his or her offences, in order to promote the long-term protection of the public.

Among other things, the Youth Criminal Justice Act (YCJA) sought to end transfers of youth to adult court, but it enabled a judge to impose an adult sentence on a youth from within a youth court. The YCJA also lowered the "age of presumption" to 14 years. Whereas under the YOA, it was presumed youths aged 16 and over convicted of a serious offence such as murder would be transferred to adult court, the new act lowered the age to 14 (individual provinces can adjust the age to 15 or 16).

On the sentencing and custodial side, the YCJA was also an attempt to lower the numbers of youth in prisons by placing less emphasis on custody as a sentence for non-violent or less serious offences. The new Act also emphasized alternative youth sentencing methods (out of court), such as referrals to community programs, formal letters of warning to parents and meetings with police.

• Youth Crime Today

Public concerns concerning youth crime (or juvenile delinquency, as it was previously called) began in the late 1950s. This early concern reflected a real increase in youth crime at the time. Table 6.3 (adjacent) illustrates the increase during this period. This trend in rising youth crime rates continued during the 1970s. The government responded by completely reviewing the youth justice system (resulting in the 1984 *Young Offenders Act*). The federal government hoped the YOA would ease public concerns, but the 1980s witnessed a continued increase in youth crime, particularly violent crimes. Public criticism of the legislation reflected the rising statistics.

However, in the 1990s, the pattern began to reverse with a steady drop in youth crime. Youth court cases related to Criminal Code offences decreased 29 percent between 1991 and 1992, and 2002 and 2003. Nevertheless, during this time, there has been a widening gap between public perceptions of youth crime (that it is high and growing) and the actual statistics (declining). Overall rates of youth crime decreased since 1992, while violent youth crime rates have been steadily decreasing since 1995.

Pre-YOA: Reason for Concern, 1957–1966

Year	Convictions
1957	9,679
1960	13,965
1964	16,608
1966	20,310

Table 6.3: Total Convictions of Juvenile Delinquents, Ages 7–15.

Carrigan, Owen. 1998. *Juvenile Delinquency in Canada: A History.* Concord (Ontario), Irwin Publishing, p.160.

TRENDS IN YOUTH CRIME

Of the Criminal Code offence categories, the largest decrease is in crimes against property (47%), which has declined every year since 1991–92.

Only crimes against the person has shown an increase (25%) since 1991–92. Most Criminal Code offences have decreased, the main exception being uttering threats (169%).

The Criminal Code offence groups with the largest decreases since 1991–92 relate to crimes against property: break and enter (-53%), fraud (-52%), theft (-48%) and possession of stolen property (-47%).

Source: "Youth Court Statistics, 2002/03," by Paul Robinson. *Juristat*, Vol. 24, No. 2. Statistics Canada, Catalogue No. 85–002–XPE.

• **Fighting Root Causes**

Given the reduction in youth crime, many argue that alternative approaches are needed that are more in keeping with the actual trends. Front-line social workers in correction facilities, child welfare services and youth service have advocated for an approach that recognizes the many factors that are at the root of youth crime.

- *Societal factors* include poverty and unemployment, substandard housing, high urban mobility, racism, homophobia and lack of resources in the community.

- *Family factors* include abuse of children, the witnessing of violence, usually against the mother, lack of supervision by parents, excessive discipline, spousal conflict, the father's absence, alcohol or substance abuse and parental and sibling psychiatric problems.

- *Individual factors* include poor school performance and learning disabilities, school attendance problems and drop out, low self-esteem, rejection by peers and/or association with a delinquent peer group, alcohol or substance abuse and psychiatric problems (Child Welfare League of Canada 1995, 8).

Social workers point out that the courts and prisons often fail to combat the youth crime problem because its roots lie outside the reach of these institutions (Waller 1989). The late Solicitor General Herb Grey perhaps summed it up best when he said that if the answer to youth crime was longer sentences, then the United States (with its punishment-oriented approach to crime) would be the safest place in the world.

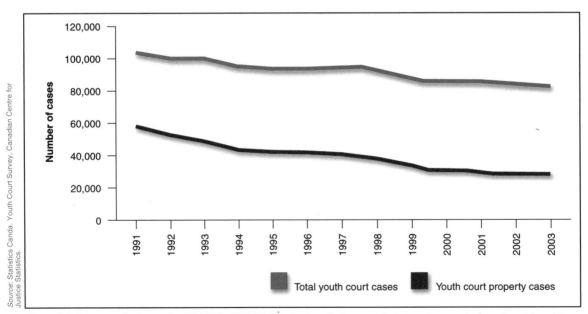

Source: Statistics Canda. Youth Court Survey, Canadian Centre for Justice Statistics.

Figure 6.4: Crimes against property, 1991-92 to 2002-03. The number of crimes against property cases in Canada continued to decrease in 2002-03.

Early Learning and Child Care Services

Many countries have publicly funded systems of early education and development for children. In the United Kingdom, for example, 60 percent of young children are in regulated care; in Denmark, 78 percent. Canada has a shortage of regulated childcare spaces — enough for less than 20 percent of children under six with working parents. The 2004 Organisation for Economic Co-operation and Development (OECD) International Report on Early Childhood Education and Care in Canada recommended that Canada should increase funding to OECD levels (Canada now spends 0.2 percent of its GDP on early education and development), with Ottawa and the provinces each paying 40 percent and parents the remaining 20 percent. It also recommends that there should be integrated child care and kindergarten as well as improved training and recruitment for child care workers.

Since its inception, Quebec's universal child care program has been seen across Canada as an exceptional model and the standard to which other provinces should aspire. The best-known feature of the Quebec model is the $7–a-day daycare program, attended by about 130,000 children. Quebec also provides full-day kindergarten for five-year-olds and after-school care for kindergarten and primary school children. Overall, Quebec spends about $3 billion a year on child care for families. It is estimated that a similar Canada-wide child care program would cost in excess of $10 billion annually.

Table 6.4: Percentage of children 0-12 years for whom there is a regulated child care space by province/territory: 1992, 1995, 1998, 2001, 2004

Province/Territory	1992	1995	1998	2001	2004
Newfoundland and Labrador	3.3	4.3	5.0	5.5	6.8
Prince Edward Island	16.2	15.5	15.4	14.0	18.9
Nova Scotia	6.8	6.8	7.3	8.1	9.6
New Brunswick	5.5	6.3	7.7	9.9	11.0
Quebec	6.8	9.4	14.9	21.1	29.9
Ontario	8.1	7.7	8.5	8.9	10.7
Manitoba	9.1	9.5	10.5	12.4	14.3
Saskatchewan	3.1	3.8	3.9	4.2	4.9
Alberta	9.7	9.6	8.8	9.1	9.3 (12.7)★
British Columbia	7.4	9.6	10.8	12.1	13.7
Northwest Territories	5.7	n/a	n/a	n/a	13.1
Nunavut	n/a	n/a	n/a	n/a	11.6
Yukon Territory	16.7	n/a	n/a	n/a	29.2
Canada	7.5	8.4	10.0	12.1	15.5

★ School-age child care in Alberta became regulated for the first time in 2004. For purpose of comparison, the 2003/04 percentage has been calculated from a figure without school-age; the percentage using school-age spaces in the calculation appears in brackets.

Source: From data supplied by Martha Friendly. See also: Friendly, M., Beach, J. and Turiano, M. 2002. *Early Childhood Education and Care in Canada*. Childcare Resource and Reserach Unit. Univeristy of Toronto.

• Policy Issues

Campaign 2000 points out that early learning and child care in Canada are characterized by two fundamental problems: public policy at national and provincial levels is patchwork (i.e., not a system at all), and public financing is inadequate and varies widely. "In 2001, there were only enough regulated child care spaces to accommodate 12.1% of children aged 0–12, up from 7.5% in 1992. Growth in regulated child care slowed dramatically in the 1990s. Most of the increase in regulated child care was in Quebec." (*Report Card on Child Poverty in Canada*, 2004).

The federal government recently announced a package of $5 billion for child care over the next five years. Advocates of universal child care estimate that it would cost $10 billion per year for an adequate program. Without federal funding on this scale, individual provinces will be left to make up the shortfall — a small likelihood in many provinces.

The recent commitment by the federal government to the development of a national system of early learning and child care is to be welcomed. "Such a system," notes Campaign 2000, "would be the most important social policy advance of the decade." Its success will depend on adhering to the principles of quality, universality, accessibility with a developmental focus and inclusiveness for all children. Funding will need to increase to at least $4 billion by the fifth year of the plan to lay the foundations for a comprehensive system.

Child Protection Worker "Burnout"

Child social work is a noble profession to be sure, but a disconcerting phenomenon has recently received considerable attention — the extent of worker "burnout" among dedicated child welfare workers. Now that we are at the end of this chapter, it is perhaps wise, to raise a note of concern about this problem.

The term burnout refers to the anxiety resulting from increased workplace pressure and increased workloads. This type of stress occurs among social workers and others who are faced with increasing responsibility and less and less control over how the work is to be completed. Across Canada, this condition seems increasingly to have become the norm for child welfare workers.

• Paperwork and Cutbacks

A recent study found that social workers employed by the Children's Aid Society of Toronto showed traumatic stress scores "considerably higher" than those of workers in other emergency services, such as firefighters and ambulance paramedics (Philip 2001). The study, conducted by the Ontario Association of Children's Aid Societies, found that mounting caseloads and a mismatch between the time allotted by provincial regulations for investigation and assessment (12.5 hours) and the actual required time of 19.3 hours are causing undue stress and the departure of many workers. Workers that successfully remain in child welfare tend to artfully manage the paper and computer work. For example, they may choose to compile all the paperwork only on cases that have a high potential for problems in the future.

In response to a number of high-profile inquests into the deaths of children in care, provincial governments are mandating new administrative requirements. It is quickly becoming impossible for the workers to comply with the mounting paperwork and computer work within the time allotted. And, of course, a failure to comply with administrative requirements places the onus for any mistakes squarely on the worker. Undoubtedly, such high levels of stress are directly linked to the workers' lack of control over work processes and the total responsibility they bear for the outcomes. When combined with larger caseloads and the significant emotional stress of the work, it should not be surprising that worker burnout results.

The ultimate victims of this state of affairs are the children themselves. Dedicated individuals enter this area of the profession with the intention of doing good work and helping children and families as best they can. If they are to remain, and if others are to be attracted to this important field of social work practice, working conditions must be improved. The current round of government cutbacks is taking a severe toll on these social workers and, in turn, on the children they are seeking to help.

Researcher Linda Duxbury found stress has major effect on families.

Conclusion

Only recently has child maltreatment received recognition as a significant social problem, although child abuse and neglect has a long history. In 1893, the passing of the *Children's Protection Act* in Ontario ushered in a new era in modern child welfare legislation protecting children from abuse and neglect. The following years saw a range of provincial legislative Acts, as child welfare was, and still is, defined in the Constitution as a provincial jurisdiction. Modern child welfare work has continued to struggle with dilemmas such as protection versus family preservation, or the "best interests" of the child versus the "least restrictive" measures of intervention.

Child welfare work is one of the most common fields of work for graduating social workers today. The field is changing rapidly and workers need continually to update their skills and learn new techniques. For example, research has been done to identify the risk assessment factors that correlate with the abuse of children, and workers are expected to apply this in their practice. The first step in the overall process of child protection is to obtain and record the initial response from a variety of sources to the report of abuse. Next, the worker determines if the child has been abused, any safety concerns, future risk, the capacity of the family to protect the child and any services that will be required. Verification decisions are critical in today's litigation-filled society, so the worker must document both the evidence of abuse and standard of proof. Finally, the social worker needs to complete a plan of service for both the child and family and keep careful records of the implementation of the plan.

Doing social work on behalf of, or with, children and youth includes more than child protection work. Social workers work with children and youth in variety of roles. Other social work settings include day care, foster care, adoptions, residential group homes, youth corrections, various income security programs and child care, to name a few. In all these settings, social workers have always been at the forefront in advocating for improvements in policy and services for children and youth.

Social workers continue to enter the child welfare field, despite its difficult conditions and high attrition rates. While working with abused children and their abusers may not be pleasant, this work is indispensable in a civilized and just society.

Chapter 6 Review
Social Work with Children and Youth

Discussion Questions

1. Identify and discuss three phases in the history of child welfare.

2. Explain what is meant by the "least restrictive" and the "best interests" approaches to child protection cases.

3. What is the extent of youth in care in Canada and how does this match up with government policy in this area?

4. What is the extent of child abuse today in Canada?

5. What are the steps to be followed in providing child welfare services?

6. What are some of the issues that trouble youth who are in care?

7. How has provincial child welfare legislation changed in the past few years in ways that you see as positive? How has it changed in ways that you see as negative?

Websites

● Child & Family Canada
http://www.cfc-efc.ca

A unique Canadian public education website. Fifty Canadian non-profit organizations have come together under the banner of Child & Family Canada to provide quality credible resources on children and families on an easy-to-navigate website. The "library" provides access to over 1,300 documents on child welfare.

● Child Welfare League of Canada
http://www.cwlc.ca

The CWLC is an organization active in Canadian policy, research and advocacy. The site contains an issue-specific search engine for those doing research in the child welfare area.

● The Ontario Association of Children's Aid Societies
http://www.oacas.org

The voice of child welfare in Ontario, dedicated to providing leadership for the achievement of excellence in the protection of children and in the promotion of their well-being within their families and communities.

● Child Welfare Resource Centre
http://www.childwelfare.ca

This website offers an excellent list of web links, an on-line CHAT group, and an e-mail discussion list. This would be a good place to start exploring the field of Canadian child welfare.

● First Nations Child & Family Caring Society of Canada
http://fncfcs.com

This site provides an excellent collection of publications about First Nations children, youth and families.

Key Terms

- **In-home services**
- **Out-of-home services**
- **"Best interests" approach**
- **"Least restrictive" approach**
- **Child abuse**
- **Neglect**
- **Physical abuse**
- **Sexual abuse**
- **Emotional abuse**
- **Risk assessment**
- **Duty to report**
- **Court order**
- **Youth Criminal Justice Act**
- **Early education and development**
- **Universal child care program**
- **"Burnout"**

Katherine Langley signs a petition that was sent to the Romanow Commission on the Future of Health Care in Canada during a rally to mark National Medicare Day at a park in Peterborough, Ontario (May 2002).

7

Social Work and the Health of Canadians

—

Medicare at Risk

ocial workers play a key role in the provision of health services in Canada. In hospital settings, social workers are often part of multidisciplinary teams that provide a unique holistic perspective to health care. This holistic perspective is not only concerned with the treatment of illness, but also with the promotion of wellness and the consideration of the social, economic, spiritual and cultural needs of the health services client.

This chapter provides an overview of the history of public medical care in Canada. Several contemporary issues are discussed, including universality, privatization, extra billing and user fees. It also looks at the recent agreement between the federal government and the provinces to restore federal funding to the health care system. Finally, the chapter examines the role of social workers who are involved in medical social work, community health centres and social work with people who have contracted HIV/AIDS.

Canadians generally see their health care system as exemplifying many deeply held Canadian values — equity, fairness, compassion and respect for the fundamental dignity of all. Social workers have been at the forefront of defending this publicly funded system and promoting healthy living and illness prevention. They have an increasingly important role in health care delivery.

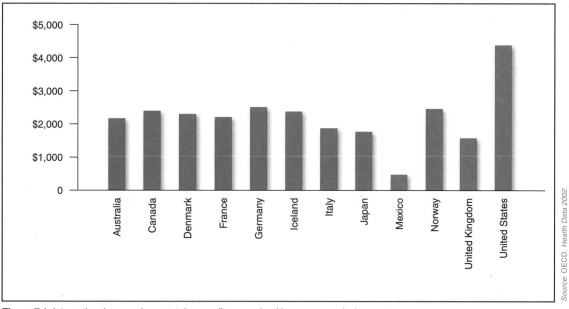

Source: OECD. Health Data 2002.

Figure 7.1: International comparisons: total expenditures on health care per capita by country.

Health and Inequality

Despite the availability of public health care across the country, there is a serious health gap between the rich and the poor in Canada — the rich are healthier than the middle class, who are in turn healthier than the poor. The well educated are healthier than the less educated, the employed are healthier than the unemployed and so on.

A 1990 report by the National Council of Welfare focused on the link between health status and income. The analysis examined a number of measures of health status in relation to the distribution of income. The report found that the poorer the neighbourhood, the shorter the average life expectancy of its residents. Fifty percent of men residing in the poorest neighbourhoods will live to age seventy-five, while almost 70 percent of men who live in the richest neighbourhoods will reach this age. Similarly, babies born to parents in the poorest neighbourhoods are twice as likely to die before their first birthday than babies born to parents in the richest neighbourhoods. And lower-income Canadians experience fewer years of good health throughout their lives (National Council of Welfare 1990a, 99).

• Income Distribution and Poverty

A more recent 1996 study found that there is a gap between the rich and the poor for most types of illnesses and for almost all causes of death. Moreover, only 47 percent of low-income Canadians rate their health as excellent or very good compared to 73 percent of Canadians in the high-income group. Commenting on the importance of relative poverty in 1999, the same committee stated that "there is strong evidence that the health of a given population depends on the equality of income distribution rather than on average income. The greater the disparities between rich and poor, the greater the health consequences" (Federal, Provincial, and Territorial Advisory Committee on Population Health 1999, 49).

In other words, the "health gap" in Canada is serious — people who are living at a socioeconomic disadvantage are more susceptible to illness and early death. Moreover, there is evidence that new immigrants and visible minorities are at an even greater disadvantage when it comes to health care. And, located as they are in the lowest quintile of the Canadian socioeconomic hierarchy, Aboriginal peoples have the poorest levels of overall health of all. For status Indians living on reserves, the average life expectancy in 2000 was 68.9 years for men and 76.6 for women (compared to 77 for men and 82.1 for women in the general population). As well, infant mortality for status Indians was 16.4 deaths per thousand in 2000 compared with the Canadian average of 5.2. Diabetes rates among Aboriginal peoples in Canada are three to five times the national average (Assembly of First Nations 1999; Indian and Northern Affairs Canada, 2001).

History of Health Policy

Universal public health care, as it came to be called and as we know it today, involving publicly funded quality health care for all Canadian citizens, took some time to evolve. Prior to the late 1940s, access to health care was based solely on one's ability to pay. Access did not become a concern of governments until illness threatened to hamper the supply of workers for industry, and even then, the road to a state-funded health insurance plan was not smooth.

Early in Canada's history, doctors and barber-surgeons served the European populations in towns and military forts, while women provided in-home care as midwives and caregivers. Within First Nations communities, healers and shamans undertook to cure illness. By the late 1700s, increasing numbers of immigrants and towns meant that doctors provided more "complete" health care services to the European population, while First Nations communities were confronted with new European illnesses for which their traditional methods were not equipped. The first Canadian medical school was established in 1824, and in 1869, government legislation gave the male allopathic practitioners (male doctors who provided diagnosis, surgery, obstetrics and whatever else was needed) control over medical education (Clarke 1990). At the time, women were excluded from access to medical schools by the male-dominated medical associations.

One of the first pieces of government health care regulation was a directive in 1832 by the Upper Canada Sanitary Commission and Board of Health pertaining to the quarantine and sanitation of immigrants infected with cholera. More extensive public health measures were introduced later in the nineteenth century (Clarke 1990). The *British North America Act* of 1867 established the jurisdictions of the federal and provincial governments in delivering health services. The management and maintenance of health institutions fell to the provinces. The larger tax base of the federal government allowed it to exert a strong influence on Canadian health delivery, as it continues to do today.

From 1880 to the 1950s, there were a variety of **pre-payment health plans** in place across Canada, sponsored by local governments, industries and volunteer agencies (Vayda and Deber 1995). By 1934, there were 27 different hospital-sponsored pre-payment plans in six provinces. For example, a payroll-deduction plan existed for miners in Nova Scotia and Ontario, and the Municipal Doctor System, which paid physicians on an annual contract basis, had been established in Saskatchewan in 1914. Medical associations and hospitals also developed health insurance plans in Ontario, Manitoba and Nova Scotia. In 1939, the first Canadian Blue Cross plan was formed in Manitoba, with most provinces following suit in the 1940s. These voluntary insurance plans did not cover all medical services, and they were available only to those who could afford to pay the premiums.

ABORIGINAL PEOPLES

The Canadian Institute of Child Health describes the problems faced by Canada's Aboriginal peoples:

"*The pattern of disease among Canada's Native people resembles the main killers of the developing world. Infections and parasitic and respiratory diseases, often helped by malnutrition, account for most deaths under one year of age. Accompanying these are "diseases" of economic under-development. Many Native people live in poverty and consequently, when compounded by the implicit and explicit racism of our society, they are doubly oppressed. The state of poverty in which they live makes them particularly vulnerable to health hazards.*"

Source: National Council of Welfare, 1990a, 108.

Universal public health care has long been a goal of Canadians.

While people struggled to obtain health insurance, provincial governments often backed down from its provision under pressure from the medical profession. For example, in British Columbia, relief workers, the One Big Union and the Co-operative Commonwealth Federation (CCF) put intense pressure on the Patullo government to institute comprehensive health insurance in the 1930s. In 1933, the Patullo government included health care as a key component of its election platform. The Bill passed a third reading, but because of opposition from doctors, Patullo refused to give effect to the legislation. In Alberta, health insurance plans were blocked by the powerful Medical Association.

Debates about health insurance also occurred within the field of social work. The 1942 Heagerty Report and the 1943 Marsh Report both recommended comprehensive state-funded health insurance. The more conservative Social Service Council, led by Charlotte Whitton (see page 52), opposed state-funded health insurance.

• Federal Involvement

Several factors precipitated more active federal involvement in medical insurance. When the issue of public medical insurance first arose in the 1920s in British Columbia, it was considered to be a provincial matter. But in the 1930s, working Canadians were devastated by the Great Depression, and political unrest was widespread. Because many people were unable to pay medical expenses, some doctors found the idea of public medical insurance attractive — at least their bills for medical care would be paid.

In 1942, the Heagerty Report proposed a federally funded, two-stage health insurance scheme. The plan was accepted by labour and the medical profession but foundered because of federal-provincial disagreements. In 1945, the Royal Commission on Dominion Provincial Relations (established in 1939) produced the Green Book, which placed on the table a whole series of proposals, including proposals regarding health care, to the provinces. The proposals reflected a reasonable ordering of priorities — extending the unemployment insurance system, instituting federal programs of unemployment assistance and health insurance, and improving old age pensions — and called for the federal government to help finance health and social services programs in return for the provinces' renouncement of their claim to income and corporate taxes.

The provinces, particularly Ontario and Quebec, turned the federal offer down. There was a "lack of agreement on the tax-sharing formula and federal interference in matters that were considered to be provincial jurisdiction under the B.N.A. Act. Ontario considered health insurance in particular, to be the responsibility of the provincial government" (Cumming 1985, 51).

With medicare, the individual's health became a public concern.

National Archives of Canada, PA165610.

By the end of World War II, however, children's allowances and unemployment insurance were in place. And in 1947, the first scheme for the public insurance plan for hospital services was instituted in Saskatchewan. The scheme did not provide funding for personal medical care received in a doctor's office, but it did provide financing for emergency services, curative medicine and surgery in hospitals.

In 1957, the *Hospital Insurance and Diagnostic Services Act* was passed. Under the Act, the federal government agreed to finance 50 percent of the cost of provincial acute and chronic hospital care (although mental hospitals, tuberculosis sanatoria and custodial care institutions, such as nursing homes, were excluded, and patients still had to pay a daily user fee for hospital services). This legislation encouraged the development of hospital insurance plans, and by 1961, all provinces and territories had signed agreements with the federal government for limited, in-patient hospital care that qualified for federal cost sharing.

The impetus for comprehensive public medical care insurance that included coverage for visits to, and services provided by, physicians outside of a hospital began in Saskatchewan. At the time, the Co-operative Commonwealth Federation provincial government in that province under the leadership of T.C. (Tommy) Douglas considered more comprehensive medical coverage to be an absolute necessity and, in the end, won the day in a major confrontation with the powerful medical establishment. Even though the plan was limited, the Saskatchewan model provided the foundation for future progress.

• Medical Care Act, 1968

In 1964, Conservative Prime Minister John Diefenbaker appointed Justice Emmett Hall to chair a Royal Commission on Health Care. In 1964, the **Hall Report** disclosed that 7.5 million Canadians did not have medical coverage and recommended that a comprehensive, publicly administered universal health service plan be implemented.

Hall's proposal received massive grassroots support. Women's organizations and organized labour were particularly positive about national medical care insurance. The federal minority Liberal government that followed Diefenbaker's Conservative government was supported by the newly established New Democratic Party, which advocated universal health care. The physicians threatened to strike but were unsuccessful in reversing the tide, and the *Medical Care Act* was passed in 1968.

The Medical Care Act of 1968 provided for equal federal-provincial cost sharing of non-hospital medical services. By 1972, all provinces and territories had extended their plans to include physician's services. Funding was made available to provinces if their services met the criteria of comprehensiveness, accessibility, universality, portability and public administration. Under the new legislation, physicians were permitted to opt out of the plan and extra billing was permitted.

CANADA HEALTH ACT, 1984

The primary objective of the health policy is stated in section 3 of the Act: "It is hereby declared that the primary objective of Canadian health care policy is to protect, promote and restore the physical and mental well-being of residents of Canada and to facilitate reasonable access to health services without financial or other barriers."

That Act goes on to state that health insurance "must provide for insured health services on uniform terms and conditions and on a basis that does not impede or preclude, either directly or indirectly whether by charges made to insured persons or otherwise."

The *Canada Health Act*, as with all of Canada's legislation, is available on-line at: http://laws.justice.gc.ca

National Archives of Canada, PA1130735.

John Diefenbaker initiated the Royal Commission on Health Care (1964).

"It is a perversion of Canadian values to accept a system where money — rather than need — determines who gets access to care."

Source: Roy Romanow

Medicare Under the Microscope — From Hall to Romanow

In 2001, Allan Rock, the federal Minister of Health, announced the formation of the Commission on the Future of Health Care in Canada under the leadership of Roy Romanow. Its mandate was to engage Canadians in a national dialogue on the future of health care and to make recommendations to preserve the long-term sustainability of Canada's universally accessible, publicly funded health care system.

In 2002 the Final Report of the Romanow Commission on the Future of Health Care in Canada was released. In his work, Romanow said he was guided by two things: Canadian values of fairness, equity and solidarity, and by the evidence. This approach led him to recommend expanding public, not-for-profit medicare and to include home care and pharmacare, and to recommend a genuine system of primary health care. "In the coming months, the choices we make, or the consequences of those we fail to make," Romanow declared in his Final Report, "will decide medicare's future. I believe Canadians are prepared to embark on the journey together and build on the proud legacy they have inherited."

The Romanow report has been the backdrop for the major debates and disagreements between the federal and provincial governments over health care in recent years.

• Main Recommendations of the Romanow Commission

The Commission's final report (*Building on Values: The Future of Health Care in Canada,*) comprises 47 detailed, costed recommendations that include implementation time frames.

"My recommendations are premised on three overarching themes," Commissioner Romanow explained. "First, that we require strong leadership and improved governance to keep Medicare a national asset. Second, that we need to make the system more responsive and efficient as well as more accountable to Canadians. And third, that we need to make strategic investments over the short-term to address priority concerns, as well as over the long-term to place the system on a more sustainable footing."

Report highlights include:

- Renewing the foundations of the health care system by establishing a Canadian Health Covenant to express Canadians' collective vision for health care and by updating the *Canada Health Act*.

- Fostering collaboration among governments, providers and citizens through a new Health Council of Canada.

- Achieving the goal of adequate, stable and predictable funding by:
  - Setting a federal cash funding floor of 25 percent of the cost of insured health services under the *Canada Health Act* by 2005–06.

CP PHOTO/Fred Chartrand.

Roy Romanow displays his report released November 28, 2002.

Under this scenario, federal funding for health care would be $6.5 billion above currently forecast levels.

- Establishing a dedicated, cash-only, multi-year (5-year) Canada Health Transfer that includes a built-in escalator provision.
- Creating five new targeted funds to address immediate renewal priorities until the minimum federal funding threshold is attained in 2005–06:
  - A Rural and Remote Access Fund ($1.5 billion total over two years) to improve timely access to care in rural and remote areas
  - A Diagnostic Services Fund ($1.5 billion total over two years) to improve wait times for diagnostic services
  - A Primary Health Care Transfer ($2.5 billion total over two years) to support efforts to remove obstacles to renewing primary care delivery
  - A Home Care Transfer ($2 billion total over two years) to provide a foundation for an eventual national home care strategy
  - A Catastrophic Drug Transfer ($1 billion beginning in 2004–05) to protect Canadians in instances where they require expensive drug therapies to remain healthy.

These new funds amount to additional federal funding above current forecasts of approximately $3.5 billion in 2003–04, $5 billion in 2004–05, and, once the 25 percent funding floor is achieved, $6.5 billion in 2005–06.

- Making the system more comprehensive by integrating priority home care services (home mental health case management and intervention services; post-acute home care, and palliative home care) within the *Canada Health Act*, as well as improving prescription drug coverage. Improving timely access to quality care for all Canadians through special initiatives to improve wait-list management, by removing obstacles to primary care reform, and by increasing the supply of advanced diagnostic services and of health care providers across Canada.
- Encouraging a national personal electronic health record system and protecting the security and privacy of Canadians' personal health information through amendments to the *Criminal Code*.

The Commission's report also addressed, among others, such diverse issues as Aboriginal health care, culturally sensitive access and the impact of globalization and applied research. It is worth noting, as well, that the Romanow Commission set something of a new standard for transparency in commissions of enquiry of this type. It released, in advance of its final report, all of the submissions it had received, all the research it had commissioned and summaries from all of the consultative activities in which it had been engaged.

CANADIAN INSTITUTE FOR HEALTH INFORMATION

Launched in 1994, the Canadian Institute for Health Information (CIHI) is an independent, pan-Canadian, not-for-profit organization working to improve the health of Canadians and the health care system by providing quality health information.

CIHI's mandate is to coordinate the development and maintenance of a common approach to health information for Canada. To this end, CIHI is responsible for providing accurate and timely information that is needed to establish sound health policies, manage the Canadian health system effectively and create public awareness of factors affecting good health.

For more information, go to: http://www.cihi.ca

• First Ministers Conferences on Health Care

With Romanow's landmark report in hand, in February 2003, the prime minister, premiers and territorial leaders met to try to turn some of Romanow's recommendations into action. They agreed on several major improvements to the system, as outlined in the First Minister's Health Accord:

- $16–billion, five-year fund for primary care, home care and catastrophic drug coverage
- $13.5 billion in new funding to the provinces over three years
- $2.5 billion cash infusion for 2003
- $600 million for information technology
- $500 million for research.

In the end, the premiers argued that they were getting about half of what Romanow recommended. The territorial leaders didn't even sign the agreement, arguing that the North would be receiving the same per capita as the rest of the country, despite much higher costs.

Subsequently, the 2004 federal election turned into a debate about the future of health care in this country. The Liberals accused the newly united Conservatives of plotting to turn medicare into a two-tiered system. The Liberals won the election, but with a substantial loss of seats, and formed a minority government in Ottawa.

CP PHOTO/Fred Chartrand.

Prime Minister Paul Martin, first ministers and Aboriginal leaders meet at the Government Conference Centre in Ottawa in September 2004 to discuss health care.

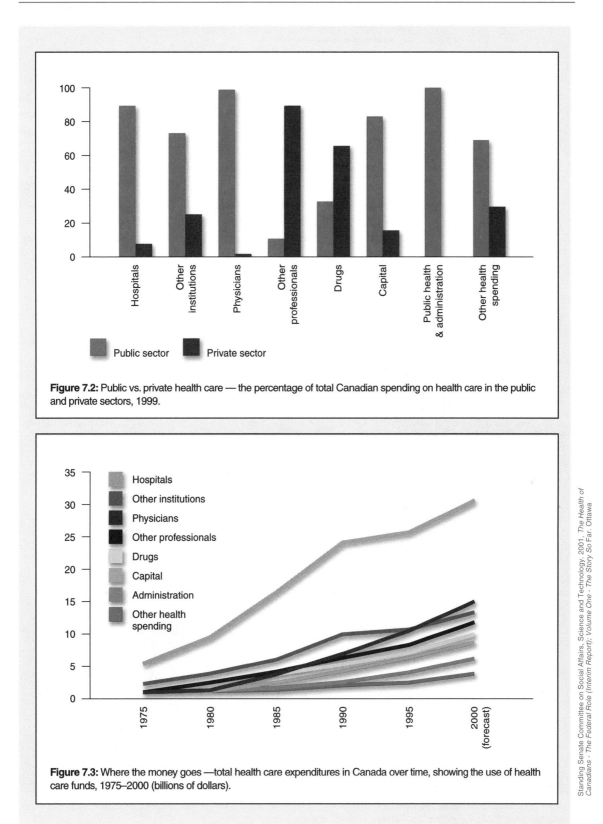

Figure 7.2: Public vs. private health care — the percentage of total Canadian spending on health care in the public and private sectors, 1999.

Figure 7.3: Where the money goes —total health care expenditures in Canada over time, showing the use of health care funds, 1975–2000 (billions of dollars).

Standing Senate Committee on Social Affairs, Science and Technology. 2001. *The Health of Canadians - The Federal Role (Interim Report): Volume One - The Story So Far.* Ottawa

Canada's Health Care Spending

Canada's public share of total health spending is smaller than most countries'. In 2001, public funding accounted for 71 percent of total health care expenditures in Canada, 44 percent in the US, and about 85 percent in Denmark, Norway and Sweden (OECD Health Data, 2003). The other 29 percent of Canada's health spending was funded through private insurance and directly out-of-pocket by Canadians.

Funds from private insurance support health services such as dental, eye and chiropractic care and drugs. Private spending rose by 57 percent after inflation in the decade leading to 2003. Household out-of-pocket spending typically includes items such as over-the-counter drugs and personal health supplies, fees, hospital expenditures (for a private room, for example) and residential care facility fees (Canadian Institute for Health Information 2003).

CP PHOTO/Tobin Grimshaw.

A team of health care professionals, including two doctors, a pharmacist and a social worker, display their concerns for improving medicare during the First Ministers' Conference on Health in 2004.

Five Principles of Medicare

Today, Canada has a health care system that is funded by government insurance. Medicare, as it is called, is publicly delivered by hospitals and privately delivered by physicians (who are self-employed or employed by physician-owned corporations). Each province must meet the following five criteria in order to receive funding from the federal government. These are known as the Five Principles of Medicare:

- **Public administration.** Pursuant to section 8, the health care insurance plan must be administered and operated on a non-profit basis by a public authority, responsible to the provincial government, and be subject to audit of its accounts and financial transactions.

- **Comprehensiveness.** Pursuant to section 9, the plan must cover all insured health services ("medically necessary services") provided by hospitals, medical practitioners or dentists, and, where permitted, cover services rendered by other health care practitioners.

- **Universality.** Section 10 requires that 100 percent of the insured persons of a province be entitled to the insured health services provided for by the plan on uniform terms and conditions.

- **Portability.** In accordance with section 11, residents moving to another province must continue to be covered for insured health services by the home province during any minimum waiting period imposed by the new province of residence, not to exceed three months.

- **Accessibility.** By virtue of section 12, the health care insurance plan of a province must provide for: (a) insured health services on uniform terms and conditions and reasonable access by insured persons to insured health services unprecluded or unimpeded, either directly or indirectly, by charges or other means; (b) reasonable compensation to physicians and dentists for all insured health services rendered; payments to hospitals in respect of the cost of insured health services.

Commitment to these "five principles" was reaffirmed, after intense negotiations, in the Social Union Agreement of 1999 between the federal government and all provinces and territories (except Quebec). The Agreement, entitled *A Framework to Improve the Social Union for Canadians*, attempted to define how power and responsibility would be divided. It also attempted to smooth relations between the federal government and the provinces following the fallout from the unilateral federal changes to funding in the *Canada Health and Social Transfer Act* (CHST). (For background information on the Social Union Agreement, see Chapter 2, page 37.)

SOCIALIZED MEDICINE?

Canada does not have a system of fully "socialized medicine," with doctors employed by the government. Most doctors are private practitioners who work in independent or group practices and enjoy a high degree of autonomy.

Private practitioners are generally paid on a fee-for-service basis and submit their service claims directly to the provincial health insurance plan for payment.

WHAT THE ACT SAYS

EXTRA-BILLING: In order that a province may qualify for a full cash contribution referred to in section 5 for a fiscal year, no payments may be permitted by the province for that fiscal year under the health care insurance plan of the province in respect to insured health services that have been subject to extra-billing by medical practitioners or dentists.

USER CHARGES: In order that a province may qualify for a full cash contribution referred to in section 5 for a fiscal year, user charges must not be permitted by the province for that fiscal year under the health care insurance plan of the province.

———
Source: Canada Health Act, 1984, c. 6, s. 18. 19.

User Fees and Extra-Billing Controversy

By the early 1980s, doctors were charging fees beyond the scale of payments established by the provinces in negotiation with the Canadian Medical Association. Many doctors maintained that **extra-billing** was their right in a free-enterprise society — if patients did not want to pay the fees, they could try to find a doctor who did not charge extra fees. For its part, the federal government argued that extra-billing made it impossible to ensure the same health services for all citizens at a reasonable cost. For example, if a majority of specialists in a certain field practised extra-billing, it would be difficult for patients to locate a specialist who did not charge fees beyond those prescribed by the Medicare system.

At the same time, **user fees** — an extra fee above the scale rate — were being charged by hospitals and other medical institutions for individual use. For example, the Quebec government wanted to introduce user fees to raise revenue and deter what it called the "frivolous" or unnecessary use of medical facilities. It was also argued that user fees would establish a direct relationship between the patient and the service provider and would allow the individual to contribute to his or her own medical health care.

In response, in 1984 the federal government brought in the *Canada Health Act*, reiterating the five principles. The purposes of the *Hospital Insurance and Diagnostic Services Act* of 1957 and the *Medical Care Act* of 1968 were reasserted. Under the *Canada Health Act*, the federal government could levy penalties on provinces and territories that did not comply with the Act. The provinces were permitted user fees and extra-billing, but the federal government reduced the grant to the provinces by a dollar for every dollar raised through either user fees or extra-billing. Consequently, the provinces gained no additional funds and extra-billing and user fees had disappeared by 1987.

• Which Way Forward?

The issue of extra-billing has by no means disappeared, however. Indeed, it is a recurring public policy issue and still the focal point of debates over the future of public health care in Canada. Those who support it argue that doctors should have the same right as others to charge what the market will bear. Doctors' incomes are, they argue, not keeping pace with inflation and are regulated by medicare. Extra fees ensure that the client determines the service. They also reduce the frivolous use of medical services, promote efficiency and lower health care expenditures.

Opponents of extra-billing argue that, with extra-billing, health care is not free to each individual. People with low incomes are deterred from obtaining health care, and a two-class system of health care is thereby created.

THE FATHER OF MEDICARE — THE "GREATEST CANADIAN"

Tommy Douglas, who died in 1986, was the Saskatchewan premier who was, and is still, recognized for his tireless role in developing and promoting Canada's national medicare program.

In 1944, the Co-operative Commonwealth Federation (CCF), under Douglas, won the provincial election to become the first socialist government in North America. The CCF election slogan was "Humanity First" and the government's budget allocated 70 percent of expenditure to social services.

Douglas emphasized that his brand of socialism depended on political and economic democracy, and Saskatchewan listened. In 1944, the old age pension plan was expanded to include medical, hospital and dental services. Douglas' government also radically changed the education system. It established larger school units and provided the University of Saskatchewan with a medical school.

In his first four years in government, Douglas paid off the provincial debt, created a province-wide hospitalization plan, paved the roads and provided electricity and sewage pipes.

The North American medical establishment tried to defy medicare, Douglas's top priority project, and Saskatchewan became an intense battleground. This turbulent time was marked by the Doctor's Strike, as the physicians of the province protested socialized health care.

However, the striking doctors were no match for Douglas. When the dust settled with the resolution of the strike, medicare in Saskatchewan was born. Douglas showed Canada two things: that it was possible to develop and finance a universal medicare system and that the medical profession could be confronted. Had Douglas not taken these first groundbreaking steps, national medicare would never have happened.

———
Taken with permission from: http://www.sfn.saskatoon.sk.ca/business/cupe1975/ burs5.html

The debate is similar with user fees — the small charges that the patient must assume for hospital services. Those in favour contend that user fees prevent the frivolous use of services, raise revenue, remind the user that the service is not truly free and therefore begin a shift towards more of a private market for medical services.

For their part, opponents of user fees contend that such additional fees prevent access to services by people who are most vulnerable, especially those with low incomes. Moreover, they argue that user fees do not prevent the abuse of health services because small fees do not deter the more affluent users of services, who therefore tend to benefit more than low-income users. As well, user fees establish a **two-tiered system** of health service, with those who can pay the extra fee or who work for employers who have extended health benefits being more privileged than others.

In many respects, of course, these debates are old hat. They are the same issues that were faced by the CCF government under Tommy Douglas, when, against formidable opponents in the medical establishment, it introduced public health care in Saskatchewan and led the way for the rest of the country to follow.

National Archives of Canada. C36222 (1961).

Tommy Douglas, the "Greatest Canadian" in a 2004 CBC survey.

PROVINCIAL HEALTH CARE WEBSITES

Provincial and territorial governments are responsible for the delivery of Canada's health care and hospital services. To find out more about health care in your province or territory, go to:

- BC Ministry of Health
  http://www.gov.bc.ca/healthplanning
- PEI Health
  http://www.gov.pe.ca/infopei/Health
- Alberta Health
  http://www.health.gov.ab.ca
- Saskatchewan Health
  http://www.gov.sk.ca
- Manitoba Health
  http://www.gov.mb.ca/health
- Ontario Ministry of Health and Long Term Care
  http://www.health.gov.on.ca
- Ministère de la Santé et des Services sociaux du Québec [French only]
  http://www.msss.gouv.qc.ca
- New Brunswick Department of Health & Community Services
  http://www.gov.nb.ca/hcs
- Nova Scotia
  http://www.gov.ns.ca
- Newfoundland Dept. of Health
  http://www.gov.nf.ca/health
- NWT Dept. of Health & Social Services
  http://www.hlthss.gov.nt.ca
- Nunavut Department of Health and Social Services
  http://www.gov.nu.ca/hss.htm
- The Yukon
  http://www.gov.yk.ca

The provincial websites change occasionally. An up-to-date list is available at Health Canada: http://www.hc-sc.gc.ca/english/about.htm.

The Debate Over Privatized Health Care

The case for public health care is by no means universally accepted. Many argue that the system is seriously flawed in practice (long wait times) and in theory (insufficiently in line with what markets might otherwise dictate). But organizations such as the Canadian Health Coalition, a coalition favouring quality public health care, argue that the costs of privatization far outweigh the benefits (Canadian Health Coalition, 2000).

Their research reveals that:

- *A private system is more complex to administer, and therefore, more costly.* In the US, health care administration cost $361 per capita in 1995, compared to $119 in Canada. Health consumes 14 percent of economic resources in the US, compared with nine percent in Canada.

- *A private system provides less coverage.* Private insurance firms refuse insurance to those with known medical conditions, or set rates so high that the average person cannot afford them. In the US, about 44 million citizens are unable to afford health insurance.

- *A private system yields poorer results.* Infant mortality and social inequality are higher with a private system; the US has the highest infant mortality rate among countries belonging to the Organization for Economic Co-operation and Development (OEDC).

- *A private system is more prone to fraud.* A national study produced by Harvard Medical School in 1998 concluded that "large scale fraud has become routine" in the profit-driven health care sector. The study cited US General Accounting Office estimates that "about 25 percent of all home care agencies (most of which are for-profit) defraud Medicare" (Center for Health Program Studies 1998).

- *A private system removes money from the system.* In the private sector, some money is always used to pay back investors. The average health maintenance organization (HMO) in the US, for example, devotes 14 percent of its premiums to overhead and profits (Canada's public system uses a mere 0.9 percent) (Evans 1998, 45). In Canada, much of this profit would go to US companies.

- *A private system raises costs.* Private firms, being private firms, have a stake in costs going up, because higher costs mean naturally higher profits for them; and there are no automatic internal checks and balances to control costs within the private sector. This, says University of British Columbia health economist Robert Evans, is the real agenda behind corporate pressure to reduce public health spending (Evans 1998). According to Professor Pat Armstrong of York University, "it is mainly [this] increase in private expenditures that makes Canadian spending on health amongst the highest in the world" (Armstrong 1997, 21).

Threats to Universal Health Care

Canadians are entering a period of intense discussion over whether public health care should be privatized along the American model. Although the Romanow Commission report came down firmly on the side of publicly funded health care, the final outcome of this debate, in terms of continuing universal medical care, is by no means certain.

An ageing population and ever-spiralling health care costs will mean that the defenders of universal care will need to be even more alert to the following danger signs:

- *Privatization.* One the biggest threats to our public system of health care is the current movement to privatize care in some provinces, particularly in Alberta and Ontario. Several trends indicate increased **privatization** in our health care system, including:
    - the "de-listing" of services covered by medicare (e.g., specific medical procedures, support services, and drugs);
    - the transferring of care out of areas covered by medicare (e.g., acute care in hospitals) to areas that are not (e.g., home care);
    - the contracting out of "non-core" medical services (labs, ambulances and rehab services) to private companies;
    - the contracting out of services (laundry, meal preparation, cleaning and maintenance, materials handling, information management and disposal services) to private companies;
    - the contracting in of management services, leading to the redesign of management practices in accordance with private sector criteria.

- *Comprehensiveness.* Some provinces have attempted to reduce medical costs by reducing comprehensiveness — that is, the range of what are considered to be "medically necessary" services. Because the *Canada Health Act* states that the provinces should determine which services are "medically necessary," there is some room for provinces to limit the the range of "necessary" services.

- *Contracting out.* There are also concerns regarding the administration of hospitals. Governments are **contracting out** the management of some hospitals to private companies. If the company generates additional funds for the hospital, it can claim those funds as profit. For example, in Alberta, Bill C-11 of 2000 encourages the establishment of private, for-profit hospitals. Also, some services, such as catering, laundry and cleaning, have been contracted out to private, for-profit organizations. While not contrary to the letter of the *Canada Health Act*, the Alberta legislation threatens universal health care in Canada as it builds into hospital care the concept that patients can be charged privately for non-insured clinical services while they are receiving an insured service. It may also activate troublesome provisions under the North American Free Trade

Technician operates MRI machine at a private clinic in Calgary, 2005.

"It's difficult to justify [a Third Way in health care] when [Klein] himself in his speech acknowledged it would cost more.

"Canadians have been very clear. They love the Canada Health Act. They count on it and they expect us to enforce it, and we will."

———

Source: Carolyn Bennett, Minister of State for Public Health, responds to Premier Ralph Klein's proposal for a "Third Way" that would undermine the principle of universal medicare across Canada. (*"Canada AM,"* January 13, 2005).

Agreement (NAFTA) by binding succeeding Alberta governments to deal with for-profit hospitals and by allowing foreign companies to claim to an international arbitration tribunal that they should be allowed into all provinces because the Alberta law has the effect of changing federal legislation.

Apart from being more effective as a delivery method, public medicare has several important advantages over a private health care system. First, public financing spreads the cost of health care across society, rather than only to those who are unfortunate or sick. Second, financing health insurance through the taxation system is efficient, since it does not require the creation of a separate collection process. Third, medicare encourages Canadians to seek preventive care services and to treat problems before they worsen and treatment becomes more costly. Fourth, the government can cut costs, as it is largely a single buyer of health care supplies and services.

Many Canadian businesses also recognize and support Canada's universal medicare system, since it provides a competitive advantage with other countries. Lower employee benefit costs and a healthy and mobile workforce are advantageous. Also, the portability principle of medicare ensures that workers can move from province to province and still be covered by health insurance. Provincial governments have also begun to address **preventive medicine** and community-based care and have considered experimentation with community-based health and social service centres, such as the community health centres in Ontario.

• Cost Reduction and Containment

Medical care costs in Canada have been rising steadily because of the ageing of the Canadian population, the emphasis on curative and high technology medicine, the increasing demand for hospital services and for expensive equipment and the increasing fees of medical personnel. Cost containment has become an area of major concern and will certainly be a focus of attention in the coming years.

The issue of spiralling costs is one that advocates of public health care take very seriously. Nevertheless, they insist that keeping operating costs under control should not be used as a justification for greater privatization. For example, under pressure to meet overall provincial budgets without raising taxes, many provincial governments have attempted to lower hospital costs by reducing the range of services or by approving smaller budgets. They have also permitted hospitals to introduce cost-cutting measures, such as fees for emergency care, fees for use of ward beds, contracts with private companies to manage hospitals and contracts for services such as food or laundry. In practice, such measures are counterproductive insofar as they undermine public confidence in medicare and open the door to even wider privatization.

Local residents protest against cutbacks at the Miramichi Hospital.

Community Health Centres

In the 1970s, the federal government recommended the establishment of a network of **community health centres** (CHCs) with the intention of providing primary care, health promotion and prevention services using salaried primary health care professionals.

The idea of community-based health centres as a serious alternative to individual physician care has existed since early in the twentieth century, with the first examples appearing in the United Kingdom and the United States. Canada's first CHC — the Mount Carmel Clinic in Winnipeg — opened some 80 years ago (1926) and is still in operation. Ontario's first CHC opened in Sault Sainte Marie in 1963. Whereas they were once considered the "poor cousins" of the mainstream health care system (because of their association with low-income and disadvantaged populations), CHCs have grown in numbers and size. Since the mid-1980s, they have offered an ever-broadening range of client services to the general public as well as to specialized client groups such as parents, seniors, and ethnic and immigrant populations.

• Community Control

CHCs tend to network with other health and social services agencies and are accountable to their communities through community boards. They operate on the premise that communities should work together to "own" health care services. They frequently address a variety of issues affecting health, such as violence, housing, literacy, workplace hazards and poverty through programs and social action.

An important advantage of the CHC model is the focus on prevention, education, community development, social action and health promotion. CHCs tend to address four determinants of health: living and working conditions, social support, individual behaviour and genetic makeup. Located as they are between the patient and the medical practitioners, social workers are central to the provision of both direct care and community development in the community health centres model of health care delivery.

CHCs are funded primarily by provincial grants. Additional funding is often obtained from the United Way, foundations and federal government programs. Funding is allocated either through a global budgeting process, based on services directed at populations, or through capitalization funding, where fixed sums are established for each registered client based on need as a reflection of age, sex, key demographic factors and prevalence and severity of chronic illness. The use of CHCs (centres locaux des services communautaires) is most widespread in Quebec. Ontario is second highest. There is, however, a growing interest in the CHC model across the country, both as a way to cut costs and as a community-based approach.

A protester at her community's medical centre in Fredericton, NB.

Medical Social Work Practice

One of the chief settings for **medical social work practice** (also referred to as health care social work) is the hospital. Almost every hospital in Canada has social workers in its departments, including emergency services, oncology, pediatrics, surgery, intensive care, rehabilitation, gerontology and orthopaedics. The type of work performed by social workers in hospitals is wide ranging and includes direct casework, group work, discharge planning, family consultation, advocating for patients, counselling terminally ill patients, training other professionals and policy and administration. The role of social workers in health care is of vital importance and is increasing along with the understanding that illness is greatly affected by social and environmental factors, and that preventive and educational approaches are both effective and cost-efficient.

When working in a hospital setting, the social worker is a member of a team that includes other health professionals. The team approach is increasingly used to help ensure that each patient's physical, psychological, social and cultural needs are being met. The role of social workers is becoming more central in this holistic approach to health care. The **holistic approach to health care** involves taking into account not only the physical aspects of health, which have commonly been addressed by physicians, but also the social, cultural, mental and spiritual aspects.

In addition to hospital work, social workers are also involved in other health care settings, such as local medical clinics, community health centres and specialized care agencies (such as HIV/AIDS clinics, addiction treatment centres, family planning, prenatal care, long-term care, home care, hospice care, nursing homes and services for people with disabilities). Social workers are also active as health promoters, community developers and policy advocates in the health field. For example, a social worker may work with a community health centre to promote an aspect of healthy living in the community. Through this work, social workers are at the forefront in addressing primary health care prevention, health promotion and self-care.

Three health areas where the role of social work is growing are in mental health, HIV/AIDS and addictions treatment. Within all three areas, social workers are developing innovative treatment and health promotion methods.

• Mental Health and Social Work

Mental illness is the term used to refer to a variety of diagnosable mental disorders. Mental disorders are health conditions that are characterized by alterations in thinking, mood or behaviour (or some combination thereof) associated with distress and/or impaired functioning. Mental illness implies significant clinical patterns of behaviour or emotions associated with some level of distress, suffering or

Inside Seaton House, Canada's largest shelter for the homeless.

CP PHOTO/Victoria Times Colonist-Bruce Stotesbury.

An outreach worker with the Housing Registry of Greater Victoria, shows a room occupied by a mentally ill client in a rooming house. Settings such as these show a need to find long-term housing solutions, along with community support for those in need.

impairment in one or more areas of functioning (school, work, social and family interactions). At the root of this impairment is biological, psychological or behavioral dysfunction, or a combination of these (Canadian Psychiatric Association 1996).

It is estimated that one in five Canadians will be affected by a mental illness at some time in their lives. The World Health Organization (WHO) considers mental well-being as an integral part of the general definition of health. In the Preamble to the WHO Constitution, for example, health is defined as "a state of complete physical, mental and social well-being and not merely the absence of disease or infirmity."

Social workers are playing an increasingly important role in promoting the mental health of Canadians with respect to prevention, treatment and rehabilitation. Social workers may specialize in one of the settings or work across all three. Prevention aims to reduce the incidence or numbers of people with mental illness through awareness, standards development and avoidance of risk factors. Treatment aims to reduce the prevalence (number of existing cases) of mental illness through counselling, intervention, or therapy and advocacy. Rehabilitation intends to reduce the after-effects of a mental illness and maximize the use of remaining capacities by the individual. Rehabilitation activities may focus on clients who are disabled by mental illness and include the building of knowledge and skills in coping or the provision of specialized residential, vocational and leisure services.

Social work in the mental health field requires the ability to work collaboratively with family members and with the community. Social workers in the mental health field deliver any of the following services:

* Direct Services — to individuals, couples, families and groups in the form of counselling, crisis intervention, advocacy and management of resources.
* Case Management — coordinating interdisciplinary services to a specified client, group or population.
* Community Development — working with communities to identify mental health needs and issues and development of capacity to deliver services.
* Administration — putting systems in place and directly supervising to maintain effectiveness of mental health.
* Program Management — development, implementation and evaluation of a mental health program.
* Teaching and Research — providing university and college courses or other workshops, conferences and professional in-services.
* Policy Analysis — analysis of mental health policies.
* Social Action — organizing people to change mental health policy or advocate for system or program changes.

Social workers have contributed two key ideas to the mental health field. First, they have expanded on the understanding of mental health. Until recently, the conception of mental health came from the study and treatment of mental disorders. It emphasized the psychological and behavioural characteristics of individuals, largely ignoring conditions in society. Social work has highlighted the centrality of social and economic factors, family and other relationships, and the physical and organizational environment as they influence individual mental health. The role of physiological processes, human biology and human experience are now viewed within the wider social context.

Second, social workers have worked to avoid labelling those with mental illness. Using labels such as depressed, schizophrenic, manic or hyperactive in a negative way can lead to branding and indignity. Stigmatizing labels are a barrier and discourage individuals and their families from getting the help they need.

The **Canadian Mental Health Association** (CMHA) exists to promote the mental health of Canadians, and employs an increasing number of social workers. Each year, CMHA provides direct service to more than 100,000 Canadians through the combined efforts of more than 10,000 volunteers and staff in locally run organizations in all provinces and territories, with branches in more than 135 communities. Each region, city or province has a CMHA that has social workers providing services to the local community. They operate on principles' of empowerment, peer and family support, participation in decision-making, citizenship and inclusion in community life.

CP PHOTO/Adrian Wyld.

"Your Education, Your Future" helps students with psychiatric disabilities.

Social workers in CMHA-run programs assist with employment, housing, early intervention for youth, peer support and recreation services for people with mental illness, stress reduction workshops and public education campaigns for the community. In addition, social workers act as advocates to encourage public action and commitment towards strengthening community mental health services and legislation and policies affecting services.

● Social Work and HIV/AIDS

The human immunodeficiency virus (HIV) is a sexually transmitted and blood-borne retrovirus that undermines a person's immune system. AIDS is the final stage of HIV in which the immune system is destroyed. At the end of 2003, there were an estimated 56,000 people in Canada living with HIV (including those living with AIDS). Of these, perhaps one-third were unaware of their infection.

HIV/AIDS has been identified as the leading contemporary global health concern. Estimates by the Joint United Nations Programme on HIV/AIDS (UNAIDS) and the World Health Organization (WHO) indicate that, in 2004, almost 40 million people had been infected with HIV and over 20 million people around the world had already lost their lives to the disease. The virus is reported to be spreading, with nearly 16,000 new infections a day. In 2000, one in every 100 adults in the most sexually active age bracket (ages fifteen to forty-nine) was living with HIV. However, only a tiny fraction are aware that they have been infected. As people can live for many years before showing any sign of illness, the HIV virus can spread undetected (UNAIDS/WHO 2004).

People diagnosed with HIV/AIDS face a great many difficult issues. Upon detection, an individual must first deal with the illness itself and the possiblity of impending death. He or she must also confront social and economic problems, such as dealing with social stigma, rejection by friends and relatives, maintaining a work life, health insurance and medication costs and maintaining interpersonal relationships. Women face special challenges, as often services do not exist specifically for them and they must frequently deal with child care concerns.

The services that social workers deliver for people with HIV/AIDS include public education and prevention initiatives, primary care, hospital care, home care, hospice care, support groups, family support and advocacy. Social workers provide information and education, form support groups, make referrals to community resources and prepare discharge plans. In a hospital setting, social workers play a pivotal role as part of the health care team. In many cases, the social worker is the only person in the hospital who deals with non-medical or non-physical needs. They also work with family members and friends to provide both information and support.

HIV/AIDS IN CANADA

The number of positive HIV test results increased between 2000 and 2003, following a steady decline since 1995. This rise may be partly due to recent changes in immigration policies that were introduced in 2002. HIV tests are now part of the routine assessment for immigrants and most provinces and territories include these results in their reports.

Women have accounted for around a quarter of adult HIV diagnoses reported with known gender in each year since 2000. This proportion has more than doubled from 12% in the period from 1985 to 1997.

Trends in AIDS diagnoses

Since the beginning of the epidemic in the early 1980s, there have been 19,468 AIDS diagnoses reported to CIDPC. The number of annual diagnoses reached a peak in the mid-1990s and has since declined. A major factor in the initial drop was the delayed or prevented onset of AIDS due to highly active antiretroviral therapy (HAART). Use of these drugs has become widespread since 1996.

Females accounted for 7% of AIDS cases reported with known gender in the period from 1979 to 1994; in 2003, this figure was 25%.

Sources: Public Health Agency of Canada. HIV and AIDS in Canada. Surveillance report to June 30, 2004. Surveillance and Risk Assessment Division, Centre for Infectious Disease Prevention and Control, Health Canada, November 2004.
Health Canada. HIV/AIDS EPI Updates, May 2004, Surveillance and Risk Assessment Division, Centre for Infectious Disease Prevention and Control, Health Canada, 2004.

• Addictions and Social Work

The treatment of addictions is a growing concern of governments and increasingly, social workers and social service workers are being called upon to address problems of this kind. Addiction can be defined as a compulsive need for, or persistent use of, a substance known to be harmful. Nearly one in 10 adult Canadians (9.2 percent) have problems with excessive alcohol consumption. Others experience problems with narcotics, tranquilizers, sleeping pills, cocaine, LSD and cannabis.

Social workers are at the forefront in developing innovative ways to help people with addictions. Increasingly social workers in addiction treatment programs are taking a harm-reduction approach instead of an abstinence approach to treatment. Just over one-half of the Ottawa-area programs, for example, list abstinence as their treatment goal, while the other agencies list reduced consumption as the treatment goal. Social workers using a harm-reduction approach believe that people can overcome an addiction in incremental steps and be successful. The focus may be on safer use patterns for addicts rather than on immediate suspension of use. The successful needle exchange program in Vancouver is a prime example of such an approach.

Health Canada.

Addiction of various kinds is a serious problem in Canada today. According to Statistics Canada, more than 600,000 Canadians were dependent on alcohol and 200,000 on illicit drugs in 2002 (Statistics Canada 2004).

First Nations Health

As noted earlier, the federal government through Health Canada has a special responsibility for the delivery of health care services to First Nations and Inuit communities. They are obligated through treaties to fund 100 percent of the cost of First Nations health care.

The Aboriginal population in Canada is quite varied, with numerous distinct cultural and political organizational structures, each with unique concerns and needs. In general, poverty and a lack of economic and educational opportunity have severely affected the health of the Aboriginal population. The health status of Aboriginal people is much worse than that of the average Canadian, and the Assembly of First Nations (AFN) states that the health gap between First Nations people and the general population is widening.

While health care services have eased this situation somewhat, they have also contributed to the gradual erosion of traditional Aboriginal holistic approaches to health and healing. The Assembly of First Nations Health Secretariat, AFN National First Nations Health Technicians Network (NFNHTN) and the AFN Chiefs Committee on Health (CCOH) have identified seven health priorities: sustainability, health research, jurisdictional issues, mental health, children's health/gender health, smoking and environmental health and infrastructure (Assembly of First Nations 2000).

Generally, First Nations leaders wish to see an integrated, holistic, interdepartmental and inter-organizational strategy to address the inequities in health and social service delivery. They also believe that jurisdictional issues between the federal and provincial governments with respect to responsibility for First Nations health care need to be removed, particularly in light of provincial health care reform. They also support the Canadian public's demands to save medicare and eliminate the widening health status gap between First Nations and the general population (Assembly of First Nations 2000).

Table 7.1: Health Care in Northern Canada

	Population	Number of hospitals	Number of communities	Number of resident physicians
Yukon	31,000	2	31	51
Northwest Territories	42,083	1 + 2 health centres	33	55
Nunavut	28,000	1	26	Approximately 10

Source: Rachelle Younglai, *Canada's North and Health Care*, CBC News On-line. Available at http://www.cbc.ca

Conclusion

The *Canada Health Act* (CHA) of 1984 laid the foundation of the Canadian health system. The CHA establishes the federal government's commitment to transfer money to each province and territory in Canada to enable them to deliver universal, accessible, comprehensive, portable and publicly administered health insurance.

Recent provincial trends indicate that equal access to the same health care services is diminishing and that the gap between the rich and poor is increasing. Several provinces are trying to move towards user fees, extra- billing and the privatization of some services. This movement has the potential to lead to a two-tier health care system in Canada. The experience in the US shows us that this type of system increases the disparity between the rich and poor and leads to a more costly, wasteful and inefficient system of delivery.

On a positive note, our public system is enabling all provinces to shift away from an emphasis on health treatment towards a more comprehensive and integrated view of health. All levels of government are looking at ways to adapt our current system. The emphasis within the health care system is moving increasingly towards community-based models that focus on health promotion and prevention. Social workers are often at the forefront in advocating for, and providing, primary, community-based and preventive health care.

In the health field, social workers work in a variety of capacities. While the primary setting for medical social work is the hospital, social workers also provide direct services in community centres, specialized facilities and alternative care settings. While social workers in hospitals frequently feel that their role is not respected, it is quickly becoming more central as health care becomes more holistic in its approach. The holistic approach is one that takes into account not only the physical aspects of health that are commonly addressed by physicians, but also the social, cultural, mental and spiritual aspects of the patient.

The wide skill set of social workers ensures that they will continue to be an essential part of multidisciplinary health care teams in Canadian health care settings.

8

Social Work with Women

A Feminist Approach

One of the defining social characteristics of the second half of the twentieth century was the increased labour force participation of women. Indeed, the participation rate for Canadian women more than doubled over the thirty-year period from 1961 (29 percent) to 1991 (60 percent). The social implications of this economic fact were phenomenal (Gunderson 1998). Among other things, it gave rise to the dominance of the two-earner family. It precipitated a marked increase in the demand for child care, part-time work, flexible work arrangements, and in pressure for legislation that would foster and ensure equality between men and women. What feminist author Betty Friedan referred to in the 1950s as "the problem with no name" very soon received a name and a solution — women's inequality and women's liberation.

As with other approaches to social work, feminist social work practice seeks to understand a client's situation by acquiring knowledge of the client's history, family and social relations, and cultural context. However, in analyzing individual problems and working out effective interventions, the feminist approach gives greater emphasis to the harmful role of patriarchal relations within the family and within the wider society.

This chapter begins by looking briefly at the important role women have played in the history of Canadian social work. It reviews the current economic context and the serious individual and social problems inherent in a society organized along patriarchal lines. Finally, it outlines the main principles of the "feminist approach" to social work practice and the role of social workers in dealing with key problems faced by women in Canadian society today.

Social Work Beginnings

In Canada, the movement for greater participation of women in public life arose at the end of the nineteenth century. It had a number of major strands, including the temperance movement, women's missionary and charitable activities, and the suffragette movement. The temperance movement focused on the abolition of alcohol (because of its devastating effects on male breadwinners and therefore on women and children); missionary and charitable activities were an opportunity for women to become involved in public life beyond their role as caregivers in the family; and the suffragette movement sought to establish the voting rights of women. Women became involved in the Women's Christian Temperance Union, the National Council of Women (founded by Lady Aberdeen), the Young Women's Christian

Nellie McClung (1873-1951), women's rights activist.

WOMEN CONCENTRATED IN TRADITIONAL FEMALE OCCUPATIONS

The bulk of working women continue to work in occupations in which women have traditionally been concentrated. In 2003, 70% of all employed women were working in one of teaching, nursing and related health occupations, clerical or other administrative positions or sales and service occupations compared with 31% of employed men.

——

Source: Colin Lindsay and Marcia Almey. 2004. *A Quarter Century of Change: Young Women in Canada in the 1970s and Today.* Status of Women Canada and Statistics Canada.

During wartime, females workers were needed at munitions factories.

Association (YWCA) and church missionary societies and charities, such as the Protestant Orphans Homes, homes for unmarried mothers, homes for the aged and settlement houses.

Women were also involved in campaigns to improve the conditions for nursing mothers through the provision of pure milk, in organizations that provided care for victims of tuberculosis and other illnesses, and in providing assistance to families of veterans during and after World War I. When the federal government agreed to pay an allowance to support the families of men who died in the war, a group of Manitoba women (including suffragette leader Nellie McClung) campaigned for a similar benefit for the widows and children of men who died in peacetime. The Mothers' Allowance established by the Manitoba government in 1916 was the first legislated welfare program, and it soon became available in all Canadian provinces.

These early women's organizations were the forerunners to the profession of social work. Participation in these organizations as well as in employment during the war in jobs vacated by men at the front led to an increased role for women in public life, and to the acquisition of the vote. Together these political and social changes opened the door for women who wanted to participate in public affairs.

In the early period, women in social work were typically maternal feminists. They felt that women's nurturing and caring qualities and their understanding of children were critical in the reformation of society. The Child Welfare Council, for example, was composed of the early feminists who entered social work because of their primary concern for families, mothers and poor children in particular. Although they brought women into public life and social work, these early activists now tend to be viewed as being quite conservative in outlook, insofar as they supported more traditional conceptions of the family in which women were expected to stay in the home.

Given the expectations on women to maintain family life, it is not surprising that it was largely single women who sought employment in the social work field and in other helping professions. Moreover, at this time salaries were typically low in comparison to those of men with similar qualifications: "excluded in large part from the male-dominated fields of business, government, and the professions, a new generation of college-educated middle class women after the turn of the century, provided a large pool of available labour for the emerging fields of nursing, teaching, library science and social work (Struthers 1991, 128). Delegates to a 1929 conference on equal pay pointed out that "the same salary which will attract superior women will interest only mediocre men" (ibid.).

The ensuing Depression of the 1930s did little to change this situation. It was only later, in the 1960s, that this began to change dramatically with the wholesale expansion of employment in the social services sector.

Equal Pay and Employment Equity

Although more and more Canadian women entered the labour force from the 1950s onward, they seldom did so on equal terms with men. The industries and occupations initially open to women were generally less prestigious. Women's incomes were far inferior to those of men in the same occupations, and justifications for this fundamental inequality seemed to be readily available. In addition to economic inequality, patriarchal family and social relations were still in force. In many households, women were expected to tend to their children, husband and household affairs as well as earn an income outside the home.

Nevertheless, many legislative changes and important policy initiatives in the post-war period were aimed at fostering greater equality for women at work. These included: (1) equal pay policies (including pay equity or equal pay for work of equal value) designed to improve women's pay; (2) equal employment policies (including employment equity) designed to help women's employment and promotion opportunities; and (3) other facilitating policies (such as child care and parental leave) designed to put women on an equal footing in the labour market. (For a discussion of the women and the labour market, from which much of this is derived, see Gunderson 1998.)

- **Equal-pay policies**. During the 1950s and 1960s, every Canadian province enacted legislation requiring equal pay for similar or substantially similar work. During the 1970s, both Quebec and the federal government introduced pay equity legislation that required equal pay for work of equal value (allowing comparisons between occupations). In the 1980s, most jurisdictions followed suit, at least with respect to public sector employment. In Ontario, most establishments are required to have a pay equity plan in place regardless of whether there has been a complaint, and this applies to the private and public sector.

- **Equal employment and employment equity**. All Canadian provinces now have equal employment opportunity legislation in place, usually as part of their human rights codes. This legislation prohibits discrimination on the basis of race, age, religion, nationality and sex. The prohibition of discrimination on the basis of sex was generally added during the 1960s and 1970s. Employment equity legislation, however, was not introduced in Canada until the 1980s. The first legislation took effect in 1986 and applied only to Crown corporations and federally regulated employers with 100 or more employees. In 1996, it was expanded to include the federal public service. Employment equity is also required of federal contractors. In Ontario, employment equity was legislated in 1994 but was repealed in 1995. Employment equity may also be required by cities and municipalities. Canadian research evidence as to the effect of employment equity legislation is thin, although what does

PROMOTING GENDER EQUALITY

In 1995, the federal government adopted a policy requiring federal departments and agencies to conduct a gender-based analysis of future policies and legislation, where appropriate. *Gender-based Analysis: A Guide for Policy Makers* is a "hands-on" working document developed by Status of Women Canada to assist in the implementation of this government-wide policy.

The guide details how government policies and social programs can be analyzed to ensure that they promote gender equality. It is available on-line at: http://www.swc-cfc.gc.ca/pubs/pubs_e.html

Table 8.1: Full-year Work as a Share of All Work in Selected Occupations

Occupation	Total	Male	Female
Total all occupations (economy-wide)	51.6%	57.6%	44.7%
Social service managers	71.8%	78.2%	68.1%
Social workers	63.5%	73.2%	60.4%
Family, marriage and related counsellors	52.8%	62.6%	48.8%
Probation officers and related occupations	74.7%	77.8%	71.6%
Community and social service workers	51.0%	56.6%	49.0%
Head nurses	60.9%	68.6%	60.4%
Registered nurses	45.7%	62.7%	44.7%
Psychologists	50.0%	62.3%	42.7%
Secondary school teachers	67.2%	75.5%	59.1%
School and guidance counsellors	48.9%	58.5%	43.4%

Source: CASSW. 2001. *In Critical Demand: Social Work in Canada, Final Report.* Ottawa.

exist suggests small improvements in occupational advancement and wages for women and visible minorities. One study, reported by Gunderson, found that only slightly more than one-third of firms where employment equity was required had effective procedures in place to administer the policy (Gunderson 1998).

• **Facilitating policies.** Many other changes have been introduced to help put Canadian women on an equal footing with men in the labour market. These include changes in divorce laws, policies against sexual harassment at work, expanded maternity leave provisions, policies to protect part-time and temporary workers and policies designed to ensure women have equal access to higher education.

Such policies have undoubtedly helped to equalize the situation for women, though there is still the overriding concern that women leave their places of work only to find that they have still to assume the main burden of work at home and in the family. Over this period, the woman's role in the household has shifted from that of "stay-at-home mother" to "worker-mother." This shift may have reduced the economic dependency of women somewhat, but it has not eliminated the disadvantages that women face.

Dick Hemingway.

Many women perform double duty, labouring at home and at work.

Persistent Problems

While the new legislation and strategic policy initiatives have undoubtedly helped to improve the position of women in Canadian society, there is a growing realization that employment legislation in itself has not resolved many of the underlying problems. In many areas of economic and social life, women are still vulnerable. Even with advances in labour force participation, women dominate the ranks of those living in poverty. An examination of the situation reveals persistent problems for women in many areas of economic life.

- *Poverty*. Women constitute a substantial segment of the working poor. High poverty rates are concentrated in three family types: unattached women under 65 (40.3 percent, compared to 29.8 percent for men), unattached women 65 and older (45.6 percent, compared with 32.8 percent for men) and single mothers with children under 18 (45.4 percent, compared to 10.8 percent for men) (Statistics Canada 2001).

- *Part-time work*. Women still constitute a large proportion of part-time workers in Canada and, as such, are usually underpaid and therefore particularly vulnerable to economic downturns. As discussed in Chapter 4, part-time employment as a percentage of total employment has grown steadily from 3.8 percent in 1953, to 12 percent in 1973, to 16.9 percent in 1983, to 18.5 percent in 1999 (Broad 2000, 13). Seventy percent of these part-time workers are women.

- *Minimum wage legislation*. Because women hold 64 percent of minimum wage jobs, they are the group most in need of minimum wage legislation. For example, although Ontario's minimum wage was recently increased, it had been fixed since 1995. Providing a living wage for women can be a policy instrument for promoting greater wage equity and anti-poverty policy goals.

- *Maternity and parental leave*. Women still perform a double duty — even if they work outside the home, women are most often the primary caregivers for dependent relatives and therefore have to work another "full shift" with the family. Employment Insurance (EI) benefits can play a significant role in addressing this issue, if women are eligible for the benefits. EI was expanded in 2000, allowing parents to receive benefits for up to one year while caring for a child, but many women find that they are not eligible.

- *Dependent care*. Because women are most often the primary caregivers of dependent relatives, Canada's lack of universal day care (child care) programs is a significant barrier to women's full participation in the labour force. Day care is a necessity for many employed mothers.

PART-TIME WORKERS

An increasing number of young men and women are working part-time, usually because they cannot find full-time employment. Nearly 43% of young workers had part-time jobs in 1994, up from 30% a decade earlier. Among young women, the rate rose from 34% to 48%; for young men, the rate increased from 27% to 38%.

In the social work field, full-year, full-time work as a percentage of all work is as follows:

- Social Workers, 63.5% (Males, 73.2%; Females, 60.4%)
- Community & Social Service Worker, 51.0% (Males, 56.6%; Females, 49.0%)

Source: CASSW, *In Critical Demand*, p.40.

In considering Canada's adherence to Articles 16 and 17 of the covenant, the United Nations concluded:

"The Committee notes with grave concern that with the repeal of CAP and cuts to social assistance rates, social services and programmes have had a particularly harsh impact on women, in particular single mothers."

——

Source: Report of the Committee on Economic, Social and Cultural Rights, United Nations, Concluding observations, Section 22 (1998).

- *Free trade and globalization.* These global trends, involving competition from low-wage countries, particularly affect women who find themselves in low-wage jobs.

- *Pension programs.* These programs are of special significance to women, because women are often employed in jobs that do not give them access to private pension plans.

- *Recessions.* Economic downturns affect women disproportionately — they are typically the last employees to be hired and the first employees to be fired.

- *Employment insurance programs.* Even those programs that are designed to assist workers can place women at a disadvantage. Increases in the required eligibility periods make it more difficult for women than men to collect Employment Insurance.

Despite all the changes in the area of pay equity and employment equity, there is a continuing need for social policy makers and social work practitioners to be aware of the economic problems women still face *as women*.

To be sure, the problems Canadian women still face are widespread, persistent and undoubtedly factor into many problems social workers encounter in their practices. The economic and psychological stresses resulting from such inequalities take a toll on women and their families, and social workers are often the first to be called upon to deal with the unfortunate consequences.

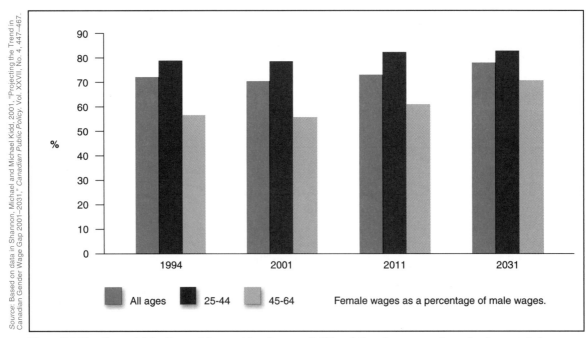

Source: Based on data in Shannon, Michael and Michael Kidd, 2001, "Projecting the Trend in Canadian Gender Wage Gap 2001–2031," *Canadian Public Policy*, Vol. XXVII, No. 4, 447–467.

All ages   25-44   45-64   Female wages as a percentage of male wages.

Figure 8.1: Equality much later. Economists expect female wages (full-time, full-year) as a percentage of male wages to increase, but a 22% gap may still exist in 2031. Female labour force participation and educational attainment contribute to the closure.

Sexism and Gender Equality

Before going on, it may be useful to distinguish several key terms.

- **Gender** has come to refer to the characteristics that identify the social relations between men and women or the way that this relationship is socially constructed. Gender is a relational term similar to the concepts of class and race, and it is an analytical tool for understanding social relations and processes.

- **Gender equality** means that women and men live in an environment that affords them equal opportunity to realize full human rights, to contribute to national, political, economic, social and cultural development, and to benefit from the results. In this context, gender equity programs refer to measures taken to compensate women for historical and social disadvantages they have suffered, which lead to gender equality. Gender equity and gender equality form the basis upon which the principles of a feminist social work practice are based.

- **Sexism** refers to prejudice or discrimination based on a person's sex. It is a system of discriminatory interrelated physical and social controls, derogatory beliefs and institutional- and societal-level policies. Sexism can be both blatant and subtle; it can take the form of derogatory language and put-downs or result in the denial of job or career opportunities based on a person's sex. Sexism can be so extensive, commonplace and internalized that it is not initially visible. Acknowledging that sexism can and does have a significant impact on the daily lives of women in Canada can be a difficult process for many individuals. It is sometimes easier to accept traditional roles and norms, which are comfortably familiar. Sexism is rooted in the patriarchal family system.

- **Patriarchy** literally means the "rule by the father" but, in a broader sense, it has come to mean the domination of society by men. Men are still the major stakeholders in Canadian society, men continue to be represented in higher numbers in positions of authority and male interests continue to take precedence over those of females.

Given the deep-rootedness of the patriarchal family system — and with it sexism and gender inequality — the prospect of eradicating widespread sex discrimination in Canadian society may seem a little daunting. However, while one should not minimize the difficulties ahead, it is important to note that great strides have been made by the women's movement. Without wishing to diminish the obstacles, the future looks brighter than ever and social workers and others have every reason to be optimistic as they join this long struggle for full gender equality.

"A feminist perspective means inserting an additional level of understanding: that women stand at the crossroads between production and reproduction, between economic activity and the care of human beings."

———
Source: Isabella Bakker, School of Women's Studies, York University.

A stereotypical image of the patriarchal family, circa 1914.

Principles of Feminist Practice

Social work, like many other fields of study and practice, was greatly influenced by the women's movement of the 1960s and 1970s. Students were demanding that social work schools look more critically at social problems and develop programs that would be more responsive to women's issues. The feminist movement dramatically changed social work thinking as well as social work practice. Feminist theories offered different ways of seeing and understanding women's lives and experiences, the nature of sexual inequality and gender relations. Feminist therapy, for example, has its origins in the women's liberation movement of the 1960s and 1970s. Women's **consciousness-raising groups** began to question gender-based roles and power relations in society. By sharing experiences, women began to understand how their own experiences were not unique.

There are different definitions of feminism and numerous formulations and debates within **feminist theory**. There is, however, a common core belief that sex-role stereotypes and social structures perpetuate women's subordination. Fundamentally, many feminist principles and concepts are similar to those of social work practice, such as the empowerment of the individual and the examination of society through a critical lens. In her book *Feminist Practice in the 21st Century*, Helen Land, a University of Southern California professor and accomplished feminist clinical practitioner, outlines the following 13 components of **feminist social work practice**:

- *Validating the social context.* Feminist approaches emphasize the effects of social context or structures on the difficulties of the client as the client and the worker jointly assess them.

- *Re-valuing positions enacted by women.* Social workers see the activities and stances assumed by women, such as nurturing, cooperating and caregiving, as vitally important and valuable. Society and mainstream psychotherapies, on the other hand, are viewed as placing more value on the activities of men, such as competition and upward mobility.

- *Recognizing difference in male and female experiences.* Feminist social workers maintain that mainstream theories are gender-blind and ignore the different experiences of women and men. To understand the emotional worlds of women, therapists must understand how the oppressive structures in society affect women.

- *Re-balancing perceptions of normality and deviance.* The need for re-balancing perceptions of normality refers to the belief "that behaviour which is conceived as being dysfunctional or deviant by our society often reflects behaviour of less-privileged groups, such as women, people of colour, poor people, older people, and gay men and lesbians" (p.6).

CP PHOTO/Frant Webber (National Action Committee on the Status of Women).

Sunera Thobani speaks at a NAC rally on women and poverty in 1996.

- *Taking an inclusive stance.* This enables feminist counsellors to challenge narrow assumptions and to include the experiences and values of all, regardless of ethnicity, class, sexual orientation, age or ability.

- *Paying attention to power dynamics in the therapeutic relationship.* This aspect ensures that the therapist works towards an egalitarian relationship between client and worker. It also serves to empower the client and thereby fosters lasting solutions.

- *Recognizing how "the personal is political."* This important component acknowledges that very personal difficulties faced by clients may reflect historical and political contexts (e.g., patriarchy). Such wider structures and ideologies influence how we think, feel and experience events.

- *Taking a deconstructive stance.* The deconstructive stance attempts to uncover and examine how social relations of patriarchy support and perpetuate a male-dominated world. The feminist approach therefore continually questions commonplace notions of what is "right" and "wrong," "normal" and "abnormal."

- *Taking a partnering stance.* This refers to the belief that disclosure of personal experiences by a therapist is helpful to a client, especially if common experiences are apparent. This practice is quite contrary to traditional psychotherapy, which holds that professional distance between the therapist and client is required.

- *Fostering inclusive scholarship.* In challenging the traditional notions of objective science, feminist scholarship frequently emphasizes both qualitative (such as interviews or case studies) and quantitative (numerical frequencies and statistics) research methods. As well, it stresses beginning with women's experience and what actually happens in the world, rather than with abstract theoretical models that claim to represent reality.

- *Challenging reductionist models.* "Reductionism" refers to the practice of reducing behaviours to simple cause-and-effect models, which often amount to stereotypes and severely limit one's ability to understand complex issues. For example, there is a stereotype of women as being naturally more emotional, and men, more objective. Feminist social workers resoundingly challenge such views.

- *Adopting empowerment practice.* Empowerment practice means that the worker and client develop goals together, with the focus on empowering the client to change structures and environments, rather than on helping the client adapt to, and cope with, existing oppressive structures.

- *Countering the myth of value-free psychotherapy.* In general, feminist therapists reject the idea that a person can be value-free in their practice and believe that therapists must be explicit about their own

WHITE RIBBON CAMPAIGN

On December 6, 1989, a man walked into a classroom at Montreal's École Polytechnique, ordered the men to leave, and proceeded to shoot and kill 14 women in what is now referred to as the Montreal Massacre.

In 1991, sparked by this horrifying event, a handful of men in Canada decided they had a responsibility to urge men to speak out against violence against women. They decided that wearing a white ribbon would symbolize this opposition.

The White Ribbon Campaign is likely the largest effort in the world of men working to end men's violence against women. In addition to wearing a white ribbon — the symbol of commitment to end violence against women — the campaign provides educational programs in high schools, community centres and workplaces, along with local shelters, help lines and other women's anti-violence programs.

WHAT IS DATE RAPE?

Date or acquaintance rape is sexual assault, which is a forced, unwanted act of a sexual nature, by someone the victim knows — a friend, a partner, someone they just met, a boss, a teacher and so on. Date rape is an act of violence and is a crime of power and control.

Women from all age groups, racial and ethnic groups, social classes, sexual orientations, abilities, and religious groups are at risk. The risk of rape is four times higher for women aged 16–24. The risk is even higher for women with disabilities.

Date rape also occurs in same-sex relationships.

——
Source:
http://www.region.halton.on.ca/heal
th/programs/sexualhealth/violence/
date_rape.htm

biases and values. As well, they would assist clients in discovering and taking ownership of their own beliefs and values.

Regardless of the particular emphasis, these components of feminist social work practice offer a way of seeing and understanding women's lives that will help individual clients and begin to change wider structures and policies that foster gender inequality and oppression. Indeed, so important are they that gradually these principles are becoming an accepted part of standard social work practice.

Incorporating feminist principles into one's social work practice is not an easy task, however. To begin, it is important to value women's experience and identity, and recognize that women have been socially subjected to unfounded negative stereotypes. Myths, such as "women are the weaker sex" and "a woman is nothing without a man," must be rejected, and the important contributions women have made must be stressed. Social workers who incorporate these principles value the diverse experience of all their clients, women and men.

In addition, social work practice informed by feminist principles seeks to identify power differences and examines how they affect both the therapeutic relationship and the client's life, thereby linking the "personal" and "political." For example, while a client is recounting a bad experience, the worker may ask, "How does this experience relate to the fact that you are a woman?" or "How is your situation similar to that of other women?" This type of question may help a client analyze their situation or experience. Identifying and critically analyzing behaviours, rather than labelling them, enables women to replace powerlessness and helplessness with strength and determination. This in turn fosters self-esteem and an egalitarian client-therapist relationship.

Another process that encourages self-esteem and egalitarianism is worker self-disclosure. The sharing of relevant personal information with a client on the part of the social worker allows the client to see that they have a common experience of oppression and face many of the same problems. This helps women to differentiate between individual and social problems and thereby eliminates some of their self-blame. Listening and validating the experiences of women is one of the most important aspects of applying feminist principles. This voicing of her experiences begins the process of healing.

There are obviously many occasions when it is only appropriate that a female worker, rather than a male, work with a woman in need. This is the case, for example, when working with women who have been sexually abused or raped, where the presence of a male social worker is clearly inappropriate. It is widely recognized that women should counsel such individuals. This work normally takes place in settings such as rape crisis centres and women's shelters where an experienced staff of women is equipped to deal with such emergency situations and provide the necessary support and assistance.

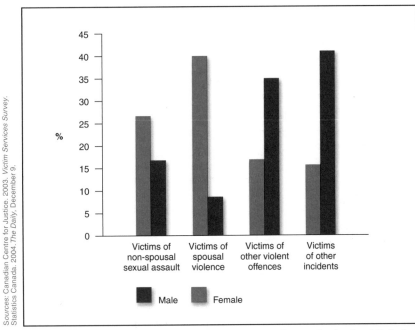

Sources: Canadian Centre for Justice. 2003. *Victim Services Survey*. Statistics Canada. 2004. *The Daily*, December 9.

Figure 8.2: Over 8 in of the 10 females helped by victim services on the day the victimization survey (October 22, 2003) was held were victims of violent crimes.

However, male social workers can, should, and do incorporate feminist principles into their practice as well. Male practitioners working with the New Directions program in Ottawa, for example, use feminist principles to help men who have abused women in relationships. The program helps men take responsibility for their abusive behaviour and to view it within the context of a male-dominated society. This includes helping them see their behaviour within the wider political context. The history of abuse that many of the men themselves may have experienced is also addressed and common experience between the men is explored.

• Record Keeping

As in all types of social work practice, social workers must keep case records or written documents that detail the client's situation, the intervention and the outcomes. However, practitioners who follow feminist principles and who work with abused women increasingly find the requirements of case records to be troublesome; they find it difficult to keep accurate records that might be used against a woman if a defence lawyer subpoenaed them.

Bill C-46, the Rape Shield Law, for example, is intended to protect women from character attacks by defence lawyers and restricts the questioning of women regarding their sexual histories. To compensate for this restriction, lawyers are subpoenaing women's counselling and medical records. Social workers need to be mindful of this when writing case notes and be careful not to write items that might be misinterpreted. Subjective comments and judgments should be avoided.

VICTIMIZATION SURVEY

There were 606 victim service agencies in Canada in 2002/03. The majority of the agencies were police-based (41%), followed by community-based (19%), then sexual assault centres (17%), court-based (10%) and system-based (8%).

A one-day survey snapshot, taken on October 22, 2003, showed that more than three-quarters of the people who sought assistance were victims, either directly or indirectly, of violent crime, and the majority were women or girls.

Overall, women and girls accounted for about three-quarters of the almost 4,400 people helped by victim service agencies on the day of the survey. Even when clients of sexual assault centres are excluded from the total, females still account for over 7 in 10 victims helped that day.

Of the over 3,300 females assisted by these agencies, about 84% had been the direct or indirect victims of a violent crime. This compares with 59% of the almost 1,000 males served that day.

In addition, about 40%, or more than 1,300 females, were victims of violence by a spouse, ex-spouse or intimate partner.

SHELTERS, TRANSITION HOUSES AND ADVOCACY FOR
ABUSED WOMEN

The feminist approach to social work is perhaps best illustrated by social work practice as it is implemented at transition houses for battered women and their children.

Transition houses are responsive to the needs of the abused woman and her children, are sensitive to the power relations within traditional family structures and emphasize social change. Because of their success, the number of transition houses or shelters is growing. A total of 96,359 women and children were admitted to 448 shelters for battered women across Canada in 1997–98. As of 2002, there were 466 transition houses in Canada. While they are becoming a primary resource for women and their children, they face serious funding problems.

The women's movement in the 1970s struggled hard for the funding and development of shelters. Today they are the primary resource for protecting assaulted women from violent partners and to assist women in moving on with their lives. Services dedicated to responding to the abuse of women include transition houses and shelters, second-stage housing, safe houses and family resource centres. Each province and territory has a unique array, with varied funding arrangements and availability.

All of the services are residential, meaning that they can provide accommodation for abused women and their children as required. The services provide counselling and other support programs, such as safe and secure emergency housing, crisis intervention, emotional support, information and referral, food, shelter, advocacy, a crisis telephone line and children's programs. Some of the centres provide outreach services to former residents and non-residents with newsletters, walk-in services or support groups.

Research has shown that an effective shelter provides the following kinds of services:

* emergency access to a safe place (including emergency transportation and overnight accommodation, particularly for those in rural and isolated areas);
* counselling and emotional support (immediately following a crisis and through follow-up and outreach on a residential or non-residential basis);
* information and referral;
* access to affordable and safe housing, and to legal and medical services;
* employment and income support;
* mental health and addiction services where required;
* child care, child support and counselling for children to overcome trauma;
* safety planning; and
* assistance with the family law system (spousal maintenance, custody and access, child support and accommodation).

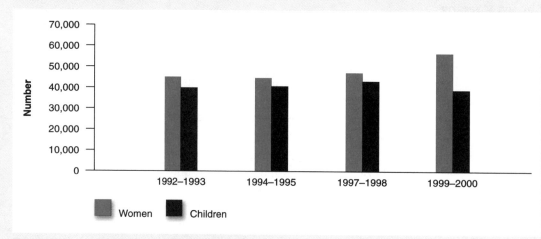

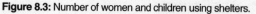

Figure 8.3: Number of women and children using shelters.

Violence Against Women

While wife-beating has never been a legal act in Canada, historically, women who were financially dependant on their husbands found that they had little recourse if their husbands should become abusive. In fact, the view that men should have complete authority over women met with general acceptance, in part because men held the economic power in the marriage.

Indeed, it was not until the late nineteenth and early twentieth century that women were recognized as having legal and political rights. The suffragette movement campaigned for the right for all women to vote, and most Canadian women were given the right to vote between 1916 and 1922 (those who resided in Quebec did not receive the right to vote until 1940).

Meanwhile, the status quo prevailed with respect to domestic violence — what happened behind closed doors was considered to be nobody else's business. Police were reluctant to respond to calls of domestic dispute, and the courts did not take the matter seriously. As a result, many assaults on women were not reported to the authorities. It was not until the 1980s that mandatory charging policies took effect across Canada. Formal training was established in Canadian police forces to assist officers in determining a proper course of action when responding to domestic disputes, as well as to help them recognize chargeable assaults.

• Statistics on Family Violence

Many social workers take exception to the phrase "family violence" or "domestic violence"; they believe it glosses over the fact that it is usually men who are violent against women. Statistics Canada reports that the rate of violence experienced in a marriage or common-law relationship is eight percent for women and seven percent for men (Statistics Canada 2000, 5). However, statistics on violence reported to police show a different picture, with women being much more likely than their male counterparts to be victims of spousal violence (85 percent versus 15 percent). Young females aged 25 to 34 experienced the highest rates of spousal violence.

This information is based on the Canadian Centre for Justice Statistics annual data collected from a number of police departments through the Incident-based Uniform Crime Reporting (UCR2) Survey. In 2002, the Survey found that there were more than 205,000 victims of violent crime reported to a subset of 94 police departments across Canada (103,001 female and 102,447 male victims). Of these, 27 percent involved violence within a family or household (40 percent involved violence by friends or acquaintances). Among all family violence victims, 62 percent were victims of violence by a spouse.

MYTHS AND FACTS ABOUT DOMESTIC VIOLENCE

MYTH. Family violence occurs most often in lower-income families.

FACT: Family violence is not related to economic status or to ethnic, racial, social or particular age groups. Family violence cuts across all age and social boundaries.

MYTH. Family violence is only about physical abuse.

FACT: Family violence includes physical and sexual assault, emotional and psychological abuse, intimidation, neglect and financial and personal exploitation. Abuse may result in injury or significant emotional or psychological harm.

MYTH. People who are abusive are "mentally ill."

FACT: People try to explain or excuse family violence by saying abusers are "mentally ill." This implies that abusers are not responsible for their actions. People who work with family violence problems say that most abusers are not mentally ill. They take advantage of a power imbalance to hurt and control others.

Source: Adapted from the National Clearinghouse on Family Violence, *Family Violence Awareness Information for People in the Workplace* (Ottawa: Health Canada, 2001).

Source: Ontario Women's Directorate: http://www.gov.on.ca/citizenship/owd/english/wapm/wapm.htm#statistics

STATISTICS ON VIOLENCE AGAINST WOMEN

- 25% of Ontario women experience spousal assault at least once in their lifetime.
- There is an average of 25 female victims of spousal homicide in Ontario each year.
- Women represent 85% of spousal assault victims in Canada.
- Aboriginal women are three times more likely to experience spousal violence than non-Aboriginal women.
- Only 27% of spousal assaults perpetrated against women are reported to police.
- 37% of spousal assaults are witnessed by children. Children who witness violence at home are more likely to grow up to be perpetrators, or victims, of violence themselves.

• Forms of Violence

Women and men also report very different forms of violence. Women in violent relationships are more likely to report more severe forms of violence — for example, women are more than twice as likely as men to report being beaten (25 percent verses 10 percent) and five times more likely to report being choked (20 percent verses 4 percent). Men, on the other hand, are more likely to report being slapped or having something thrown at them. Unfortunately, Statistics Canada combines these very different "forms of violence" into one statistic. To put this in context, from 1974 to 1992, a married woman was nine times more likely to be murdered by her partner than by a complete stranger.

Other figures indicate that about 29 percent of women married or living in a common-law relationship are likely to be abused (Rodgers 1994). The National Clearinghouse on Family Violence reports that nearly 22 percent of the women who experienced violence never told anyone about the abuse.

Evidence also shows that for a woman who is leaving an abusive relationship the period immediately following her departure is the most dangerous, and that women are more at risk of being murdered or experiencing severe violence at this point than at any other. Several attempts at violence might be made before a final separation results.

Table 8.2: Victims of Spousal Violence by Offence, 2002[1,2,3,4]

Offense	Total	%	Female No.	%	Male No.	%
Homicide/attempt	132	0	105	0	27	1
Sexual assault	521	2	514	2	7	0
Major assault (assault levels 2 & 3)	4,446	13	3,355	12	1,091	21
Criminal harassment	2,453	7	2,159	7	294	6
Uttering threats	4,167	12	3,592	12	575	11
Other violent offences[5]						
Total offences	**34,107**	**100**	**28,953**	**100**	**5,154**	**100**

Note: Percentages may not add up to 100% due to rounding. 0 is a true zero or a value rounded to zero.

[1.] Excludes incidents where the sex and/or the age of the victim was unknown.

[2.] Data are not nationally representative. Based on data from 94 police departments representing 56% of the national volume of crime in 2002.

[3.] Includes victims aged 15 to 89.

[4.] Spousal violence refers to violence committed by legally married, common-law, separated and divorced partners.

[5.] Other violent offences include robbery, unlawfully causing bodily harm, discharge firearm with intent, assault against peace-public officer, criminal negligence causing bodily harm, other assaults, kidnapping, hostage-taking, explosives causing death/bodily harm, arson, and other violent violations.

Source: Statistics Canada. 2000. Centre for Justice Statistics. Incident-based Uniform Crime Reporting (UCR2) Survey.

Sexual Assault and Sexual Harassment

Sexual violence in a major social problem is Canada today. Indeed, the level of violence against women, in whatever form it takes, is one of the strongest indicators of prevailing societal attitudes towards women.

- **Sexual assault** is any form of unwanted sexual activity including fondling, touching, and/or penetration that is forced upon another person without that person's consent. It includes a wide range of criminal acts ranging from rape to sexual harassment. All forms of sexual assault are crimes under the Criminal Code. Consent is a key component of defining an act as sexual assault. Consent is an active choice and the voluntary agreement of two adults to engage in sexual activity. Someone who is under the influence of medication, drugs or alcohol is not considered to be in the position to give consent (Federal-Provincial-Territorial Ministers' Responsible for the Status of Women 2002, 19).

- **Sexual Harassment** is any behaviour, comment, gesture or contact of a sexual nature that treats the person receiving it as a sexual object and is considered offensive.

• Statistics on Sexual Assault

In 2001, 24,419 sexual assaults were reported, but only 43 percent of the reported sexual assault cases resulted in a conviction. Women made up the majority of victims of sexual assault (86 percent) and other types of sexual offences. Most sexual assaults are not reported, because women often feel afraid to report or don't want to go to court or know the probability of conviction is low. In addition, most sexual assaults occur when women are on a date, and these assaults are reported far less frequently than assault by a stranger. Forty percent of female victims of sexual assault were assaulted by a friend or casual acquaintance, 23 percent by a stranger and 23 percent by a family member, including a spouse or ex-spouse (Statistics Canada 2001).

Recovering from a sexual assault can often be a long and painful process. Often women feel as though they should have done more to prevent the situation or are worried that people will not believe them. Many women seek support to help them deal with ongoing nightmares, distrust, fear, anxiety, difficulties with sex, depression, guilt, shame — and social workers are often at the frontline working with these women. They work for rape crisis centres, sexual assault centres and helplines, sexual assault and domestic violence care and treatment centres, sexual assault survivors' centres, and shelters or transition houses. For an idea of the sheer number of shelters and sexual assault centres in Canada, browse the Health Canada listing of Transition Houses and Shelters for Abused Women (http://www.hc-sc.gc.ca) and the Canadian Association of Sexual Assault Centres (http://www.casac.ca).

KEY STATISTICS

- Sexual assault is vastly under-reported. Studies indicate that fewer than 10% of sexual assaults are reported to police.
- Women are twice as likely to be sexually assaulted by a man known to them than by a stranger.
- The vast majority of victims of sexual assault are women.
- Young women under the age of 25, women with disabilities and Aboriginal women are at highest risk of sexual assault.
- An estimated 572,000 women in Canada were sexually assaulted in one year alone. That's more than one per minute!
- Over one-third of adult women report being sexually assaulted since they were 16 years old.

For more statistics, see "Assessing Violence Against Women: A Statistical Profile," Federal-Provincial-Territorial Ministers Responsible for the Status of Women.

DISPELLING MYTHS ABOUT SEXUAL ASSAULT

Our society's understanding of sexual assault is complicated by widespread myths. To dispel these myths we need to ask ourselves: Do I believe that …

MYTH: Women often provoke sexual assault by their behaviour or manner of dress?

Fact: No behaviour or manner of dress justifies an assault. Such a belief takes the onus off the offender and places it on the victim. In fact, a man should always ask to ensure his advances are wanted. The idea that women "ask for it" is often used by offenders to rationalize their behaviour. Offenders are solely responsible for their own behaviour. A woman may put herself at risk by using poor judgment. However, this is not cause for the assault.

MYTH: Most women lie about sexual assault?

Fact: Statistics show that more than 98% of sexual assault allegations are true. Other crimes have a higher percentage of false allegations. Also, sexual assault is one of the most under-reported crimes.

MYTH: When a woman says "no" she secretly enjoys being forced, teased or coerced into having sex?

Fact: No one enjoys being assaulted. No one asks to be assaulted. "No" means "no." It's the law. If a woman says no, it is the responsibility of the man to accept and respect her "no." Sexual assault can have serious effects on people's health and well-being. People who have been sexually assaulted feel fear, depression and anger. Victims can experience harmful physical and emotional effects that influence future relations and cause the individual to become more cautious and less trusting.

MYTH: Saying "no" is the only way of expressing your desire to not continue?

Fact: There are many ways of communicating non-compliance.

- "I have to go" / "I'm going to be late."

- "My friend is waiting."

- "I'm not into this right now."

- silence

- crying

- body language (squirming, stiffness, shaking)

Remember: Many offenders will rationalize their behaviour by saying that because she didn't actually say "no,"

they thought a woman was consenting, that she really wanted sexual contact).

MYTH: Sexual assault only occurs when there is a struggle or physical injury?

Fact: Many victims are too afraid to struggle. They may freeze in terror or realize that the overwhelming size and strength of their attacker makes resistance very dangerous. Eighty-five percent of sexual assaults are committed by someone the victim knows and trusts. Acquaintances, friends or relatives are more likely to use tricks, verbal pressure, threats or mild force like arm twisting or pinning their victim down during an assault. Assaults may also be drug assisted. Lack of obvious physical injury or knowing the attacker doesn't change the nature of the act.

MYTH: If it really happened, victims would be able to recount all the facts in the proper order?

Fact: Shock, fear and trauma impair memory, temporarily and/or long term.

MYTH: A woman who has agreed to sex previously with the offender (for example, her husband, boyfriend or acquaintance) cannot be sexually assaulted?

Fact: Sexual assault is any unwanted sexual activity forced on one person by another. Sexual assault occurs whenever a person does not want to have sex but is forced into the act, regardless of previous consensual sexual relations. The Canadian Panel on Violence Against Women found that 38 percent of sexually assaulted women were assaulted by their husbands, common-law partners or boyfriends. Although illegal since 1983, few of these assaults are reported to police

MYTH: My personal biases or stereotypes might interfere with my ability to openly listen to complaints of sexual assault by gays/lesbians, women of diverse cultures, the disabled, sex trade workers, etc?

Fact: Many of the above-mentioned groups are at higher risk for any type of violence, including sexual violence.

- More than 90 percent of gay and lesbian youth suffer verbal and physical assault because of their sexual orientation.

- Two-thirds of disabled women have been physically or sexually abused before they reach puberty.

- One-third of these women continue to be abused as adults.

STATISTICS ON VIOLENCE AGAINST WOMEN AND GIRLS

- Every week, at least one woman in Canada is murdered by her boyfriend or spouse.
- Of women who were murdered by their partners, more than one half had previously reported domestic violence to the police.
- As many as 1 out of 5 young women in high school are in abusive relationships.
- 60% of all sexual assault victims are children under 18 years of age.
- More than 13 women and girls are sexually assaulted in BC every day.
- Some women have been beaten by their partners 35 times before they ever call police.
- Every year, over 90,000 Canadian women and children are admitted to shelters for battered women.
- 45% of women assaulted by a male partner suffered physical injuries that include bruising, cuts, burns, broken bones, fractures, internal injuries and miscarriages.

- Girl children are targets of abuse in the family more so than boys. 4 out of 5 family related sexual assaults are against girls and over half of physical assaults are against girls by family members.
- In 1997, fathers accounted for 97% of sexual assaults and 71% of physical assaults of children.
- Only 10% of sexual assaults on women are reported to the police.
- In Canada, there are approximately 509,860 cases of reported and unreported sexual assault incidents per year, which amounts to 1,397 sexual assaults per day. This daily figure is refined into one woman or child being sexually assaulted every minute of every day.

Source: Compiled from: B.C. Ministry of Community, Aboriginal, and Women's Services. "A minute of silence." (http://www.mcaws.gov.bc.ca/womens_services/a-minute-of-silence/weq_print.htm) and M. Morris (2002, March). "Fact sheet: Violence against women and girls." Canadian Research Institute for the Advancement of Women (http://www.criaw-icref.ca/factSheets.

Source: SANE Program. 2003. Fraser Health. Surrey Memorial Hospital. Surrey, British Columbia.

- In Canada today, women with disabilities are at least one and one-half times more likely than non-disabled women to experience some form of violence during their lifetime.
- Sixty-seven percent of those disabled women surveyed had been physically or sexually assaulted as children, compared with 44 percent of non-disabled women.

MYTH: If a man — for example, a husband, boyfriend or acquaintance — buys a woman dinner or drinks, gives her a present or does her a favour, she owes him sex?

Fact: No one owes anyone sex. It cannot be assumed that friendliness and openness are an invitation to sex.

MYTH: Once a sexual assault report has been made, the alleged offender will eventually be prosecuted and found guilty?

Fact: As with all types of charges before the Criminal Courts, not every sexual assault reported ends in prosecution and certainly not every prosecution ends in a conviction or a finding of guilt. Each case is dealt with on its own merits. It requires tremendous courage and strength to come forward and disclose sexual violence, and to participate in the criminal justice process. There

is no statute of limitation for reporting and prosecuting sexual assault.

MYTH: There is no such thing as a male victim of sexual assault?

Fact: Anyone can be a victim. Men and boys can be attacked by sexual offenders too. One-third of the males and just over one-half of the females surveyed reported that they had been the victims of at least one unwanted sexual act. Women are considerably more likely than men to report being victims of sexual abuse.

MYTH: Most sexual assault crimes are reported to police?

Fact: Only one in ten sexual assaults are reported to the police. There are many reasons that people don't report their sexual assault. Fear of not being believed or fear of being blamed for the assault are very common. Some believe the myth that they are to blame for being sexually assaulted. Males are often not recognized as victims because society does not define assault as something that happens to males.

Taken with permission from:
http://www.region.halton.on.ca/health/programs/sexualhealth/violence/Myths.htm.

Social workers support and assist women who have been sexually assaulted in numerous ways. Figure 8.4 illustrates the range of counselling, legal and medical services that a sexually assaulted woman might need. Social workers also act to educate the public about sexual violence, advocate for women and campaign for government policy and systemic change. Social workers in this field recognize that sexual violence is not only an individual problem, but reflects wider social and structural dimensions.

The Vancouver Rape Relief and Women's Shelter provides a typical range of services for both abused and sexually assaulted women. They provide a 24–hour emergency call line. They operate for women and their children, offering a safe place to stay in order to escape or prevent an attack. They offer support groups to help counter feelings of isolation, including an ex-residents' group. They believe that sharing emotional support and knowledge helps all women to join together to act for change. They offer information for women interacting with the Ministry of Social Services, the police, the court or the hospital. Finally they will accompany women to the hospital, to the police, through court proceedings, to appointments with lawyers, financial aid workers, and social workers, providing emotional support and advocacy.

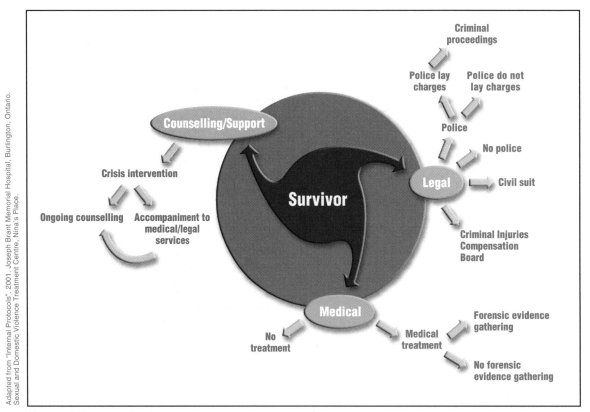

Adapted from "Internal Protocols". 2001. Joseph Brant Memorial Hospital, Burlington, Ontario. Sexual and Domestic Violence Treatment Centre, Nina's Place.

Figure 8.4: Flow chart of system access.

What Is the Role of a Social Worker?

The role of social workers in helping abused women may include crisis intervention, support and empowerment, support group facilitation and the provision of information. A social worker in a shelter will frequently be the first person a woman meets when she flees a violent situation. At this critical time, it may be necessary to discuss the cycle of violence and point out that the violence is likely to occur again. The social work process will be assisted by conveying the message that the violence is not her fault and that she is not the only woman to experience this kind of violence.

The social worker should ultimately support the woman in whatever decision she makes and provide her with the kind of support and education she needs to make a good decision. While it is very frustrating for a social worker to see a woman go back to an abusive relationship, sometimes several times, the worker must be sure not to take the power of decision away from the woman, as that has been her experience throughout her relationship. The social worker should empower the woman to make this important decision about her life.

In all such situations the first priority is the safety of the woman. Within this context, the social worker may partake in one or several of the following activities:

- Intervene in a crisis, which may involve the identification and assessment of danger to the woman and her children;

- Facilitate an empowerment approach with the woman;

- Listen to what the woman has to say and empathetically respond, sharing one's personal experience if appropriate;

- Connect the woman to a support group of women who have had a common experience;

- Teach the woman how to assess the assault/homicide potential in domestic and other situations;

- Make an appropriate referral, for example, if the woman has immediate financial needs;

- Teach the woman how to recognize abuse, name the problem and its source and avoid self-blame;

- Advise the abused woman of her legal rights and link her to legal resources, thereby avoiding the traditional practice of "re-victimization";

- Mobilize safety, legal and community resources effectively (e.g., linking children to a children's protective service, arranging admission to a shelter for abused women, finding a translator for an immigrant woman, linking a rape victim with an advocate);

Yolande James, the first black woman in the Quebec legislature.

- Implement agency policy regarding mandated reporting and keep accurate records, including dental and other X-rays, as these can possibly aid later legal action;

- Use the consultative process (know whom to call under what circumstances, and do it) and review one's referrals and interventions with other health care providers;

- Complete the crisis management and follow-up referral or treatment steps while withholding judgment and the imposition of values on the woman and her significant others; and

- Provide follow-up counselling to the woman and her assailant.

• Role of Support Groups

Support groups are a key component of social work with abused women. They can empower women in a number of ways. They can:

- help reduce isolation and allow women to meet other women who share their experience;

- help women to develop an understanding of the power and control that are at the root of battering and learn what actions they can take to change the situation;

- be a forum for women to exchange information, practical help and emotional support; and

- allow women to explore their self-image and appreciate their own strengths and accomplishments.

Traci Healy is a volunteer at Sheena's Place, a community support centre for people with eating disorders. Healy says that she is living proof that, with help, anorexia can be conquered.

EXPLAINING VIOLENCE AGAINST WOMEN

Violence against a woman by a man is a social act, a behaviour for which the perpetrator is accountable to the community. A variety of theories have been advanced to explain why this phenomenon occurs in Canadian society. Each of these attempts to conceptualize violence against women contains a great deal of truth, and any social work assessment of a situation of violence by a man against a woman needs to consider the following major theories: power theory, learning theory, anger-control theory and cycle-of-violence theory.

- **Power theory.** This theory argues that wife abuse is a societal problem that occurs because of the power imbalance between men and women, specifically, because of the dominance of men and men's roles. Wife abuse continues because there has been historical acceptance of abuse and of men's right to control women, even by force. This theory maintains that society must change its attitudes, values and responses with respect to women if wife abuse is to be prevented. This theory is consistent with a structural or feminist approach to social work.

- **Learning theory.** The main idea behind this theory is that violence is a behaviour learned in childhood. Boys learn that it is okay to be violent, and girls learn that it is okay to be on the receiving end of violence — this is what relationships are about. This theory holds that all children in our society are socialized to accept violence and that this, coupled with the different roles into which boys and girls are socialized, supports and perpetuates abuse. Children who witness violence in the home are much more likely to become abusers or be abused. The emphasis here is on changing the behaviour of the perpetrator.

- **Anger-control theory.** This theory focuses on the idea that men must be held accountable for their violent behaviour. They must learn to deal with and control their anger and express it in more appropriate ways. This theory does not attempt to explain the root cause of wife abuse, and in that, it is different from the other two theories. Instead, it focuses on poor anger control — if men could control their anger, violence would stop. It is a changed-behaviour model. Within this theory, a criminalization and a punishment-based social work approach would be the most successful.

- **Cycle-of-violence theory.** This theory does not explain why violence occurs; rather, it explains what happens in individual relationships in terms of a three-step process. First is the tension-building phase. In this phase, the woman sees that tension is building in the relationship and that there is going to be an explosion. The man is expressing more anger every day. He may be kicking the dog or yelling at the children. The second phase in the process involves an acute battering incident. The tension has reached a point where the violence erupts against the woman. She is abused, hit, bruised and battered. This is usually a shorter phase than the first, lasting from between two and twenty-four hours. The third phase is called the honeymoon period. In this phase, the man says he is sorry; he should not have done it; he loves her; he begs her not to leave him; he promises it will never happen again. The man will call relatives to ask them to convince the woman to return to him. If the woman has left during the second phase, she might return to him during this phase. Statistics show that a woman is usually abused and leaves many times before she leaves for the final time. The honeymoon period is a very powerful phase. Women want to believe that their partner has changed; they may also feel that it will be their fault if the marriage breaks down as they perhaps didn't work hard enough at the relationship. Some women stay for the sake of the children or believe that a bad marriage is better than no marriage at all. Statistics show that single mothers are among the poorest in our society, and this is where income security programs come into play.

These theories are useful in that they look at different aspects of the problem of violence against women. In one's daily practice, a concrete assessment that takes account of the specifics of the situation will always be needed so as to ensure that any intervention addresses the full range of possible solutions.

The Quebec Federation of Women march for equality and justice, October 2000.

CP PHOTO/La Presse-Bernard Brault.

Other Areas of Social Work Intervention

Violence against women is one of the main areas where social workers intervene directly on behalf of women in need. Two other areas are discussed briefly below: women in poverty and women battling with HIV/AIDS.

• Women and Poverty

Mounting numbers of low-income women, and especially lone-parent mothers, are receiving social services across Canada. Indeed, so disturbing is the problem that a phrase has been coined to capture it — the **feminization of poverty**.

Currently, almost 15 percent of adult women live below Statistics Canada's Low Income Cut-off (LICO). In 2002, 51.6 percent of female lone-parent families lived below LICO (Statistics Canada 2004). This is up dramatically from 2001 when it stood at 44.9 percent. In 1997, there were a total of 93,000 lone-parent mothers with incomes of less than 50 percent of the poverty line. This was roughly double that of 47,000 in 1989, a year before the 1990–91 recession (National Council of Welfare 1999, 54).

Another way to look at the feminization of poverty is to calculate the severity of poverty, or what is referred to as the **poverty gap**. This is done by examining how far below the LICO women fall. This type of analysis reveals that many women are not only poor, but that they live far below the poverty line. Both unattached women and men who are below the poverty line have an income that is only 55 percent of the poverty-line income. Overall, lone-parent mothers earn 61 percent of the poverty line and unattached women over 65 earn 84 percent of the poverty line (National Council of Welfare 1999, 54).

In working with low-income women, social workers need to be aware that women's poverty is caused by different factors than men's poverty. Canadian studies have found that men's poverty is usually more directly related to low-wage employment, whereas women's poverty arises from additional factors such as divorce and separation, and their responsibilities as mothers, homemakers, caregivers and nurturers. Even though more and more women have paid employment, many are still dependent on the income of a spouse. This has led many women to conclude that they are "only one man away from welfare" (Townson 2000, 6).

Issues pertaining to gender inequality need to be addressed in order to tackle women's poverty in Canada. Beyond understanding the unique issues affecting low-income women, social workers should challenge governments at all levels to develop specific strategies to deal with women's employment, child care, old age security, family law, social assistance rates and general income security.

CP PHOTO/Fred Chartrand (1989).

Civil servants win the long fight for equal pay for work of equal value.

• Women and HIV/AIDS

HIV/AIDS in Canada has changed from the early epidemic, which affected primarily men who have sex with men (MSM), to the current epidemic, which increasingly affects other groups such as injecting drug users (IDU) and heterosexuals. As a result, the number and percentage of women living with HIV/AIDS is increasing. The HIV/AIDS epidemic among women is of particular concern because of the potential for transmission to their infants.

In Canada, of the 18,713 cumulative AIDS cases in adults reported up to June 30, 2003, to the Centre for Infectious Disease Prevention and Control (CIDPC), 1,555 (8.3 percent) were women. The proportion of all reported adult AIDS cases (for which gender and age are known) occurring in women has increased over time, from 6.1 percent before 1994 to 15.8 percent in 1999; in 2002, the proportion of women was 16.5 percent. Of all cumulative reported AIDS cases in women up to June 30, 2003, 67.9 percent were attributed to heterosexual contact (this category includes three subcategories: sexual contact with a person at risk, origin from a country where HIV is endemic and sex with the opposite gender as the only identified risk), 23.3 percent to injected drug use and 8.5 percent to receiving of blood or blood products. The proportion of adult female AIDS cases attributed to IDU increased from 20.1 percent before 1998 to 46.2 percent in 1998 and has since dropped to 29.3 percent in 2002.

Social work practitioners are increasingly engaged in efforts to secure specific services for women affected by AIDS. Because they are at the front lines, they are in an ideal position to address the AIDS problem.

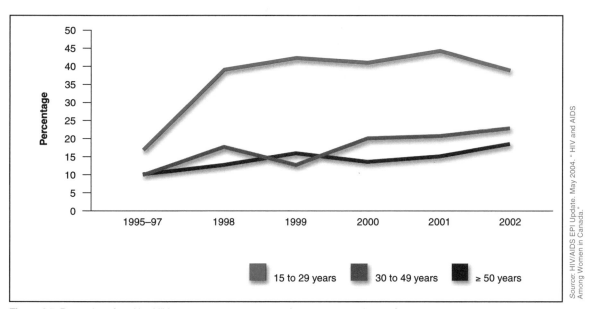

Source: HIV/AIDS EPI Update. May 2004. "HIV and AIDS Among Women in Canada."

Figure 8.5: Proportion of positive HIV test reports among women by age group and year of test.

Conclusion

The women's movement has dramatically changed the status of women in Canadian society. Legislation and policies on employment equity, pay equity, abortion rights, discrimination in employment and education, and specialized health programs have been pursued and important gains have been made — yet equality for women is still far from being achieved. Increasingly, it seems, women who are not attached to a man are poor. Women of colour and Aboriginal women are even poorer, and employed women tend to be sex-segregated in low-wage jobs.

Social workers need to help women at both the personal and political level. In helping women deal with personal problems, social workers need to analyze the social and economic context of women's problems. The feminist approach emphasizes the harmful role of patriarchal relations within the family and within the wider society. The recognition that sex-role stereotypes and social structures perpetuate women's subordination also necessitates a response that addresses the institutions, structures and policies in Canadian society. Social workers should not minimize the importance of helping women deal with personal changes in their attitudes, behaviours and relationships, but workers also need to challenge the ways in which sexism supports oppression and inequality.

Since the early 1970s, social workers have been concerned with eliminating sexism from social work education and thereby enabling graduating social workers to work more effectively with women. Facts about the historical roots of patriarchy and gender inequality are now generally woven into the curriculum, and feminist social work practice skills are increasingly taught in both core and specialized courses. To be effective, practitioners need continually to be aware of how sexism pervades social work practice, and understand the social, economic and cultural context of women's problems.

Chapter 8 Review
Social Work with Women

Discussion Questions

1. What was the general approach of the early women who were involved in social work?

2. List and define five persistent problems that women in Canadian society confront.

3. What is meant by *the feminization of poverty*?

4. Define and compare the terms *gender equity* and *gender equality*.

5. List and define five components of feminist social work practice.

6. Describe two ways in which social workers put feminist principles into practice.

7. What is the generational cycle of violence?

8. What are two theories that explain violence against women?

9. What is the role of social workers when working with women who have been abused?

Websites

* **Status of Women of Canada**
  http://www.swc-cfc.gc.ca

  Status of Women Canada (SWC) is the federal government agency that promotes gender equality and the full participation of women in the economic, social, cultural and political life of the country. SWC focuses its work in three areas: improving women's economic autonomy and well-being, eliminating systemic violence against women and children and advancing women's human rights.

* **Gender-based Analysis: A Guide for Policy-making**
  http://www.swc-cfc.gc.ca/publish/gbagid-e.html

  This "hands-on" working document developed by Status of Women Canada is a must read for social workers interested in analyzing social policy to assess the differential impact of proposed or existing policies, programs and legislation on women and men. The guide is divided into three sections: Section 1 defines key concepts and provides the rationale for gender-based analysis; Section 2, Policy Development and Analysis Process, outlines a commonly accepted policy analysis process and highlights how sensitivity to gender can be integrated into this process; and Section 3, Gender-Based Analysis Methodology, offers a step-by-step process for gender-based analysis.

* **National Clearinghouse on Family Violence**
  http://www.hc-sc.gc.ca/hppb/familyviolence

  National Clearinghouse on Family Violence is a national resource centre for those seeking information about violence within the family and new resources being used to address it.

Key Terms

* **Maternal feminists**
* **Equal-pay policies**
* **Equal employment and employment equity**
* **Facilitating programs**
* **Gender**
* **Gender equality**
* **Sexism**
* **Patriarchy**
* **Consciousness-raising groups**
* **Feminist theory**
* **Feminist social work practice**
* **Transition houses**
* **Suffragette movement**
* **Sexual assault**
* **Sexual harassment**
* **Power theory**
* **Learning theory**
* **Anger-control theory**
* **Cycle-of-violence theory**
* **Feminization of poverty**
* **Poverty gap**

Poundmaker's Lodge in Edmonton, Alberta, offers programs for Aboriginal people seeking addiction treatment. The Lodge draws heavily on Native traditions and the real-life stories of people before they came to Poundmaker's Lodge.

9

Social Work and Aboriginal Peoples

The Canadian Legacy

This chapter examines social work with Aboriginal peoples. To understand this aspect of contemporary social work and social welfare, however, it is necessary to begin with the history of relations between Aboriginal peoples and the European settlers who made Canada a colony, first of France and then of Britain. With the founding of Canada, the social relations between the original inhabitants and the colonizer were expressed in the *Indian Act* and the reserve system. These continue to shape contemporary relations between Aboriginal peoples and mainstream Canadian society.

The chapter begins by briefly describing the Aboriginal peoples of Canada. It continues with a review of the history of colonialism in Canada and its legacy today. It then goes on to examine the residential schools and early child welfare systems, which were nothing less than attempts to wipe out Aboriginal societies altogether. The chapter examines some of the issues pertaining to providing welfare and social services to Aboriginal peoples, and it outlines the basic principles that underlie an Aboriginal approach to a social work practice. The factors that make various social work interventions successful are discussed, as well as the question of who will provide services to Aboriginal peoples.

"Government policies have been singularly aimed, for over a century, at reducing the differences that exist between Aboriginal life and the mainstream of Canadian society in the hope that Aboriginal peoples would disappear as distinct societies. The extent to which Aboriginal peoples have retained their distinctiveness is a testimonial to their strength and endurance as peoples."

Source: *Justice Murray Sinclair,*
Aboriginal Justice Inquiry of Manitoba
(Manitoba 1991, 97).

Who Are the Aboriginal Peoples?

Aboriginal peoples are the original inhabitants of this portion of the North American landmass known as Canada. Aboriginal peoples have lived upon this land for thousands of years. The term *Indian* is widely understood to have originated with the early explorers who thought they had reached India in their search for a passage to the east. Whether this story is true or not, today the term is used to define a group of indigenous people registered as such according to the *Indian Act*. Menno Boldt notes that the term *Indian* "serves the Canadian government as a convenient political, legal, and administrative categorization of the culturally diverse first peoples of Canada" (1993, 192). It is used in much the same way as *Native,* as a means of "outside-naming" those "who are descendants of the first inhabitants of what is now Canada" (Chartrand 1991, 3–4).

Land claims focus on the need for Aboriginal self-government.

The term *Aboriginal,* another all-encompassing term, "appears to be associated with a general, emerging emancipation of Aboriginal peoples from domination of all sorts by the settler society" (Chartrand 1991, 3–4). Of course, the Aboriginal peoples have their own names for themselves in their respective languages: Anishnaabe, Inuit, Innu, Nuu-chah-nulth, and Métis. The Inuit are Aboriginal peoples of Canada "that have traditionally used and occupied, and currently use and occupy, the lands and waters" ranging from the Yukon and Northwest Territories to northern Quebec and Labrador (Indian and Northern Affairs Canada and Tungavik 1993, 4). On April 1, 1999 marked the creation of Nunavut, a new territory was born from the eastern part of the Northwest Territories. The agreement between the Inuit of Nunavut and the federal government recognizes that the Inuit are best able to define who is an Inuk according to their own understanding of themselves. Like other Aboriginal peoples, the Inuit have a diversity of cultures and ways of living.

The Métis have often been neglected in the consideration of the Aboriginal peoples of Canada, an injustice that obscures their role in the westward expansion of this country. Unlike other Aboriginal peoples, the Métis cannot assert that they have inhabited this continent *as a distinct people* for many thousands of years. According to Purich,

> most often, the term Métis is used to refer to the descendants of the historic Métis — that is, those whose origin can be traced back to the Red River in the early 1800s. These are the people, now located mainly in the prairies and the north, who formed a language and culture, which was a unique blend of Indian, and European cultures (Purich 1988).

When Europeans began to arrive on this continent, Aboriginal peoples numbered between 500,000 and two million. They lived a wide variety of lifestyles, depending on the natural resources available to them. The oral traditions of some Aboriginal cultures assert that the pre-contact population was even greater than the estimates of anthropologists and historians. Across Canada, there were approximately 50 Aboriginal languages spoken, which made up 11 main language groups. Within each Aboriginal language there are also several dialects. For example, the Algonkian language group includes the Ojibway language, which in turn includes the Saulteaux, Odawa, Potowatomi and other dialects.

Aboriginal nations were also characterized by a rich diversity of social organization, including systems of governance, health care practices, and cultural and spiritual rituals. These social aspects were not separated into functionally specialized institutions, but were organized holistically. Such social organization usually included some formal means by which different nations agreed to coexist. Some, such as the Haudenousaunee or the Mi'kmaq, formed confederacies. Much of Aboriginal history is based on unwritten oral accounts passed down over generations. These accounts often contain spiritual concepts foreign to European minds.

Canadian Tourism Commission.

The age profile of the Aboriginal population is relatively young.

• Relationship with Europeans

The relationship between Aboriginal peoples and Europeans was initially harmonious. During the sixteenth and seventeenth centuries, Aboriginal peoples served as partners in exploration and trading. Later, as the English and the French became locked in an imperialistic struggle for control over North America, the relationship with the Aboriginal peoples evolved into a military alliance. As European peoples and their governments exerted dominance over the territories that had been inhabited by the indigenous peoples, the role of Aboriginal peoples gradually changed from one of military allies to one of irrelevance — or worse, an obstacle to imperial domination (Miller 1989, 84).

The movement westward in the later eighteenth and nineteenth centuries caused increasing displacement and conflict for the Aboriginal peoples who lived on the land that the newcomers wanted for agriculture and homesteads. The presence of Aboriginal peoples on these lands demanded a response from the European governments. With the colonization of what would become known as Canada, the land's original inhabitants became "**the Indian problem**," and impediments to "civilization." Colonial representatives and, later, government officials devised various schemes to address the problem, including land-cession treaties and assimilation policies. Such schemes came at an exorbitant cost to the original inhabitants, not only financially, but more importantly in terms of the loss of Aboriginal lives and ways of living.

The interior of a Nootka house, Nootka Sound, circa 1780. The Nootka lived along the west coast of Vancouver Island and the northwest part of Washington. They had a rich culture based on whaling and river fishing.

National Archives of Canada, C70626.

The Colonial Legacy

The policy subsequently adopted by the settlers, best described as colonialism, amounted to nothing less than an attempt to completely subjugate the Aboriginal peoples. As a direct result, among other things, to this day living conditions and income levels for the Aboriginal communities and those living off reserves continue to be lower than for the rest of Canada. Aboriginal people are also more reliant on various forms of social assistance. Typical of this colonial legacy, a primary factor contributing to the high rates of poverty among Aboriginal people is unemployment. According to the 2001 Census data, the unemployment rate for the "Aboriginal Identity Population" was 19.1 percent and the percentage of Aboriginal households living below Low-Income Cut-off (LICO) was 31.2 percent (Statistics Canada 2001).

Aboriginal peoples are also incarcerated in correctional centres and penitentiaries more than other groups. They are twice as likely to be imprisoned in the first place and are more likely to receive a full prison sentence than non-Aboriginal people. The rate of suicide and suicide attempts is at least three to four times higher among Aboriginal peoples, especially among those 15 to 20 years old, than among the rest of Canadians (Royal Commission on Aboriginal Peoples 1995).

These poor social conditions have caused many Aboriginal peoples to leave their own communities for urban centres, particularly within the last thirty years. However, poverty doesn't disappear when Aboriginal people reside in cities. In 1996, 44.5 percent of Aboriginal people lived in metropolitan areas of Canada. Half of these lived in the prairie provinces. Winnipeg has by far the largest Aboriginal population at 43,200 or almost 20 percent of the total urban Aboriginal population (Lee 1999, 9). Of the total Aboriginal urban population, 50.4 percent live below LICO, sometimes referred to as the poverty line, as compared to 21.2 percent of the non-Aboriginal population. Perhaps the most shocking statistic is that 77 percent of Aboriginal lone-parent families live below this line. The poorest urban Aboriginal people live in Saskatoon (63.7 percent), Regina (62.2 percent) and Winnipeg (60.5 percent) (Lee 1999, 10).

Interestingly, while the mainstream Canadian population ages and its birth rate declines, the Aboriginal population continues to grow. Currently, the median age of status Indians recognized as Indians under the *Indian Act* is 10 years younger than the Canadian median age, and for Inuit it is 12 years. While the Canadian population, as a whole, is ageing into retirement, Aboriginal populations are moving from youth into working age (Canadian Medical Association 1993, 7).

Unless real action is taken soon to address and resolve the serious social problems in Aboriginal communities, social alienation and unrest, especially on the part of the growing numbers of Aboriginal youth, is likely to become even more acute.

National Archives of Canada, PA048475.

Aboriginal worker ploughing on a reserve (c. 1920).

• The Indian Act

With the signing of **land-cession treaties** and the adoption of a succession of *Indian Acts*, the government of Canada changed its relationship with the continent's first inhabitants in the later nineteenth century. "The intention of the civil government, now that Indians no longer were militarily useful, was to concentrate Indians in settled areas, or reserves; to subject them to as much proselytization, schooling, and instruction in agriculture as 'circumstances' made necessary" (Miller 1989, 100). The legal instrument for this was the *Indian Act*.

The **Indian Act of 1876** sought to define strictly who would be considered an Indian so as to exert government authority over Aboriginal peoples. The Act fragmented the Aboriginal population into legally distinct groups with different rights, restrictions and obligations. As a consequence, Canada is one of the few countries to have legislated separate laws for a specific group based on race or ethnicity. The *Indian Act* was, and still is, a piece of social legislation of very broad scope that regulates and controls virtually every aspect of Native life.

The so-called **Indian Agent** administered the Act in the Aboriginal communities. These agents were to displace traditional Aboriginal leaders so as to institute a new way of living consistent with the intentions of the Canadian government at the time. The Indian Agents had extraordinary administrative and discretionary powers. In order to ensure this, Clause 25 of the Act established the government's guardianship over Indian lands.

I AM ... FIRST NATIONS

I am First Nations...
no longer burdened with weakness,
from grief and pain of humiliation.
I now stand with dignity and strength
within my Native spirit for I am free.

——
Source: Shirley Kiju Kawi. 1994. I am First Nations. Chester Basin, NS: Mulda'qati Books.

Dr. Clement Bourget, an Indian Agent for the Canadian government, examines an Aboriginal child. Bourget was the Indian Agent for the Fort Resolution agency, which was established in 1923 in the Northwest Territories.

National Archives of Canada, PA102608.

ABORIGINAL WOMEN IN PRISON

The over-representation of Aboriginal people within the Canadian criminal justice system is indisputably the most egregious example of the racist legacy of colonization.

- Aboriginal peoples are 9 times more likely to go to prison than the majority of the non-Aboriginal population in Canada.

- The proportion of Aboriginal women in the federal prisons has been steadily increasing over the past decade. Overall, Aboriginal prisoners were 11% of the jail population in 1992, 16% in 1999, 20% in 2001, and 27% in 2003.

- 45% of Aboriginal women make up the overall prison population, and are estimated to represent 90-99% of the population in some provincial jails, even though Aboriginal women only make up 1-2% of the Canadian population.

- In 1998-1999, of all adult women admitted into provincial prisons in Alberta, 56% were of Aboriginal ancestry.

- Aboriginal women are also disproportionately over classified as maximum security prisoners. 40-50% of federally sentenced women who are classified as maximum security prisoners are Aboriginal.

Source: Factsheet. Elizabeth Fry Week 2003 . Available at: http://www.elizabethfry.ca/eweek03/factsht.htm#prison

The social control aspects of the *Indian Act* placed Canada's First Nations firmly in the position of a colonized people. The Act spelled out a process of enfranchisement whereby Indians could acquire full Canadian citizenship only by relinquishing their ties to their community; that is, by giving up their culture and traditions and any rights to land. Consequently, the cost of Canadian citizenship demanded of an Aboriginal person far surpassed that for an immigrant to Canada. The Canadian government saw the *Indian Act* as a temporary measure to control Aboriginal peoples until they had been fully assimilated through enfranchisement. Assimilation refers to the absorbing of one cultural group into another. It was not until 1960, however, that the government granted Indians the right to vote in federal elections — for the first time, citizenship for Aboriginal peoples was not conditional upon their assimilation into mainstream Canadian society.

Once land was ceded and Canadian settlements had been established, Aboriginal peoples were shunted aside onto small parcels of land largely devoid of any economic potential. This land could not even be used as collateral to develop business ventures, since that land was held "in trust." It has been argued that by confining Aboriginal peoples to reserves, Inuit communities and Métis settlements

> the welfare of Aboriginal societies was systematically neglected. Famines and tuberculosis were allowed to virtually decimate Aboriginal communities, unaided except for relocation of survivors to state institutions. Housing provided was of the poorest quality, and health care and education were until quite recently, left to the Church (Scott 1994, 7).

The federal government then established the Department of Indian Affairs as the main vehicle to regulate and control Aboriginal movement and ways of living.

• Racist Legislation

The *Indian Act*, still in force, certainly seems to be wildly out of step with the bulk of Canadian law. It singles out a segment of society — largely on the basis of race — removes much of their land and property from the commercial mainstream, and gives the Minister of Indian and Northern Affairs and other government officials a degree of discretion that is not only intrusive but frequently offensive.

The Act has been roundly criticized. Many want it abolished because it violates normative standards of equality, and these critics tend to be non-Aboriginal; others want First Nations to be able to make their own decisions as self-governing polities and see the Act as inhibiting that freedom. Even within its provisions, others see unfair treatment between, for example, Indians who live on reserves and those who reside elsewhere. In short, this is a statute of which few speak well. (Bill Henderson has annotated the *Indian Act*, and placed it on-line at http://www.bloorstreet.com/200block/sindact.htm.)

• The Métis and Inuit

The situation among the Métis in the late nineteenth and early twentieth centuries was unique. The Métis in western Canada could seek to become status Indians by aligning themselves to certain treaty areas or they could "take scrip." The **scrip system** entitled the bearer of a scrip certificate to either land or money; in exchange, the person who took scrip gave up all further claims to land. Although the scrip system offered to the Métis was different from the treaty-making process for Indians, the result was the same. Neither Métis nor Indian had been treated fairly (Purich 1988, 125).

The *Indian Act* also governed the Inuit. No land was formally set aside for their use nor were any treaties signed with the Inuit peoples. Because of the extensive mineral and oil exploration on their lands, Inuit communities have been relocated, forcing a change in their lifestyle.

One gross example of the nature of state intervention in Inuit lives is the **disk list system**. As bureaucrats could not or would not acknowledge the Inuktitut names for individuals, the disk list system assigned a numbered disk to each Inuk. Although not universally employed, the disk list system "ultimately came to define the quasi-legal Eskimo status which had an impact on virtually all aspects of Eskimo social life as an intensely administered population within Canadian society" (Smith 1993, 64). (The term *Eskimo* in references to the Native peoples of the Canadian Arctic and Greenland is now considered to be offensive.)

National Archives of Canada. PA012854.

Councillors of the Provincial Government of the Métis Nation. Louis Riel is located in the centre row, third from left. Manitoba, c. 1870.

Child Welfare and Residential School System

The now-infamous **residential school system** was established in the mid-1900s by Indian Affairs in conjunction with several Christian churches. Native children were removed from their Native communities and placed in residential schools. By restricting Native culture and language, the schools sought to fulfill the **assimilationist policies** of the federal government. The children were denied their language, spiritual rituals and, more importantly, access to their families. Aboriginal children were often subjected to emotional, physical and sexual abuse.

As a result of their having resided within an institution that regulated every aspect of their lives, the Aboriginals' decision-making skills were impaired: "residential schools were no preparation for life in any type of community" (Armitage 1993, 142). Some struggled with drug and alcohol addiction and problems with mental health that arose from the psychological trauma they had endured. Many found themselves with a limited ability to parent their own children, as parenting models had been unavailable to them.

While many individuals who emerged from these institutions retained a positive outlook, a true testament to their adaptability and resilience, it must be stressed that the residential school experience systematically crippled many Aboriginal children and families. This legacy will take many generations to heal.

National Archives of Canada, PA42122.

The intent of the residential schools policy was to erase Aboriginal identity by separating generations of children from their families and socializing them in mainstream culture. Above: Aboriginal pupils at the Roman Catholic Mission in Fort Resolution, NT.

• "The Scoop"

In 1951, the *Indian Act* was amended such that provincial laws of application (and therefore child welfare legislation) applied to reserves (Timpson 1990, 54). With this legislative change, the government's approach to Aboriginal assimilation veered from residential schools towards the apprehension and placement of Native children in non-Native foster homes. Child welfare agencies assumed responsibility for services to Aboriginal communities.

One result is what is known as "the Scoop." In the 1960s, massive numbers of children were removed from their communities and placed in non-Aboriginal foster and adoptive homes. By the late 1970s and early 1980s, at any given time one in seven status Indian children was not in the care of his or her parents, and as many as one in four status Indian children was spending at least some time away from the parental home (Armitage 1993, 147). Between 1959 and 1970, the percentage of Native children made legal wards of the state increased from 1 percent of all children in care to 30–40 percent (Fournier and Crey 1998, 83). Recently, Assembly of First Nations Chief Phil Fontaine reported that the number of status Indians removed from their homes and into care comprises 30–40 percent of all children in care in Canada. This represents 8,000 status Indian children on reserve in Care. When non-status Indians, Inuit and Métis are brought into the picture, over one half of the children currently in care are Aboriginal (Curry 2005).

• Aboriginal Child Welfare Agencies

In 1981, the federal government entered into agreements with the provinces, insisting that child and family services for Aboriginal peoples adhere to provincial standards and regulations. Under this legislative mandate, many Aboriginal welfare agencies came to resemble mainstream service providers. While it was recognized that a distinctive Aboriginal approach was required in order to redress the damage done over generations, the provincial welfare system did not foster it.

Canadian child welfare authorities subsequently recognized the damage caused by this approach, and the federal government has made efforts to fund Aboriginal child welfare agencies. In 1990–91, the federal government funded 36 Aboriginal child and family agencies, covering 212 bands; in this same period, a total of $1.5 million over a period of two years was allocated to First Nations for the development of Aboriginal child and family service standards.

Most Aboriginal child care agencies have adopted placement protocols that specify the following placement preferences: first, with the extended family; second, with Aboriginal members of the community with the same cultural and linguistic identification; and third, other alternative Aboriginal caregivers. As a last resort, placement is considered with non-Aboriginal caregivers.

ABORIGINAL CHILDREN IN CARE TODAY

"The Scoop" of the 1960s appears to be occurring again today, and recent data shows that it may, in fact, be worse.

According to Cindy Blackstock, a member of the Gitksan Nation and Executive Director of the First Nations Child and Family Caring Society of Canada (FNCFCS), there are currently over 22,500 First Nations children in the care of child welfare authorities and few of these children will be placed with Aboriginal families.

The rate at which First Nations children on reserve are entering foster care has increased by 71.5% from 1995–2001 based on Indian and Northern Affairs Canada (INAC) data.

Source: Blackstock, Cindy (2003) Pre-Conference Interview, Social Inclusion Research Conference, Canadian Council on Social Development, Ottawa. Retrieved from: http://www.ccsd.ca/events/inclusion/papers/interview-blackstock.htm on April 10, 2005.

There needs to be a respect for Aboriginal traditions in child care.

Government Policy Objectives

In *Arduous Journey: Canadian Indians and Decolonization*, Roger Gibbins and Rick Pointing outline the major goals of national government public policy towards Aboriginal peoples (Gibbins and Ponting 1986). While these are historical, many remain with us today.

Protection. Some officials developing policy at the time were very aware of the problems of alcoholism, greed and prostitution that flourished on the frontier of Canada. Some had "humanitarian" goals and sought to protect Aboriginal people until they could be assimilated into white society. This led to laws prohibiting the sale of Aboriginal land, the use of alcohol by Aboriginal people and the prostitution of Aboriginal women. These officials saw the reservation system as a way to isolate and protect Aboriginal people. It can also be argued that these goals of protection were mostly illusory, glossing over the underlying goal of exploitation. For example, by isolating Aboriginals on reserves the government was free to exploit the vast Aboriginal lands.

Assimilation. The central pillar or thrust of federal government policy was assimilation — that is, to prepare Aboriginal peoples for complete absorption into Canadian society. It was desired and expected that eventually all Aboriginal people would give up their Native customs, culture and beliefs and become like those of the dominant society. The failure of this assimilation process can largely be attributed to barriers posed by systemic and societal discrimination. As Gibbins and Pointing state, "government policy tried to induce Indians into a mainstream that was unwilling to receive them." Another aspect of this failure is the extent and success of Aboriginal activism today.

Christanization. To the colonial government, the civilizing of the Aboriginal peoples was synonymous with their Christanization. Aboriginal ceremonies and cultural practices were officially discouraged or outlawed. Education through church residential schools was seen as a way to destroy the social, spiritual and cultural systems and relations of the Aboriginal people. Because the residential schools isolated Aboriginal people from the mainstream, they worked at cross purposes to the goal of assimilation.

Land surrender. The desire by the government to obtain land held by Aboriginal peoples for the settlement of non-Aboriginal people was a primary goal. Reserves were seen as a way to move them into agriculturally based communities, both to assimilate them and to free vast tracks of land for non-Aboriginal settlement. As immigration increased, the government moved to make more and more "excess Indian land available for non-Indian settlement." Further to this end, numerous treaties were signed between First Nations peoples and colonial officials between 1670 and 1923. While the treaties were quite different in their terms and complexity, they generally served to establish peaceful relations, institute payments and gain the surrender of land. The major

WHAT MAKES YOU THINK YOU'RE DISTINCT?

Susan Dewar.

Assimilationist policies run counter to Aboriginal self-government.

treaties were signed in the west, starting with Treaty #1 in 1871 and ending with Treaty #10 in 1906. This allowed the vast territories of the west to be settled and the construction of the CP railway. It is important to note that no treaties were signed between the First Peoples of Quebec, the Maritimes and most of British Columbia. In fact, almost half of the population of registered Indians did not sign land treaties. These treaties (in many cases, the lack of them) are now disputed across the country.

Government authority. As discussed above, a major goal of the *Indian Act* was to give sweeping power and authority to the colonial administrators. This external political control is a fundamental aspect of colonization. In the case of Canada, it was explicitly embodied in the *Indian Act*. The assistant deputy minister of Indian Affairs branch described the *Indian Act* as follows: "The Indian Act is a lands act. It is a municipal act, an educational act, and a societies act. It is primarily social legislation, but it has a very broad scope: there are provisions about liquor, agricultural and mining as well as Indian lands, band membership and so forth. It has elements that are embodied in perhaps two dozen different acts of any of the provinces and overrides some federal legislation in some respects... It has the force of the criminal Code and the impact of a constitution on those people and communities that come within its purview" (Gibbins and Ponting 1986, 19).

"it is crucial to recognize that the social condition of Aboriginal people is a direct result of the discriminatory and repressive policies that successive European and Canadian governments have directed towards Aboriginal people."

Source: Manitoba Justice Murray Sinclair.

National Archives of Canada, PA129879.

Inuit mother and children sign for family allowance at Royal Canadian Mounted Police office in Coppermine, Northwest Territories, in 1949. Income security programs like this were available, but not without conditions.

THE INNU OF LABRADOR

The terms of union under which Newfoundland joined Confederation in 1949 make no mention of Aboriginal peoples. Arrangements for service delivery to the Innu and others were made later, under a series of federal-provincial agreements. Until recently, the government of Newfoundland provided all health, education, welfare and related services, and the federal government contributed 90 percent of the cost of programs the province chose to deliver. The federal government has now begun to provide direct funding to the Innu for some–but not all– health and social programs.

The Innu have long held that federal refusal to treat them in the same way they treat First Nations registered under the *Indian Act* for purposes of program and service delivery constitutes discrimination, an infringement of their rights as Aboriginal people, and an abrogation of fundamental federal responsibilities.

_____

Source: The Final Report of the Royal Commission on Aboriginal Peoples (1996). The Institute of Indigenous Government makes this material freely available: http://www.indigenous.bc.ca/rcap.htm

Income Security and Health Care

Although income security and health care in Canada are available to every citizen who meets the conditions of a particular program, a double standard has existed for Aboriginal peoples.

• Income Security

Until the early 1900s, any kind of relief taken from the trust accounts of Indian bands was granted at the discretion of the local Indian Agent. The decision to grant relief was based on the old practice of distinguishing between the "deserving" and the "undeserving" poor — and Aboriginal people were generally considered undeserving. These rations were grossly inadequate and were used just as much as a means to sanction behaviour as for relief (Moscovitch and Webster 1995, 211). When "the first universal and statutory old age pension was enacted in 1927 it excluded Indians and Inuit, but was available to the Métis" (Scott 1994, 18). The first *Unemployment Insurance Act*, passed in 1940, also excluded most Aboriginal people from eligibility (ibid., 20).

Between 1951 and 1966 the Indian relief system collapsed and was replaced by access to the mainstream welfare state (Moscovitch and Webster 1995). This occurred after the development of several federal Acts related to income security, amendments to the *Indian Act* in 1951 and the establishment of the Canada Assistance Plan. Through the development of an administrative structure with huge discretionary powers that minimized community control, the government of Canada effectively came to control the day-to-day lives of Aboriginal peoples across the country.

• Health Care

Until the mid-1900s, the federal government directly delivered virtually all programs and services to First Nations. In the 1950s, the responsibility for health care was transferred to the medical services branch of the Department of Health and Welfare. This led to the development of a system of primary care clinics, public health programs and regional hospitals for Aboriginal peoples. Unfortunately, this change did not mean an end to the denigration of Aboriginal cultures or the isolation of Aboriginal peoples from their own societies. Health care was still provided by non-Aboriginal practitioners who had little or no sensitivity to the differing cultural and social systems among Aboriginal peoples. Well into the twentieth century, for example, the *Indian Act* outlawed the spiritual ceremonies of Aboriginal peoples, reflecting the assumption that indigenous healing methods were non-existent or ineffective. As a result, "encounters were often clouded by suspicion, misunderstanding, resentment, and racism" (Scott 1994, 8). These feelings were exacerbated when Aboriginal peoples were removed from their communities to outside medical facilities for treatment.

Young Innu of Labrador

Perhaps nothing better illustrates the tragedy bestowed on Aboriginal peoples by successive federal and provincial governments than the plight of the Innu of Labrador.

• Sheshatshiu

In November 2000, Peter Penashue, president of the Innu Nation, reported that there were at least thirty children sniffing gas in Sheshatshiu, a village of 1,200 people and part of an Innu community of about 1,800 in Labrador. What was unique was the fact that the chief of Labrador's largest Innu community was requesting that the provincial government get involved and take the children out of the community to ensure that they received the treatment that they needed.

This situation sparked debate about the role of non-Aboriginal social workers. The legacy of government policy had left the Innu community without opportunities or prospects and many were rightly skeptical of the help that outsiders could provide. Yet the situation in Sheshatshiu was clearly desperate and the leaders were calling for help. (In the end, these children were taken to centres elsewhere for treatment.)

• Davis Inlet

Meanwhile, Davis Inlet, another Innu community in Labrador, had even bigger problems. The town had been established in 1967 after government officials decided the nomadic Innu should settle down. They were promised comfortable homes with indoor plumbing. Instead, the residents found themselves living in squalor and slipping out of touch with their traditional way of life. Violence and addiction were widespread in the community. In 1993, Davis Inlet made headlines in Canada and around the world after a police officer released a video-tape showing six Innu children getting high by sniffing gasoline and shouting that they wanted to die. A government response was required.

The federal government finally moved into action and subsequently spent about $200 million carving out the new community of Natuashish, 15 kilometres away on the Labrador mainland, where they built and furnished modern split-level bungalows for the Innu to live in. The move began in December 2002 and was completed within seven months. However, as might have been expected, the new houses in Natuashish became homes to the same old social problems in Davis Inlet. A recent report by an Ottawa-based consulting company warned that, despite the millions of dollars spent by the federal government on this new town, there was virtually no progress. Moreover, there are only two social workers trying to cope with a staggering caseload. And, according to a report on child, youth and family services, the social work system is in a crisis and about to tip over into disaster.

The community of Natuashish was created on the Labrador mainland.

The Institute of Indigenous Government makes the entire 3,200–page Report accessible through on-line search features and download capabilities.

The Report can be found at: http://www.indigenous.bc.ca

Royal Commission on Aboriginal Peoples

The **Royal Commission on Aboriginal Peoples (RCAP)** of 1996 brought together six years of research and public consultation on First Nations issues. It was the most concise and comprehensive distillation of material on First Nations issues ever published and provides the factual basis for significant strides forward. Among the many issues discussed, the Report examines the need for Aboriginal people to heal from the consequences of domination, displacement and assimilation.

The conclusion of the Commission was that the relationship between Aboriginal and non-Aboriginal people for the last 400 years was built on "false premises" — government policies over this period that were always presented as beneficial invariably resulted in harm. The foundation for a renewed relationship, according to the Report, involves a recognition of Aboriginal nations as political entities.

• Core Recommendations

At the core of the Report's 440 recommendations is a rebalancing of political and economic power between Aboriginal nations and other Canadian governments. The Report points to five key themes:

1. Aboriginal nations have to be reconstituted.
2. A process must be established for the assumption of powers by Aboriginal nations.
3. There must be a reallocation of lands and resources.
4. Aboriginal people need education and crucial skills for governance and economic self-reliance.
5. There must be economic development if the poverty and despondency of lives defined by unemployment and welfare are to change.

As part of this, there also has to be a sincere acknowledgment by non-Aboriginal people of the injustices of the past.

• Aboriginal Social Services

With respect to social services, the Commission recommended incorporating traditional knowledge and training in the development of Aboriginal health and social work. It also recommended that mainstream social work and social service systems be adapted to complement Aboriginal institutions.

The Report notes that Aboriginal peoples want to develop and control health and social services for both urban and on-reserve communities. The control of social services by external agencies and bureaucracies continues to frustrate attempts to organize holistic responses to need, and variations in available services reflect systematic inequities rather than adaptations to community diversity. The fact that

health and social services are under the authority of provincial legislation while funding obligations are a federal responsibility often creates barriers. First Nations are asking that federal, provincial and territorial governments, in consultation with Aboriginal nations and urban communities, cooperate to establish new funding and programs.

Beyond the development of services controlled by Aboriginal people, the Report outlines how the transformation of mainstream social services could make a more positive contribution to the well-being of Aboriginal people. Owing to the small population and remoteness of many Aboriginal communities, some health and social services, particularly specialized services, may be available only from mainstream providers. Initiatives to improve the effectiveness of mainstream health and social service programs will need to take many forms, including:

- affirmative action and employment equity hiring policies;
- specialized Aboriginal units staffed by Aboriginal employees within larger mainstream programs;
- cross-cultural education programs for non-Aboriginal staff;
- Aboriginal input into mainstream programs and decisions; and
- Aboriginal customary practices included in the services offered by mainstream agencies.

CP PHOTO/Shaney Komulainen,

Canadian soldier Patrick Cloutier and Aboriginal activist come face-to-face in a tense standoff at the Kahnesatake reserve in Oka, Quebec (September 1, 1990). The "Oka Crisis" reflected the growing frustrations in Aboriginal communities across Canada.

• Aboriginal Healing

A prominent theme throughout the Report is the restoration of Aboriginal health from the wounds of culture loss, paternalistic and racist treatment, and official policies of assimilation. The Report details how healing is already underway in many communities and how restoring communities and nations to unity and harmony is an extension of healing at the personal level.

The Royal Commission on Aboriginal Peoples acknowledged that the convergence between Aboriginal perspectives and Western science provides a powerful foundation for moving forward. The core of the strategy is to develop a system of healing centres in urban, rural and reserve settings for front-line services and healing lodges for residential treatment. These would operate under Aboriginal control and deliver integrated health and social services. Sagamok Anishnabek First Nation, a reserve of just over 1,000 people located in the village of Blind River along the north shores of Lake Huron, developed such a centre.

The Report acknowledges that Aboriginal people have also developed alternative correction programs that actually work. Although they are still few and far between, they bear little resemblance to conventional correctional services. The Aboriginal approach typically involves a healing lodge, bush camps and wilderness programs. They also work with traditional skills and spiritual practices. In taking a "justice as healing" approach, they look at the whole of the person's life.

CP PHOTO/Winnipeg Free Press-Joe Bryksa.

Volunteers of Ganootamaage Justice Services in Winnipeg hand down the first sentence by a healing circle under a new provincial program for Aboriginal offenders in Winnipeg, Manitoba.

Aboriginal Social Work Practice — Four Principles

Two factors make it difficult to formulate a comprehensive **Aboriginal approach to social work practice.** First, the Aboriginal peoples of Canada are exceedingly diverse, with many languages, cultures and traditions, and Aboriginal peoples have a variety of healing and helping philosophies and techniques. Second, a legacy of mistrust and animosity exists towards those in the helping professions, including social work. An Aboriginal approach to social work needs to be flexible enough to incorporate a variety of healing methods and must avoid repeating the mistakes of the past. It is imperative that the approach be based on the wants of Aboriginal peoples and give power to Aboriginal communities.

An Aboriginal approach to social work does not mean that mainstream methods are of no value. The Nechi Institute, founded in 1974 by a group of elders located in Edmonton, is a good example of a training organization that incorporates both traditional Aboriginal and mainstream standards (http://www.nechi.com). Their holistic approach is based on the belief that true physical, mental, emotional and spiritual healing occurs when an individual is in harmony with his or her environment. They also contend that problems must be understood within the context of history, community setting, personal experience, culture and the social institutions that have had influence on the individual.

The development of an Aboriginal approach to social work practice should be consistent with four key principles. These principles are:

(1) the recognition of a distinct Aboriginal worldview;

(2) the development of Aboriginal consciousness regarding the impact of colonialism;

(3) an emphasis on the importance of cultural knowledge and traditions; and

(4) the use of the concept of Aboriginal empowerment.

These principles need to be practiced alongside adherence to a holistic approach, a belief in equity, Aboriginal self-control and a respect for diversity (Morrissette, McKenzie, and Morrissette 1993, 91).

• Distinct Aboriginal Worldview

The first principle acknowledges that there is a distinct **Aboriginal worldview.** The First Nations of Canada are diverse and culturally distinct, and therefore each may have a different approach to healing and helping. While Aboriginal peoples do not have one single philosophy or worldview, one can draw upon the fundamental differences between non-Aboriginal and Aboriginal worldviews. For example, the concept of the circle captured in the Medicine Wheel illustrates the notion of balance prevalent in Aboriginal societies, in contrast to the typically linear models of cause and effect common in Western society.

Aboriginal social work starts with an appreciation of a unique world view.

TEP Photo Archives.

• Impact of Colonialism

The second principle involves an analysis of the impact of colonization, which has greatly contributed to the current situation in Aboriginal communities. Colonizers attempted to subordinate Aboriginal peoples and displace traditional spirituality, governance systems, leadership and knowledge by using missionaries, residential schools, child welfare and artificial legal distinctions in the *Indian Act*. Using the reserve system and treaties, the colonizers also sought to subordinate Aboriginal economic systems in order to facilitate the extraction of benefits for themselves. A recognition and analysis of colonialism will assist the social worker in framing problems, in recognizing solutions that emphasize self-determination and in seeing the importance of the reclamation of Aboriginal culture and identity in the social work process.

Residential schools and child welfare work in First Nations communities are illustrative of the damage done by colonialism. Even today, social work with Native families is premised on the Western perception that individuals are members of nuclear families that provide economic support and affection, and that individuals can turn to specialized institutions for problem-specific help. This is not consistent with the Aboriginal view. Aboriginal peoples often perceive themselves to be members of a family network in which everyone is obliged to contribute their resources and support all community members.

These dissimilar conceptions of family, community and social obligation lead to different ideas about how to carry out social work, as described by an Anishnabe social worker and his colleagues:

> Members of the Aboriginal community potentially (and normally do) play multiple roles in relation to one another — friend, neighbour, relative, and community service volunteer, as well as job-related service giver and receiver roles. All of these roles are reciprocal, each (at least potentially) being played by each person in relation to all others in the community.

> The individual or family who is the focus of concern assumes the role of "client" [in the] system — a more dependent and generally stigmatized role. In like manner, the community member functioning in the job of human service worker is cast in the role of "worker" — a more powerful and generally more expert role. The worker is not seen by formal human service agencies as an individual simply fulfilling an expected role in the mutual aid system of the Aboriginal community. In the formal system, the worker-client role relationship becomes single faceted rather than multiple, and uni-directional (helper-helped) rather than reciprocal. Both worker and client become removed and isolated from the interpersonal network that gives their needs and behaviour meaning and that will ultimately provide the support and resources, or obstacles, to satisfaction of those needs.

CP PHOTO/Ryan Remiorz.

Legacy of colonialism: substance abuse today is a serious problem.

The discrepancy between Aboriginal ways of helping and conventional social work services are even more pronounced when the worker is an outsider to the community. The conventional methods of social work, in which community members are required to turn to outside agencies for help, weakens internal bonds of mutual aid. People in Aboriginal communities begin to question their ability to help one another as they are unable to contribute to the external social work process that becomes the community's source of help. This situation fosters dependent relationships and weakens the traditional community bonds of mutual aid.

• Cultural Knowledge and Traditions

The third principle of reclaiming Aboriginal culture emphasizes an awareness of and reflection on common aspects of culture and identity. By examining Aboriginal history, culture and traditions and dispelling the conventional views of Aboriginal reality flowing from colonialism, Aboriginal people can begin to see the underlying causes of their individual problems. Of course, there may be differences in how much individuals identify with traditional Aboriginal culture and therefore in how much the reclamation of Aboriginal culture will assist in social work intervention. Some will adhere to the teaching of elders and follow traditional ways, while others may not.

CP PHOTO/Medicine Hat News-Ryan Taplin.

Social workers examine rock formations thought to be Aboriginal burial grounds in Medicine Hat, Alberta, showing a new sensitivity to Aborginal history and cultural traditions.

In many cases, traditional healing techniques and teachings will be combined with non-traditional methods. This combining of traditional healing and mainstream techniques is evident at the Strong Earth Woman Lodge in Manitoba, where the power of Aboriginal spirituality and traditional teachings are combined with crisis intervention techniques. Working with the Sagkeeng First Nation, Strong Earth Woman Lodge has a holistic healing centre based on Native spirituality and traditional teachings. They see holistic healing as the healing of the mind, body, emotions and spirit. Traditionally, this is done through sweat lodges; fasts; vision quests; herbal medicines; ceremonial healing with the eagle fan and rattles, in which sacred songs and the drum are key components; traditional teachings at the sacred fire; sharing circles; individualized counselling; and guidance and direction through traditional teachings.

The Strong Earth Woman Lodge incorporates any or all of these into an individualized program based on the needs of each client. All clients are instructed in the seven sacred teachings and are encouraged to seek understanding of the four elements — fire, earth, water and air — and the four directions. The seven sacred teachings are respect, love, courage, humility, honesty, wisdom and truth. These teachings are carried by the spirits of the Buffalo, Eagle, Bear, Wolf, and Sabe, which is the Giant Beaver and Turtle respectively. The Lodge offers 24–hour care service towards holistic healing for grieving, loss of identity and suicide crisis intervention.

• Empowerment

In the context of social work, the principle of **Aboriginal empowerment** emphasizes the participation of community members in bring about lasting social change. For example, the National Aboriginal Women's Association (NAWA), a not-for-profit, non-governmental, membership-based organization formed in 2001, stresses empowerment of Aboriginal women as the means to provide for the betterment of the political, economic, and social conditions for Aboriginal peoples, families, communities, and Nations.

The tragedy of the Innu Nation of Labrador illustrates how important empowerment is to community healing (see page 207). Chief Tshakapesh stressed the need to involve Innu members in finding long-term solutions to the problems of substance abuse and suicide among their children. He criticized the federal and Newfoundland governments for imposing unsuccessful programs on his community in the past: "We are here today because the solutions didn't work. We will never allow others to control our future."

At its most basic level, the principle of empowerment implies that services must be defined and controlled by those persons or groups seeking help.

TEP Photo Archives.

Young Aboriginal social worker speaks at CASSW meeting, 2004.

Holistic Healing

Traditionally, many Aboriginal people have used some form of the "healing circle" to underpin their approach to healing. The circle is representative of the fact that we are all one and that the entire universe is connected. The circle appraoch can also serve to teach social workers to balance or consider all aspects of a presenting problem. Another basic teaching common to many First Nations is the four sacred directions of North, South, East and West. These directions likewise represent aspects of life that must be considered when looking at a situation.

In many Aboriginal societies, the circle and the four sacred directions are the symbols of holistic healing, embodying the four elements of whole health:

- spiritual health, which can mean many things depending on the individual's approach to spirituality, and may include participating in ceremonies, gaining traditional knowledge and exploring his or her spiritual heritage;
- mental health, which includes education, knowledge of Aboriginal history and cultural contributions, and activities that promote self-confidence;
- physical health, including nutrition, sports and recreation, and cultural activities; and
- emotional health, gained through access to sharing circles, counsellors and elders.

The circle best captures what is often referred to as a **holistic approach to healing** (looking at the physical, emotional, spiritual and mental aspects of a problem or situation). For example, an approach that stresses only the psychological aspects of a problem would not be consistent with these teachings. Social workers using the circle to inform their practice would begin with the physical aspect, and then move to the mental, the emotional, and the spiritual. After going around the wheel completely, the social work practitioner would begin again, ony at a deeper level.

The tragedy of the Innu of Davis Inlet in Labrador illustrates the importance of the healing circle (see page 207). The community captured national attention in January 1993 when television stations across the country reported youth suicide attempts. Seventeen youths were sent to the Poundmaker Lodge in Alberta for substance abuse treatment, yet when the youth returned to the community, many resumed abusing substances. Their bodies had been healed, but there was nothing to nourish their minds, emotions or spirits. In order to have a lasting effect, healing must address not only individuals, but also the community; not only the physical, but also the spiritual, emotional and mental aspects of life. The initiative to heal must be holistic and must come from, and be rooted in, the community.

A healing lodge participant holds a "talking stick" and feathers.

CP PHOTO/David McCord.

The holistic approach to healing at Matootoo Lake, near the Peguis First Nation in Manitoba, successfully benefits young women and men. Traditional teachings are offered. *Matootoo* is the Ojibwa word for sweat lodge and is a place where traditional elders used to come for specific medicines. The teachings presented at Matootoo Lake prepare young women for their emotional, physical and spiritual transition to womanhood. A major goal of the program is to reduce the number of unplanned pregnancies by helping young women acquire confidence in their ability to deal with sexuality. A parallel program for boys is designed to enhance their self-esteem, develop respect for girls and women, and raise awareness of issues such as violence against women. The program has a great deal of local credibility, and the demand for services outstrips availability. The program exemplifies how a properly structured social work approach, rooted in the community, can successfully heal.

• Healing Lodges

Community healing centres that incorporate an Aboriginal approach to social work are opening across Canada. They provide a forum for exploring how Aboriginal and mainstream approaches can be brought together to meet Aboriginal community needs. Traditional healers, elders, community health representatives, medical interpreters, nurses, addiction counsellors, midwives, therapists, social workers, doctors, psychologists and rehabilitation specialists may all come together, depending on the situation in the community.

There has also been a marked increase in the number of **healing lodges** that provide residential treatment for people who are overwhelmed by social, emotional and spiritual problems. There are currently approximately 50 such treatment facilities that provide Aboriginal residential healing. The Nechi Institute and Poundmaker's Lodge in Alberta, for example, provide healing and lodging for people dealing with addictions. First Nations and Inuit have identified the need for such lodges, since most Aboriginal people suffering from addictions and substance abuse continue to receive treatment in urban medical facilities, isolated from their communities and culture.

The integration of an Aboriginal approach to mainstream social work services is not always straightforward. Federal and provincial governments often legislate the work of social workers in state agencies. To secure funding for these needed services, First Nations are obliged to follow rules and procedures. However, First Nations are developing intervention processes that slot Aboriginal healing practices into the legislated practices. For example, a child welfare worker may apprehend a child who has been abused as stipulated by legislation and the court system. The next step, however, may be a holistic conflict-resolution sentencing circle based on an Aboriginal approach to healing.

CP PHOTO/Ruth Bonneville.

Garette Courchene finds healing in Winnipeg's urban sweat lodge.

In their *Atikamekw Social Policy* regulations, the Atikamekw Nation stipulates an intervention process that is responsive to the social needs of Atikamekw communities and is a part of a self-government process, but also complies with provincial government legislation. They outline fairly typical mainstream "temporary measures for protection of a child or youth," and then proceed to detail Aboriginal processes of healing. These processes include Family Council, the Circle of the Wise Counsel, and a Circle of Helpers. The Family Council process involves numerous family members and community participants. In a case where the family, friends and community cannot resolve the problem adequately, a Circle of the Wise Counsel replaces the Family Council. The Circle of Helpers, which includes social workers, is responsible for implementing the intervention plan. The social worker is called a Community Protection Delegate, signifying that the worker represents the protection interests of the community.

The community healing centres and the child welfare policy of the Atikamekw demonstrate how the incorporation of mainstream social work techniques into an Aboriginal approach to healing can work as effective social work practice models. Once again, at the root of this success is the recognition of a distinct Aboriginal worldview, the development of Aboriginal consciousness regarding the impact of colonialism, an emphasis on cultural knowledge and traditions, and the empowerment of communities to control their own futures.

Clare McNab of the Okimas Ohci Healing Lodge in Maple Creek, Saskatchewan, talks about the spiritual aspects of Okimaw Ohci. In the background is the spiritual lodge where the morning healing circle is held.

THE KEKINAN CENTRE

The KeKiNan Centre was started by the Manitoba Indian Nurses Association and the Indian and Métis Senior Citizens Group of Winnipeg in 1991 to provide culturally appropriate services. It was the first urban senior citizens home for Aboriginal people.

The Centre provides geriatric care for Aboriginal elders in Winnipeg, 30 enriched (or supportive) housing units and a number of personal care (geriatric) units. The philosophy of KeKiNan is consistent with an Aboriginal approach to social work, as it seeks to ensure that the people at the Centre play a major role in making decisions that affect their lives.

The seniors become role models for the Aboriginal youth by teaching them about culture and traditions.

Assembly of First Nations logo, with an explanation: http://www.afn.ca.

Urban Social Services for Aboriginal Peoples

Many Canadians think of Aboriginal people as living on reserves or in rural areas. This is a misperception, since almost half of Aboriginal people in Canada live in cities and towns. As many Aboriginal people live in Winnipeg as in the whole of the Northwest Territories. Aboriginal people who live off the reserve are often left with no alternative to mainstream conventional social work services, as few urban centres offer distinct Aboriginal social services.

Many Aboriginal people migrating to urban centres are women moving to the city to escape abuse, seek healing or find employment. This naturally distances Aboriginal women from their community support networks and makes it very difficult for them to maintain a connection to their culture. Access to their teachers, grandmothers, clan mothers and healers is limited.

Off-reserve Aboriginal women have also found mainstream social work services to be less than welcoming. At the Royal Commission on Aboriginal Peoples hearings, women stated that the existing services were not culturally sensitive nor designed with an Aboriginal approach to social work in mind.

> When a non-native woman goes in they don't even bother to take her children away. They are there to comfort her and give her counselling. When people like me or someone else goes in, right away they take their children. You really have to fight to hang on to them. You really have to prove yourself as a mother, and the other non-native women do not have to do so (Ellison 1992).

Aboriginal people have found that mainstream social work services rarely offer traditional spiritual practices, access to elders, healing medicines or women's teachings that reflect Aboriginal values. They have also found that the social workers in mainstream agencies are not trained to be culturally aware and sensitive nor do they know how to deal with issues critical to Aboriginal women, such as cultural expectations with regard to family roles and the impact of colonization.

Social work for Aboriginal people living in non-Aboriginal communities requires a combination of specific services geared to the distinct needs of Aboriginal women and men, and the development of culturally competent social workers in mainstream services that do not re-victimize and isolate. Aboriginal men and women have voiced a strong desire for culturally appropriate services, and have worked to develop Aboriginal urban institutions and networks.

Non-Aboriginal social work practitioners can play an important role in providing social services to Aboriginal people, both in Aboriginal communities and in urban settings. To do so, however, requires a commitment on their part to develop and apply knowledge and skills that are attuned to the culture and traditions of Aboriginal peoples.

Towards Aboriginal Self-Government

The social service and health problems that have long plagued Aboriginal peoples are well documented, although much more remains to be changed before their state of health and well-being is comparable to that of the general population. Individuals, private organizations and governments have had much to say about what is needed to address these issues. However, these recommendations still tend to be embedded in attempts to define the role of Aboriginal peoples in Canadian society and to impose that role upon them, attempts that have to this point abjectly failed.

As part of a lasting solution, it is time to acknowledge that non-Aboriginals can no longer presume to institute their will upon the First Nations, Métis and the Inuit. Aboriginal peoples across Canada are finding their own voice and, with that, the hope of establishing political, financial and moral control over their lives. Eventually, there will be a dialogue and partnership with the rest of Canada in addressing the issues facing their communities, whether those communities are on traditional lands or within urban centres.

• Who Will Provide Services to Aboriginal Peoples?

Aboriginal people today are healing from the ravages wreaked upon them by the residential schools and child welfare system and from the results of the systemic racism and discrimination within Canadian society. They are in the process of redefining themselves in the context of their traditional cultural practices.

Perhaps most important in this process is the reaffirmation of Aboriginal rights to land, rights that are inextricably linked to the principle of Aboriginal self-government. Such an affirmation is one of the key recommendations of the Royal Commissions and the foremost demand of Aboriginal leaders. Aboriginal peoples are seeking the formal recognition of rights that already exist, rights that existed prior to the European incursions.

An important factor today is the tenacious resistance on the part of Aboriginal people, over a very long period of time, to all efforts to eradicate both them and their distinct ways of living. Also important are the beginnings of Aboriginal economic development, the resurgence of Aboriginal languages, the establishment of Aboriginal education with a culturally based curriculum, the development of working models of Aboriginal justice systems, and Aboriginal control of social services that are no longer based exclusively upon the mainstream social work model but increasingly integrating an Aboriginal approach to social work practice. All these positive developments point a way out of the present predicament toward one that allows Aboriginal people their rightful place in Canadian society.

"The number of status Indians removed from their homes and placed in foster care now makes up 30% to 40% of all children in care in Canada, according to Indian Affairs documents.

"The briefing documents prepared for Indian Affairs Minister Andy Scott and obtained through Access to Information legislation, say the problem is First Nations Child and Family Services agencies are 'woefully underfunded,' even with an annual budget of nearly $400 million."

———

Source: Vancouver Sun, January 5, 2005, A4.

Former AFN Chief Ovide Mercredi speaks on the Royal Commission.

Aboriginal Political Activism

The resurgence of Aboriginal political activism that began in the 1970s has helped to move this process of redefinition along. It has led to the development of several national organizations representing and uniting distinct constituent groups. Among these organizations are: (1) the Assembly of First Nations, which represents status Indians who reside on Indian reserves across Canada; (2) the Inuit Tapirisat of Canada, representing Canada's Inuit population; (3) the Métis National Council; (4) the Congress of Aboriginal Peoples, representing off-reserve Aboriginal peoples; and (5) the Native Women's Association of Canada. These national organizations are generally affiliated with provincial and/or territorial and local groups that lobby the Canadian government to develop inclusive policies to protect the rights and interests of Aboriginal peoples, rights guaranteed in section 35 of the *Canadian Charter of Rights and Freedoms*. They also seek to educate governments and Canadians about the issues facing Aboriginal peoples.

In addition to these national organizations, there are grassroots organizations that are taking responsibility for the administration of social programs devolved to them from the federal government. The Métis have historically advocated for inclusion within mainstream services, but have recently made strides in developing their own services related to education, economic development and social support, among others. The Nunavut Land Claims Agreement provides for mechanisms to

Dick Hemingway.

Part of a support rally during the "Oka Crisis" in 1990. The conflict drew worldwide attention, catapulting Aboriginal land rights into the spotlight. Banner reads: "In Support of Mohawk/Native Sovereignty."

assist the majority of Inuit living in Canada in developing cultural and social services in the new territory of Nunavut. Tripartite agreements between an individual Aboriginal organization and the federal and provincial governments are another means of enabling Aboriginal peoples to deliver services. These include agreements that provide for child welfare services, law enforcement and elementary and secondary education, as well as social assistance and community health prevention and treatment programs.

In some cases, provincially funded organizations are the main service providers, especially in the case of elementary and secondary education or child welfare services. However, since the late 1970s, there has been an overall shift towards community control. For example, in 1969 the YWCA opened a second-stage supportive housing facility (first stage is an emergency shelter) for status Indian women in downtown Toronto. When it opened, it was called simply "Y Place." Aboriginal women gradually became more involved in the operation of the facility and, in 1973, renamed it *Anduhyaun*, Ojibwa for "our home." Anduhyaun still provides Aboriginal women and their children with a culturally based supportive environment and the resources to work on a variety of problems, including abusive relationships, family and marital breakdown, legal and financial difficulties, and alcohol and drug abuse. Other services help the women find housing, medical services, further education, skills development and employment. It also operates a food bank.

Within grassroots organizations such as Anduhyaun, it is still a challenge to balance the dictates of provincial or federal legislation and administrative criteria with the determination to provide culturally based and culturally appropriate services. This means that it has been difficult for Aboriginal peoples to secure stable funding for programs and services that supersede the limitations of the funding criteria for mainstream programs and services. For example, Indian Child and Welfare Services for reserves are funded by Indian Affairs, who may not necessarily provide funding for prevention programs such as courses in traditional parenting styles; instead, funding may be based simply upon the number of children taken into care.

In the past, service providers (including social workers) have usually been non-Aboriginal people who lived outside the community or only lived in the community for a short period of time. This too is beginning to change. Communities are increasingly looking within their own ranks to find the human resources to build an infrastructure to heal and foster well-being. This option is becoming more and more viable as more Aboriginal people complete a mainstream professional education, and as the communities themselves create training programs that prepare community members to deliver social services to their own communities. Genuine self-government will create the conditions where Aboriginal peoples take greater control of their own destinies in the social services field as well.

Aboriginal community worker and activist addresss CASSW, 2004.

Conclusion

Aboriginal peoples in Canada comprise four to five percent of Canada's total population. They include the Métis, the Inuit and a wide variety of other First Nations. Many endure conditions found only in the poorest countries of the world. Poverty (35 percent below LICO) and unemployment (38.4 percent) are widespread. The situation is not only unjust, it is a national disgrace.

The *Indian Act*, residential schools and other government policies are the immediate roots of today's problems, which began with attempts by the European settlers to subjugate Aboriginal peoples and take away their rights to the land. Gradually, much of this is being acknowledged, as evidenced by the 1996 Royal Commission on Aboriginal Peoples and its 440 recommendations.

Social justice and self-determination for the First Nations of Canada are principles upon which to build effective social work with Aboriginal peoples. The Aboriginal holistic approach to healing provides a useful starting point. It encourages service providers to consider all aspects of problems that arise. Social workers with an understanding of such an approach are already breaking new ground by initiating community healing centres, implementing restorative justice, setting up healing lodges, developing innovative child welfare policies, creating culturally appropriate urban social services and establishing holistic health care programs.

There is much that remains to be done to reverse the damage done to Aboriginal communities across Canada, and social workers, Aboriginal and non-Aboriginal, will play an important part in this process.

Chapter 9 Review
Social Work and Aboriginal Peoples

Discussion Questions

1. What bearing does the history of the relationship between Aboriginal peoples and the people of Canada have on the social welfare of Aboriginal peoples?

2. What was the reasoning behind the residential schools?

3. What were the six major goals of public policy in relation to Aboriginal peoples as identified by Gibbins and Ponting?

3. What are the four principles of an Aboriginal approach to social work?

4. Why does one need to be careful in describing a uniform Aboriginal approach?

5. What is the relevance of the circle for social work? How can it inform our approach to social work practice?

6. Is there a way for non-Aboriginal people to work productively with Aboriginal peoples and under what circumstances might this take place?

Websites

* **Aboriginal Canada Portal**
  http://www.aboriginalcanada.gc.ca

  This is a window to Canadian Aboriginal on-line resources, contacts, information and government programs and services. The portal offers ease of access and navigation to listings of Aboriginal associations, businesses, organizations, bands, communities, groups, news and so forth.

* **Report of the Royal Commission on Aboriginal Peoples (RCAP)**
  http://www.indigenous.bc.ca/rcap.htm

  The Final Report of the Royal Commission on Aboriginal Peoples brings together six years of research and public consultation on Indigenous issues. This website makes the entire report accessible through on-line search features and download capabilities.

* **Assembly of First Nations (AFN)**
  http://www.afn.ca

  The AFN is the national representative/lobby organization of the First Nations in Canada. Their website has up-to-date news and information about First Nations people.

* **Congress of Aboriginal Peoples (CAP)**
  http://www.abo-peoples.org

  The Congress of Aboriginal Peoples was founded in 1971 as the Native Council of Canada (NCC). It was established to represent the interests nationally of Métis and non-status Indians, a population that out-numbered all other Native people combined. This is an excellent website with statistics, history and news.

Key Terms

* **Aboriginal peoples**
* **The "Indian problem"**
* **Colonialism**
* **Land-cession treaties**
* **Indian Act of 1876**
* **Indian Agent**
* **Scrip system**
* **Disk list system**
* **Residential school system**
* **Assimilationist policies**
* **"The Scoop"**
* **Royal Commission on Aboriginal Peoples**
* **Aboriginal approach to social work practice**
* **Aboriginal worldview**
* **Reclaiming Aboriginal culture**
* **Aboriginal empowerment**
* **Holistic approach to healing**
* **Healing lodges**
* **Aboriginal self-government**
* **Aboriginal political activism**

CP PHOTO/Victoria Times-Colonist-Ray Smith.

Members of the "Gettin' Higher Choir" sing at an anti-racism rally held on the front steps of the legislature in Victoria, British Columbia (March 21, 2002), to mark the United Nations' International Day for the Elimination of Racial Discrimination.

10

Anti-Racist Social Work Today

—

Resisting Resistance to Change

Canada is one of the most culturally diverse nations in the world and, based on current immigration trends, this is not about to change. According to a 2004 poll (Ipsos World Monitor), Canada is also one of the most accepting nations of ethnic diversity — it sees itself as more of a "mosaic" than a "melting-pot." Four out of five Canadians (85 percent) agreed that "multiculturalism" is important to Canadian identity (Statistics Canada 2004).

However, this widespread acceptance of racial and cultural diversity should be contrasted with the belief of many visible minority Canadians (36 percent) that they had experienced discrimination or unfair treatment in the past five years. The current trend towards increasing numbers of immigrants from Asia, Africa and Central and South America means that there is a strong likelihood of persistent problems in this area in the future. Racial prejudice and discrimination are not simply random discriminatory acts by individuals against "visible minorities" — they include much more. There is a deep-seated ideology underlying racial prejudice and this belief system needs to be combatted. Front-line Canadian social workers need to be armed with tools to address such problems head-on.

In order to practice anti-racist social work, it is necessary to have a sense of the history of racism and its extent in Canada today and to be aware of one's own preconceptions in this area. This chapter introduces the basic concepts, themes, strategies and practices associated with anti-racism and the role of social work and social workers in combatting racial prejudices and stereotypes — within themselves, their organizations and wider society. It touches on the following points: the history of racism in Canada in relation to various minority groups (Aboriginal, Chinese, Japanese and Blacks), Canadian immigration policy and the impact of the recent shift in immigration away from Europe to Third World countries, the history and impact of Canada's multicultural policy, the nature and scope of provincial and federal human rights legislation and the prevalence of hate crimes in Canada today.

Finally, the chapter outlines the basis of the new "anti-racism approach" to social work practice today.

Racism is the subordination of one group by another using arbitrary physical features such as skin colour. It can occur at individual, institutional or societal levels in the form of attitudes, beliefs, policies or procedures. Anti-racist social work is an approach to practice that aggressively combats racism on all three levels.

Celebrating ethnic diversity in the Canadian mosaic.

The forced eviction of the
Japanese Canadians from the
Pacific Coast in the early months
of 1942 is said by some to have
been the greatest mass
movement in the history of
Canada.

It was not until 1949, four years
after Japan had surrendered,
that the majority of displaced
Japanese Canadians were
allowed to return to British
Columbia. By then, most had
begun a new life elsewhere in
Canada. Their property had long
before been confiscated and sold
at a fraction of its worth.

In 1988, Prime Minister Brian
Mulroney formally apologized to
Japanese Canadians and
authorized the provision of
$21,000 to each of the survivors
of wartime detention.

History of "Race Relations" in Canada

Canadians take great pride in the ethnic and racial diversity of their country. By comparison with many other countries, there is much to feel good about. However, one need not reach too far back into Canadian history to see that ethnic conflict and racism are not at all foreign to the Canadian experience and that problems in this area continue to the present day.

Racism persists and even thrives in Canada, according to Lincoln Alexander, chair of the Canadian Race Relations Foundation:

> Today I stand before you to say: As Canadians, we are not doing a very good job. We're not making the grade. We get a failing grade when police officers in Saskatoon drive Aboriginal men to the outskirts of town and leave them in sub-zero temperatures without winter coats. We get a failing grade when 600 Chinese arrive by ships off the coast of British Columbia looking for sanctuary in Canada only to be met with fear and even hatred. They were handcuffed like criminals, and today, the future for some of these refugee claimants is uncertain and 35 of them remain in provincial jails. We get a failing grade when our schoolyards become a war zone for some visible minority youth because they're bullied on a regular basis, sometimes with fatal results. We get a failing grade when new immigrants, especially non-white immigrants, subsidize Canada's economy to the tune of 55 billion dollars each year, according to a study done by the University of Toronto, because skills acquired in their homelands are not recognized in this country (Alexander 2001).

To begin with, then, let us briefly review some of the historical background that contributes to this troubling state of affairs.

• Native Canadians and the Residential School System

The history of injustice wreaked upon Canada's founding peoples since the Europeans first arrived in North America is widely documented and quite widely known. Perhaps its worst expression is found in the infamous residential school system, which was, for all intents and purposes, designed to obliterate Native society and culture altogether.

The church-government partnership for Aboriginal education lasted from the 1840s to 1969 (the last residential school, Christie Roman Catholic School in Tofino, BC, didn't close until 1983). It is estimated that between 100,000 and 150,000 Aboriginal children attended residential schools. A 1920 amendment to the *Indian Act* made it mandatory for every First Nations child to attend. Children stayed at the residence for most of the year, and family visits were limited. The use of the English language was mandatory.

The intent of the residential school policy was to erase Aboriginal identity by separating children from their families and socializing them, not in the culture of their ancestors, but in the culture of the Canadian

Vancouver City Archives.

Japanese-Canadian fishing boats
confiscated during World War II.

mainstream. This process was often done by force, which resulted in psychological damage to the students. This was social welfare at its worst, and its effects (poverty, family disintegration, poor health, high rates of suicide, high incarceration rates) remain with us today.

One of the main arenas of conflict today is Native land claims. All Aboriginal groups (Inuit, First Nations and Métis) have placed claims before provincial and federal governments. More often than not, the desire to expand mineral and resource exploration on Native lands has brought the federal and provincial governments into conflict with the First Nations. These clashes escalated in the 1990s, with the Oka Crisis outside Montreal over incursions into Native land areas, and the celebrated struggle over Clayoquot Sound on Vancouver Island, where Native groups and environmentalists resisted the clear-cutting of ancient forests.

• Chinese Canadians

Between 1881 and 1884, 15,700 Chinese workers were brought over from China as contract labourers to work on the Canadian Pacific Railway (Isajiw 1999). Thereafter, a series of laws were put in place to exclude or limit the number of Chinese and South Asian immigrants to Canada: the *Chinese Immigration Act* of 1885; the Head Tax of $50 on Chinese immigrants set in 1885 (raised to $100 in 1901 and to $500 in 1904, an average two-year wage for a Chinese person in Canada); the *Immigration Act* of 1910 (which established "undesirable" classes of immigrants); and the *Chinese Exclusion Act* of 1923 (which admitted to

CHINESE PEOPLE IN CANADA

In 1885, federal legislation was passed to restrict the immigration of Chinese people into Canada. A $50 Head Tax was imposed on every Chinese immigrant entering Canada. In January 1901, the tax was increased to $100 per head and raised again in January 1904 to $500.

An excellent website summarizing facts and accounts of the lives of Chinese-Canadians since 1858, using text articles and an extensive photo gallery, is located at: http://www.ccnc.ca/toronto/history/index.html

Certificate of Head Tax paid by Quan Lum, 1912. Once the CPR was completed, the Federal Government moved to restrict immigration. The first anti-Chinese bill was passed in 1885.

REMEMBER AFRICVILLE

Canada is a country that prides itself on its multiculturalism and ethnic diversity. But, in the 1960s, a different approach was evidenced in a small village on the edge of Halifax, named Africville.

In the name of urban renewal, this poor African-Canadian community, pictured below, was erased. Civil servants insisted that this action was above board and legal and that it was not a example of racism, but few people now see it this way.

Africville was plowed under to make way for a park and a new bridge over the narrows to Dartmouth, between 1964 and 1969. Former residents were moved to nearby public housing in the depressed north end of Halifax.

Africville in the 1960s; now a largely abandoned park.

Canada only certain specified classes of Chinese and almost stopped Chinese immigration completely). William Lyon Mackenzie King, then Deputy Minister of Labour, claimed in 1907, that it was "natural that Canada should remain a White man's country." The tax was eliminated in 1923, but other laws, which made it nearly impossible for Chinese men to bring their families to Canada and forced many to be separated from their wives and children for years at a time, remained in place until 1947. Recently, the Canadian government was faced with a lawsuit by Chinese-Canadians who were demanding compensation for the Head Tax and other racially motivated measures aimed at limiting immigration from China in the first half of the twentieth century. In July 2001, however, a court ruled that the claim could not proceed.

Japanese-Canadians

In World Wars I and II, the Canadian government instituted a policy of internment of members of ethnic minority groups whom it defined as "enemy aliens." Immigrants from the Austro-Hungarian Empire, with whom the Allies were at war, were interned, as well the Japanese-Canadians. In both cases, the basic human rights of the respective minorities were violated. The homes, businesses and property of Japanese-Canadians were confiscated and their lives were turned on end (Isajiw 1999). It was not until four decades later, in 1988, that the government announced a comprehensive settlement with surviving members of the Japanese wartime community.

Jews

In addition to racial categories, racist ideologies may be focused through policies directed towards specific ethnic groups. During and immediately after World War II, the Canadian government was reluctant to admit Jews as refugees to Canada. It undertook informal measures to restrict their immigration. When asked how many Jews would be allowed into Canada after the war, a senior immigration official issued his famous reply: "None is too many." The Canadian government refused entry to a ship called the *St. Louis*, which carried a shipload of Jews desperate to be admitted to Canada. Instead, they were compelled to sail back to Europe on a voyage of the damned. Anti-Semitic beliefs and practices are still widespread today.

Blacks in Canada

The first account of the presence of Black people in Canada was in 1605. Mattheu de Costa was one of the team members with the French explorers who landed in Nova Scotia (formerly Port Royal) in the early seventeenth century. Later, Black slaves were brought to Canada by the French. Slavery was officially introduced in Canada by the French in 1628 and continued by the British until 1833–1834, when slavery was abolished in the British Empire.

The next significant early migration of Black people into Canada was that of the Black Loyalists, brought by the British in 1784 following the American War of Independence. Hundreds, who had fought for their freedom on the side of the British against the Americans, were brought to Nova Scotia. They were emancipated and promised education, employment and citizenship, but were instead left to fend for themselves. Many were forced back into slavery through abject poverty. The situation forced them to ask the British government in England to send them to Africa. Their request was granted, and in the late 1790s, many were shipped to West Africa to the British colony of Sierra Leone. In response to the need for cheap labour, the British also deceived and brought Maroons (runaway slaves) from Jamaica to work on the fortifications at Citadel Hill in Halifax. The Maroons were militant and refused to be controlled as slaves by white Nova Scotians, who used them as forced labourers. Many were also shipped to Sierra Leone.

Another group of Black people taken to Nova Scotia were refugees from the War of 1812 between Britain and the US. Most black Nova Scotians today are offspring of these refugees. Finally, Black people used what is known as the Underground Railroad to escape slavery in the United States between 1820 and 1860. These Black Americans, as fugitives, slaves and as freedmen, formed sizable settlements, particularly in southwestern Ontario and the Maritimes. More recently, immigration from the Caribbean accounts for the majority of Black Canadians.

The history of racism towards Black people in Canada should not be minimized. Canada actively practised slavery until early in the nineteenth century (Sheppard 1997), and even the Black Loyalists who entered Canada as free persons were subject to racist policies. Black Canadians were subject to legislation that enforced segregated schools and communities and limitations on property rights. In 1939, Canada's highest court concluded that racial discrimination was legally enforceable (Walker 1997). It was not until 1953–54 that Canada deleted from its statutes discriminatory laws that denied Black citizens the right to freely pursue formal education, respectable jobs, welfare assistance and civil and humanitarian rights. For over four hundred years, white Canadians have discriminated against Black Canadians.

There have been a great many newspaper reports and research documenting continuing anti-Black racism and suggesting that much of it is systemic. For example, according to Frances Henry, relations between police and the Black community are "fraught with tensions." She notes in particular that "stop-and-search procedures and other forms of harassment have exacerbated tensions and contributed to the 'criminalization' of young Black males" (Henry 1994). Similar serious conclusions were reached by the Ontario Commission on Systemic Racism in the Ontario Criminal Justice System, which reported that discriminatory practices by police against Black men were widespread (Ontario 1995).

MARY ANN SHADD CARY

Teacher, abolitionist, civil rights advocate, feminist and newspaper editor, Mary Ann Shadd (1823–1893) was an influential voice in the Underground Railroad community in Upper Canada. She was active in Sandwich, Toronto and Chatham, teaching and editing the *Provincial Freeman*, an important newspaper of the Canadian Underground Railroad community.

Shadd broke new ground for women, being not only an early woman newspaper editor, but also the first Black female editor in Canada. She claimed equal rights under the law regardless of colour or gender, while exhorting her community to realize the benefits of self-sufficiency.

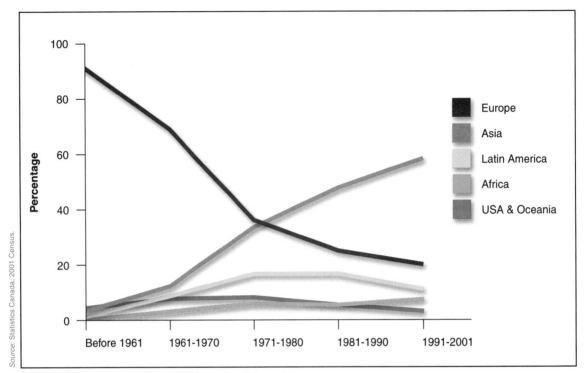

Source: Statistics Canada, 2001 Census.

Figure 10.1: Canada's immigrants by region and period of arrival.

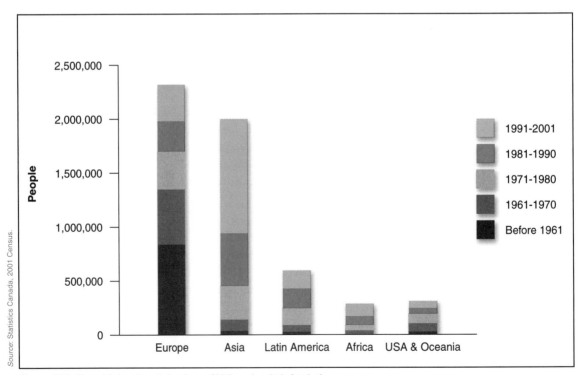

Source: Statistics Canada, 2001 Census.

Figure 10.2: Canada's immigrants by place of birth and period of arrival.

The New Immigration

As might be expected in a country comprised largely of immigrants and their descendants, ethnic and race relations in Canada have been heavily influenced by immigration policy. Prior to 1967, when important new immigration legislation came into force, "Nationality" was one of the criteria used to qualify for admission to Canada. Canadian immigration policy was undoubtedly Eurocentric; immigration was encouraged from (white) Europe and discouraged from the rest of the world. In 1967, new legislation introduced a point system, whereby prospective immigrants had to qualify based on such criteria as education, work experience, language fluency and age. "Country-of-origin" was no longer an explicit criterion in the selection process. The inevitable consequence of the new legislation was a new wave of skilled immigrants from Asia, Africa and South and Central America.

The shift was dramatic. Prior to 1961, over 90 percent of all immigrants were from Europe, and over half of these were from Northern and Western Europe and the United Kingdom. Immigrants from Asia constituted only a small percentage (3.1 percent) of all immigrants arriving in the country. By the 1990s, Europeans made up only about one-fifth of all the immigrants, and the largest number, close to 60 percent, came from Asia. The remaining proportion — almost one-fifth (16.6 percent) — came from Central and South America, the Caribbean and Bermuda and from the United States. The largest proportion of European immigrants came, not from the United Kingdom or Northern and Western continental Europe, but from Eastern Europe.

• "Visible Minorities"

With this shift came a substantial increase in the "visible minority" population in Canada. Close to four million Canadians (or 13.4 percent of the population) identified themselves as members of "visible minorities" in the 2001 census. According to Statistics Canada projections, the number of Canadians in visible minority groups is expected to increase to 7.1 million by 2016, up from 2.7 million in 1991. As a proportion of the overall population, this represents a doubling to 20 percent in 2016 from 10 percent in 1991.

It is projected that roughly one-half of all visible minorities in Canada will belong to two groups by 2017: South Asian or Chinese. The projections show that the population of each group would be around 1.8 million. In 2001, Chinese and South Asians were already the largest visible minority groups in Canada, but their share of the total population differed. According to the 2001 Census, 1,029,000 individuals identified themselves as Chinese, and they accounted for 26% of the visible minority population. In comparison, the 917,000 South Asians represented 23% of the visible minority population.

RACIALIZED GROUP

The term *racialized group* is preferred to the commonly used *visible minority*.

The term *racialized group* makes it clear that race is not determined by biology, but is socially constructed.

Further, the term reflects the process by which non-white groups are considered almost solely by race while white people are not.

Finally, the term *visible minority* is often used with the intention of negative connotation (Smith and Jackson, 2002).

By 2016, one in five Canadians will be a "visible minority."

RACISM DEFINED

Racism, as defined in Article 1(1) of the International Convention on the Elimination of Racial Discrimination (1966), includes all three levels of racism:

"Any distinction, exclusion, restriction or preference based on race, colour, descent, or national or ethnic origin which has the purpose or effect of nullifying or impairing the recognition, enjoyment or exercise, on an equal footing, of human rights and fundamental freedoms; in the political, economic, social, cultural or any other field of public life."

Projections show that the Black population will remain the third largest visible minority. It would reach around 1.0 million in 2017, compared with about 662,000 in the 2001 Census. The visible minority groups that would grow fastest between now and 2017 are the West Asian, Korean and Arab groups. Under most of the projection scenarios, the population of each group would more than double.

The substantial increase in the visible minority population in recent years has already dramatically affected public policy (e.g., multiculturalism and anti-racism policy), and it seems likely to continue to do so in the future. The new period of ethnic and racial diversity has undoubtedly enriched Canada and the lives of each of its citizens. Certainly, there is no reason the demographic changes need to result in serious ethnic and racial conflict. However, other factors, such as a serious downturn in the economy, and policies and institutional procedures that intervene and foster ethnic and racial divisions, will likely affect the social impact of this underlying demographic change.

As a result of the recent wave of immigration, a new set of issues confront social workers and others working in the social services. Social worker practitioners are now required to have a greater sensitivity to religious beliefs and cultural background, and they will not only need to deal with the effects of discrimination and racism, but also find ways actively to combat it.

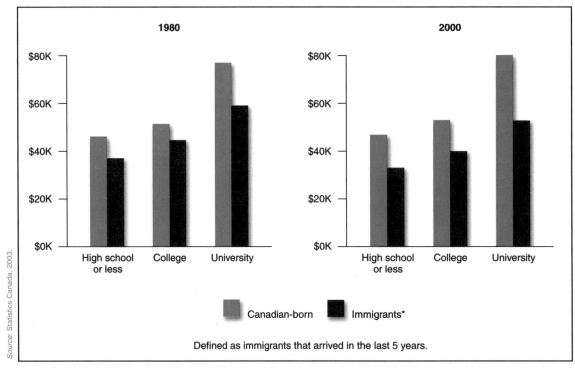

Source: Statistics Canada, 2003.

Figure 10.3: Mean earnings of male workers (aged 30 to 54) by education and country of origin.

Multiculturalism Policy

In 1971, Canada became the first country to adopt multiculturalism as an official policy. The policy was aimed at a greater integration of Canadian society by providing the diverse ethnic minority groups with a sense of belonging to Canada. Its original aim was to give ethnic minority groups a public recognition of their identity. The policy gave them a chance to reinforce their identity, but within the Canadian context, and with the recognition that ethnic diversity is part of Canadian identity (Isajiw 1999). The basic principles of the policy were expressed by Prime Minister Pierre Elliott Trudeau in his introduction of the policy in the Canadian Parliament on October 8, 1971:

> A policy of multiculturalism within a bilingual framework commends itself to the government as the most suitable means of assuring the cultural freedom of Canadians. Such a policy should help to break down discriminatory attitudes and cultural jealousies. National unity if it is to mean anything in the deeply personal sense must be founded on confidence in one's own individual identity; out of this can grow respect for that of others and a willingness to share ideas, attitudes and assumptions. A vigorous policy of multiculturalism will help to create this initial confidence. It can form the base of a society which is based on fair play for all.

In 1988, the *Multiculturalism Act* was passed, restating and reinforcing the 1971 policy and mandating federal departments to ensure equal opportunities in employment for all ethnic and racial groups. In order to implement the policy, the Canadian government created the Multicultural Directorate, which in turn developed a range of programs designed to help it fulfill the policy's objectives. The federal multicultural program stimulated the development of other programs and the establishment of other agencies and institutions. For example, in many Canadian provinces, particularly Alberta, Saskatchewan and Manitoba, the idea of multiculturalism has been instrumental in the inclusion of a number of "heritage" languages into regular secondary school programs. In 1996, by a special Act of the federal Parliament, the Canadian Race Relations Foundation was established to deal more directly with issues of race.

Canada's multiculturalism policy has set a positive framework within which all issues relating to ethnic and racial equality are now discussed. Nevertheless, while the policy's impact on Canadian society has been significant, and ethnic and racial groups have experienced some improvement in their conditions, they are still relatively disadvantaged. In a recent report, for example, the Canadian Race Relations Foundation notes that members of visible minority groups continue to have poorer outcomes with respect to employment and income and still face barriers to socioeconomic equality (Canadian Race Relations Foundation 2000).

CONSTITUTION ACT

"Every individual is equal before and under the law and has the right to the equal protection and equal benefit of the law without discrimination based on race, national or ethnic origin, colour, religion, sex, age, or mental or physical disability."

———

Source: Constitution Act, 1982, s.15, pt.1.

Multiculturalism ensures that all citizens have a sense of belonging.

RESPONDING TO ON-LINE HATE

What do you do if you come across hateful on-line content or e-mails? Youth are often the targets, but are sometimes left wondering, "What can I do about it?"

Well, the content is not only offensive but it is illegal in Canada, so there is plenty you can do. First, you can contact the website's Internet Service Provider (ISP). Most ISPs now have Acceptable Use Policies that clearly define the guidelines for using their services, as well as the penalties for violating those guidelines.

Second, you can contact the police or Cybertip's on-line reporting form or toll-free phone line (1–866–658–9022) to make a complaint.

Finally, check out the "hate watch" websites. A number of Canadian sites, such as the B'nai Brith Canada's League for Human Rights, monitor and document illegal material on the Internet.

Check out the Media Awareness Network at:
http://www.media-awareness.ca

Human Rights Legislation

National **human rights legislation** in Canada began with the passage of the Canadian *Bill of Rights* in 1960. Later in that decade other provinces enacted similar legislation, and by 1975, all provinces in Canada had human rights codes.

Whether a rights violation complaint is heard at the federal or provincial levels is determined by the constitutional division of powers: Complaints involving banking, national airlines, railways or federal government employees are in the federal jurisdiction, whereas complaints involving school boards, city government or restaurants are in the provincial jurisdiction. In general, both federal and provincial human rights law prohibits the dissemination of hate propaganda and discrimination in all aspects of employment, the leasing and sale of property, public accommodation, services and facilities, and membership in labour unions and professional associations. Grounds of discrimination vary slightly depending on the jurisdiction.

In 1982, the Canadian *Bill of Rights* was superseded by the **Charter of Rights and Freedoms**. The *Charter* guaranteed the fundamental freedoms of conscience and religion, thought, belief, opinion and expression (including freedom of the press and other media of communication), peaceful assembly and association. It guaranteed democratic rights, geographical mobility rights, legal rights (including the right to life, liberty and security of person), and equality rights that protect against "discrimination based on race, national or ethnic origin, colour, religion, sex, age or mental or physical disability." The *Charter* reinforced official bilingualism in Canada by affirming the equality of the English and French languages and by affirming the rights of children to be educated in either language. It also affirmed the multicultural character of Canada and recognized the rights of Canada's Aboriginal peoples. Finally, it emphasized that all the rights and freedoms referred to within it are guaranteed equally to male and female persons (Isajiw 1999).

In 1986, the Canadian *Human Rights Act* and the *Employment Equity Act* were passed with the purpose of redressing some of the past injustices against designated groups in Canada. The designated groups are women, persons with disabilities, Aboriginal peoples and visible minorities. The purpose of the **Employment Equity Act** is to ensure equity in the workplace so that no one is denied access to employment for reasons unrelated to merit and skills.

In relation to its own minority groups, Canada is also bound by the international covenants on human rights to which it is a signatory. These include the United Nations Charter of 1945, the Universal Declaration of Human Rights adopted by the United Nations in 1948, the International Convention on the Prevention and Punishment of the Crime of Genocide of 1948, the International Convention Concerning

Discrimination in Respect of Employment and Occupation of 1958, the International Convention on All Forms of Racial Discrimination of 1965 (ratified in 1969), the International Covenant on Economic, Social and Cultural Rights of 1966 (ratified in 1976), the International Covenant on Civil and Political Rights (ratified in 1976) and various other resolutions of United Nations assemblies and international conferences (Isajiw 1999).

Passing laws is one thing; implementing them is another. The provinces and territories, and the federal government, have **human rights commissions** charged with dealing with human rights abuses. While these commissions have had some success, they have unfortunately often been hampered by limited resources and case backlogs. Furthermore, since such commissions are by their nature complaints-driven, it is generally felt that many victims of discrimination, perhaps themselves new to the country, do not have the financial resources or even the time to report discrimination and initiate the lengthy complaints process.

TOUR OF HUMAN RIGHTS IN CANADA

The Canadian Human Rights Commission has created an extensive website on the evolution of human rights. You can explore the key court cases and laws, historical background material, case studies, cross references and anecdotal information that have shaped human rights in our country since 1900. The tour is divided into four periods: 1900–1924; 1925–1949; 1950–1974 and 1975–2000.

Start the tour at: http://www.chrc-ccdp.ca/en/

Dick Hemingway.

The *Canadian Charter of Rights and Freedoms* guarantees equality rights that are designed to protect Canadians against all forms of discrimination, including institutional racism, which is highlighted in this contingent at an anti-racism rally.

Combatting Hate Crime

When people are the targets of violence solely because of who they are, or who they are thought to be, they are the victims of hate crimes. The most common targets of hate-motivated crime are Black people, Jews and gay people. Canada's police agencies report that just after September 11, 2001, there were increased numbers of hate crimes with 15 percent of incidents directly attributed to those events.

More than half (57 percent) of the reported 2001–02 hate crimes were motivated by racial and ethnic origins, 43 percent involved religious motivations and issues of sexual orientation motivated 10 percent. Members of visible minorities report fearing victimization of hate crime at a percentage rate more than twice that of Canadians generally, and fears of victimization are also heightened for members of Hindu, Jewish and Muslim religions (Juristat, *Hate Crime in Canada*, Vol. 24, no. 44). Such crimes create a climate of fear within the entire targeted group.

The promotion of hate based on race, religion, ethnic origin or sexual orientation is widespread. Hate sites on the Internet increased from 50 to more than 800 in the period from 1998 to 2001. The Toronto Police Hate Crimes Unit reports that 19 percent more hate crimes, or 110 incidents, were reported in the first six months of 1999 compared with the previous six-month period. There were 584 reported incidents of anti-Semitic harassment and vandalism in Canada in 2003, according to the League for Human Rights of B'nai Brith. This represents a doubling of rates in the later 1990s and early 2000s (League for Human Rights of B'nai Brith, *Audit of Anti-Semitic Incidents*, 2003).

Individuals acting out conscious feelings of hate, bias or prejudice commit most hate crimes in Canada. A survey in 1994 by Canada's Department of Justice to assess the tone of race relations found that people involved in racially motivated hate crimes tend to be young — in their teens or early twenties — and that the perpetrators of such crimes are not, as some have suggested, experiencing bouts of teenage angst and rebellion (Roberts 1995). To the contrary, the study concluded that it is young people who are acting out on long-held views shared by their families and friends about those unlike themselves. Organized hate groups are responsible for about 5 percent of hate-motivated activities in this country.

There is a growing consensus on the need for consistent policy and service delivery responses from the criminal justice system at all levels. The federal government demonstrated strong leadership in this area by amending the *Criminal Code* in 1996 to strengthen sentencing for any *Criminal Code* offence that is motivated by hate (Bill C-41). The move prompted community discussion, raised overall awareness of the issues and helped to mobilize communities. It also highlighted the need for stronger responses in the communities where hate-motivated incidents occur and may go unreported.

CP PHOTO/Ottawa Citizen-Nicki Corrigall.

Simon I. Kerzner surveys graffiti on the side of Ottawa synagogue.

For their part, front-line social workers are using innovative anti-racist approaches that emphasize community empowerment to combat hate crimes. Since hate crimes do not occur in a vacuum, education and community work can prevent hate crimes and act as an important complement to hate crime laws. Social workers are involved in outreach and consultation, education and awareness activities and fostering the creation of advocacy and support groups. In struggling against overt racism of this kind, social workers also work closely with community organizations to promote an anti-racist perspective through education. This may involve producing brochures on anti-racism, going into schools and engaging students in the issues or speaking out about community conditions and government inaction.

With their roots firmly in the locality, community workers can also provide feedback on what works and what does not. This kind of collaborative, community-based approach to combatting overt racism can help to minimize the extent of hate crime activity and strengthen the resolve and solidarity of its victims.

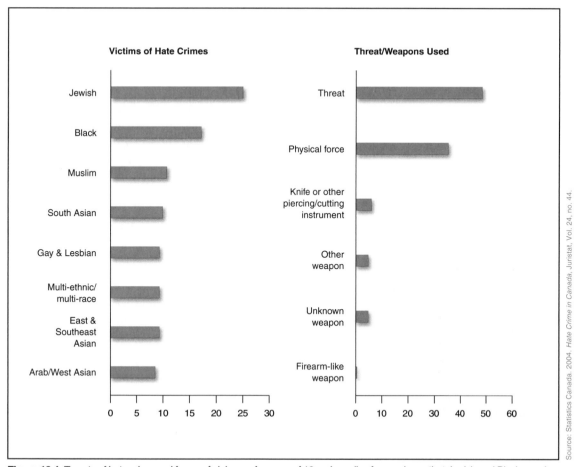

Source: Statistics Canada. 2004. *Hate Crime in Canada*, Juristat, Vol. 24, no. 44.

Figure 10.4: Targets of hate crime and forms of violence. A survey of 12 major police forces shows that Jewish and Black people are the most likely to be targets and that victims of hate crimes are most likely to encounter threats and physical force.

"Schools shall be expected to provide evidence of effective progress in attaining multicultural/multiracial diversity given the school's context and mission. Such progress should be evident in curriculum, administration, the selection of faculty and professional staff and in initiatives directed toward their self-awareness and education, in student admissions, and in external relations."

Source: CASSW Accreditation Standards, Sec. 1.11.

Canada today is one of the world's most multi-ethnic nations.

Health Canada.

Concepts and Terms

The terms used to describe and understand complex social issues such as race and racism evolve over time. In the 1970s, for example, racism tended to be seen as the result of individual prejudice. Negative and stereotypical attitudes were deemed to be "the cause" of racist discrimination; if individual attitudes were corrected through education and the sharing of cultures, racism would no longer exist. Much of federal multicultural policy is premised on this understanding.

More recently, we have seen the emergence of a comprehensive "anti-racist" approach. In general, this has involved a shift from seeing the causes of racism as lying only within personal prejudice and individual behaviour to seeing racism as interlinked with the larger structures and social systems in Canadian society.

Some of the key concepts in this area are reviewed below.

- **Stereotype**. When applied to people, stereotyping refers to the forming of a fixed picture of a group of people, usually based on false or incomplete information.

- **Prejudice**. Prejudice literally means to "prejudge" others based on preconceived ideas. No law can prevent prejudiced attitudes. However, the law can prohibit discriminatory practices and behaviours that flow from prejudice.

- **Ethnicity/ethnic group**. The term ethnicity refers to the characteristics of a group of people who share a common heritage, identity or origin or are descendants of those who have shared a distinct culture and who identify with their ancestors, their culture or their group. Most commonly, the term *ethnic group* is used to mean minority ethnic groups, for example, Black, Chinese or Sikh Canadians (as opposed to the majority ethnic group, white Anglo-Saxons). Interestingly, in today's multicultural Canadian society, the term *ethnic* is used both in a derogatory sense (i.e., as a racist slur) and in a positive sense as describing a group and its food, customs and so forth as being different and interesting.

- **Culture**. The concept of culture generally refers to behaviours, beliefs and practices that are meaningful in terms of some shared, even if implicit, cognitive and value assumptions derived from a unique historical community experience (Isajiw 1999).

- **Ethnocentrism**. Ethnocentrism is an attitude by which members of a group tend to consider their group to be in some or all ways better or superior to other groups. Such an attitude is especially significant in relation to the majority groups because it is conditioned by the positions of power that members of a group hold.

- **Race**. Race is an arbitrary classification of human beings based on skin colour and other superficial physical characteristics. This classification, conceived in Europe in the colonial period, placed the populations of the world in a hierarchical order with white Europeans superior to all others. Modern biologists do not recognize "race" as a meaningful scientific category and recent human genome research is conclusive on this point.

- **Visible minorities.** Canadian legislation, such as the *Employment Equity Act*, even today refers to "visible minorities" — defined as "persons, other than Aboriginal peoples, who are non-Caucasian in race or non-white in colour." However the term begs the question: visible to whom? It is probably time to abandon this term.

- **Racism.** Racism is a relationship or attitude based on the subordination of one group by another using arbitrary physical features such as skin colour. One can identify three types of racism: personal racism, cultural racism and institutional racism. Racism is manifested in overt (obvious and unconcealed) and covert (subtle and hidden) forms.

- **Discrimination.** Discrimination refers to actions, situations or policies that have the effect, whether intentional or not, of putting some people at an unnecessary disadvantage on grounds such as race, sex or religion. Discrimination is usually based on prejudice and stereotypes. Canadian courts have recognized two types of illegal discrimination: (1) direct discrimination; and (2) adverse effects discrimination (also called indirect discrimination or systemic discrimination).

- **Systemic discrimination (or institutionalized racism).** Systemic racism refers to the existence of policies and structures built into our social institutions that serve to subjugate, oppress and force the dependence of individuals or groups. The recent finding by a commission of inquiry of systemic racial discrimination within the Ontario criminal justice system is an example. The forced-assimilationist policies underlying the residential schools were of this kind, as were the pre-1968 Canadian immigration laws that explicitly excluded persons based on their country of origin.

- **Anti-racist social work.** In the past, racism tended to be presented as if it took place only at the individual level (i.e., that there were individuals with racist opinions), and there was a belief that it could be eliminated at this level by education alone. The new anti-racist approach goes beyond this and recognizes that racism is also deeply rooted in the wider institutions of our society — most notably, in employment, education, justice, media, policing, immigration and government policies. Certainly, there is now ample evidence that deep-rooted racism exists. Since social service practitioners carry out their work within these institutions, it is incumbent upon them in the course of their daily work to be aware of this wider problem and to combat racism fully and comprehensively wherever and however it manifests itself.

ANTI-RACIST TRAINING AND MATERIALS PROJECT

Social work professional associations are taking up the challenge of implementing an anti-racist model that respects difference and acknowledges oppression. The Anti-Racist Training and Materials Project, a project of the Canadian Association of Schools of Social Work (CASSW), was designed to build a national infrastructure of regionally strong collegial educational support and scholarship in the areas of anti-racism and anti-oppression.

The project participants concluded that, because racism and diversity are so multi-layered, social work educators need to address them across the curriculum.

For more information, go to: http://www.cassw-acess.ca

Rallies across Canada unite the forces opposed to racism.

TRANSFORMING OUR
ORGANIZATIONS

Social workers sometimes find themselves employed by agencies that do not operate with what they would consider to be an appropriate anti-racism perspective. Doing something about this (hopefully, without losing one's job) is part of anti-racist social work.

How does one approach this difficult task of organizational change? Social workers can promote anti-racist organizational change by using "Transforming Our Organizations," a tool kit for planning and monitoring anti-racism and/or multicultural change in organizations.

For more information on this anti-racism tool, go to: http://www.multiculturalism.org

Towards an "Anti-Racist" Social Work: The Personal, Institutional and Societal

What does it mean to practice anti-racist social work? The Canadian Association of Social Workers' code of ethics states that "a social worker shall identify, document, and advocate the elimination of discrimination." As part of this, there is an obligation to not only challenge and eradicate racism in others, and in policies and organizations, but also to examine one's own beliefs and behaviours.

Lena Dominelli, one of the pioneers in developing anti-racist social work, summarized anti-racist social work: "Social work, redefined according to anti-racist criteria, is about realizing significant improvement in the life chances and well-being of individuals regardless of their gender, race, class, age, physical or intellectual abilities, sexual orientation, religious affiliation or linguistic capabilities. Anti-racist social work, therefore, is a bridge between social work in a racist society and social work in a non-racist one" (Dominelli 1988, 164). At the same time, many practitioners have emphasized a broad anti-oppressive framework that recognizes the need to continue the fight against racial oppression but to do so alongside combatting oppression based on class, gender and other factors.

Effective anti-racist social work practice addresses these issues at the personal, institutional and societal levels. At the personal level, social workers must ensure that their own practices are free of racism and challenge what are considered to be individual racist practices by others. In other words, workers should be "culturally competent" and aware that cultural practices will vary among the different groups of people with whom they work. At the institutional and societal levels, social service agencies must pursue policies and practices that are non-discriminatory, and legislation and government policies must be changed to remove barriers to racial groups. This includes working to eliminate unintentional racism in policy and procedures.

• Exemplary Practice

There are many examples of social workers and social service agencies that integrate an anti-racist approach to their practices. Take, for example, the work done by the Nanaimo Youth Services Association in Vancouver, which serves youth and integrates an anti-racism approach within its social services. Social workers at the agency focus on youth with difficulties that affect their physical and/or emotional well-being and development. Services offered include job-readiness training, employment counselling, wage subsidies, community development, internships, housing, supportive living, student summer programs, a youth drop-in centre, a youth newspaper, work experience, meal programs, a recycling building materials centre, and a teen talkline. The Supportive Living Program within the association helps facilitate the

Health Canada.

Dialogue between ethnic groups builds tolerance and trust.

process of the youths' transition from residential care to successful independent living. The program objective is to obtain input from the caseworker, youth and, when appropriate, the caregiver to develop an individual program plan for the youth. The work done by social workers at the association does not stop with the individual youth. First Nations youth often face racism in finding employment and training opportunities. In this case, social workers relate directly with the community and employers in undertaking awareness training and organizational development activities directed at systemic changes. The workers understand that the youths' difficulties in finding employment cannot be addressed only through education and training of the youth. Barriers and systemic discrimination must also be tackled.

Anti-racist social workers often use an empowerment approach or elicit the direct participation of those affected by racism in developing solutions. The Urban Native Youth Association (UNYA) in Vancouver, for example, was formed to address Aboriginal youth issues when it became apparent that growing numbers of young people were leaving reserves for the city of Vancouver. A disproportionate number of First Nations youth end up on the streets with little or no knowledge of where to go for help. UNYA's goal is to serve as a safe place for Native youth to come and find out about other services in the community and to develop their own solutions. Their involvement in the development of youth services has enabled the youth to raise difficult questions around racism in the community, suggest solutions and work towards implementing the changes. The youth have taken it upon themselves to work with social workers to challenge the racism they confront in their daily lives.

When faced with mainstream services that are not fully meeting their needs, minority communities have sometimes needed to create separate social service agencies to act on their behalf. The Black Community Resource Centre in Montreal helps Black English-speaking youth and advocates for systemic change. The centre promotes the social, health, education and economic needs of the youth by collaborating and partnering with Black community organizations, public agencies and community-wide agencies. Ethnicity-specific centres organize services not only to help people from their particular group, but also to collaborate with other groups to address systemic or structural racism. The Black Community Centre works with community organizations to monitor and review public policy that affects Black youth. The Centre attempts to improve the cultural and racial appropriateness of other public and para-public agencies by organizing cultural and racial sensitization workshops, and it works with other Black organizations in providing operational support and training. The Centre's approach is two-pronged — it has created a separate agency to address unmet needs, while also working to improve the cultural appropriateness and anti-racist perspective of mainstream agencies.

A CANADA FOR ALL

In 2005, the federal government announced a $56 million plan to get tough on racism through a wide-ranging action plan that deals with everything from attacking discrimination in the workplace to setting up a snitch line to report Internet hate sites.

Called "A Canada for All: Canada's Action Plan Against Racism" the plan has six priority areas:

- Assist victims and groups vulnerable to racism and related forms of discrimination;
- Develop forward-looking approaches to promote diversity and combat racism;
- Strengthen the role of civil society;
- Strengthen regional and international cooperation;
- Educate children and youth on diversity and anti-racism; and
- Counter hate and bias.

Racial divides often disappear in the closeness of the workplace.

Anti-Racism Analysis Tool

An anti-racist approach to social work practice emphasizes placing personal difficulties within the larger social context. Not doing so leads to viewing problems as personal pathologies or problems of interpersonal relations and can result in "blaming the victim," thereby diverting attention away from social structures and thus inhibiting social change. The **anti-racism analysis tool** provides a way to apply this approach.

Take, for example, racism in relation to First Nations youth caught up in the criminal justice system, which continues to be one of the most readily apparent examples of institutionalized racism. Studies show that, provincially, First Nations peoples are incarcerated at rates that are six to seven times higher than the overall provincial rate. The anti-racist analysis tool can be used to examine issues arising in the context of the overrepresentation of First Nations people in the criminal justice system. In this context, it redirects us to examine personal, institutional and ideological aspects of the problem:

- Personal racism can be found in policing practices, since First Nations people are three times more likely to be charged after arrest than non-Aboriginal people. Instances of overt racism by police officers have also been widely reported.

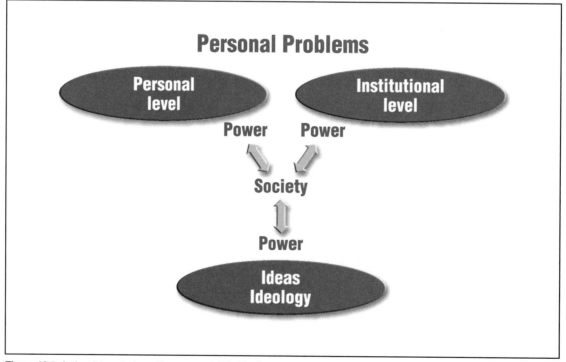

Figure 10.5: Anti-racist analysis: putting personal difficulties in context.

- At the institutional level, social workers find that few police officers are Aboriginal, almost all judges are white and less than one
percent of lawyers are First Nations people. This combination
often results in lawyers advising First Nations people to plead
guilty (75 percent do so) to charges even when they are innocent.

- At the ideological level, First Nations people are alienated from the
mainstream justice system, which emphasizes an adversarial rather
than a healing and community approach. Cultural differences and
language barriers also compound the problem — for example,
almost one-third did not understand the sentencing process
(Satzewich 1998). This cultural racism continues in prison where
ceremonial and spiritual practices are often forbidden. And, later,
only 18 percent of First Nations inmates are released on parole as
compared to 42 percent of the general inmate population (ibid.).

It is important for social workers addressing the problem of the
overrepresentation of First Nations people in prisons to work on all
levels to achieve a complete and effective solution. Using this tool may
enable you, as the social worker, to view an Aboriginal client who is in
conflict with the law in a different light. While not ignoring individual
problems and individual responsibilities, the anti-racism tool places the
person within broader historical and contemporary context.

Example Using the Anti-Racist Tool

Tom is an 18–year-old living in a large hostel run by a family as a
profit-making business. The hostel mainly houses young single people
with mild disabilities. Tom is Aboriginal and has mild brain damage
incurred in a car accident four years ago. He currently works in a day
program for people with mild disabilities. The manager at the hostel
referred Tom to a social worker in a local community health centre
because Tom is creating problems at the hostel (refusing to clean his
room, arguing with the other residents and causing damage to the
common living areas). It is rumoured that he is an alcoholic (these are
rumours, without definite evidence). For the first four months Tom
lived at the hostel, there were no problems; it has only been recently that
problems have been reported. Tom will not discuss the reasons for his
behaviour, and has not responded to requests to follow hostel rules.

The hostel owner arranges an interview between Tom and the social
worker. Tom does not want to see the worker, but the owner threatens
to evict him if he does not. He admits to the worker that he has caused
some damage, but claims that the other hostel residents are ganging up
on him and spreading rumours about him because he is Native. He has
no friends at the hostel, and no family with whom he could live. His
mother has thrown him out of her house because he argued with her
new boyfriend. He does not know what he will do if he has to leave the
hostel, and would continue to stay there if the other residents would

CANADIAN RACE RELATIONS FOUNDATION

The Canadian Race Relations Foundation is committed to building a national framework for the fight against racism in Canada.

The CRR Web site features resources and reports on topics such as racism in our schools, racism and representation in Canadian media, and analysis of curricula and special programs appropriate for the study of portrayal of diversity in the media.

To access the Foundation's resources, go to: http://www.crr.ca

only get off his back. However, he would consider going somewhere else if something became available. He agrees that his behaviour has not been without fault, but blames the manager and residents for setting him off.

There are numerous ways to approach this case, but the social worker who is taking an anti-racist approach avoids jumping to conclusions about Tom's rumoured alcohol abuse. The worker explores the issue with Tom and discovers that Tom does not drink at all. He produces a letter from an Elder stating that Tom once had an alcohol problem, but that he has been dry for years. In exploring what "sets Tom off" or makes him angry, the worker discovers that several of the hostel residents taunt him and call him names, such as "drunken Indian."

Working at the personal, institutional and societal levels, the worker undertakes sensitivity training with the hostel residents and the owner, emphasizing the importance of managing an environment that is non-racist. The worker also investigates the reasons for the lack of other hostel opportunities closer to Tom's community, and connects with Native Friendship Centres or other organizations in advocating for such facilities in First Nations communities. There are a wide variety of options, but the anti-racist social worker addresses the multi-level aspects of the problem and avoids racist stereotyping.

Conclusion

Anti-racist social work has an important role to play in creating a non-racist society. It demands that practitioners work to change their own awareness and practices, the practice of those around them, institutional policies and procedures and social relations and systems that operate, both overtly and covertly, to perpetuate racism. The implementation of anti-racist approach requires the employment of workers who have an ability to work across racial divides, and who have an empathy based on knowledge of the differences between people. It also means asserting the values of being human, of respect and dignity to all.

The anti-racist approach to social work is gaining acceptance in the profession, but challenges remain. Anti-racist social work writers and researchers are few in number, and as a result, it is often necessary to go beyond social work literature. Additionally, social workers who confront racism sometimes face opposition because they are often challenging deeply held beliefs and values. Responding to this will often involve joining with other advocacy and social action groups.

Anti-racist social work practice is a framework for analysis as well as a form of practice pertinent to all aspects of social work, including individual and group counselling, community work, social policy development and advocacy. It is multifaceted and relevant for practitioners from all backgrounds.

Chapter 10 Review
Anti-Racist Social Work Today

Questions

1. Describe three major events in Canadian history that illustrate racial injustice.

2. How has immigration changed in the past 20 years?

3. Describe the origins and basic principles of Canada's multiculturalism policy.

4. What is meant by a "hate crime"? What is the extent of hate crime in Canada? What is the best way to combat such crimes?

5. Explain what is meant by systemic racism and give some examples of systemic racism in Canada.

5. What is anti-racist social work? How has the approach to racism changed in the last decade?

Websites

- **Canadian Race Relations Foundation**
  http://www.crr.ca

  The Canadian Race Relations Foundation is committed to building a national framework for the fight against racism in Canadian society. They have an excellent on-line media centre with access to their publications.

- **Canadian Association of Schools of Social Work — Anti-Racist Training and Materials Project**
  http://www.cassw-acess.ca

  This is a site with an extensive list of resources and materials. These include print journals, organizations, publishers, videos and films, websites, virtual libraries and teaching tools. There are course outlines and papers available for downloading as well. This site also includes numerous bibliographic citations organized by theme. Five themes have been selected as entry points. There are definitions to help you access the right category for your needs. Full-text searches are also available.

- **The World Conference Against Racism, Racial Discrimination, Xenophobia and Related Intolerance (WCAR)**
  http://www.unhchr.ch/html/racism

  The World Conference Against Racism, Racial Discrimination, Xenophobia and Related Intolerance was held in South Africa in 2001. The conference focused on developing practical, action-oriented measures and strategies to combat contemporary forms of racism and intolerance.

Key Terms

- **Immigration policy**
- **Multiculturalism**
- **Human rights legislation**
- *Charter of Rights and Freedoms*
- *Employment Equity Act*
- **Human rights commissions**
- **Hate crimes**
- **Stereotype**
- **Prejudice**
- **Ethnicity/ethnic group**
- **Culture**
- **Ethnocentrism**
- **Race**
- **Visible minorities**
- **Racism**
- **Discrimination**
- **Systemic discrimination (institutionalized racism)**
- **Anti-racist social work**
- **Anti-racism analysis tool**

The Raging Grannies at an anti-war demonstration in Fredericton, New Brunswick. The protest group consists of older women who try to raise awareness of issues relating to peace, the environment and social justice through satirical songs and skits.

▌▌
Social Work with the Elderly

The Implications of an Ageing Society

The elderly are the most rapidly increasing age cohort in Canada. In the coming years, this demographic fact will increasingly affect most aspects of our society, particularly health care needs and health care provision across the country. As a result, in the coming years, social workers will focus more and more of their time and efforts on addressing the concerns and issues of this group.

In 2000, there were an estimated 3.8 million Canadians aged 65 and older, up 62 percent from 2.4 million in 1981 (see Table 11.1). Statistics Canada projects that by 2021 there will be almost seven million seniors comprising 19 percent of the total population; by 2041 there will be over nine million seniors comprising 25 percent of the population. Twenty-seven percent of seniors are immigrants, which presents special issues for social work practice with the elderly.

The ageing of the Canadian population can be attributed to three main factors:

- the large cohort of persons (the baby boomers) born between 1946 and 1966 who will begin turning 65 starting in 2011;
- the decline in the fertility rate and birth rate; and
- increases in life expectancy at birth.

Certainly the main factor contributing to the ageing of the Canadian population is the so-called baby boomers — those born during the years from 1946 to 1966. The eldest of this age group are now approaching retirement age (and vast numbers are immediately behind them). In addition, their consumer patterns are unique since, growing up in the prosperity of the post-World War II period, as a group they are relatively well educated and affluent.

The second trend causing the increase in the elderly age cohort is the fact that many younger couples are postponing having families, and many are deciding not to have children at all. This trend is due to a number of reasons, among which are the increased participation of women in the labour force, the importance of women establishing their own careers and the increasing economic demands placed on young families.

Because seniors are such a diverse group, it is impossible to provide a single approach to social work with them. However, knowledge of the particular health and emotional challenges faced by older Canadians can greatly assist those providing social work services.

Canadian Tourism Commission.

The baby boomers are rapidly approaching retirement.

Table 11.1: Population Profile and Projections – Percentage Over 65 Years, 1921–2051

Year	Men (000s)	Women (000s)	Total (000s)	As a % of the Canadian population
1921	215.0	205.3	420.2	4.8
1931	294.6	281.5	576.1	5.6
1941	390.9	376.9	767.8	6.7
1951	551.3	535.0	1,086.3	7.8
1961	674.1	717.0	1,391.1	7.6
1971	790.3	972.0	1,762.3	8.0
1981	1,017.2	1,360.1	2,377.3	9.6
1986	1,147.6	1,589.3	2,737.0	10.4
1991	1,349.8	1,867.4	3,217.2	11.4
1996	1,515.3	2,066.7	3,582.0	12.1
1998	1,587.4	2,142.3	3,729.8	12.3
2000	1,645.4	2,204.4	3,849.9	12.5
Projections				
2016	2,521.2	3,181.2	5,702.4	16.6
2021	2,989.6	3,681.1	6,670.6	18.9
2026	3,515.5	4,237.4	7,753,0	21.4
2031	3,950.2	4,705.9	8,656.1	23.6
2036	4,132.7	4,934.0	9,066.7	24.4
2041	4,197.1	5,035.8	9,232.9	24.9
2046	4,231.4	5,087.2	9,618.7	25.2
2051	4,257.5	5,108.9	9,366.4	25.4

Source: Statistics Canada. 2001. *Population projections for Canada, provinces and territories, 2000–2026*. Catalogue No. 91–520–XIB

In addition to these two factors, Canadians' life expectancies have increased as a result of healthier lifestyles and universal health care. Many of the baby boomer generation's grandparents, for example, are still alive. A woman born in today can expect to live 82.1 years; a man's life expectancy at birth is 77.2 years (Statistics Canada, *The Daily*, September 27, 2004).

• Demand for Social Workers

All of these contributing factors will mean that the issues affecting older Canadians will become increasingly prominent. And because of the sheer size of this cohort, their concerns will be heard. They will have a bigger influence in social and political matters generally, and especially in matters pertaining to their own welfare and health.

Already an important area of activity, social work with the elderly is set to become a veritable growth industry.

A Portrait of Canada's Seniors

The senior population in Canada, as elsewhere, is not a homogeneous group. Seniors aged 85 and over are obviously the most likely to have serious medical conditions and disabilities. About one in 10 seniors is now 85 or over, up from one in 20 in the early 1920s. Statistics Canada estimates that there will be almost two million people aged 85 and over in 2051, almost five times the current figure. Needless to say, older people in this age range generally have greater needs for social support and health care than younger seniors .

The living arrangements of older Canadians are also varied. Most (93 percent) live in a household and many (68 percent) live in their own household. Ninety percent of senior homeowners have paid off their mortgage. Fifty-seven percent live with a spouse; seven percent live with members of their extended family; 29 percent live on their own; and seven percent live in a long-term care institution of some kind (Chappell 2001, 3).

Women comprise an ever larger share of the senior population, and in the oldest categories, they are even more numerous. In 2000, women made up 70 percent of those aged 85 and older, 60 percent of those aged from 75 to 84, and 53 percent of people aged from 65 to 74.

Each of these sectors has special needs, and unique methods of social work practice need to be applied in each case.

GERONTOLOGY

Gerontology is a multidisciplinary field of study that encompasses the biological, psychological, sociological, health and economic aspects of ageing.

Elie Metchnikoff, the originator of gerontology, was a scientist at the Pasteur Institute in Paris during the early twentieth century. He wrote two important books: *The Nature of Man: Studies in Optimistic Philosophy* (1903) and *The Prolongation of Life: Optimistic Studies* (1907). The optimism in the subtitles was intentional, as Metchnikoff thought the negative effects of the ageing process could be eliminated or reduced.

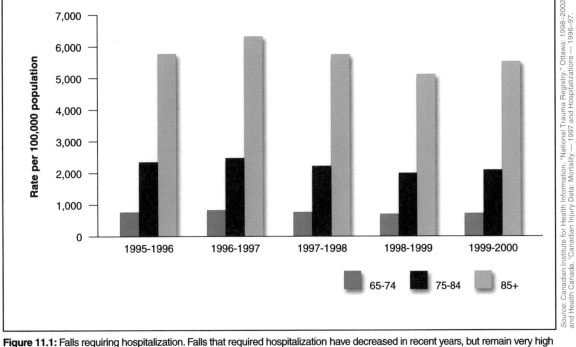

Source: Canadian Institute for Health Information. "National Trauma Registry." Ottawa: 1998–2002 and Health Canada. "Canadian Injury Data: Mortality — 1997 and Hospitalizations — 1996–97.

Figure 11.1: Falls requiring hospitalization. Falls that required hospitalization have decreased in recent years, but remain very high for senior citizens over age 85. (Most recent data not yet available.)

• The Incomes of Seniors

In the past two decades, the incomes of seniors have increased significantly. According to Statistics Canada, the average real income of seniors (after adjusting for inflation) rose 22 percent between 1981 and 1998. In contrast, the average income of people aged from 16 to 64 rose only two percent in the same period.

Nevertheless, seniors have lower incomes than Canadians who are under age 65. In 2002, seniors had an average income of just over $55,200, compared with over $77,000 for non-elderly families. The only age group with a lower income than seniors are those from 16 to 24 years of age. In 2002, a single elderly woman averaged only $24,000 per year.

Most Canadian seniors are retired, but six percent are still in the paid labour force. The largest shares of the income of seniors come from: (1) private pensions, including RRSPs; (2) the Old Age Security (OAS) program; and (3) Canada and Quebec Pension Plans (C/QPP). Because, historically, men have had better access to private pensions due to higher labour force participation and higher-paying jobs, women obtain the largest share of their income from the income security programs. In 2002, senior families received $20,200 in government transfers on average. This accounted for 41 percent of their total income before taxes (Statistics Canada 2002).

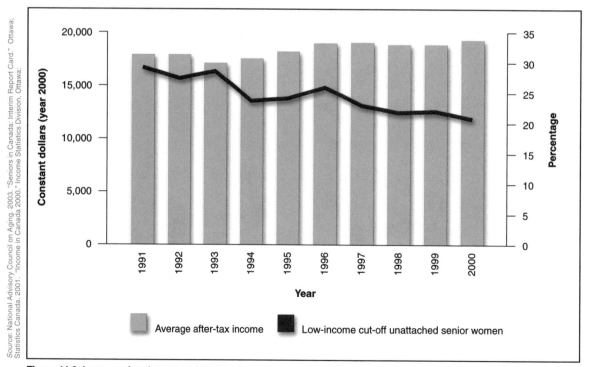

Source: National Advisory Council on Aging. 2003. "Seniors in Canada: Interim Report Card." Ottawa; Statistics Canada. 2001. "Income in Canada 2000." Income Statistics Division. Ottawa:

Figure 11.2: Incomes of senior men and women. A small increase in the average after-tax income for unattached senior women lifts them above the low-income cut-off line.

Theories of Ageing

Two early micro-level theories that have held considerable sway over social work practice with the elderly are activity theory and disengagement theory. Activity theory holds that, as people age, they have a decrease in life satisfaction and that this can be relieved by engaging in various activities such as joining clubs, doing volunteer work or participating in sports. Disengagement theory, by contrast, asserts that individual adjustment to ageing is accomplished by withdrawing from social life and that this is a natural and inevitable process.

These theories or approaches focus almost exclusively on individuals and how seniors adjust to ageing. There are other, more contemporary theories that are beginning to inform social work practice with the elderly. For example, continuity theory suggests that to age successfully, one must maintain a consistent lifestyle. According to this view, older Canadians will be most satisfied if they continue the roles and activities of their middle years. This theory is based on the notion that old age is a continuation of a person's past, rather than a break with it.

Role theory, a expansion on the above approaches, seeks to understand the "adjustment" of ageing people to the new roles entailed in getting older. In the context of disengagement, for example, role theory looks at how "normal ageing" involves a functional and voluntary process in which the elderly withdraw from social life, letting go of social roles and activities. In the context of seniors' activity, role theory focuses on how successful ageing involves "slowing down but keeping active" — that is, as people age, they may need to replace old roles with new and equally fulfilling ones.

• "Life Course" Theory

An alternative to these is the life course theory or approach, which focuses more on how individuals take various distinct pathways through life as they move through different periods. This approach does not view old age as any less satisfying as other periods of life, such as early parenthood. Rather, it views each period as having particular benefits, limitations and characteristics. The approach is also unique in that it discusses issues in terms of life events rather than age.

"Life course" theory sees old age as a new but equally satisfying stage.

The life course theory likely has the largest potential with respect to informing effective social work practice. Glen Elder (2002), the originator of the life course theory, posits four main principles for the approach:

- the life course of a person is shaped by his or her historical and geographic placement;

- the impact of a transition or event depends on when it occurs in a person's life;

- lives are lived interdependently in that the actions and relationships of one person can affect the lives of others; and

- individuals construct their own life course through choices and action, but these are contingent upon the constraints and opportunities presented.

The life course theoretical approach has the advantage of addressing both the individual and broader contextual issues surrounding ageing. Being broader in scope, it also allows for the incorporation of ideas from feminist theory, critical theory and political economy theory (see social work theories discussion at the end of Chapter 5, p.106).

Ageism: Negative Images of the Elderly

Common phrases such as "over the hill" and "don't be an old fuddy-duddy" symbolize society's negative image of old age and elderly people in general. Ageism, as this kind of discrimination is called, can be defined as any attitude, action or institutional structure that subordinates or oppresses a person or group on the basis of age. Of course, ageism is different from other "isms," such as discrimination on the basis of race or gender, in that everyone will at some point be old (unless, of course, he or she dies young) and will therefore likely experience ageism.

Researchers have found that different cultures regard their elderly in a variety of ways. Lena Dominelli, a professor of Social and Community Development at Southampton University in England, believes that the decline in the economic status of older people in the West is part of the explanation for ageism (Dominelli 2004, 135). Ageism, according to Dominelli, is oppression of people on the basis of age where seniors are presented as a homogeneous group that are a burden to society. Western countries generally, she argues, tends to regard people in materialist terms — people's worth or value to society is often based on how much they make, the size of their house or the kind of car they drive. In retirement, the income of seniors usually drops, and this may have the effect of lower self-esteem on the part of the seniors themselves and negative views from other Canadians. Furthermore, with urbanization, and especially with the breakdown of the extended family, the elderly have tended to lose their status in the family and in society as a whole.

Indeed, North Americans and Western societies generally may fear ageing more (and be more ageist) than others. This is perhaps best exemplified by the sales of beauty products and the use of painful plastic surgery to restore a youthful look. However, not all societies and cultures view the elderly this way. Many Aboriginal, Asian and African societies (and many cultures within Western societies) place a higher value on the wisdom and traditions of the elderly. In many societies, the elderly are traditionally viewed as sources of guidance and knowledge.

Health Canada.

Aboriginal elders are viewed as sources of knowledge for the young.

IN THE EYE OF THE BEHOLDER — FEAR OF AGEING

The "fear of ageing" is largely based on a series of myths about old age and the elderly. Some such views depict ageing negatively, while others portray an unrealistic picture of the joys of later life — travel, golf, dinner and dancing. The following are a few of these myths.

- **Myth**: "To be old is to be sick."

  Reality: Most seniors are relatively healthy and active. Three-quarters of Canadian seniors report that their health is good, very good or excellent.

- **Myth**: "Seniors and technology don't mix."

  Reality: Seniors are the fastest growing group on-line, and they are not incapable of using the new technology for more than just e-mail. For example, seniors in the Seniors' Education program at Ryerson University developed, produced and moderate an interactive website. The webmaster and all those working on the site came to computers with no background in the field.

- **Myth**: "Most seniors live in nursing homes."

  Reality: Just five percent of men and nine percent of women over age 65 live in health care institutions; most are 85 or older. And the percentages have declined.

- **Myth**: "Seniors don't pull their own weight."

  Reality: Up to a third of seniors provide help to friends and family, including caregiving for spouses and grandchildren and financial assistance to children. Senior volunteers (about 18 percent of all seniors) spend an average of five hours a week on their activities. Seventy-seven percent of seniors donated money to a charity in 2000 — the greatest proportion of any age group. And seniors pay taxes — just as they've done all their lives. So the argument is based on a misunderstanding..

- **Myth**: "Seniors are too set in their ways to undertake new things."

  Reality: The evidence points in a different direction, or at least suggests that the opposite can occur. For example, Dorothy Rungeling of Fonthill, Ontario, published her first book, *The Road to Home*, at the age of 91 and the second, *It's Fun to Grow Old*, a year later in 2002. A third book, about her experiences as a pilot in the 1950s and 1960s, is in the works. One might equally say that the senior years are a time when more time and more security can open up new and exciting vistas that were simply not available to individuals earlier in their lives.

Health Canada.

How Healthy Are Seniors?

Life expectancy has doubled over the past one hundred years, and, as the chart indicates, seniors in Canada seem to be enjoying their improving health in most instances (see Table 11.2). Men aged 65 can expect to live the equivalent of 82 percent of their remaining years in good health, and women, 80 percent. Moreover, the majority of seniors do not engage in behaviours harmful to their health (National Advisory Council on Aging 2001, 5). Many analysts believe that our public health care system plays a particularly important part in preventing seniors' health problems, promoting and restoring health and preventing further health deterioration.

Nevertheless, there is, as is the case with other age groups, a health gap between seniors with low income and those with higher income. Seniors with low income are more likely to have chronic conditions or long-term activity limitations. In 1998–99, 30 percent of seniors with household incomes of less than $20,000 saw themselves as being in fair to poor health and 69 percent of these persons were physically inactive. In comparison, 20 percent of seniors with incomes over $20,000 rated themselves as being in fair to poor health and 58 percent were physically inactive (National Population Health Survey 1998–99).

• Pain and Suffering

A major concern for older Canadians is pain. Pain not only causes physical suffering, but also affects emotional and mental well-being. Seniors are more likely to have conditions that cause pain, such as arthritis, osteoporosis or diabetes. Regrettably, seniors are also more likely to suffer untreated pain. Over one-third report some level of pain or discomfort, and the figure is higher for those over age 75.

To an extent, perhaps, some pain is subjective — each person feels and reports pain differently, and identical injuries can cause widely different perceptions of pain. However, most of it is real and it is crucial for social workers to understand the nature of pain and the terminology used by medical professionals. Pain can be of two types:

• **Acute pain** is temporary. It may be severe at the beginning but decline over time, lasting from a few seconds to several days or weeks.

• **Chronic pain** lingers, lasting from a few months to many years. It can be mild or excruciating, episodic or continuous, merely inconvenient or totally incapacitating.

Sometimes chronic pain begins as acute pain. It can also stem from disease, such as arthritis, diabetes or shingles, but often an immediate cause cannot be found. Both types of pain need to be addressed before intervention around other issues can be undertaken.

Health Canada.

Most seniors keep active and many find time to pursue new hobbies.

Table 11.2: How Healthy Are Seniors?

Indicator	Definition	Trend Direction Indicates
Life expectancy at age 65	Average number of years of life remaining after age 65	Situation improving
Health expectancy	The average number of years after age 65 that in individual can expect to live in good health	Situation improving
Perceived health status	How seniors assess their own health	Situation improving
Chronic disease prevalence	Percentage of seniors with key chronic diseases	Mixed situation
Activity limitations	Restriction in activities of daily living resulting from a long-term health problem	Situation improving
Personal health practices	Percentage of seniors who are physically inactive	Situation improving
Lifestyle issues	Percentage of seniors who smoke	Situation improving
Unintentional injuries	Number of seniors' unintentional injuries resulting in hospitalization	Stable situation
Hospitalizations due to falls	Number of seniors' injuries resulting in hospitalizations that are due to falls	Stable situation
Suicide rate	Number of suicide deaths per 100,000 persons in the same age group	Mixed situation
Sense of coherence	Percentage of seniors reporting that life is meaningful, that events are comprehensible and that challenges are manageable	Situation improving

Source: National Advisory Council on Aging. 2001. *Seniors in Canada: A Report Card.* Reproduced with the permission of the Minister of Public Works and Government Services Canada, 2005.

Because they often work with individuals closely over an extended period of time, social worker practitioners may be in a better position than other heath care professionals to listen to the reports of pain from seniors and communicate these concerns to the medical team. Social workers also need to be aware of the reasons for undertreatment of pain with seniors. First, seniors may be reluctant to report pain, believing that they are supposed to just bear it. Second, medical professionals may lack training and experience in managing pain and may hold myths about seniors — these myths might include the belief that seniors are less sensitive to pain or can tolerate it better than younger people, that pain is a natural part of ageing or that older patients cannot tolerate strong painkillers.

SOCIAL ISOLATION AND LONELINESS

Researchers and medical practitioners differentiate between social isolation and social loneliness, and knowledge of the distinction is necessary for social work practice.

• **Social isolation** involves being separated from one's environment to the point of having few satisfying and rewarding relationships. It is measured by the number of personal contacts people have — including relatives, friends, neighbours and co-workers.

• **Social loneliness** is one's feeling of dissatisfaction with social contacts in terms of quantity and quality of the relationships or both.

A recent "Aging in Manitoba" study found that four out of five participants aged seventy-two and over expressed some degree of loneliness, with 38 percent expressing low levels of loneliness and 45 percent expressing high levels.

CP PHOTO/John Lehmann (1998).

Two older women examine a new anti-fraud program for seniors.

Issues of Increasing Concern

While they are all different in many respects, seniors also face a number of issues in common. Below, we examine a few of these issues — inadequate levels of physical activity, the risk of injury, fraud and employment discrimination.

• Inactivity

Physical activity may not appear to be a social work issue, but many emotional, spiritual and mental health issues — perhaps especially among seniors — are directly related to it. Inactivity can lead to preventable health problems, such as heart disease and stroke. According to the Fitness and Lifestyle Research Institute, physical inactivity can also lead to depression, lack of energy, chronic disease, weight problems, disability and premature death. The Canadian government estimates that billions of dollars per year could be saved if physical activity rates increased. For many seniors, walks, gardening or light sports could lead to a better emotional state.

Unfortunately, the majority of seniors are inactive, with 55 percent of men and 67 percent of women reporting being physically inactive in 1998–99. There is recent evidence that this trend may be reversing in the younger elderly age categories. Seniors aged 65 to 74 had an improvement in their physical activity levels, with 51.1 percent reporting being physically inactive in 2000–01 compared with 54.7 percent in 1998–99. Seniors 75 and older reported inactivity levels of 63.3 percent in 2000–01, a little worse than the 62.5 percent in 1998–99 (Statistics Canada and Canadian Institute for Health Information 2002).

• Accidents

Canadian seniors also face significant risks due to common accidents such as falling. Hospital admissions for unintentional injuries occur most often among seniors. The situation has not improved, as 36 percent of all injury admissions in 1997–98 involved seniors, up slightly from 33 percent in 1995–96 (Canadian Institute for Health Information 1999).

• Victims of Fraud

Often isolated in their homes, seniors are also the leading targets of fraudulent crimes, such as fake investment opportunities, phony contests and false fundraising campaigns. People over the age of 60 comprised three-quarters of those defrauded of more than $5,000 in 1997 and the vast majority were victimized more than once (National Advisory Council on Aging 2001). In some cases, seniors have lost their life savings. Criminals are using more and more sophisticated techniques, often misrepresenting themselves as employees of the person's bank or other financial institution.

• Mandatory Retirement

Finally, retirement is often presented to Canadians as something that enables hard-working seniors to take a break from the grind of work and to relax, travel and enjoy life — "Freedom 55." Unfortunately, the reality is often quite different, since retirement usually means a substantial drop in income as well as greater social isolation. Taken on its own, forced or unexpected retirement can be bad enough, but when combined with other misfortunes (illness or illness of a spouse) it can be particularly stressful.

Forced retirement, whether it is early or not, can create financial and emotional troubles that seniors are subsequently left to face alone. This can affect women even more negatively, since many women enter the labour force later, after they have raised their children. Mandatory retirement in such cases dramatically reduces the pension income of senior women.

NEW COMPASSIONATE CARE BENEFITS

As of January 4, 2004, there is a new type of special benefit through Employment Insurance (EI) administered by Human Resources and Skills Development Canada (HRSDC), called compassionate care benefits.

The federal government expanded the Employment Insurance (EI) program to extend compassionate care benefits to a person who must be absent from work to provide care or support to a gravely ill family member. Benefits may be paid up to a maximum of six weeks to an employee looking after a loved one who is at risk of dying within 26 weeks. Unemployed persons on EI can also ask for this type of benefit. Benefits can be shared with other members of the applicant's family, but they also must be eligible and must apply for them.

Providing care to a family member means providing psychological or emotional support, arranging for care or directly providing or participating in the care. More information is available on the Social Development Canada website, at http://www.http://www.sdc.gc.ca.

Caregiver Tax Credit

Canada Revenue Agency (CRA) allows Canadians to claim deductions and credits for individuals supporting people with disabilities. For example, care could have been provided to parents, parents-in-law and grandparents. The caregiver amount is a non-refundable tax credit which reduces the amount of federal income tax paid.

<hr>

For more information, consult the CRA website at: www.ccra-adrc.gc.ca

Health Canada.

Abuse and Neglect of Seniors

Often called elder abuse, a straightforward definition of abuse and neglect of seniors is mistreatment of older people by those in a position of trust, power or responsibility for their care. Neglect is frequently associated with abuse. The abuse may take place in the home or in an institutional care setting. Like other forms of violence within families, senior abuse is largely hidden from view. Isolated and often frail, seniors are highly vulnerable to mistreatment, for whatever reason, by those closest to them and responsible for caring for them. Hard data are difficult to come by, however.

Though dated, the study most cited is the 1990 national telephone survey of 2,000 older adults in private dwellings (Podnieks, Pillemer, Nicholson and Shillington 1990). The findings were as follows:

- Approximately four percent of older adults living in private homes reported experiencing abuse or neglect.
- The most prevalent mistreatment reported was mental abuse, most often involving widowed older adults living alone and perpetrated by a relative or a non-relative rather than by a close family member.
- Chronic verbal aggression, a component of psychological abuse, ranked as the second most prevalent form of abuse. Victims were usually abused by their spouse.
- Physical abuse ranked third. Again, in the majority of cases the abusers were spouses of the victims.

While these data are dated, they provide a comparison point in relation to more recent data on the problem of elder abuse in Canada.

Table 11.3: Over One-Quarter of Senior Victims of Violent Crime Victimized by a Family Member

Victimized by:	Number			Victims (%)		
Family member	1,660	649	357	28	36	19
Spouse	312	236	76	31	36	21
Parent	53	28	25	5	4	7
Adult child	398	243	155	40	67	43
Sibling	110	60	50	11	9	14
Extended family	133	82	51	13	13	14
Non-family person	2,407	1,052	1,355	66	59	74
Unknown person	214	91	123	6	5	7
Total	**3,627**	**1,792**	**1,835**	**100**	**100**	**100**

Note: Data are not nationally representative, being based on data from 166 police departments representing 53% of the national volume of crime in 2000.
Source: Statistics Canada. 2000. Centre for Justice Statistics. Incident-based Uniform Crime Reporting (UCR2) Survey.

• The General Social Survey (GSS) and Police Statistics

Essentially, there are two sources of more recent data on senior abuse: victimization surveys and police-reported statistics. Victimization surveys tell us only what the victims themselves report — and there are many reasons why seniors may not respond, even when they are reached with the survey. On the other hand, police statistics are reliable but only for cases where abuse is reported. Both types of data therefore seriously under-report the extent of senior abuse in our society.

Perhaps the most reliable source of data is the 1999 General Social Survey (GSS), which shows that about seven percent of seniors report experiencing some form of emotional or financial abuse by an adult child, caregiver or spouse (in the five-year period preceding this survey) (Dauvergne 2003). The breakdown by types of abuse is as follows:

- emotional abuse (seven percent);

- financial abuse (one percent); and

- physical or sexual violence (one percent).

In addition, almost two percent of older Canadians said they had experienced more than one type of such abuse.

Police-reported statistics from 2000 indicate that common assault by family members was the most frequent experience. Twenty-one percent were cases of uttering threats and 13 percent were cases of assault with a weapon or causing bodily harm. The pattern was the same for senior males and females. As might be expected, the most common form of abuse by non-family members was robbery (67 percent against older women and 56 percent against older men).

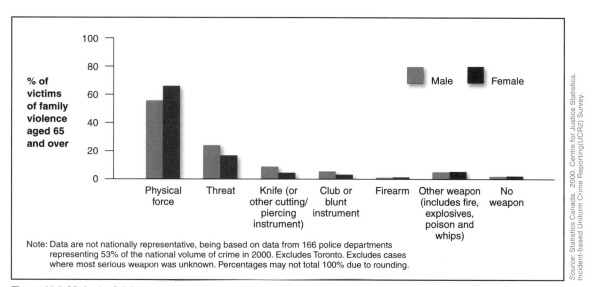

Note: Data are not nationally representative, being based on data from 166 police departments representing 53% of the national volume of crime in 2000. Excludes Toronto. Excludes cases where most serious weapon was unknown. Percentages may not total 100% due to rounding.

Source: Statistics Canada. 2000. Centre for Justice Statistics. Incident-based Uniform Crime Reporting(UCR2) Survey.

Figure 11.3: Methods of violence against seniors.

DETECTING ABUSE

- Physical abuse: Fear of caregivers; unexplained injuries; delay in seeking treatment; over-sedation; unusual patterns of bruises; history of changing doctors; scalp injuries.

- Psychological abuse: Low self-esteem; appears nervous around caregiver; confused; suicidal; avoids eye contact with caregiver; fear of abandonment; lethargic or withdrawn.

- Financial abuse: Unexplained missing items; failure to pay bills; inaccurate knowledge of finances; suddenly changing a will; going without affordable necessities; unusual withdrawals from bank account.

- Neglect: Malnourishment; wandering without supervision; lack of heat or electricity; unkempt appearance; missing dentures, glasses or hearing aids; skin conditions or pressure sores; untreated medical problems; alcohol or medication abuse.

Source: National Advisory Council on Aging. 2004. *Hidden Harm: The Abuse of Seniors*. Reproduced with the permission of the Minister of Public Works and Government Services Canada, 2005.

Occasional Relief from Caregiving

One step in preventing senior abuse within families is to understand the possible causes. Dauvergne (2003) discusses several lines of reasoning that have been advanced: the stressfulness of a family situation; the fact that some of this violence may have been learned earlier and is simply a way of responding to stressful situations; the fact that the lives of the senior and family care giver are so intricately intertwined; and the possible effects of discriminatory attitudes towards the ageing members. Doubtless all of these are contributing factors, but a major factor must be the seemingly relentless strain put on family members who have responsibility for caring for seniors.

The extent of informal caregiving is often understated. Over 1.7 million adults in Canada aged 45 to 64 are providing informal care to almost 2.3 million seniors with a long-term disability of physical limitation. According to Stobert and Cranswick, "most are looking after their own parents (67 percent) and their spouse's parents (24 percent). Many (24 percent) are providing help to close friends and neighbours." Women dedicate almost twice as much time to the task, and working outside the home does not appear to reduce the amount of time middle-aged women spend providing care — 26.4 hours a month for women and 14.5 for men. "In other words," Stobert and Cranswick note, "the caregiving labour is divided along traditional gender lines, which may reflect the provider's level of comfort performing tasks that mirror their areas of competence in their own homes."

Equally troubling is the fact that less than one in five of the care providers reported that they received help if they needed a break. Yet, when asked to identify the most useful thing to allow them to continue providing help, the most common answer (51 percent of those aged 45 to 64) was "occasional relief or sharing of responsibilities." Flexible work arrangements and financial compensation were also on the list.

There is the additional complication of seniors looking after seniors. Stobert and Cranswick report that over one in 12 seniors (321,000) is also looking after at least one other senior: a spouse (25 percent), a close friend (33 percent) or a neighbour (19 percent). The gap between men and women with respect to giving care in this age group is higher than for younger caregivers. Moreover, only 18 percent of the senior caregivers indicated that someone else could take over should they need, or want, time off — pointing to an even greater need for support.

The physical and psychological effects of violence against seniors is traumatic, if not completely devastating, for the senior and perhaps even the abuser. In the face of all these concerns, and the growing senior population, it is a primary concern that governments at all levels (as well as family members and friends) find more ways to provide those who are giving care to seniors the relief they need when they feel need it.

Table 11.4: Caregiving — Only About One in Five Care Providers Get Help When They Need a Break

	Caregivers aged 45 to 64		Caregivers aged 65 and over	
	'000	%	'000	%
People providing informal care to seniors	1,748	16	321	8
Male	861	49	133	41
Female	886	51	188	59
Marital status of caregivers				
Living common law	108	6	F	F
Married	1,255	72	218	68
Widowed	45	3	67	21
Divorced	158	9	17[E]	5[E]
Separated	45	3	F	F
Single (never married)	132	8	11[E]	3[E]
Total	1,744	100	320	100
Main activity of respondent in the past 12 months				
Working at a paid job or business	1,221	70	20[E]	6[E]
Looking for paid work	35[E]	2[E]	0	0
Going to school	F	F	F	F
Caring for children	23[E]	1[E]	F	F
Household work	116	7	34	11
Retired	247	14	245	77
Long-term illness	57	3	F	F
Other	38[E]	2[E]	16[E]	5[E]
Total	1,745	100	319	100
Person gets assistance if he/she needs a break	305	17	58	18
From whom does he/she receive assistance?				
Sister	83	27	F	F
Brother	63	21	F	F
Spouse	56	18	F	F
Daughter	26[E]	9	18[E]	37[E]
Son	22[E]	7	8[E]	31[E]
Friend or neighbour	36[E]	12	6[E]	11[E]
Formal help (paid or government)	50	16	12[E]	20[E]
Other family (includes in-laws)	41	13	7[E]	13[E]

[E] Use with caution.
[F] Too unreliable to be published.
Source: Statistics Canada. 2002. General Social Survey, Cycle 16.

Abuse in Institutional Settings

Another issue of concern to social workers is abuse in facilities providing care to older people, including acute care hospitals, nursing homes and retirement homes. In this context, **institutional abuse** is any act or omission directed at a resident that causes the person harm, or that wrongfully deprives that person of her or his independence.

This definition focuses on the consequences or impact of acts on residents and less on the intent. The abuse could be of an individual nature, whereby a staff member at the institution directly abuses the resident. But often the abuse is systemic, whereby situations are allowed to develop that facilitate or permit abuse and neglect. It could also involve the failure to provide adequate safeguards for residents and staff. Guarding against such forms of abuse and neglect, both intentional and unintentional, is important not only for family members and relatives but for social workers associated with these seniors and the institutions in which they find themselves.

• Combatting the Abuse of Seniors in Institutions

Systemic abuse in institutional settings often results from policies, procedures and processes that appear to be designed to maximize care. For example, a facility may have a policy that permits staff members to search residents' rooms at any time for alcohol or medication. The intent of the policy may be protecting cognitively impaired residents from harm, but the outcome is an invasion of privacy. Institutions typically have numerous policies regarding eating, wake-up and sleep times. Often, these conflict with residents' lifelong eating and sleeping patterns. Residents also might find it difficult to question these policies as they are framed in terms of protection. One important way that social workers can assist with preventing abuse of seniors is by using various advocacy strategies, resident councils and family councils. Ongoing staff training and policy reviews are also important.

The "home" or "residence" model for long-term care can help overcome some of the problems of abuse in institutional settings. Some facilities have found that developing a charter of rights works well in addressing abuse. An example is the Yvon Brunet seniors' residence in Montreal. Their Charter includes five basic rights: information and freedom of expression, privacy, dignity and respect, continuity, and responsibility and participation. These rights translate into a variety of procedures that ensure that residents' needs are being met, such as a residents' council, flexible schedules and consultation about medications and menu choices. (National Advisory Council on Aging 2004).

Awareness of the widespread abuse of older adults is growing and social service agencies are responding with community-based initiatives that are more effective in reducing the incidence and eliminating some of the causes.

Elizabeth Podnieks, Chair, Network for the Prevention of Elder Abuse.

EXAMPLES OF SIGNS AND SYMPTOMS OF ABUSE AND NEGLECT IN INSTITUTIONS

Neglect

- Dehydration, malnourishment
- Missing dentures, glasses, hearing aids
- Poor hygiene, lack of inappropriate clothing
- Untreated medical problems
- Poor condition of skin
- Being left unattended or tied to a bed or chair
- Failure to monitor restraints
- Failure to allow outside services; no outside medical appointments

Physical Abuse

- Unexplained injuries — fractures, bruises
- Unexplained falls
- Unauthorized or inappropriate restraints
- Delay in seeking and receiving medical treatment

Sexual Abuse

- Pain, swelling, bleeding in the genital area
- Fear of specific persons or of being alone with them
- Sexually transmitted disease
- Drawing back from touching

Psychological/Emotional Abuse

- Feelings of fear, passivity, shame, or guilt
- Extreme passivity and withdrawal
- Symptoms of depression
- Exclusion from activity and family
- The use or threat of punishment
- Decisions made for resident

Financial Abuse

- Lack of necessities or comforts
- Unauthorized use of resident's money or property
- Disappearance of resident's property
- Unexplained changes in a deed or will
- Inadequate facilities to protect resident's property
- Resident constantly lacking money to buy small personal comforts
- Lack of accounting for way finances have been spent

Medical Abuse

- Reduced/absent therapeutic response
- Poor documentation of medical records
- Improper administration of drugs
- No reason for treatment given

Violation of Rights

- Difficulty visiting, calling, or contacting resident
- Resident not permitted to manage their own financial affairs
- Lack of choices in life
- Lack of privacy
- Resident not permitted to participate in decision-making about his or her own affairs
- Lack of confidentiality in use of health care records

Source: L. McDonald and A. Colins. 2000. *Abuse and Neglect of Older Canadians: A Discussion Paper*. Ottawa, ON: Health Canada. Adapted from: Spencer, C. 1994. Abuse and Neglect of Older Adults in Institutional Settings: An

Social Work in Long-Term Care Settings

Social workers play an important role in the provision of long-term care. The percentage of seniors living in institutions declined from 8.1 percent in 1991 to 7.3 percent in 1996 (Lindsay 1999), but it remains a key area of social work practice. Projections for 2031 estimate that the number of long-term care beds will triple or even quadruple. The percentage of the population aged 85 and over is growing at the fastest rate, and it is this group that is most likely to require long-term care.

Long-term care commonly means nursing home or rehabilitation centre care, primarily for the elderly. Often, this care involves specialty programs for persons with developmental, physical, mental or emotional impairments. In some provinces the term has a wider meaning and may be used to refer to ongoing care within day programs or even within home-based programs. The 1995 Canadian National Population Health Survey established that 75 percent of long-term care residents required help with one or more activities of daily living (i.e., personal care, moving about the institution, getting in and out of bed, getting in and out of a chair) and 39 percent needed help with all of these activities (Tully and Mohl 1995, 27–30).

Work in this field is multidisciplinary, thereby providing an opportunity for social workers to practice collaboratively with allied professionals. The principal components of long-term care are health care and social services designed to provide assessment, treatment, rehabilitation and supportive care, as well as to prevent the increased disability of individuals of all age groups who have chronic physical, developmental or emotional impairments (NASW 1981).

● Phases of Long-Term Care

Social workers in long-term care settings are involved during all the phases of care, from pre-admission through residency to the termination of residency at the time of discharge or death. The four phases in long-term care are briefly described below.

● **Pre-admission phase.** As the first contact with the resident and family, the social worker deals with feelings about placement and provides information about the facility and its services. This is an important phase, as potential future issues with the resident and the family can be identified here.

● **Admission phase.** Social workers are generally responsible for the admission process. During admission, the social worker helps the resident and family become familiar with the facility and its services. He or she is the first liaison between the resident and family and any other community agency that was previously involved. Often social workers engage in counselling during this phase as the resident and family members adjust to their new reality.

ALZHEIMER'S DISEASE AND DEMENTIA

First described by Alois Alzheimer, a German physician, Alzheimer's disease is the most common form of dementia — a condition that results in progressive loss of mental functions.

Dementia involves mental impairment caused by chronic, irreversible brain damage, whether that damage is caused by multiple strokes or by a deterioration of the brain cells of the Alzheimer's type. About 60 percent of persons with dementia (cognitive impairment) are believed to have a cerebral degeneration of the Alzheimer's type (Lyons 1995).

Prevalence and Effects

Approximately 250,000 Canadians, representing eight percent of the population aged 65 and over, met the criteria for dementia. Among those aged 85 and over, the prevalence of dementia rose to 34.5 percent. The vast majority of people with dementia are elderly. The impact of losing one's cognitive abilities is momentous and is generally accompanied by feelings of fear, loss of self-esteem, resentment and even anger.

People with Alzheimer's gradually lose their independence, becoming incapable by degrees of performing simple tasks, remembering recent events, controlling thoughts or moods, or relating to others. The most common form of dementia (from the Latin *demens*, "out of one's mind"), Alzheimer's slowly destroys nerve cells in the brain. It affects primarily those over the age of 65, but it is considered to be an illness and not a normal part of ageing.

There is no cure for Alzheimer's, but there are medications that can help relieve some of the symptoms. According to Health Canada, Canadians spend about $3.9 billion each year for the treatment of persons with Alzheimer's disease and other dementias.

Family Crisis

The onset of Alzheimer's has distressing reverberations. It can cause emotional and financial stresses. Often, spouses or children are left in a precarious position, attempting to care for their loved ones and earn a living at the same time. It is not only the victims of the disease that become increasingly dependent, but also the families and primary caregivers. Family caregivers become dependent upon physicians, other family members, friends, household help, a variety of health and social services and institutional services.

Family members have mixed feelings about entrusting the care of a helpless relative to strangers over whom they have little control. Dealing with these feelings and reactions is often the job of the social worker.

Role of the Social Worker

The first activity of the social worker is to help the family examine different possible courses of action. Family members close to the illness may not see all the options available. And, in other cases, family members may think that they can do it all and may not be open to a stranger's suggestions. The social worker needs to assess the family's feelings and desires before making recommendations.

It is imperative that the social worker has a basic clarity about his or her task: It is to help the family of people with dementia and its members to develop an understanding among themselves about the situation that enables them to act. This helps the family to gain a sense of direction in what seems to be an impossible situation.

The Alzheimer Society of Canada's website (www.alzheimer.ca) is an excellent resource for information about Alzheimer's and working with those who suffer from it.

CP PHOTO/Judy Creighton.

Ewart Angus Home in Toronto takes an active approach to caring for people with Alzheimers or related dementia.

- **Residency phase.** A variety of interventions may occur that involve the social worker. Social workers regularly work at the individual, family, community and policy levels. Work at the individual level focuses on the social and emotional impacts of physical and mental illness or impairment and the prevention of further physical and mental health problems. Social workers work with families in discussing palliative care and end-of-life issues, dealing with the resident's family members who are feeling guilt related to placement or providing information regarding care and prevention issues. Commonly, social workers are involved in locating and arranging resources and in developing or implementing innovative programs and policy.

- **Discharge, transfer or death phase.** Discharge planning is a key aspect of social work in long-term care. In the case of the death of the resident, social workers may provide grief counselling for the family.

Hospice Palliative Care

Palliative care is a special kind of health care for individuals and families who are living with a life-threatening illness, usually at an advanced stage. The goal is to provide the best quality of life for the critically or terminally ill by ensuring their comfort and dignity.

Hospice palliative care focuses on holistic care by offering a wide range of health, emotional and spiritual support services. Palliative care expert Madeleine Saint-Michel emphasizes that a terminally ill person requires much more than physical comfort — they need help in addressing the deep-seated emotions and feelings related to dying. In Canada, we tend to use the terms hospice and palliative care interchangeably. When the distinction is drawn, people use the term hospice to refer to care in the home or community and palliative care to refer to care in the hospital.

Palliative care is provided in a variety of places — at home, in long-term facilities, in hospitals and occasionally in hospices. Hospitals either admit patients into a general ward or, if available, a special palliative care unit. The Sunnybrook Health Science Centre in North York, Ontario, for example, has a palliative care unit that serves cancer patients. Other centres, such as the Maison Michel Sarrazin facility in Quebec (the first opened in Canada in 1985), offer a network of care, providing care at the facility and support in the home.

Social workers offer hands-on support and assistance in such situations. They provide instruction on how to care for the person, for example, or how to give medication, recognize signs of pending problems or how and where to call for assistance in an emergency. They may also help family members work through emotions and grief regarding the illness and death of a loved one.

Social Work and Home Care

In the past two decades, there has been a devolution from institutional-based services to the community- or home-based services. Recent studies have estimated that between 85 and 90 percent of care for the elderly is provided in the home by relatives. This has resulted in an increasing need for support for those providing home care.

Home care involves a range of services, including health promotion, curative medicine, end-of-life care, rehabilitation, support and maintenance, social adaptation and integration and support for the informal (family) caregiver. Home care programs also link formalized health care delivery services in the home setting with community-based services (e.g., Meals on Wheels, respite care and volunteer services). While the recipients of home care are often elderly Canadians, these services are also provided for infants, children and adults.

Home care services include:

- Assessment of client needs (medical and social) and determination of the "best setting of care" based on a client's health and social situation and support network.

- Development of an in-home care plan, which includes family involvement, teaching, interventions and community support.

- Provision of nursing services, therapy services, and home support services.

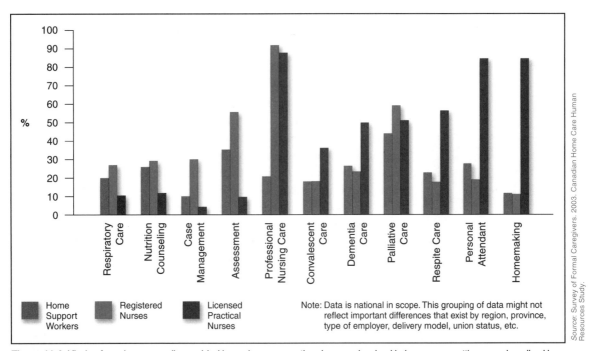

Source: Survey of Formal Caregivers. 2003. Canadian Home Care Human Resources Study.

Figure 11.4: Kinds of services normally provided by various occupational groups involved in home care settings, as described by respondents in a survey of formal caregivers.

CARE BY DEFAULT, NOT BY DESIGN

A report card issued in August 2001 by Canada's Association for Retired Persons (CARP), entitled *Home Care by* Default, *Not by Design,* states that the responsibility for home care is being dumped by governments onto families, not-for-profit groups, volunteers and the private sector. Moreover, no improvement has been made since a similar CARP study in 1999.

Other key problem areas include the need for the development of a country-wide home care strategy, the lack of national standards and difficulty attracting and retaining qualified staff.

CARP notes that the problems with home care will approach a crisis level as Canada's population ages.

The home care report is available on-line at: http://www.50plus.com

A progress report on home care in Canada.

• Coordination of medical supplies, equipment, pharmaceuticals and assistive devices.

• Ongoing monitoring and evaluation of the client, family and caregiver's status and needs.

• Respite care to assist informal caregivers and support families in their role as caregivers.

• Discharge planning and coordination of placement services to long-term care facilities (if required).

Additional services, such as long-term care placement, ambulatory care clinics, home adaptation and home maintenance, are coordinated and provided through or in conjunction with home care programs. Home care services generally include the provision of health services by two tiers of workers: professionals, such as social workers, physicians, nurses, physiotherapists, occupational therapists, speech therapists and dieticians; and unregulated workers, such as homemakers, personal support workers and personal care attendants.

• A Provincial Responsibility

Home care falls within provincial jurisdiction. In Canada, there are at least 663 agencies providing home care services, with 93 percent of delivery agencies receiving some government funding and just over 50 percent receiving all of their funding from government sources. Under the *Canada Health Act,* home care is an extended health service, which is not insured and to which the principles of the Act do not apply. The home care workforce is largely unregulated and largely composed of women. Many work part-time and must hold multiple jobs to make an adequate income. They receive few fringe benefits and face limited career options within the field.

As of 2003, nine provinces had legislation related to home care. The type of services, the amount of service, and the criteria for accessing services vary from province to province. The responsibility for home care has been delegated to a regional or local health authority in ten of thirteen jurisdictions. Six provinces require an income test to obtain public funding for home care. Veterans Affairs Canada provides home care services to clients with wartime or special-duty area service when the service is not available to them through provincial and territorial programs. Home care services are also offered jointly by the Department of Indian Affairs and Northern Development (DIAND) and Health Canada, which have joint responsibility for on-reserve First Nations home care.

Many Canadian social workers are convinced that nothing short of a universal and comprehensive national home care system is necessary, since home care is not currently regulated by any provincial or federal legislation, nor is it included in the *Canada Health Act.* In 1997–98,

PROVINCIAL AND TERRITORIAL HOME CARE
INITIATIVES

The following represent some of the provincial and territorial special home care initiatives:

- British Columbia's Home and Community Care Program, which provides a continuum of supportive health care services from community care to residential care, has focused on the development of their Independent Living and Assisted Living programs. The program is also developing a comprehensive strategy for better end-of-life care.

- Alberta's Home Care Program has provided education and training for home care personnel, including continuing care support workers and health professionals. Areas of particular focus include the care of individuals with Alzheimer's, dementia and the special needs of the geriatric population. The program has also completed a prototype provincial curriculum for support workers.

- Saskatchewan Home Care has set up a course in diabetes education for health care providers that is targeted to home care and others working in the community. (Although unrelated to the elderly, they also have assisted their health regions with supports for children with complex needs.)

- Manitoba Home Care has initiated computerized scheduling in two communities and has tele-monitoring home care pilot programs in two regions. Additionally, they have a Palliative Care Drug Program that improves coverage for drugs for palliative clients, including home care clients.

- Community Care Access Centres in Ontario are implementing the Resident Assessment Instrument for home care (RAI-HC) province-wide. They are also involved with the implementation of management information systems, reporting standards and automation.

- Quebec is implementing standardized home care practices across the province and is collaborating with hospitals and other CLSCs to develop specialty services. In addition, a pilot home chemotherapy initiative is being considered for expansion across the province.

- New Brunswick is involved in the development of a tele-health strategy for the Extra-Mural Program (EMP), the development and implementation of palliative care strategies and preferred practice models for all disciplines.

- Nova Scotia's Continuing Care Home Care Program has adopted the RAI-HC assessment tool, and care coordinators use laptops to complete assessments in their clients' homes. Automated service planning and case management modules have also been implemented to augment the assessment component.

- Prince Edward Island Home Care initiatives include formalizing the case management process, developing integrated palliative care programs, improving support for the frail elderly and offering tele-home care services.

- Newfoundland and Labrador are in the process of conducting a Home Support Review in order to recommend options for controlling costs and developing alternative program models. The province is also involved with the development of a Long-Term Care and Support Services Strategy.

- The Nunavut Home Care Program has been enhanced by the First Nations and Inuit Home and Community Care Initiative (FNICCI). It was designed to establish a complete range of home care services that reflect the health and social needs of Nunavut citizens.

- The Northwest Territories Home Care Program has also been enhanced by the FNICCI, which provides additional resources for increased support services in the community. In addition, a Palliative Care initiative has been developed with an education and support focus, including a palliative care conference and palliative care certification for 44 home support workers.

- The Yukon Home Care Program has started implementation of an Electronic Health Record and Client Database and has trained workers to use it and to gather statistics from it.

Taken with permission from the Canadian Home Care Association, *Portraits of Home Care: A Picture of Progress and Innovation* (Canadian Home Care Association, 2002).

Canada spent only four percent of total public health care dollars on home care. Public home care expenditures reached $2.1 billion in 1997–98, an increase of $1.1 billion, or 104 percent, from 1990–91. By 2001, spending had climbed to $2.5 billion (Statistics Canada E-book 2001). Yet the slow pace and the piecemeal development of these services has left many without programs that properly meet their physical, emotional and social needs.

Conclusion

Of course, becoming a senior does not automatically mean that you will need the services of a social worker. People age differently. Some will remain physically and mentally fit; others will face a number of problems such as isolation, health problems, loss of mobility, inadequate income and housing, discrimination, crime victimization and abuse. It is in these more difficult situations that the social worker and other social service professionals get involved.

With the rapidly ageing population, issues around home care for the elderly are increasingly important. Caring for the elderly at home puts enormous strains on their family members, not to mention the seniors themselves. However, the availability of publicly supported home care is uneven across Canada. In some provinces, such as Ontario, home care is increasingly being provided by large American health care corporations. There is a strong case that home care provision needs more public support if it is to reach all citizens and not just those who can pay for it.

As knowledge of the ageing process increases, social service providers are looking at innovative ways to meet the needs of older citizens. One model or approach that appears to have wide usefulness is "life course" theory. Using this approach, social workers relate to seniors in different ways as they move through the different periods of their life. Every senior's life experience is unique, but it may also have certain similarities with the experiences of others. As a way of approaching social work with the elderly, the "life course" model seems to have wide applicability.

Social work with the elderly is a growing field of social work practice. It offers not only abundant employment opportunities but also the satisfaction of helping those who are, in some cases, less able to help themselves. It is challenging, yet it is also a rewarding and highly important field of social work today and will continue to be so in the decades to come.

Chapter 11 Review
Social Work with the Elderly

Discussion Questions

1. What are the primary issues facing Canada's ageing population with which social workers will increasingly be involved?

2. What special problems are experienced by elderly women in Canada?

3. Should the mandatory age of retirement be extended? Why or why not?

4. What are the advantages of using the life course theory as a lens for effective social work practice?

5. How does the contemporary western view of ageing differ from that of other societies?

6. What are some of the issues of increasing concern regarding the elderly in Canada?

7. Define and explore the causes of the abuse and neglect of seniors in institutional settings.

8. How are seniors affected by social isolation and loneliness?

9. What are the three types of care provided by social workers who work with the elderly?

10. Discuss the role of home care in social work with the elderly.

Websites

- **The National Advisory Council on Aging**
  http://www.naca.ca

  The National Advisory Council on Aging was created in 1980 to assist and advise the Minister of Health on matters related to the ageing of the Canadian population and the quality of life of seniors. Their A-Z index of publications is large and comprehensive.

- **Seniors Canada On-line**
  http://www.seniors.gc.ca

  This site provides access to Web-based information and services that are relevant to seniors 55 and older, their families, caregivers and supporting service organizations. The publications section is great, and the listing of services available for seniors is a good resource for social workers.

- **Canadian Association on Gerontology (CAG)**
  http://www.cagacg.ca/

  Founded in 1971, the Canadian Association on Gerontology (CAG) is a national, multidisciplinary scientific and educational association established to provide leadership in matters related to the ageing population.

Key Terms

- **Gerontology**
- **Activity theory**
- **Disengagement theory**
- **Continuity theory**
- **Role theory**
- **Life course theory**
- **Ageism**
- **Acute pain**
- **Chronic pain**
- **Elder abuse**
- **General Social Survey (GSS)**
- **Institutional abuse**
- **Social isolation**
- **Social loneliness**
- **Phases of long-term care**
- **Palliative care**
- **Home care**

The Gay Pride Parade in Toronto is the final event of Pride Week, Canada's largest gay and lesbian celebration. "Everyone's welcome in our city, and Pride is a celebration of respect for everybody," mayor David Miller told local TV.

12

Social Work and Sexual and Gender Diversity

Celebrating Human Diversity

Sarah Todd

In recent decades Canadians have become increasingly aware of sexual and gender diversity. As a result of significant activism on behalf of lesbians, gay men, bisexuals, transgendered persons and people who identify as queer (**LGBTQ**), discriminatory laws and practices are changing to ensure that people of all sexual orientations and gender identities have equal rights and protection in our society.

Such changes challenge what is sometimes referred to as **heterosexual privilege** — the comfort and power accorded to people who are in, or are expected to be in, a relationship with a person of a different sex and who conform to dominant gender norms. Those who conform to conventional gender norms do not have to worry, for example, whether the neighbourhood they choose will approve of their family and can expect that the people they meet will consider their marital relationship an asset. Straight people do not have to worry about gay bashing or about being disowned by family members upon disclosing their gender identity or their sexual orientation. Straight people rarely, if ever, lose jobs, promotions, political positions or social status because they are straight. These specific social risks, dangers and costs, and a long list of others, are borne by anyone in our society who transgresses norms of gender and/or sexual orientation.

Social work is a profession that is committed to the celebration of diversity, equality and social justice. This chapter considers how sexual and gender diversity is expressed and regulated in our society. It places the discussion within a historical context and considers issues that are relevant to social workers in individual practice, community organizing and policy making. As social work is a profession dedicated to the support and struggle of peoples whose interests are underserved by mainstream society, it will examine issues facing people who belong to sexual and gender minorities.

While many of the gay, lesbian, bisexual and transgendered people with whom social workers work have the same needs as their non-gay counterparts, sexual orientation and gender identity may shape how members of LGBTQ communities experience their problems, what resources are available to them and the ways in which their problems are shaped by the broader society. This is the subject matter of this chapter.

With the rise of LGBTQ activism and the 1973 removal of "homosexuality" from the Diagnostic and Statistical Manual of Mental Disorders (DSM), social workers are increasingly working to challenge homophobia and heterosexism and are celebrating what sexual and gender diversity contributes to the profession and to society in general.

People celebrate at the annual Gay Pride week in Toronto.

VANCOUVER, HOME TO THE
FIRST GAY RIGHTS
ORGANIZATION

In 1964 the first Canadian gay
rights organization, the
Association for Social
Knowledge (ASK), was formed in
Vancouver. They would go on to
open the first gay and lesbian
community centre.

Religious protesters show their
opposition to homosexuality.

The Historical Context of Gender and Sexuality

There are two histories that have shaped thinking about gender and sexuality. The first is the history of sexology, which is the area of science that invented the identities of heterosexual and homosexual. The second is the history of community activism that evolved once the identity of "homosexual" emerged to signify a shared history of oppression and marginalization. To understand the contemporary experience of gender and sexuality, practitioners need to be aware of both.

• Sexology

In the late nineteenth century, scientists and philosophers in Europe and North America increasingly used notions of science and reason to explain and categorize the world around them. Part of that categorization involved documenting what they considered to be proper sexual attraction (Katz 1995, 51). It is through this process that the science of sex — **sexology** — was invented, and the "heterosexual" emerged.

It is not that same-sex and different sex desire did not exist before this point in time, but the turn of the century marked a shift in how we made sense of these desires and behaviours. So, for example, while there are historical records throughout time of men having sex with men, such behaviour was not considered to reflect a "homosexual" or "gay" identity. In other words, before the late 1800s, the concept of "a homosexual" — a person whose identity was defined by their sexual practice — did not really exist.

Another aspect of the invention of sexual identities that occurred at the turn of the century is often termed *medical colonization*. The end of the nineteenth and beginning of the twentieth century was a time when medical authority increasingly began to replace pre-existing religious and judicial authority. Before this transition, gender and sexual non-conventionality were most often understood as sinful and/or illegal. With the rise of professional "scientific medicine," sexologists were called into courtrooms to provide evidence that such transgressions were caused by biological or neurological abnormalities that required treatment, rather than punishment.

At the turn of the century, much of the concern around sexual normality and abnormality was focused on whether people were engaging in sex primarily for reproduction (normal) or pleasure (deviant). One of the ·pioneers in creating categories of normal and abnormal was Richard von Krafft-Ebing (1840–1902). His most famous piece of writing is a categorization of abnormal sexual behaviour entitled *Psychopathia Sexualis*. It is in Krafft-Ebing's work that the heterosexual begins to represent normality — he implicitly defined heterosexuality as reproductive sex between a man and a woman, and homosexuality as same-sex desire.

While some researchers were inventing the heterosexual, others were developing scientific theories of homosexuality. Karl Heinrich Urlichs (1825–1895), an Hanoverian lawyer, was one of the first to do so and was vocal in the fight to decriminalize sodomy — anal sex. Urlichs created categories of the Urning (a female caught in a male body) and Urningin (a male caught in a female body) to make sense of same-sex attraction. He saw homosexuality as inborn and natural — in other words, it was a biological variation, like blue eyes or red hair. Urlichs was also one of the pioneers of gay and lesbian movements. In 1885, as a result of activists such as Urlichs, Berlin police were convinced to stop closing gay bars. By 1897 the first gay rights organization, The Scientific Humanitarian Committee, had been founded. The creation of spaces for "homosexual" congregation and interaction was an important step in the development of homosexuality as an identity and homosexuals as a type of person.

Magnus Hirschfeld (1868–1935) was a psychiatrist in Germany who founded the Scientific Humanitarian Committee. Hirschfeld was one of the strongest advocates for the progressive liberalization of laws against "deviant" sexual behaviour. He fought tirelessly against paragraph 175 of the German Criminal Code that made male homosexuality a crime. He was the first person to systematically describe and work with people whom we would now call transsexuals — people whose gender identity is inconsistent with their biological sex. Most importantly, he challenged the notions of sexual polarity that existed at the time in favour of sexual pluralism. Hirschfeld suggested that gender and sex were not limited to the polar opposites of man/male and woman/female, but were instead spread across a spectrum of sexual diversity.

In their efforts to provide ever-finer classifications of sexual difference, researchers sought physical markers of perversion. Scientists argued that one could determine an invert (homosexual) by the way that he walked, the size of his hips, the shape of his penis or by his "womanly" behaviour. Female homosexuality was seldom explored scientifically until the end of the nineteenth century. This inattention was to some extent a result of prevailing beliefs that women lacked sexual desire and did not enjoy sex. When women did fall under the gaze of sexologists, female homosexuality was largely considered in relation to "abnormal" or enlarged clitorises, hermaphroditism and gender-reversed body types. By the 1920s, lesbianism was linked with "inappropriate female behaviour," such as avoiding motherhood, or political activism.

Many of the beliefs of early sexologists remain part of our common-sense thinking about sexuality. So, for instance, many people still have the stereotype that a man whose gait or speech patterns do not fit within masculine norms is gay. While there has been progress, the desire to find biological and/or physical causes and markers of gay sexuality remains strong in today's culture.

THE HETEROSEXUAL IS INVENTED!

In 1892, American doctor James Kiernan was the first to use the term *heterosexual*. He used the term to describe people who were seen as deviant because they had sex primarily for pleasure, not procreation, and were erotically attracted to people of both sexes. In other words "heterosexuality" was initially a perversion.

Kiernan's 1892 article was also the first North American publication to use the term *homosexual*, which described persons whom we would now think of as transgendered — people who bend or cross conventional gender roles (Katz 1995).

THE POLITICS OF LANGUAGE

While we now consider the term *homosexuality* to be medicalized and usually prefer the terms *gay* and *lesbian*, at the turn of the nineteenth century, the new homosexual identity provided a radical opportunity for people with same-sex desires to see others with whom they had some shared experiences and could build communities.

Language around sexuality and gender continues to change and evolve. It is also quite "political" as groups reclaim and invent language to give meaning to their experience.

In the years following, a second generation of sexologists emerged. Probably one of the most well-known scientists of this generation was Alfred Kinsey (1894–1956). The Kinsey Report, published in 1948 under the title *Sexual Behavior in the Human Male*, surveyed a variety of people about their sexual habits and surprised (at least some of) the American public by revealing that 37 percent of men in his survey reported some homosexual experiences to the point of orgasm. He also reported that most Americans masturbated. Most significantly, he showed that people's sexual behaviours combined so-called perverse behaviours with those considered normal. In 1953, he published *Sexual Behavior in the Human Female* along similar lines.

This type of research was groundbreaking because it suggested that everyday sexual behaviour often transgressed laws, public opinion and social norms. However, with the rise of anti-communism in the 1950s, Kinsey's work was viewed with suspicion. Rumours spread that he was a communist, working to destroy American values. He lost his research funding and died of a heart attack two years later. Kinsey's research provided much of the basis for the political analysis that was developed by members of the gay liberation movement in the early 1970s.

The second generation of sexologists suggested that our social world plays a significant role in shaping our sexual desires and behaviour. In other words, they felt that changes in the sociocultural environment could result in changes to what was understood as normal sexual behaviour. This transformation in the scientific understanding of sexuality was, in itself, a result of social and political changes. Second-generation sexologists were, for instance, influenced by the feminist movement that had challenged the notion of a women's "natural" place in society, suggesting that the "female" gender role is as much or more about socialization and social expectations as any innate or essential characteristics of womanhood.

"We are recorders and reporters of facts ..." — Alfred Kinsey.

• The Rise of Community Activism

In spite of these new understandings, the psychiatric profession in the 1950s had officially labelled homosexuality as a mental disorder caused by an individual's psycho-social environment — a deviation from the heterosexual norm. Their response to such deviance included administering drugs, giving people lobotomies and having gay men and lesbians undergo electroshock treatment. In addition, some lesbians endured hysterectomies and estrogen injections (Warner 2002, 24). Early gay and lesbian organizing would challenge this medical authority by demanding to have homosexuality declassified as a mental illness. After years of activism, public and political pressure from gay and lesbian rights organizations and their supporters resulted in the removal of homosexuality from the Diagnostic and Statistical Manual of Mental Disorders (DSM) in 1973.

World War II was an important period in the emergence of gay communities. During this period of time, the traditional patriarchal family structure was to some extent disrupted. There were increasing opportunities for people to socialize in predominantly same-sex groups. Men were in the army and at war, while many women were working together in large factories. Many people moved to cities where anonymity and lack of parental supervision also allowed more opportunities for sexual exploration. However, this freedom was quickly circumscribed by the hunt for subversives that characterized the Cold War in the 1950s. Any kind of deviance became suspect, because the logic of the day was that if someone had anything to hide (and same-sex attraction was considered something to hide) then the individual had a greater likelihood of being blackmailed into work for a foreign government (Girard 1987).

Thus, the 1950s were a terrible time for gay men and lesbians in the Canadian civil service. The RCMP collected close to 9,000 names of people within the civil service who were suspected to be lesbians or gay men (Kinsman 2003). Many of these people were subjected to police interrogation and surveillance. It was within this climate that, in 1952, homosexuals were prohibited from entering Canada under the *Immigration Act*. While the next few decades were a period of easing anxieties over communism, it would not be until 1976, after significant activism, that the provision denying entrance by homosexuals was removed from the Act.

Throughout the late 1950s and 1960s there was a growing gay and lesbian political movement that began to shape public discourse and scientific understandings about sexuality. This movement symbolically coalesced on June 27 and 28, 1969, when a series of riots erupted in response to a police raid on a Greenwich Village gay bar, the Stonewall Inn. The riots, which were later called the **Stonewall Rebellion**, represented the first significant collective uprising by the gay and lesbian community against state oppression. By the time of the riots, lesbian and gay organizations had had decades of experience in organizing, but were now able to take a more militant course. Stonewall marked the beginning of a much more public, large-scale movement for gay and lesbian rights. A new national organization, the Gay Liberation Front (GLF), was formed with the mandate of creating a revolutionary freedom for all oppressed people, not just members of LGBTQ communities.

In the 1970s gay and lesbian organizations were able to work systematically to begin to challenge laws that limited the civil and social rights of members of LGBTQ communities. An important year for the recognition of the civil rights of gays, lesbians, bisexual and transgendered persons was 1969. With the passing of Bill C-150 and Pierre Trudeau's statement that "there is no place for the State in the bedrooms of the

SIGMUND FREUD

Sigmund Freud (1856 -1939) critiqued much of the biological explanations for homosexuality, coming close to arguing that masculinity and femininity are socially constructed. However, Freud also suggested that homosexuality is an immature stage of development, less developed than heterosexuality.

Freud's theories about sexuality marked an important move away from biology to psychology, but his approach, as adopted by psychologists, was not necessarily liberating for gay men and lesbians. More often, Freud's theories were mobilized to further pathologize homosexuality as a mental illness that needed to be cured.

Itrath Syed, Canadian graduate student and gay rights activist.

CAN YOU CHANGE YOUR SEXUAL ORIENTATION?

Throughout the history of sexology, scientists and physicians have developed methods, such as aversion therapy, to change sexual orientation. With this technique, therapists would pair an individual's same-sex desire and arousal with painful or negative stimuli (e.g., electric shock).

In recent years aversion therapies have been largely discredited as unethical and unsuccessful.

nation," gross indecency and buggery — the legal terms used to describe gay sex — were decriminalized if committed in private between two consenting adults over the age of 21.

Since that time, there have been a number of changes to the *Criminal Code* that have provided increasing sexual freedom, though still within arbitrary limitations. The age of consent for anal sex is now 18, still four years older than the age of consent for other forms of sexual activity. This difference exists despite court decisions that confirm its unconstitutionality. While same-sex sexual activity was decriminalized in 1969, it was not until decades later that it became illegal to discriminate against gay men, lesbians and bisexual persons in immigration, employment, military service, housing, pensions and other benefits, marriage and custody of children.

• Queer Activism

The gay and lesbian movement in the 1980s became increasingly organized and began incorporating queer politics. Queer — a disparaging term often directed at gay men and lesbians – was reclaimed by LBGTQ communities to represent an inclusive celebration of all persons whose sexual and gender expression differs from heterosexual norms. The founders of the first queer activist group, Queer Nation, were from ACT UP, a radical AIDS activist group that was instrumental in having pharmaceutical companies and governments finally respond to the AIDS pandemic.

Queer activism was more confrontational than the 1990s gay and lesbian movement, demanding dramatic changes to the ways we understand difference and diversity in society. It proved to be very difficult, however, to sustain a movement with such fluid boundaries around identities. While none of the queer groups were able to resolve their own contradictions around addressing multiple systems of oppression and the tensions of exclusion/inclusion, they did infuse gay and lesbian politics with radicalism. They also popularized the use of

> "queer" to be more inclusive of sexual minorities and other marginalized people, as a replacement for the more cumbersome, "gay, lesbian, bisexual and transgendered people."... By adopting queer they reclaimed and politicized a derogatory term commonly used before gay and lesbian liberation. It represented the belief in an identity that is more ambiguous and more fluid than gay, lesbian, or homosexual (Warner 2002, 262).

Gay rights activists often align with other progressive movements.

Queer activists distanced themselves from gay and lesbian organizing by critiquing identity-based movements. As a result, queer activists are skeptical of the ways in which identities are viewed as coherent and stable, instead suggesting that they mask a significant amount of diversity within categories, and sameness across them.

AIDS AND SEXUALITY

Over the past three decades, AIDS has had a significant impact on our thinking about sexuality. It ushered in an era of safer sex practices that has broadened our discussion about sexual practices. Today at least 37 million people are HIV positive. The epidemic has hit low-income countries the hardest, affecting men and women equally. In sub-Saharan Africa alone, there are more than 12 million orphans whose parents have died from AIDS.

In North America and much of Europe AIDS has taken an enormous toll on gay communities. In the beginning of the epidemic in North America, AIDS was perceived as a gay disease. This resulted in an increase in homophobia and gay bashing. Gay men often found it hard to find doctors and dentists who would offer care, lost their jobs as a result of HIV/AIDS and/or received substandard care in hospitals. Gay and lesbian communities responded to this hostility and a lack of response by mobilizing their own creativity and resources. While governments, health care systems and pharmaceutical companies were very slow in responding to the pandemic, the GLBTQ community organized ways to take care of itself. This history of volunteerism and activism is strong within LGBTQ communities. They established educational campaigns, hospices and their own support networks. Community activists continue to be very involved in the struggle to ensure that medicine to treat HIV/AIDS is accessible to everyone.

Over the past three decades many gay men have experienced successive losses of partners, friends and colleagues, leaving many older gay men with survivor guilt and decades of loss and trauma, which can affect their well-being. Other gay men continue to live with HIV/AIDS and the uncertainty of how long new treatments will ensure they can live reasonably healthy lives. Many people who are taking protease inhibitors (AIDS drugs) are also living with the side effects of these drugs, which can be severe and disabling. Moreover, decades of using condoms and being continually concerned about the possibility of becoming infected has left some gay men longing for the intimacy of skin to skin sex; so there has been a rise in what is called barebacking — penetrative sex without a condom.

The desire for the intimacy of intercourse without condoms is not just an experience of gay men, but has been one of many reasons why people of all sexual orientations and genders continue to practice unsafe sex. For others, sex is too uncomfortable to talk about or their partners are clear that they do not want to use condoms. If people live in abusive relationships, negotiating condom use can be an impossibility. As a result, activists have increasingly focused their attention on microbicides, which are a range of products that have the ability to prevent the sexual transmission of HIV and other sexually transmitted diseases. Microbicides can be produced as gels, creams, suppositories, films, or as a sponge or ring that releases the active ingredient over time.

Microbicides are increasingly important as we realize that it is the people in our society with the least economic and social power who are at the greatest risk of HIV. For these persons, negotiating condom use or abstaining from sex is made more difficult by the structural oppression they experience in their daily lives. For example, many women around the world cannot risk angering their male partners because to do so would threaten their shelter and their access to the money and resources necessary for survival.

Dick Hemingway.

TERMINOLOGY

Homophobia, biphobia and transphobia

These are terms that are used to describe an individual's and/or society's fear and hatred of gay men, lesbians, bisexuals and transgendered persons.

Heterosexism

Heterosexism is the system of oppression that assumes that heterosexuality is normal and superior.

Sexual orientation

Sexual orientation is defined by more than the identity of the person with whom we have sex or want to have sex. Relatively few people are exclusively homosexual or heterosexual. Instead, it is an emotional, romantic, sexual or affectional attraction to another person. It is not dependent upon a person's gender identity, which is our sense of ourselves as being male, female or transgendered, or our ability or willingness to adhere to cultural norms of masculine or feminine (gender roles).

Sex and Gender

Issues of sex and gender are often conflated (or seen as the same) when, in fact, they refer to quite different aspects of our identities. Sex (usually man or woman) is what doctors attribute to babies based largely on the size of their genitalia. In fact, sex is determined by genetics, chromosomes and hormones, which can combine to create an indeterminate number of sexes. Gender has two components, first gender identity, which is the sense we have of ourselves as male, female or transgendered; and secondly our gender role, which is our adherence to cultural norms of femininity and masculinity.

Theoretical Perspectives

This short account of modern Western responses to sexual diversity highlights the shifting theoretical understandings of sexuality.

• Biological Determinism

Early sexologists attempted to explain sexuality in terms of biology. These explanations are understood as **biological determinism**, which has traditionally focused on the organic causes of non-conventional gender and sexual identities and behaviours. This tradition continues today. Most recently, Simon LeVay, a former Harvard University researcher and founder of the Institute of Gay and Lesbian Education, has argued that the brain structures of gay men are different from those of heterosexual men. We have also witnessed the contemporary hunt for the "gay gene." Such theories have been used to demand rights for queer communities on the grounds that queer persons are born queer.

While it has a certain potential for liberation, biological determinism also has serious limitations. First, the argument that sexual diversity is rooted in biology has not ended homophobia and heterosexism. In fact, it has often been used to entrench this inequality. Secondly, scientific "truths" have consistently been shown to reflect sociopolitical norms and values, rather than existing as objective facts separate from the society in which the research takes place. The search for a clear identifiable difference also raises ethical concerns; what if parents want to test their fetus for the "gay gene" and choose abortion based on the results? This research also has the effect of accentuating the differences that heterosexual privilege relies upon, rather than exploring the many ways in which people who desire those of a different sex and those who desire people of the same sex are similar.

• Social Constructionism

Another group of theories that are used to think through gender and sexual diversity fall under the heading of **social constructionism**. These are predominantly the theories of the second generation of sexologists. Using this perspective, theorists argue that sexualities are constructed by our social and cultural context and by our cultural histories. It is as a result of such theories that gender reassignment surgery at birth was introduced for babies who were determined to be intersexuals — persons whose sexual organs are not clearly male or female. It is also why psycho-therapeutic approaches to "curing" sexual orientation or gender identity (if inconsistent with an individual's sex) evolved.

While it is clear that society plays a large role in our sexual expression, this theory has a number of shortcomings. First, research has found that people cannot change their sexual orientation: While some individuals can decide not to act on their desires, the desires themselves do not disappear. Equally, babies who have been reassigned a gender at birth, either as a result of a botched circumcision or because of having ambiguous genitalia, have not easily reinvented themselves as the gendered subjects that doctors have chosen for them. Many face challenges once they enter puberty and find that their gender identity is incompatible with their sex. It seems clear that our sex, gender expression and sexual orientation rely upon at least some biological potentials.

• Queer Theory

One significant theory that has recently emerged to explain sexuality falls largely within the social constructionism school of thought — Queer theory. This body of thought raises doubts about the possibility that legislative changes within a capitalist democracy will result in liberation. Indeed, these theorists argue for radical transformation.

By the late 1980s, people began to see the ways in which people of colour, women and members of LGBTQ communities, were still marginalized, discriminated against and oppressed, despite hard-won legislative protections. Such observations led some activists to conclude that the existing social structures of Western society, while having many benefits, also have some fundamental problems that limit the possibility for freedom, equality and justice. Queer activists and theorists argue for a rethinking of the entire terrain upon which we create categories of people and distribute power among them. In part, Queer theory responds to the realization that many people do not fit easily or neatly into the binary oppositions of man-woman, heterosexual-homosexual and so on. Queer theorists suggest that identifying as gay or straight does not provide an unquestionable or complete description of who people are sexually attracted to, whom they have sex with, or with whom they share loving relationships.

Queer theory is informed by the work of Michel Foucault (1926–1984), who wrote persuasively that the entire social structure through which we make sense of sexuality is a modern invention. In short, he insisted that there is nothing "natural" about sexual expression — our behaviours and understandings are a product of the particular era (and the social regulations therein) in which we live. Foucault highlighted the social mechanisms that were at work in societies where particular sexual desires and practices were promoted, denied or punished, and how these resulted in people resisting social regulations by organizing themselves around their sexuality.

Many Queer theorists and others who theorize about sexuality have attempted to challenge the polarization that exists between biological determinism and social constructionism. From this perspective, one writer has argued that "our physiological potentialities are built upon, organized, and developed as they become part of our social bodies and lives" (Kinsman 2003b). This theory lets us attend to the ways in which our biological potentials intersect with cultural norms so as to produce us as sexed and gendered beings with particular sexual orientations.

Transgender
Transgender is inclusive of people who identify as bigender, gender benders, gender outlaws, cross-dressers, drag queens, drag-kings, transvestites and transsexuals. Some intersexuals also identify as transgender. Some transgendered persons understand their experience in dimorphic absolutes (i.e. a man trapped in a female body), while others inhabit a more ambiguous zone "between" the sexes.

Transsexuals
Transsexuals are people whose gender identity is at odds with their physical sex. Psychiatry still considers transsexualism a mental illness, which requires treatment. Some transsexuals undergo gender re-assignment surgery in order to have their anatomy coincide with their gender. Others use hormones to shape their body. Not everyone who identifies as transsexual uses medical interventions to change their physical appearance.

Intersexuals
Intersexuals are individuals whose external sex (genitalia) are indeterminant, people who appear to be males but are medically/biologically females, people with female physical attributes who are medically/biologically males as well as those of us having the external appearance of both sexes and the DNA chromosome karyotypes of both sexes.

MORE RECENT HIGHLIGHTS

In February 2001, the *Immigration and Refugee Protection Act* was reformed so that same-sex partners are recognized as members of the family class of immigrants. Now a common-law partner is recognized as someone who has been in a conjugal relationship for at least one year. If the applicant lives within Canada, then there is a cohabitation requirement in place. Refugee processes have also begun to recognize that people might have legitimate refugee claims because of fears that they will be persecuted for their sexual orientation in their country of origin.

Until 1992, gays, lesbians and bisexuals were not allowed to serve in the Canadian military. Similarly, it was not until 1996 that federal employees could receive same-sex benefits. In 1999, the Act regulating survivor benefits, the *Public Service Superannuation Act*, was amended to extend such benefits to same-sex couples. In 1996, the *Canadian Human Rights Act* was finally amended to explicitly prohibit discrimination based on sexual orientation. However, human rights protection at a national level has yet to be extended to transgendered persons.

The most comprehensive package of changes for people living in same-sex relationships came with Bill C-23, the *Act to Modernize Benefits and Obligations*. This Bill amended 68 federal statutes to provide everyone within any common-law relationship with nearly all the rights and responsibilities of heterosexual married couples under federal law.

Legal battles were also fought to challenge Canada's "obscenity" laws that allowed Canada Customs to confiscate gay literature, including safer sex material that depicted anal sex. In December 2000, the Supreme Court of Canada confirmed that Canada Customs discriminates against lesbian, gay, bisexual and transgendered materials, and placed the burden of proving obscenity on the Crown as opposed to on community bookstores or other importers.

It was not until 2001 that the Canadian Census asked whether people "were living with a common-law partner," which was defined to include both opposite and same-sex partners. For many gay men, lesbians and bisexual persons, this term still does not represent their relationships. "Common-law" is generally used to describe a heterosexual relationship. No questions were asked about Canadians' sexual orientation, nor was the opportunity provided for respondents to identify as transgendered. Such silences make the experience of people with diverse sexual identities and gender expression invisible, and thus conveys, at the best, insignificance, and at the worst, shame and disdain.

Most recently, the battle for equal marriage rights has been in front of the courts. Currently the provinces of Ontario, Saskatchewan and British Columbia, and the Northwest Territories, allow same-sex couples the right to be legally married. There is no provision as yet to allow for legal divorce.

There are still many struggles ahead. Many Canadian provinces and territories still refuse to extend equal rights to gay, lesbian, bisexual and transgendered persons. Limits still exist in terms of human rights legislative protection, the ability to make medical decisions for one's partner, workplace benefits and access to gender reassignment surgery. Despite repeated calls for human rights legislation, Nunavut is the only territory to extend human rights protection to transgendered persons. See Egale's website (http://www.egale.ca) for more details on these legal changes and all the latest national and provincial policy changes.

CP PHOTO/Tom Hanson (1999).

Supreme Court ruled in 1999 that same-sex couples should have same rights as heterosexual couples.

Diverse Communities and Sexuality

People's experiences of sexual or gender diversity are different depending upon, among other things, their ethnicity, age and physical abilities.

- **Ethnicity.** Members of LGBTQ communities are also racially and ethnically diverse. For many LGBTQ persons of colour there can be pressure to give up one identity for another. There is sometimes racism within queer communities and sometimes heterosexism in racially or ethnically diverse communities. However, communities of colour are no more bi/trans/homophobic than white communities. Our perceptions that this is otherwise are largely rooted in racist beliefs that communities of colour are "less civilized" than white communities. There are some studies that suggest communities of colour are more accepting of LGBTQ persons.

- **Age.** In North American culture, sex is largely seen as the terrain of the young. Our obsession with youthful beauty makes us uncomfortable with images of older sexuality and, in turn, results in our culture assuming that older people are asexual. This perspective may be harmful for all seniors, but has a particular texture in the lives of seniors who identify as bisexual, gay or lesbian and whose significant relationships and sexual experiences remain hidden from view. When these relationships do become more visible, seniors who identify as gay, bisexual or lesbian often face discrimination. For example, until recently, seniors' residences and nursing homes remained inattentive to seniors' needs for privacy and intimacy. While this has begun to change, it has largely only done so for heterosexual seniors.

- **Disability.** People with disabilities are typically also perceived as asexual, and most of the images around disability and sexuality are medicalized. Men who are living with disabilities are often perceived as impotent because sex is only recognized in terms of the ability to reproduce. Women with disabilities are generally perceived as victims without agency. People with psychological disabilities are often protected from sexual knowledge so as to prevent them from having sexual relationships. In fact, most people with disabilities have the same sexual feelings and needs as people without disabilities. They can also have positive sexual intimacy and healthy relationships. The main problem for most people with disabilities is not how to do it, but finding someone to do it with. There are so many negative stereotypes about disability that it is difficult for people with disabilities to feel desirable and confident enough to seek out a partner. Similarly, these negative images shape the general public's response to people with disabilities. As such, issues of poverty, marginalization and self-esteem are key for people with disabilities living sexually fulfilling lives.

SOCIAL WORK AND INTERSEXUALITY

Social workers can play a key role as society begins to struggle with the long-held misconception that sex is a binary category. In counselling, social workers can provide significant support for parents whose newborns transgress the sex binary that most of us take for granted. Parents often need reassurance, information and sometimes advocacy.

Social workers also play a role in supporting people who have undergone gender reassignment surgery as babies and who are negotiating their assigned sex in their adolescence and adulthood.

At a community and policy level, many people who identify as intersexuals have been politically active, trying to secure changes to the medical establishment, which has traditionally operated within rigid sex binaries. Intersexuals have fought against the practice of sex reassignment surgery in infancy. Social workers can play an important role supporting this activism.

Internet resources:

- http://www.isna.org/drupa
- http://www.healthyplace.com/communities/gender/intersexuals/index.html
- http://www.sexuality.org

Social Work Counselling

In her recent survey, Carol-Anne O'Brien (1999) highlighted the ways in which social work may be implicated in the pathologization of gay, lesbian and bisexual identities. She found that social workers often promote the belief that homosexuality is a passing stage. She concludes that the most common way social workers reinforce heteronormativity — the "normalcy" of heterosexuality – is through silence about non-heterosexual identities. This is exacerbated by the lack of openly gay, lesbian, bisexual or transgendered role models in the profession.

There are two extremes in social work counselling with lesbians, bisexuals, transgendered persons and gay men. The first occurs when social workers exaggerate the difficulties in living in a heterosexist society. In this situation, counsellors tend to obscure that LGBTQ persons are often happy and have positive relationships with family members, straight colleagues and friends. The second extreme occurs when workers assume that sexual orientation and gender identity make no difference to a person's experience. The challenge is to find a way of working between these extremes and providing balanced support to members of queer communities (van Wormer et al. 2001).

There has been a long history of people in social work who challenge the heterosexist norms of society. For instance, Jane Addams, one of the founders of the profession, lived a woman-identified life in Hull House (Stebner 1997). Gay men, lesbians, bisexuals and transgendered persons have enriched society as a whole and our profession specifically. Their contributions have helped to develop queer-positive practice, AIDS services, responses to women's health and activism for social justice, and have contributed to social work knowledge and practice.

The homophobia and heterosexism institutionalized within schools, the health care system and social services have led many gay, lesbian, bisexual and transgendered people to feel reluctant to ask for help. As a result, LGBTQ communities are developing queer-positive social services. These organizations are involved in policy change, community organizing, and individual advocacy and service provision. Most medium and large cities have Pink Triangle Services.

The personal experience of heterosexism and oppression is felt through stigma, stress, guilt and shame. It is often difficult to accept one's sexual and romantic attractions to people of the same sex because we live in a society that is generally hostile to such desires. As a result of the experience of stigma, many members of LGBTQ communities experience internalized homophobia — the external cultural messages that suggest lesbians and gay men are somehow failing to meet social standards are as internalized guilt, shame and stress.

This can, though does not necessarily, result in members of LGBTQ communities struggling with self-acceptance. On average gay

Same-sex marriage rally outside a Conservative Party caucus retreat.

COMING OUT

Contemporary arguments that homosexuality may be a relatively rare biological variation often leave young gay men and lesbians feeling as though they are a tiny minority and that no one in their immediate environment will be like them. While many people use biological arguments in a struggle to assert normality, it can have the effect of adding stress and increasing the sense gay youth have of being isolated. Teachers and administrators often turn a blind eye to sexist and homophobic comments. Gay teachers often have to keep their sexual orientation a secret for fear of being exposed and possibly losing their jobs. In turn, queer youth are more likely to drop out of school, especially since they have few role models.

Because many people assume that everyone, or at least the people closest to them, are straight, and because homosexuality and bisexuality and transgendered persons are stigmatized, LGBTQ persons have a particular set of challenges when it comes to openly claiming their identity. Coming out is a process through which gay and lesbian people disclose their sexual orientation to themselves and others. It is also a process through which transgendered persons can experiment with gender identities until they find one that fits. In such situations, it is often important for people to be open with their family members and friends.

Coming out can be a difficult and terrifying process, as families and friends can and sometimes do react badly. This said, many gay men, transgendered persons and lesbians report feeling relief once they have come out and no longer have to hide their feelings. People who live lives "out of the closet" tend to have fewer experiences of isolation and depression.

Some people are only out to themselves and their partners. Others are out to family and friends, but remain closeted at work. There are many variations in how "out" someone is. Social workers can help support people through the coming out process, but they need to be careful to also respect what people are saying. If people are not ready to come out, or assess the risks to be too high, it is important to trust that they are the experts in their own experience and to support them. The problem with models of coming out is that they can become prescriptive, suggesting that people have to come out. The difficulty is that few models account for the social context and the cultural and ethnic diversity of gay men, lesbians, transgendered persons and bisexuals. These contexts can have a dramatic impact on whether coming out is a possibility for people.

Families and friends of queer people also sometimes need support, and support each other. It is important to not just consider the needs of people's biological families, but also the needs of people's chosen families. The largest family organization is PFLAG, which includes parents and friends of gay men, lesbians, bisexuals and transgendered persons.

Raging Grannies parade in support of gay and lesbian rights in Fredericton, New Brunswick (1998).

adolescents and young men are six to 16 times more at risk for attempting suicide (Dorais 2004). Studies have shown that it is not gay sexuality that causes suicide, but rather having a homosexual or bisexual orientation in highly homophobic environments. Young gay men, lesbians and transgendered youth are known to experience both ostracism and harassment in their everyday lives. They are sometimes rejected by their families and end up on the streets, where they are vulnerable to sexual and physical violence.

CREATING A QUEER POSITIVE SPACE

For social workers who are not members of LGBTQ communities, the following are some preliminary guidelines for creating the space for diverse sexual and gender identities in your practice:

Never assume people are heterosexual. Use words like "partner" and other gender-inclusive language. When asking a person about their life, explicitly articulate the possibility that a person may be attracted to people of the same sex. For instance, you can ask if a person is dating a man, woman or a transgendered person — in other words, leave open the possibility of non-heterosexual relationships.

If someone discloses that they are transgendered, gay, lesbian or bisexual, it is important for social workers to affirm and validate their identity. Queer-positive counsellors view same-sex desire and transgender identities as normal human diversity. Similarly they recognize same-sex relationships as having the same value as heterosexual partnerships.

It is important to remain aware of your feelings about gender and sexual diversity. You cannot expect to grow up in a culture that is hostile to gender and sexual diversity and not internalize some of those feelings and stereotypes. If you cannot provide affirming counselling, or if someone would prefer to work with a counsellor who is a member of a LGBTQ community, then you are obliged, whenever possible, to make the appropriate referrals.

Sometimes heterosexual counsellors avoid their own discomfort with same-sex desire by letting gay, lesbian and bisexual clients talk only about their positive experiences of sexual diversity, but not their struggles with feelings of shame or ambivalence.

When working in areas of sexuality or gender that are uncomfortable, heterosexual counsellors may say supportive things, but their body language may convey discomfort. Body language may do more to alienate clients with diverse sexual and gender identities.

When working with clients to explore the problems that people bring to counselling, it is important to explore homophobia and heterosexism as problems rather than perceiving sexual or gender diversity, in themselves, as being the problem.

It is important to see a client's decision to accept a transgendered, bisexual, gay or lesbian identity as one of many positive outcomes of counselling.

Gay men, lesbians, bisexuals and transgendered persons often seek social work support for issues similar to their non-queer counterparts. These problems may also be shaped by their experience of oppression. LGBTQ persons may also struggle with issues of depression, suicide, alcoholism and drug abuse, all of which can be prevalent among persons who live in a society that is hostile to their identity, desires and relationships.

Support colleagues who are gay, lesbian, bisexual and/or transgendered. Do not rely on them to teach you about sexual or gender diversity.

The Gay Pride parade in Toronto on June 27, 2004, attracted up to one million spectators along its downtown route.

CP PHOTO/Toronto Globe and Mail-Tibor Kolley.

• Counselling Issues

For social workers who are gay, lesbian, bisexual or transgendered, there are specific counselling issues to think through when working with clients and colleagues:

* Social workers who are gay, lesbian, bisexual or transgendered can be excellent role models for people who are dealing with their own same-sex desire or transgendered identity. Hiding one's sexual orientation can send a message that gay, lesbian and bisexual persons are ashamed. However, LGTBQ social workers also have to assess the risks that might accompany coming out in your workplaces, particularly as clients are not bound to confidentiality.

* It may also be challenging for sexual or gender diverse social workers to deal with clients who are hostile to LGBTQ communities. It may be appropriate for these clients to be referred to a heterosexual counsellor, particularly if you feel threatened.

* As members of a marginalized community, often the risks of making mistakes are higher as they may be attributed to your identity or community. This may add pressure to your work if you are not practising in a queer-positive workplace. It is important to try to find allies and people who can offer support.

* Gay, lesbian, transgendered and bisexual service providers can also be uncomfortable with some forms of sexual and gender diversity. You can also have stereotypes and beliefs that you have to think through when working with members of LGBTQ communities.

Working in a small community can present particular challenges. You are much more likely to meet clients outside of the counsellor-client relationship. It is important to be aware of the possibility of roles overlapping and to get support from colleagues to help with maintaining professional boundaries.

• Social Work with Members of Intersexual Communities

Social workers can play a key role as society begins to struggle with long-held misconceptions that sex is a binary category. At the individual level, social workers can provide significant support for parents whose newborns transgress the sex binary that most of us take for granted. Parents often need reassurance that their child is normal and can have a fulfilling life.

Parents also need information, and sometimes advocacy on their behalf, so that they can negotiate with doctors regarding what medical interventions they want taken or whether they would rather wait until their child reaches puberty to see what biological potentials become visible. After many conversations with intersexuals, their families and friends, the Intrasex Society of North America has developed the

COMING OUT

Van Wormer and her colleagues (2000) identify a number of stages of coming out. It is important to understand that not everyone who is gay, lesbian or transgender goes through these stages, or necessarily goes through them in the order that van Wormer presents them. Also, people can be content without moving through all the stages:

* The first stage occurs before a person comes out. People in this stage may feel discomfort, but do not consciously recognize themselves as being attracted to people of the same sex or as not fitting within their assigned gender.

* The second stage takes place when people begin to become aware of their same-sex attraction or their gender discomfort.

* In the third stage – exploration – people develop gay, lesbian or transgender friendships and participate in the LGBTQ community.

* The final stage is marked by integration – in which people accept their identities and incorporate their identities into their lives.

following list of suggestions for responding to intersexuality (http://www.isna.org/drupal):

- Intersexuality is primarily a problem of stigma and trauma, not gender.
- Parents' distress must not be treated by surgery on the child.
- Professional mental health care is essential.
- Honest, complete disclosure is helpful.
- Children should be assigned as boys or girls, without early surgery.

• Social Work with Transgendered Persons

Social workers often work with transgendered persons around the same life issues that affect people who are not negotiating their gender identity. There are, however, some counselling issues that may arise that are specific to members of transgendered communities. Particularly, many transgendered persons experience harassment, physical violence and estrangement from families and friends.

In addition to brokering appropriate services, social work practitioners may also help to advocate for the needs of transgendered persons. The following are useful points to consider in this context:

- Just because someone presents outwardly as a particular gender, it does not mean that that person sees themselves as always, or even often, fitting within that gender norm.
- People make sense of gender discomfort in many ways. Attempting to be supportive of how people understand their gender, however complicated or counterintuitive, is important.
- There are no "cures" for transsexualism. It is not an illness. To the contrary, the problems experienced by transgendered persons are often a result of society's hostility towards people who do not fit within dominant gender norms.
- Gender transitioning, hormonal therapy and/or gender reassignment surgery are a few of the options available for people who are transgendered.
- Gender transitions can cause a great deal of anxiety and uncertainty in a family, so support for family members is also important. Couples and families do sometimes stay together during and after a gender transition.
- Employers and workplaces may also need education and sensitivity training to respond respectfully to someone who is making a gender transition.

BC transsexual filed a human rights complaint claiming discrimination.

The social and regulatory issues that surround gender reassignment are highly specialized areas of practice. In most large cities there are practitioners who specialize in gender counselling. It is important, when possible, to provide support and refer people to counsellors who have expertise in this area.

Social workers might also play an important role in challenging how we organize washrooms, personal identification and demographic forms that exclude, marginalize and silence people who do not fit within the binaries of male and female (e.g., washrooms can be dangerous spaces for someone who does not fit within gender binaries. If someone can not pass as the "appropriate" gender, transgendered persons often face verbal harassment, and sometimes physical violence).

It is also important for heterosexuals to consider heterosexuality. Instead of always looking at people who are "different," it is also important that members of dominant groups reflect on their own sexuality. As with any sexual identity, heterosexuality represents diverse gender identities and sexual practices, many of which are looked upon with suspicion by mainstream society. For example, someone can be transgendered and heterosexual. Also, despite the stereotypes, most people who are sexually aroused by children (pedophiles) are heterosexual. Many heterosexuals also practice S&M, a type of sex play where the power relations are made explicit.

Despite the range of sexual and gender variety, many heterosexuals take for granted that everyone around them is heterosexual and are often unaware of the ways they unconsciously reproduce heterosexual privilege. For example, how many heterosexuals have to think twice before putting a photograph of their partner up in their office? Without thinking through the ways in which heterosexuals move through the world, not listening to or supporting gender and sexual diversity, heterosexual social workers may consciously and unconsciously maintain heterosexual privilege.

WHAT ALLIES CAN DO TO HELP

1. Help ease the isolation felt by queer youth. Help them feel as though solidarity is possible.

2. End shame by fighting for full equality and social acceptance.

3. Use inclusive language.

3. Create a general atmosphere of respect for human diversity.

Source: Dorais, M. 2004. Dead Boys Can't Dance: Sexual Orientation, Masculinity and Suicide. Montreal: McGill-Queens University Press.

CP PHOTO/Jonathan Hayward (2002).

NDP MP Svend Robinson (right) and Bloc Quebecois MP Real Menard support a petition by the national lesbian, gay, bisexual and transgendered equality rights organization, EGALE.

THE SEX TRADE/PROSTITUTION

The exchange of sex for money is often referred to as the "oldest profession," as it can be traced far back in human history. The sex trade has a particular shape in our modern, globalized society. In Canada it is illegal to engage in activities that facilitate prostitution. However, in some Canadian cities, municipal governments have tried to regulate the sex trade by licensing escort services. By trying to legalize the sex trade, many people argue that we move to make the work safer for sex trade workers. Many sex trade workers who are victims of crimes do not go to the police because they are afraid that they will be charged with prostitution. The fear of going to jail also leaves women working in isolated, dark spaces that only increase the dangers of their work. Because of the dangers involved in prostitution, many sex trade workers rely on a pimp, a man who manages their work for a fee. Pimps often provide sex trade workers with protection from violence, bail and sometimes a place to live. For these services the pimp will take a percentage — or all — of the sex trade worker's income. Pimps are also often violent and abusive towards the women they manage.

Many, but not all, sex trade workers are poor, and in the sex trade, there is a class hierarchy. Some women work as expensive escorts and earn a great deal of money for their services. At the other end of the spectrum are women who walk the streets and receive money to help pay the rent, pay for food or to help finance their drug or alcohol addiction. There are also teenagers (many of whom are gay, lesbian, bisexual or transgendered) who work in the sex trade so that they can earn money to live. Many of these teenagers have left or been kicked out of their homes and must earn a living to survive on the streets. Prostitution is often referred to as survival sex — the only means by which people can support themselves.

At the same time, it is important to note that not everyone who works in the sex trade feels coerced into doing so. Some women, men and teenagers say that they are making a living and that sex trade work should be considered to be a job like any other type of work. Increasingly, sex trade workers have challenged social workers not to always see them as victims. Some women say that they are making good, sound choices and that sex work is only stigmatized because of the way people who are not in the sex trade perceive it.

Most people who pay for sex services are male, and they do so for a number of reasons. Some want sex without a commitment, or because they want sex that is novel or kinky. Other times men do not feel comfortable asking for certain types of sexual activities with their partners so they seek out the services of a sex trade workers. Oftentimes, men are away from home and want to purchase sex. Some men hire sex trade workers because they are lonely and are not able to have sexual intimacy in their personal relationships.

There is increasing concern about prostitution on a global scale, particularly the global trafficking in women, where women are promised citizenship in a country such as Canada, but when they arrive are kept in inhumane conditions and are forced to work as prostitutes. Also, legislatures in many income-poor countries are starting to address the problem of wealthy Westerners travelling to income-poor countries to pay for sex with children. Both of these issues present particular challenges as those who are providing services often have little, if any, choice as to whether they participate in the sex trade.

Social workers often work with sex trade workers who are in trouble with the law or who are dealing with the challenges of poverty. People who work in the sex trade are human beings who have private lives. Many of them have families; children and partners. In addition, for many women leaving the sex trade is very difficult because they have few other economic choices; without sufficient education or job experience, many women feel that the sex trade is the only way for them to support their families and pay the rent.

Children of sex-trade workers participate in World AIDS day in Calcutta, India (2001).

CP PHOTO/AP-Bikas Das.

Implications for LGBTQ-Positive Practice

- It is a mistake to make assumptions about a person's sexual behaviour based upon the way in which he or she identifies. As a society, we learned this lesson well during the AIDS crisis. Initially, it was assumed that the virus only affected gay men, and we paid no attention to the fact that straight men sleep with other men and gay men have sex with women. Social workers need to be careful not to assume that people's identities signify a set of consistent sexual practices at one time, or over their lifespans.

- The range of sexual behaviours and attractions that humans experience can at times be confusing for everyone involved. Social workers need to remain supportive in these situations, and be open-minded to new situations and the possibility of a degree of confusion on the part of the people with whom they are working.

- Social work as a field now maintains that people cannot change their sexual orientation. Sexual orientation emerges for most people in early adolescence without any prior sexual experience — choice is not a factor. While social workers are active in supporting people who may be questioning their sexual orientation or who may be struggling with homophobia and heterosexism, it is generally considered unethical to work with someone to change their sexual orientation. There are many people who, for a variety of religious or personal reasons, suppress their sexual orientation, but this is entirely different from changing it altogether.

- Gay, lesbian, bisexual or queer people often prefer working with counsellors who are members of LGBQ communities. We need to learn not to take these preferences as an attack on our abilities as social workers. It is likely that counsellors who identify as gay, lesbian, bisexual or queer know more about issues that may be of concern to someone who is negotiating their sexual orientation. LGBTQ counsellors can also be important role models and appropriate self-disclosure can help decrease a client's sense of isolation.

- If you are straight and working with a gay, lesbian, or bisexual person, or a person who is questioning their identity, it is often helpful to ask the individual if they would prefer to work with a member of an LGBTQ community and facilitate that referral. If such a connection is not possible, it is important not to rely on the client to educate you about issues of sexual orientation. You need to seek out literature and training opportunities. Heterosexual counsellors can also model respect, acceptance and admiration of a person who is lesbian, gay or bisexual.

Participants share a kiss at Halifax's Gay Pride Day Parade in 2002.

CP PHOTO/Halifax Daily News-Scott Dunlop.

For more information on counselling gay, lesbian and bisexual persons, see the resource list at the end of this chapter.

Service Agencies — Case Studies

• David Kelley Services — Toronto, Ontario

David Kelley Services was created in 1996 and is part of the Family Service Association of Toronto. This program provides a range of interventions for the gay and lesbian community at both the micro and mezzo levels. The Lesbian and Gay counselling program is a short-term service for individuals, couples or families. Following an assessment conducted by a worker, issues explored may include sexual identity, violence and isolation. The worker then assists the client in creating appropriate interventions that facilitate problem solving and working towards change. One specific intervention employed within this program is Partner Abuse Response services. This service works with abusive partners to reduce the occurrence of violence in their intimate relationships. Counsellors working within this model assist individuals in finding alternatives to abuse and violence and work with them to change their abusive behavior.

An HIV/AIDS community counselling program is also offered to gay and lesbian individuals who are dealing with HIV or AIDS. Workers provide counselling and support to individuals affected by HIV/AIDS, including those infected by the disease and those who have friends and family diagnosed with HIV/AIDS. Within this program, workers also refer clients to other services within the community and will advocate for them in areas such as housing and treatment. Workers play a brokerage role as they work to connect clients to necessary services that are essential to a client's life. As such, workers assess client needs and available resources and mutually explore such options with the client.

Finally, David Kelley Services offers many therapy and support groups for the gay and lesbian community. Such groups focus on areas such as same-sex partner abuse, living with HIV/AIDS, male survivors of sexual abuse and parenting. Workers in such groups are facilitators for personal change, educators on issues relevant to the group and of existing appropriate resources and services within the community, linkages to these resources and services, and mediators to help solve disputes and conflicts with the group.

• Transgender Health Program — Vancouver, BC

Implemented by Vancouver Coastal Health in 2003, this program strives to improve the quality of health and social services for transgendered persons. The program brings together transgendered people, health care providers, planners and researchers in pursuit of this goal.

Within this program, professionals with counselling and mental health backgrounds, as well as individuals from other disciplines, are involved in the Education Working Group. This group oversees program development and implementation of strategies created to best educate and inform health and social service professionals about issues facing the transgendered community. This group also provides input on developing best practices and standards of care within health and social services for transgendered persons. Such education is conducted through curriculum developed for workshops and seminars and print and electronic resources. Within this context, social workers are actively involved in community education and social planning. Problems in access to appropriate care and social services are identified and then solutions are designed to solve them. The Education Working Group strives to ensure the competence of health and social service professionals that interact with transgendered patients and clients.

• Youth Services Bureau — Ottawa, Ontario

The Youth Services Bureau in Ottawa provides a comprehensive offering of services to gay, lesbian, bisexual and transgendered youth and to youth who are questioning their sexual identity or sexual orientation. These services are provided to youth aged 12 and over and reflect the Youth Services Bureau's commitment to youth and their healthy development and well-being. Staff within this organization work with this population in a variety of different contexts involving individual, group and community-level interventions.

This organization offers individual and family counselling to youth struggling with issues surrounding their sexual identity or orientation. Issues such as coming out, social barriers and family reactions are all areas that are explored either individually, or with the youth's family, after a thorough assessment has been conducted by the worker. Counsellors at Youth Services Bureau also provide extensive direct service with youth groups and youth drop-in programs. These environments provide support and encourage discussion around relevant issues in the lives of LGBTQ youth. Drop-in services, such as the Bilingual Rainbow and Downtown Diversity Drop-in, provide a safe, queer-friendly atmosphere for youth to socialize with peers and to obtain relevant information and resources. Staff are able to link youth with other services or resources in the community if appropriate.

The Youth Services Bureau also provides a range of housing options for LGBTQ youth, including the Non-Profit Housing Program, the Host Homes Program and the Young Women's Shelter. These programs were developed to house LGBTQ youth who may not be safe at their homes or within other community services. Staff work with youth to access one of these shelter programs and engage in advocacy if appropriate. Workers also work with youth to acquire life skills, provide crisis intervention and support, provide counselling and link youth to services in the Ottawa community. Finally, staff within the Youth Services Bureau are also engaged in community development.

Mark Hall, Ontario teen, speaks at Gay Pride event in Halifax in 2002.

Conclusion

Across the world and throughout history there has been a broad spectrum of social responses to sexual and gender diversity. At one end of this spectrum, many indigenous cultures have traditionally been accepting of sexual and gender diversity. At the other end, non-conventional gender and sexual expression has been considered a sign of immorality that may be, even today, punishable by death.

Today, in Canada, many social work practitioners are part of the movement to challenge heterosexual privilege and to celebrate people, including colleagues, who are lesbian, gay, bisexual, transgendered and/or queer. Gay and lesbian social workers and their allies have been leaders in initiating a community response to AIDS. Social workers have also been an active part of the movement to change the laws that discriminate against members of LGBTQ communities, and have worked with queer persons to celebrate their diversity and the contributions they make to our communities. Their efforts in these arenas are exemplary.

To be sure, the struggle for sexual and gender equality is far from over, and it is important that social workers continue to be participants in this long struggle. Among other things, social workers need to reflect initially on their own practice to ensure that they do not reproduce heterosexism in their silence, or replicate myths and stereotypes about sexuality or gender diversity. In addition, gay-positive and queer-positive values must not be sidelined or ignored but rather brought to the forefront as required.

Possibly more than in other areas, the complex issues surrounding sexual and gender diversity present challenges both to social work theory and to social work practice. To be effective in addressing these issues requires not only a deeper understanding of the theoretical foundations and traditions of social work but also an openness to new ways of doing things. In their training to become social work practitioners, it is therefore especially important that students acquire a firm grasp of sexual and gender diversity principles and, drawing on the best practices in the area, develop a good understanding of the range of responses that may be effective in particular situations.

Chapter 12 Review
Social Work and Sexual and Gender Diversity

Discussion Questions

1. What are the main theories that are helpful in understanding sexuality? Briefly explain each.

2. What is "internalized homophobia," and why is it important for social workers (and others) to understand it?

3. What is the social work profession's perspective on gender and sexual diversity, and how has it changed in the last two decades?

4. What is "coming out," and what are some of the factors involved of which social workers should be aware?

5. How serious is the problem of suicide among gay, lesbian and bisexual persons, and what are its underlying causes?

6. What are important considerations when supporting parents of a new-born child who is intersexual?

7. How might social work practitioners ensure that their workplaces are supportive to those who do not fit within the expected gender binaries?

Websites

* **Equality for Gays and Lesbians Everywhere (EGALE)**
http://www.egale.ca

This national organization is committed to advancing, at the federal level, equality and justice for lesbians, gays and bisexuals. The website has a vast collection of news, articles and resources. Included is a summary of lesbian and gay rights in each jurisdiction in Canada.

* **Gender Education and Advocacy**
http://www.gender.org

Gender Education and Advocacy (GEA) is a national organization focused on the needs, issues and concerns of gender variant people. It seeks to educate and advocate for all persons who experience gender-based oppression in all of its many forms.

* **PFLAG (Formerly Parents, Families and Friends of Lesbians and Gays)**
http://www.pflag.ca

Information and resources for gay men, lesbians and bisexuals and their families and friends. Most chapters have scheduled meetings that provide support and information.

* **International Gay and Lesbian Human Rights Commission**
http://www.iglhrc.org

IGLHRC's mission is to protect and advance the human rights of all people and communities subject to discrimination or abuse on the basis of sexual orientation, gender identity, or HIV status. Their website contains excellent resources, news and urgent action items.

Key Terms

* **LGBTQ**
* **Heterosexual privilege**
* **Sexology**
* **Kinsey Report**
* **Stonewall Rebellion**
* **Queer activism**
* **Biological determinism**
* **Homophobia, biphobia and transphobia**
* **Sexuality**
* **Gender**
* **Intersexual**
* **Social constructionism**
* **Queer theory**
* **Sexual orientation**
* **Gender diversity**
* **Transgendered**
* **Transsexuals**
* **"Coming out"**

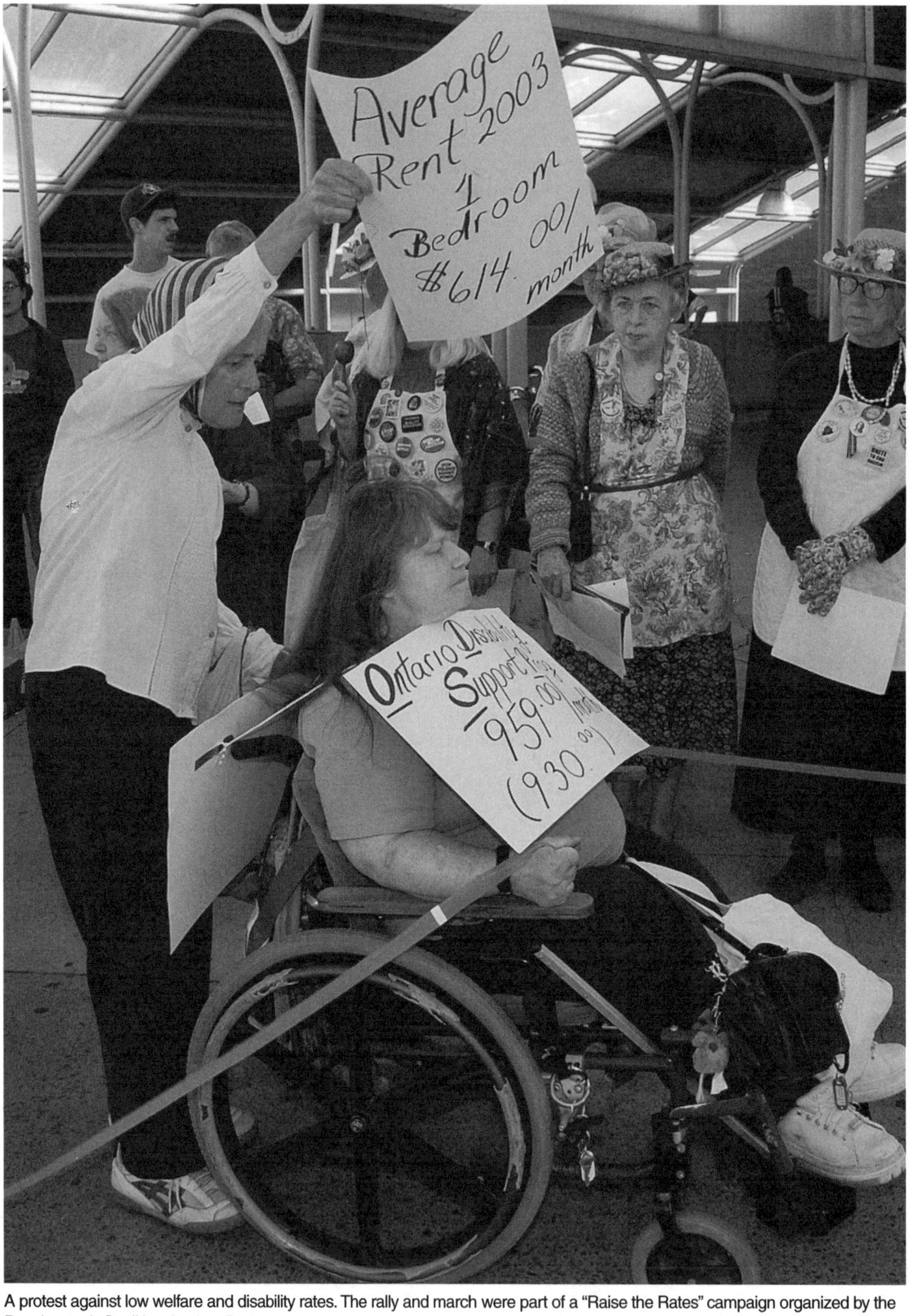
Average Rent 2003
1 Bedroom
$614.00/ month
Ontario Disability Support
959.00/ month
(930.00)

CP PHOTO/Peterborough Examiner-Clifford Skarstedt.

A protest against low welfare and disability rates. The rally and march were part of a “Raise the Rates” campaign organized by the Peterborough Coalition Against Poverty.

13

Social Work with Persons with Disabilities

Helping Individuals and Their Families

Roy Hanes

There are approximately 3.6 million Canadians with disabilities — that is, about 12 percent of the population (or one in eight Canadians). Needless to add, this is not an insignificant proportion of the Canadian population. Worldwide, it is estimated that there are about 600 million people with disabilities — again, a staggering number.

As we will see, disabilities are complex and the causes and consequences are often multifaceted. For example, a disability can be the result of sensory impairments, such as blindness and or deafness. People can also have psychiatric disabilities, developmental disabilities, learning disabilities and neurological disabilities. A great many people have mobility impairments. People can also become disabled as a result of many different factors, such as disease and/or injury. And, of course, many persons with disabilities have more than one impairment and therefore have more complex needs.

This chapter provides some essential information and guidelines for prospective social workers who may, at some point in their careers, find themselves working with persons with disabilities.

Issues pertaining to social work with persons with disabilities are very complex, and to be effective in this work requires specialized knowledge and training. The proportion of Canadians affected by some form of disability, and the sheer variety of disabling conditions they experience, will mean that in the future more resources will need to be devoted to training social workers in this field.

Who Are "People with Disabilities"?

The federal government recently carried out a detailed investigation into the nature and extent of disability in Canada. The results were reported in *A Profile of Disability in Canada, 2001*. Data on disabilities were last collected in 1991, when the Health and Limitation Survey (HALS) was conducted. Because major changes were made to the new survey, direct comparisons with the 1991 survey are unreliable. However, the **Participation Activities Limitation Survey (PALS)** provides essential information on the prevalence of disabilities, the various supports that exist for persons with disabilities, the employment profile of persons with disabilities, as well as their income and their participation in society — information that is essential in the planning of services needed by persons with activity limitations in order to help them participate fully in Canadian society. The following statistical information is based on this recent report.

About one in eight Canadians has a disabling condition.

TYPE OF DISABILITY

CHILDREN

The PALS survey questions allow the identification of the following types of disabilities among children under 15:

Hearing*: Difficulty hearing.

Seeing*: Difficulty seeing.

Speech**: Difficulty speaking and/or being understood.

Mobility**: Difficulty walking. This means walking on a flat firm surface, such as a sidewalk or floor.

Dexterity**: Difficulty using hands or fingers to grasp or hold small objects, such as a pencil or scissors.

Learning**: Difficulty learning due to the presence of a condition, such as attention problems, hyperactivity or dyslexia, whether or not the condition was diagnosed by a teacher, doctor or other health professional.

Developmental delay***: Child has a delay in his/her development, either a physical, intellectual or another type of delay.

Developmental disability or disorder**: Cognitive limitations due to the presence of a developmental disability or disorder, such as Down's syndrome, autism or mental impairment caused by a lack of oxygen at birth.

Psychological**: Limitations in the amount or kind of activities that one can do due to the presence of an emotional, psychological or behavioural condition.

Chronic condition*: Limitations in the amount or kind of activities that one can do due to the presence of one or more chronic health conditions that have lasted or are expected to last six months or more and that have been diagnosed by a health professional. Examples of chronic conditions are asthma or severe allergies, heart condition or disease, kidney condition or disease, cancer, epilepsy, cerebral palsy, Spina Bifida, Cystic Fibrosis, Muscular Dystrophy, Fetal Alcohol Syndrome, etc.

Unknown*: The type of disability is unknown if the respondent answered YES to the general questions on activity limitations, but did not provide any YES to the questions about type of disability that followed.

---

* Applicable to all children under 15.
** Applicable to children aged 5 to 14.
*** Applicable to children under 5.

ADULTS

The PALS survey questions allow the identification of the following types of disabilities among adults aged 15 and over:

Hearing: Difficulty hearing what is being said in a conversation with one other person, in a conversation with three or more persons or in a telephone conversation.

Seeing: Difficulty seeing ordinary newsprint or clearly seeing the face of someone from 4 metres (12 feet).

Speech: Difficulty speaking and/or being understood.

Mobility: Difficulty walking half a kilometre or up and down a flight of stairs, about 12 steps without resting, moving from one room to another, carrying an object of 5 kg (10 pounds) for 10 metres (30 feet) or standing for long periods.

Agility: Difficulty bending, dressing or undressing oneself, getting into and out of bed, cutting own toenails, using fingers to grasp or handling objects, reaching in any direction (for example, above one's head) or cutting own food.

Pain: Limitations in the amount or kind of activities that one can do because of a long-term pain that is constant or reoccurs from time to time, for example, recurrent back pain.

Learning: Difficulty learning because of a condition, such as attention problems, hyperactivity or dyslexia, whether or not the condition was diagnosed by a teacher, doctor or other health professional.

Memory: Limitations in the amount or kind of activities that one can do due to frequent periods of confusion or difficulty remembering things. These difficulties may be associated with Alzheimer's disease, brain injuries or other similar conditions.

Developmental: Cognitive limitations due to the presence of a developmental disability or disorder, such as Down's syndrome, autism or mental impairment caused by a lack of oxygen at birth.

Psychological: Limitations in the amount or kind of activities that one can do, due to the presence of an emotional, psychological or psychiatric condition, such as phobias, depression, schizophrenia, drinking or drug problems.

Unknown: The type of disability is unknown if the respondent answered YES to the general questions on activity limitations, but did not provide any YES to the questions about type of disability that followed.

• Children with Disabilities

Determining and diagnosing disabilities in children, particularly young children, can be quite difficult. The best estimate is that approximately 180,000 children between the ages of 0–14 have disabilities.

- **Chronic health condition.** Among children 0–14, the most widespread disability is that related to a chronic health condition. Disabilities resulting from such conditions represent about 118,000 children, or about 65 percent of children with disabilities.

- **Developmental delay.** Developmental delay is the most common disability in children aged 0–4. In this age group the PALS found that almost 18,000 young children with disabilities had a developmental delay that was reported by a parent or guardian.

- **Learning disabilities.** Among children between the ages of 5–14, learning disabilities represent a high number of disabling conditions. The number of children reported as having learning disabilities is over 100,000, representing about 65 percent of all children with disabilities between the ages of 5 to 14.

• Profile of Adults with Disabilities

Adults with disabilities report disabling conditions similar to those of children with disabilities. The three dominant categories reported were in the areas of mobility, agility and pain.

- **Adults with disabilities.** Almost 2.4 million adults representing 10.5 of the adult disabled population (aged 15 and over) reported a mobility related disability.

- **Multiple disabilities.** Disabling conditions are often quite complex and people might have one or more significant disabilities. The Participation Activity Limitation Survey found that over 80 percent of adults with disabilities over the age of 15 had multiple disabilities.

- **Severity of disability.** For adults, the PALS distinguished among four levels of severity: mild, moderate, severe, very severe. The level was determined by the intensity and frequency of factors causing limitations. For example, a person who might not have difficulty walking or climbing stairs but might have difficulty standing for long periods of time would have a mild disability. However, an individual who might require a wheelchair for mobility and might require assistance with washing, bathing, dressing and/or feeding would have a severe disability. In terms of the overall population of Canada aged 15 and over, PALS found that 5.0 percent reported a mild disability, 3.6 percent reported a moderate disability, 3.9 percent reported a severe disability and 2.0 percent reported a very severe disability.

DEFINING DISABILITY

The Participation and Activity Limitation Survey (PALS) used the World Health Organization's framework of disability provided by the International Classification of Functioning (ICF). This framework defines disability as the relationship between body structures and functions, daily activities and social participation, while recognizing the role of environmental factors.

Disability

For the purpose of PALS, persons with disabilities are those who reported difficulties with daily living activities, or who indicated that a physical or mental condition or health problem reduced the kind or amount of activities they could do. The respondents' answers to the disability questions represent their perception of the situation and are therefore subjective.

Disability Rate

Refers to the total number of persons who reported activity limitations expressed as a percentage of the population. For example, the calculation of the disability rate for the population aged 15 to 64 in Ontario is as follows: (Number of persons with disabilities aged 15–64 in Ontario/Total population aged 15–64 in Ontario)*100.

OVERVIEW — PERSONS WITH DISABILITIES

CANADA

- 12.4 % of Canadians have disabilities — one in eight
- A total of 3,601,000 Canadians have disabilities

Children 0–14

- 3.3% of children have disabilities
- A total of 181,00 children have disabilities

Adults 15–64

- 9.9% of adults 15–64 have disabilities
- A total of 1,968,000 adults 15–64 have disabilities

Adults 65 and over

- 40.5% of adults 65 and over have disabilities
- A total of 1,452,000 adults 65 and older have disabilities

Preschool Children (0–4)

- 1.6% of preschool children have disabilities
- A total of 26,210 children 0–4 have disabilities
- 57.5% (15,080) have mild to moderate disabilities
- 42.5% (11,130) have severe to very severe disabilities
- Three most common types of disabilities are: developmental delay, chronic conditions, hearing

Key issues:

- Addressing disabltity starts with identifying the condition and determining necessary supports
- 75% of parents who need help due to their child's condition don't have the help they need
- 25.3% of families of children aged 0–4 with disabilities have a low income
- 62% of families experience impacts on employment

School-Age Children (5–14)

- 4% of school-age children have disabilities
- A total of 154,720 children 5–14 have disabilities
- 57.3% (88,690) have mild to moderate disabilities
- 42.7% (66,030) have severe to very severe disabilities
- Three most common types of disabilities are: chronic conditions, learning, speech

Key issues:

- Enrolment in school and availability of necessary supports
- 65% of parents who need help due to their child's condition don't have the help they need
- 24.4% of families of children aged 5–14 with disabilities have a low income
- 54% of families experience impacts on employment

Youth (15–24)

- 3.9% of youths have disabilities
- A total of 151,030 youths have disabilities
- 69.3% (104,720) have mild to moderate disabilities
- 30.7% (46,310) have severe to very severe disabilities
- Three most common types of disabilities: pain, learning, mobility

Key issues:

- Completion of high school, access to post-secondary education and a successful initial transition from school into work or life in the community
- 48% of youths with disabilities are full-time students versus 57% of other youths
- 45.7% of youths with disabilities are employed versus 56.6% of other youths
- 53% of youths with disabilities are prevented from doing at least some desired leisure activities

Core Working-Age Adults (25–54)

- 9.2% of core working-age adults have disabilities
- A total of 1,206,660 core working-age adults with disabilities
- 58% (702,110) have mild to moderate disabilities
- 42% (504,550) have severe to very severe disabilities
- Three most common types of disabilities are: pain, mobility, agility

Key issues:

- Finding or keeping a job; for those with new disabilities, early interventions to permit return to work

- 39.4% who need help with everyday activities don't have the help they need
- 51.2% of those with disabilities are employed versus 82.3% of others
- 42.7% of those with disabilities are not in the labour force versus 12.5% of others
- 27.9% of those with disabilities experience low income versus 10.2% of others

Older Working-Age Adults (55–64)

- 21.8% of older working-age adults have disabilities
- A total of 610,800 core working-age adults with disabilities
- 55% (335,120) have mild to moderate disabilities
- 45% (275,680) have severe to very severe disabilities
- Three most common types of disabilities are: pain, mobility, agility

Key issues:

- Maintaining employment or an adequate alternative source of income; possible early retirement
- 34.5% who need help with everyday activities don't have the help they need
- 27.3% of those with disabilities are employed versus 56.2% of others
- 70.8% of those with disabilities are not in the labour force versus 40.7% of others
- 23.8% of those with disabilities experience low income versus 12.4% of others

Younger Seniors (65–74)

- 31.2% of younger seniors have disabilities
- A total of 649,180 younger seniors with disabilities
- 66.5% (431,180) have mild to moderate disabilities
- 33.6% (218,000) have severe to very severe disabilities
- Three most common types of disabilities: mobility, agility, pain

Key issues:

- Transition from work to retirement; those with new or increasing disabilities need to find and establish eligibility for the supports needed to maintain desired lifestyles
- 34.3% who need help with everyday activities don't have the help they need

- 33.4% who need assistive aids or devices don't have all they need
- Principal reason for not getting needed help is cost

Older Seniors (75+)

- 53.3% of older seniors have disabilities
- A total of 802,670 older seniors have disabilities
- 55.8% (447,660) have mild to moderate disabilities
- 44.2% (355,010) have severe to very severe disabilities
- Three most common types of disabilities are: mobility, agility, pain

Key issues:

- Maintaining community participation; obtaining necessary assistance to stay at home; for some, experiencing a loss of independence. Seniors with disabilities are often caregivers themselves
- 31.8% who need help with everyday activities don't have the help they need
- 29.2% who need assistive aids or devices don't have all they need
- Family members are a principal source of assistance

The Participation and Activity Limitation Survey (PALS) was conducted by Statistics Canada in 2001. Low-income figures are based on Statistics Canada, pre-tax Low-income Cut Off (LICO)

History of Social Welfare Services for People with Disabilities

• The Origins of the "Disability" Category

Prior to the expansion of scientific medicine in Canada, "disability" was viewed as a social and legal category based on the English Poor Laws of 1601 (Stone 1984). The Poor Laws were developed as a means of determining who would be entitled to "social support," and very restrictive parameters were used to distinguish between the "deserving poor and the non-deserving poor." The deserving poor included lepers, those who were bedridden, the impotent (meaning those unable to work), and people above the age of 60. The sociolegal criteria of disability established by the English Poor Laws in Britain were adapted in the British colonies of North America and the social and/or legal determination of disability lasted until the early years of the twentieth century. Persons were considered deserving of charitable support if a local magistrate deemed them unable to work because of a disability. Various methods of support such as outdoor relief, indoor relief and scientific charity were used throughout Canada from the late eighteenth to the early twentieth century.

Outdoor relief was a common form of assistance provided for persons with disabilities when their families could not take care of them. An early form of outdoor relief established in England and later transported to British North America was begging. Through the Poor Laws, legitimate "deserving poor" persons such as persons with disabilities were given license to beg. As time passed other forms of outdoor relief supplemented begging. When families could not provide for a family member (usually an elderly person or a person with a disability), these persons were housed in private homes, and funds to cover expenses for food, clothing, shelter and medical care were often provided through municipal taxes, charitable organizations and religious organizations. In essence, outdoor relief meant that persons with disabilities were cared for through non-institutional methods of relief and were more or less part of the community.

By the mid-nineteenth century outdoor relief came to be seen as a mechanism that created rather than relieved dependency, and institutions such as asylums, poor houses and houses of industry replaced the former methods of outdoor relief (Splane 1965). The replacement of outdoor relief measures by indoor relief measures represents a significant shift in the philosophy regarding charitable relief. Persons with disabilities, who were once considered part of the social order, were now viewed as nuisance populations, to be removed from society and placed in segregated institutions. Disability was often considered a source of shame and many persons with disabilities who were not sent to institutions were often hid away in the home by their family members. There are numerous examples of people with various forms of disabilities

Picketing at the Ontario Ministry of Community and Social Services.

being hidden or kept at home in Canada, the United States and the United Kingdom throughout the nineteenth and twentieth centuries. Hanes (1995), for example, found many examples of children with orthopaedic disabilities being hidden in their homes by parents.

Broad social, political, economic and cultural changes took root in Canada during the mid- to late nineteenth century. By the mid-nineteenth century there was a major shift in the public attitude towards social dependency and social relief, and the public's attitude to the provision of relief changed as well. The social rejection of "defective" populations was so severe that many persons with disabilities were treated as common criminals and banned from the streets of many cities in Canada. Many persons with disabilities were charged under vagrancy laws and sent to jail. Many of those who were not sent to jail were sent to a local poor house, a house of industry or an asylum. Provincial governments were reluctant to fund support programs for dependent populations, including people with disabilities, and very coercive means were used to provide for the relief of dependent populations (Hanes 1995).

By the mid-twentieth century, the institutionalization of people with disabilities was the dominant method of care and most provinces across Canada had established large facilities for this purpose. Many provinces, for example, had "special" residential schools for blind and deaf children and adolescents. Provincial institutions were established for people with psychiatric disabilities and in many provinces there were institutions for people with developmental disabilities. In addition to the provincial institutions, specialized hospitals were established for many different disabled populations including tuberculosis hospitals, orthopaedic hospitals and rehabilitation hospitals.

Within a few decades, the institutionalization of people with disabilities was so widespread that it became the common belief that this was the natural order of things, and that people with disabilities had always been separated from their communities (Bowe 1978).

• Disability as a Medical Category

Historically, people with disabilities have often been part of a "stigmatized element of society" and many people with disabilities were viewed as social outcasts. This particular view of people with disabilities was challenged with the onset of World War I when many young men from various classes of society returned home with significant impairments. The enormous tragedy of the war brought about changes in the public's attitude as people began to realize that disability was not just a problem of the poorer classes and that it did not stem from immoral character. "When Johnny came marching home without an arm, without a leg, without an eye, people started looking around for other solutions to the disability problem" (Varela, in Crewe and Zola 1983, 31).

UNITED NATIONS

In considering Canada's adherence to Articles 16 and 17 of the covenant, the United Nations concluded:

"The Committee is concerned about significant cuts to services on which people with disabilities rely, such as cuts to home care, attendant care, special needs transportation systems and tightened eligibility rules for people with disabilities. Although the government failed to provide to the Committee any information regarding homelessness among discharged psychiatric patients, the Committee was told that a large number of those patients end up on the street, while others suffer from inadequate housing and insufficient support services."

Source: *Report of the Committee on Economic, Social and Cultural Rights*, United Nations, Concluding Observations, Section 36 (1998).

PEOPLE FIRST — "PERSONS WITH DISABILITIES"

In recent years, many debates have taken place in the fields of sociology, social work, political science and disability studies with respect to the most appropriate term to be used when writing about or speaking about people who are disabled. While still commonly used in everyday conversation, terms such as "defective," "crippled," "lame" or "gimp" are now generally considered to be derogatory and certainly inappropriate.

Since the early 1980s, the terms "person with disabilities" and "people with disabilities" have come to be accepted as the most appropriate terms to be used when referring to individuals who have a disability. This new terminology was promoted by "people first" initiatives and the terms indicate that disability is one of many characteristics of the individual.

In recent years, however, many disability rights advocates and disability theorists have challenged the "person first" conceptualizations of disability. Those who do so advocate for the replacement of the terms "people with disabilities" and "person with a disability" with the term "disabled person." The argument is that "person first" language tends to minimize and de-politicize disability.

Both terms "disabled person" and "people with disabilities" are acceptable usage, providing the disadvantages of each term are properly acknowledged. But for the purposes of this book, the terms "people with disabilities" or "persons with disabilities" will mainly be used throughout.

The post-World War I era represents a significant period in the history of disability in Canada. First, there was a shift in public attitude towards people with disabilities. Second, the war brought about many advances in medicine especially in the areas of surgery, follow-up care and rehabilitation. In time, because of these changes, the disability category shifted from a social and/or legal category to a medical category and, as Stone (1984) points out, medical professionals replaced magistrates and judges in determining disability.

Another important era in the history of disability in Canada emerged following World War II. In the post-World War II era, Canada witnessed the establishment of the "welfare state" wherein social security programs such as pensions and disability benefits were established for a wide spectrum of people with disabilities. In addition to the rise of the welfare state, the post-World War II era witnessed the onset of the multidisciplinary rehabilitation team, which included the physiatrist (rehabilitation physician), nurse, occupational therapist, physiotherapist, and later, the social worker, psychologist, vocational counsellor and recreologist.

The establishment of rehabilitation services following World War II thus laid the foundation for the modern era of medical and social services for people with disabilities. During this era, medical and social services were expanded to people with disabilities, including the establishment of special schools, training programs, sheltered work shops, summer camps, recreational programs, as well as the establishment of special trades and industries and special hospitals and after-care facilities.

Two Theories: The "Medical" and "Social" Models of Disability

The dominance of medical professionals over the lives of people with disabilities that emerged following World War II remained unchallenged until the 1970s with the development of the disability rights movement in Canada. The rise of disability rights organizations in Canada is linked to the rise of the consumer movement, the civil rights movement, the peace movement, the gay rights movement and the women's movement of the late 1960s and the early 1970s. Rather than be labelled "defective" or "handicapped," disability rights advocates argued that they also should be seen as members of a minority group. "Many persons with disabilities," as Frieden suggests, "considered themselves members of a minority group related not by colour or nationality but by functional limitation and similar need" (Frieden 1983, 55).

The *American Vocational Rehabilitation Act* of 1973 represents a pivotal point in the history of persons with disabilities, because this legislation prohibited discrimination against people with disabilities. "No otherwise qualified handicapped individual in the United States as defined by Section 7 shall, solely by reason of his handicap, be excluded from participation in, be denied the benefits of, or be subject to discrimination under any program or activity receiving federal financial assistance" (Zola 1986, 1). Similar legislation followed in Canada at both the provincial and federal levels, and in 1982 the rights of people with disabilities were enshrined in the *Canadian Charter of Rights and Freedoms*.

• Approaches to Disability

Currently, two broad approaches characterize the discussions of disability. The *medical model* of disability has its roots in rehabilitation medicine, where the focus of the intervention is on the individual. It focuses on disability as an "impairment" and a "personal tragedy" and the need of the individual to adapt or otherwise to fit in as far as possible within mainstream society. The *political rights* model, on the other hand, is concerned with the broader social and political context and the need for society as a whole to adapt and to address the needs of those persons with a disability.

The shift to defining disability in terms of rights, instead of medical need, was influenced not only by the disability rights movement but also by the development of disability theories that challenged the dominant medical model view of disability. The pre-eminent British disability advocate and theorist Michael Oliver has coined the terms "personal tragedy theory" and "social oppression theory" of disability to describe the differences between a medical model of disability and a sociopolitical model of disability (Oliver 1990).

Quebec protest on behalf of people with developmental disabilities.

• "Personal Tragedy" Theory (Medical Model)

From the perspective of the **personal tragedy theory of disability**, a disabling condition is viewed as an unfortunate life event where some form of professional and medical assistance is required (Oliver 1990). This theory holds that disability is primarily a medical problem and the focus of intervention should therefore be only on the disabled individual. The various forms of interventions are therefore introduced as a means of "curing" or "fixing" the individual.

According to the personal tragedy theory, persons who become disabled, as well as their loved ones, go through various stages of psychological and emotional adjustment before they can accept themselves or their loved one as disabled. Much of the literature pertaining to the impact of disability on the individual and on the family focuses primarily on the stages of adjustment to the disability. Oliver (1996) argues that many of these explanations of adjustment to disability are based on psychological theories pertaining to or coping with death and dying — stages of shock, denial, grief, loss, reconciliation, and acceptance. Such an approach is usually based on an interpretation of coping that involves the following:

- An individual or family must move sequentially through these various stages to become fully adjusted.

- There is but one path through the sequence.

- An individual can be placed clearly in one stage or another by analyzing their behaviour.

- There is an optional length of time for staying in each stage.

• "Social Oppression" Theory (Political Rights Model)

In contrast, the social oppression theory of disability suggests that the problems faced by people with disabilities are not the result of physical impairments alone, but are also the result of the social and political inequality that exists between people with disabilities on the one hand and people without disabilities on the other. A social model of disability maintains that the difficulties faced by people with disabilities stem from the social context and not entirely from the individual impairment. This model thus challenges the widely prevalent view that disability is essentially an individual problem requiring individual treatment and individual solutions to problems.

The social oppression model tends to see people with disabilities as members of an oppressed minority population and that environmental factors — such as the lack of employment opportunities, lack of affordable housing, lack of accessible transportation as well as the presence of negative stereotypes and prejudicial attitudes — are a primary cause of problems for people with disabilities. This, in turn, has implications with respect to resolving problems. Because many problems stem from structural and attitudinal barriers, systemic change involving social and political change is required if these obstacles are to be overcome. Among other things, this requires the incorporation of a "human rights" focus for addressing the needs of people with disabilities.

Table 13.1: Theories of Disability — Contrasting Approaches

	"Personal Tragedy" Theory (Medical Model)	"Social Oppression" Theory (Political Rights Model)
Definition of problem	Physical impairment/lack of employment skills	Dependent on professionals, relatives, etc.
Locus of problem	In the individual	In the environment and rehabilitation process
Solution to problem	Professional intervention by physician, therapist, occupational therapist, vocational rehabilitation counsellor, etc.	Peer counselling, advocacy, self-help, consumer control, removal of barriers
Social role	Patient/client	Citizen/consumer
Who controls	Professional	Citizen/consumer
Desired outcome	Maximize activities, living skills and gainful employment	Independent living

CITIZENSHIP

"The concept of citizenship is central to disability issues. Citizenship is the inclusion of persons with disabilities in all aspects of Canadian society — the ability of a person to be actively involved with their community. Full citizenship depends on equality, inclusion, rights and responsibilities, and empowerment and participation...

"A person is able to exercise full citizenship when they do not face barriers that significantly reduce their ability to participate fully in their community. Persons with disabilities and their advocates have argued that ensuring full citizenship is not just the right thing to do, but is also a matter of fundamental rights under Canada's Charter of Rights and Freedoms."

Source: Federal, Provincial and Territorial Ministers Responsible for Social Services, *In Unison 2000: Persons with Disabilities in Canada* (Ottawa: Human Resources Development Canada).

The Stigma of Disability

In most social work courses nowadays, students learn about discrimination and prejudice towards people because of their race, religious beliefs, ethnic background, gender and/or sexual orientation. It is less common that social work students are informed about discrimination and prejudice towards people with disabilities. Yet, disability is a "human constant" — since disablement has always existed, there is nothing inherent in disability that should lead to the stigmatization of people with disabilities, nor is there anything inherent in disability that should lead to the development of belief systems wherein biological difference is linked to biological inferiority. But unfortunately in many countries, including Canada, disability is viewed as undesirable and people with disabilities are often stigmatized. They are discriminated against, and they often have low social status.

It is possible to identify and describe, in general, various types of stigma towards persons with disabilities as well as the possible motives that may underlie them (Livneh 1984).

- In most Western industrialized societies there is a growing cultural emphasis on the "body beautiful." Physical attractiveness, sexuality and desirability have become a valued cultural norm. People with disabilities often do not meet cultural standards of physical attractiveness and this contributes to a stigma of disability that to be disabled is to be undesirable and unlovable. For the person with the disability this has implications for many aspects of life from developing friendships, developing intimate relationships, socializing, or being involved in recreational activities.

- It is commonly believed that when people become disabled or a loved one becomes disabled, individuals and family members go through a long period of grieving. When people with disabilities do not show signs of long-term grieving and mourning, they are considered to be in a state of denial. There is a common expectation that people with disabilities should be in a continuous state of emotional distress and psychological suffering.

- A common stereotype is that people with disabilities are often psychologically damaged. This stems from the long-held belief that there is an interconnection between the physical, mental and emotional aspects of the human body. Therefore, it is theorized that if there is damage to one aspect of the system (physical disability) then there should be damage to the emotional and mental elements as well.

- Sometimes the person with the disability is portrayed as deserving the disability. For example, a young person who may have become disabled as a result of an automobile accident where that person was drunk at the wheel of the car may be viewed as someone who received what he or she deserved. Another example might be a person who became disabled as a consequence of a particular lifestyle — there tends to be little public sympathy for adults who have disabling conditions because of drug use, prostitution or through unprotected sex.

- Because of the influence of religious and/or cultural beliefs, some people believe that a disability is a consequence of sinful activities on the part of an individual or parent. Many people might view the onset of AIDS as a punishment by God for people who are involved in what are perceived as immoral acts. Some types of childhood disabilities are also stereotyped as being a form of punishment. For example, children born with fetal alcohol syndrome or AIDS-related disabilities may be seen as infants who were born with disabilities as punishment to the mother for participating in illegal and/or immoral acts.

- There is also a stereotype of the individual with a disability as an "evil person" based on the belief that the onset of disability leads that individual to participate in evil or criminal acts. There are many examples that portray persons with disabilities as evil people in folklore, in literature, TV programs and movies.

- Many people without disabilities feel physically and psychologically uncomfortable when they are in the company of people with disabilities. Such fearful and negative reactions are often more common when there is a lack of exposure and a lack of contact between those without disabilities and people with disabilities.

- A great fear that most people have is the fear of becoming disabled themselves. The presence of people with disabilities reminds some people that they too can, and likely will, become disabled. Such a fear may lead to avoidance of people with disabilities by people without disabilities and this contributes to the social isolation of people with disabilities.

- For many people, disability reminds them of their own mortality. The loss of the use of a body part and/or the loss of a bodily function often stimulates feelings associated with death. Indeed, as noted earlier, much of the literature pertaining to the psychological adjustment to the onset of disability comes from literature based on the psychological adjustment to death and dying.

- Because of internalized beliefs and values regarding what is considered beautiful and desirable, many people without disabilities view disability as non-aesthetically pleasing. Aesthetic aversion leads to a strong desire to avoid and to remain separated from people with disabilities.

Terry Fox challenged all stereotypes with his "Marathon of Hope".

CP PHOTO/Toronto Star-Boris Spremo.

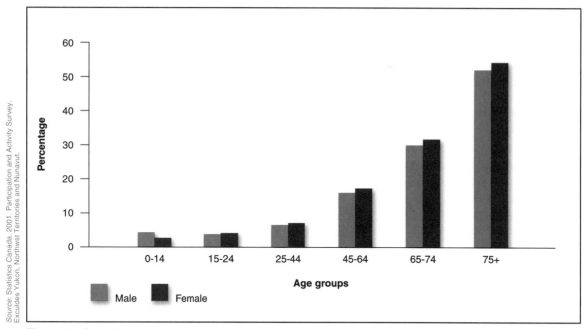

Source: Statistics Canada. 2001. Participation and Activity Survey. Excudies Yukon, Northwst Territories and Nunavut.

Figure 13.1: Disabilities by age and sex.

• Ableism

Many students of social work are familiar with terms such as racism, sexism, heterosexism and ageism but they may be unfamiliar with the term *ableism*. The stigmatization of disability and the existence of prejudicial attitudes held by people without disabilities towards people with disabilities is often referred to as "ableism."

Ableism denotes the consequences of the belief in the superiority of people without disabilities over people with disabilities. Thompson (1997) uses a "PCS" model to examine ableism:

- **P** — Prejudice towards disabled people at a personal level, which refers to revulsion, avoidance, infantalization, condescension and other forms of prejudice.

- **C** — Cultural norms, which reflect a positive image of being without disability and a negative image of being disabled (people without disabilities are valued more than people with disabilities). Culture of society stigmatizes people with disabilities and emphasizes the horror of being disabled. People with disabilities are often the brunt of many jokes and derogatory statements.

- **S** — Social stratification and social division, which focus on the manner in which people with disabilities are kept out of the mainstream. Social stratification and social division also explore ways in which people with disabilities are marginalized because of structural and attitudinal barriers.

Income Security Programs

Canada's disability income support system is based on a loosely knit set of programs. These programs have different eligibility criteria, guidelines and procedures. The social and income security programs for disabled people are derived from private and public sources in the form of contributory or non-contributory benefits.

- **Publicly funded disability programs** are programs covered by federal, provincial and municipal legislation. These programs include the Canada Pension Plan — Disability Pension (a federal program), the Family Benefits plan (a provincial program), and the General Welfare Assistance plan (a municipal program). These types of programs are funded through government taxation, and except for the Canada Pension Plan, do not require the financial contribution of recipients.

- **Privately funded disability programs** include programs that are provided through private insurance plans or through long-term disability plans as part of job benefits. These private income security programs are based on the amount of funding that the recipient has contributed directly to the plan, or funding that has been contributed to a plan on behalf of the recipient.

In 1988, in an analysis of disability benefits provided through Canada's income security programs, the G. Allen Roeher Institute (a research group associated with the Canadian Association for Community Living) noted the "insecurity" of income security programs for persons with disabilities. Between 1996 and 2004, income security was radically altered — many would say, for the worse — with the introduction of the Canada Health and Social Transfer (CHST). The CHST was a per-capita grant to the provinces, without regard to provincial circumstances or needs. The Canadian Association of Independent Living Centres maintains that this policy shift significantly jeopardized the livelihood of people with disabilities, making them even more insecure than in the mid-1980s. (Since 2004, the CHST has been divided into the Canada Social Transfer and the Canada Health Transfer.)

While Canadians have a universal health care system, the health care benefits do not extend to providing full support for all people with disabilities. The primary similarity across the provinces is the range and types of supports and services provided. For example, provincial programs, whether in Newfoundland or British Columbia, will cover the cost of wheelchairs, canes, eyeglasses, walkers, attendant care services, home care, transportation and so forth. The differences among the provinces are found in two areas. One is eligibility requirements, which may be different from one province to the next; the other is the amount of funding for supports and services, which may vary from one province to the next. Each province has its own legislation and

ADVOCACY GROUPS

- Council of Canadians with Disabilities (CCD) is a national organization representing disabled people across Canada. This organization was formerly known as the Coalition of Provincial Organizations of the Handicapped. The CCD is primarily a cross-disability advocacy group representing provincial organizations of disabled people as well as groups such as the Disabled Women's Network, the Canadian Association of the Deaf, the Thalidomide Victims Association of Canada, and the National Network for Mental Health. The CCD's objectives include promotion of full partnership of people with disabilities, self-determination, consumer control, equality and rights.

- Canadian Rehabilitation Council for the Disabled (CRCD) represents 60 organizations of service providers, professional associations and rehabilitation centres across Canada. The CRCD is also linked to international organizations such as Rehabilitation International. The primary focus of the CRCD is to develop rehabilitative programs and services that will contribute to the social and economic integration of people with disabilities.

mechanisms for providing services to people with disabilities. As a consequence of this lack of universality, the care and treatment of persons with disabilities varies across the country. For example, some provinces, such as Newfoundland, Prince Edward Island, Saskatchewan and New Brunswick, have a single-tier program wherein supports and services are directly funded by the province to the individual in need. Other provinces, such as Nova Scotia and Manitoba, have a two-tier system of support for people with disabilities — basically, the programs are funded though a system of general welfare assistance at the municipal and/or county level. The province provides the funding, and the money for supports and services is then transferred to the local government, which, in turn, funds the individual.

The types of programs indicated above (one-tier and two-tier systems) are directly related to provincial social welfare spending, but there are also provincial programs based on specific legislation aimed at people with disabilities. In Ontario, people with disabilities are covered under the *Ontario Disability Supports Program Act*; in British Columbia, they are covered under the *Disability Benefits Program Act*; and in Alberta, they receive benefits through the Assured Income for the Severely Handicapped program. These provincial programs are based on distinct legislation covering people with disabilities and are not directly connected to any provincial welfare legislation.

Melissa Webster voices her concerns during the "Ontario Needs A Raise" rally in Peterborough in June 2003. Members of the Ontario Disabilities Support Program took part in a province wide initiative to protest against low minimum wage.

• Gaining Access to Services

For people with a disability, the first step in gaining access to municipal or provincial programs, such as General Welfare Assistance or Family Benefits, is an eligibility determination carried out by a physician. The physician determines whether or not the applicant has a disability that seriously impedes his or her potential for employment. Once a medical evaluation has been carried out and the person is deemed to be disabled, a Social Assistance review takes place. First, there is an investigation of assets, which means that a person with a disability cannot have assets beyond a specific limit. For example, people with disabilities living in Ontario who receive Family Benefits are not allowed to accumulate savings beyond the amount of $3,500. Only in special circumstances can asset exemption be waived. Each province has its own types and levels of exemption. For example, in Quebec, benefits are reduced if the value of the applicant's house exceeds $50,000, and automobiles are exempt only to a certain amount.

The next step in a Social Assistance review is a needs test. A needs test consists of three basic steps:

1. The applicant's basic requirements for living are identified (food, clothing, shelter, utilities, other household and personal allowances). Each requirement is designated with a maximum dollar allotment, and the requirements are then totalled to determine the funds needed to meet basic needs.

2. The applicant's available financial resources to meet basic needs are determined, that is, income from resources such as other pensions, including public or private funds, savings, money received through paid employment or training programs.

3. The difference between total resources and total basic needs is calculated. A negative remainder indicates a "budget defect" upon which eligibility for assistance is determined.

The amount of assistance will then be assessed according to a variety of factors, including size of family, degree of employability of the family's main decision maker, size and type of accommodation and so on.

In addition to basic financial assistance, people with disabilities who receive either General Welfare Assistance, Family Benefits or who are covered by the Canada Pension Plan are also entitled to other forms of assistance. These may include dental services, prescription medication, eyeglasses, technical aids and devices, prosthetic and orthotic equipment, wheelchairs, child care subsidies and so forth. These forms of assistance are referred to as "in kind." Recipients who work must notify authorities and are allowed to keep only a percentage of the income, with the remainder being deducted from benefits.

EQUALIZING OPPORTUNITIES
(UN RESOLUTION, 1993)

Among the major outcomes of the Decade of Disabled Persons was the adoption, by the General Assembly of the United Nations, of the Standard Rules on the Equalization of Opportunities for Persons with Disabilities in 1993.

Although not a legally binding instrument, the Standard Rules represent a strong moral and political commitment of Governments to take action to attain equalization of opportunities for persons with disabilities. They are:

1. Awareness raising
2. Medical care
3. Rehabilitation
4. Support services
5. Accessibility
6. Education
7. Employment
8. Income maintenance and social security
9. Family life and personal integrity
10. Culture
11. Recreation and sports
12. Religion
13. Information and research
14. Policy making and planning
15. Legislation
16. Economic policies
17. Coordination of work
18. Organizations of persons with disabilities
19. Personnel training
20. National monitoring and evaluation of disability programs
21. Technical and economic cooperation
22. International cooperation

Available at website:
http://www.un.org/esa/socdev/enable/dissre00.htm

DISABILITY BENEFITS

From 1996 to 2003 there was a 35 % increase in disability-related expenditures. Annual spending on income support benefits rose by over $1.1 billion, a 23% increase, including an increase in the Veterans Disability Pension from $1.3 billion to over $1.5 billion in 2003–04.

• Canada Pension Plan

With work-related or contributory income security programs, contributions are made through an individual's employment, and the amount of financial benefits received is based on the amount paid into the plan. The Canada Pension Plan (CPP) is an example of an income security program based on contributory payments. Workers between the ages of 18 and 65 make contributions based on funds received. Employees and employers pay equal amounts into the plan. Persons receiving disability pensions or other pensions do not have to pay into the plan.

Eligibility for CPP benefits is based on the following:

1. A physician must first determine eligibility for benefits.

2. Benefits are granted only to individuals who have either contributed to the plan during two of the last three years or during five of the last ten years.

3. Pension benefits consist of a flat rate plus earnings equal to 75 percent of the retirement pension to which the person would be entitled.

The Canada Pension Plan does not consider the day-to-day financial needs of the disabled individual and his or her family. Low-income workers, therefore, receive lower benefits and may require additional assistance through other programs such as Family Benefits (GAINS-D) or General Welfare Assistance (Special Needs).

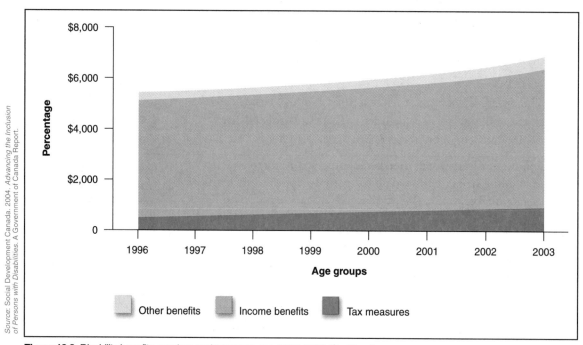

Source: Social Development Canada. 2004. Advancing the Inclusion of Persons with Disabilities. A Government of Canada Report.

Figure 13.2: Disability benefits, services and tax measures, 1996–2003 ($ millions).

Social Work Practice with Persons with Disabilities

What skills should social workers have in order to work effectively with people with disabilities? Social workers should obviously have generic practice skills, which include an understanding of individual and family counselling, as well as an understanding of group work and community organization. In addition, they should have a working knowledge of mediation and advocacy and be able to connect clients to available resources.

But, to be effective, whether working with persons with disabilities or with other groups, the social worker must be able to help an individual and family cope while at the same time recognize that many of the difficulties may stem from the social context in which the individual and family find themselves. At times this may require that the social worker become a direct advocate for social and political change with, and on behalf of, their clients. In the case of working with persons with disabilities, this may involve petitioning for more or better services, organizing clients to protest lack of accessible housing, or it might mean leading or supporting boycotts against businesses that are not accessible to people with disabilities.

• Families and Disability

Until the 1970s, the medical care and treatment of people with disabilities for both children and adults was predominantly directed at the physical needs of the individual who was disabled. Less attention was paid to the emotional needs of the individual and the family. During the past 25 years there has been a greater recognition of the importance of the family and family members.

This new focus was influenced by the introduction of "family systems theory" to social work. The idea is that the family is an interrelated network and an impact on one component has significant consequences for all others in the system. In other words:

- all parts of the family unit are interrelated,

- each member of the unit affects and is affected by other members of the unit, and

- no one part of the family system can be understood in isolation from the other parts.

Obviously, the onset of disability, whether at birth or later in life, will have a great effect on the entire family unit. Family members (especially parents of a child with a disability) therefore have a critical role to play in the care, treatment and emotional adjustment of the person who is disabled. Much of the work of the social work practitioner, therefore, needs to focus on those persons on whom the person with the disability will come increasingly to depend on to one degree or another.

Variety Village "Sunshine Games" aim to promote disability awareness.

IN UNISON

The *In Unison 2000* report marked the first time that Canada's federal, provincial and territorial governments came together to express a common vision on disability issues. This report provides Canadians with a broad view of how adults with disabilities have been faring in comparison with those without disabilities, using both statistical indicators and examples of personal experiences.

Examples of effective practices that have been implemented across Canada are also woven into the report. The situation of Aboriginal persons with disabilities is specifically highlighted. This report is available at: http://socialunion.gc.ca/ In_Unison2000

There are some basic guidelines that can be kept in mind to help social workers deal with family members' adjustment to the onset of disability on the part of a loved one:

- **Emotional coping and functioning skills.** The intensity and impact of disability on the family may be influenced by the family's ability to cope in previous life crises. Families that have dealt with previous crises, and did so effectively, may have acquired problem-solving and coping skills that can be used again to help them deal with the disablement of a family member. If the social worker is aware of this, he or she can build on these abilities and help the family or family member apply these skills in the new situation.

- **Family's post-trauma functioning.** It is important for the social worker to help individuals and family members recognize their strengths and find, maintain and develop resources and supports. These would include "internal supports" — such as strong affective relationships between family members, marital stability/partners' stability, strong parent-child bonds, as well as effective decision-making and problem-solving skills of the family members. They would also include "external supports" — such as external family members, friends, peer support, self-help groups, community resources, and supportive outside environments such as school or workplace.

- **Person's status within the family.** The impact of disability on the family is influenced by who in the family has come to be disabled. For example, is the person a newborn, an infant, the husband, the wife, the primary wage earner, the primary decision maker, or the individual who provides most of the emotional support for other family members? Each circumstance will be different and each will call for a particular type of response with respect to how family members may or may not cope with the onset of disability.

- **Stage in the life cycle of the family.** The stage in the life cycle of the family will influence how people cope with the onset of disability. For example, if the onset of disability comes late in life, family members may have had an opportunity to plan for the onset of chronic illness and/or impairment. However, if the onset of the disability comes earlier as a consequence of birth impairment or injury, the family may well be affected quite differently. For example, a young couple may have significant financial difficulties resulting from loss of income and, depending on the type of disability, there may be consequences for intimacy and sexuality. For others, the onset of disability may be with the birth of a child who has significant impairments and the hopes, plans and dreams of the parents may be dramatically altered. Again, each situation is unique and will require a unique solution.

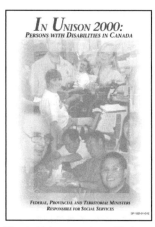

The *In Unison* report provided an overview of disability issues.

- **Understanding the nature and extent of the disability.** This relates to the relationship of the family members with professionals who may be involved (especially medical professionals). Uncertainty, use of medical jargon and lack of information can create tension and frustration for the family members. To be able to cope effectively, family members must be treated with dignity and respect and need to be involved in all aspects of treatment. In many situations, the social worker is a member of a multidisciplinary team and part of his or her role will be to serve as advocate for the individual and the family in relation to the professional support services being provided.

- **Access to resources is important.** The impact of disability on the family unit is often influenced by the availability of community resources. Such services include support networks, day care, schools, jobs, attendant care, retraining, respite care, hospice care, transportation or recreational facilities. Other important community resources include access to financial resources, including private pension plans, insurance plans or government-sponsored financial programs, such as the federal government's Canada Pension Plan or the various provincial financial assistance programs. Helping families access financial, community, social, recreational and/or medical resources is often central to the social worker's role.

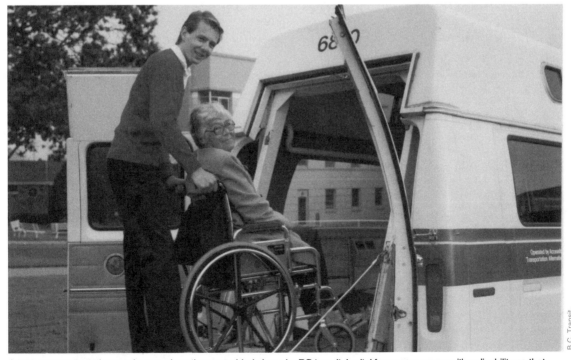

B.C. Transit.

Access to transportation services, such as those provided above by BC transit, is vital for many persons with a disability so that they can maintain a high degree of independence each day.

The Independent Living Movement

The **Independent Living Movement (ILM)** has been a key player in the struggle to achieve human rights legislation for people with disabilities. Originating in the United States during the early 1970s and introduced to Canada in 1979, the Independent Living Movement has become a dominant force in disability rights activity in Canada.

The origins of the Independent Living Movement can be traced to the Cowell Residence Program at the University of California, Berkeley. In 1962, Ed Roberts, a post-polio respiratory quadriplegic, became one of the first persons with a severe disability to be admitted to the university. A group of students with disabilities began to recognize that medical and rehabilitation professionals largely controlled their lives. They came to realize that the concerns raised by the black and student movements regarding self-determination were very relevant to their lives as people with disabilities.

This consciousness-raising process was accelerated in 1969 when the rehabilitation counsellor assigned to the Cowell Program tried to have two students with disabilities evicted because she "deemed their educational goals unfeasible and their lifestyles improper." The Cowell students fought the eviction and won. They went on to form the Physically Disabled Students' Program, which was a radical departure from former practice in the medical and rehabilitation fields.

CP PHOTO/Toronto Sun-Michael Peake.

Artist Debbie Donald of British Columbia discovered an untapped talent for art, and has become a member of The Mouth and Foot Painting Artists, a for-profit group whose works for sale provide them with the means to live an independent life.

The Independent Living Movement in Canada grew out of two central developments: (1) the existing infrastructure developed by the Canadian Consumer Movement in the 1970s, in particular the Coalition of Provincial Organizations of the Handicapped (now known as the Council of Canadians with Disabilities); and (2) the introduction of the Independent Living (IL) philosophy by American disability theorist Gerben DeJong to the Canadian disability community in 1980.

Three subsequent events in 1981 were central to the full development of the IL movement in Canada: (1) the United Nations declaration of the International Year of Disabled Persons, (2) the Canadian government's release of its Obstacles report, and (3) the personal contribution of one of its founding members, Henry Enns, to the IL philosophy. These helped provide legitimacy to the social oppression approach to disability and promoted the philosophy of IL to the various levels of government, academics and other disability organizations.

By 1985, Independent Living Resource Centres (ILRCs) were operating in Waterloo, Winnipeg, Thunder Bay, Calgary and Toronto. In 1986, at the first IL conference in Ottawa, the Canadian Association of Independent Living Centres (CAILC) was formed to act as a national coordinating body for the ILM and the definition of a Canadian ILRC was developed. In 1997, a total of 22 ILRCs were operating across Canada.

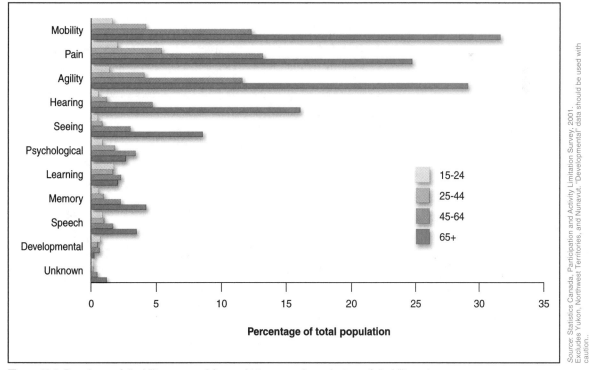

Source: Statistics Canada, Participation and Activity Limitation Survey, 2001. Excludes Yukon, Northwest Territories, and Nunavut. "Developmental" data should be used with caution.

Figure 13.3: Prevalence of disability among adults aged 15 years and over, by type of disability and age.

The Philosophy of Independent Living

The philosophy underlying the Independent Living Movement is to encourage and help persons with disabilities achieve self-direction over the personal and community services needed to attain their own independent living. The Canadian Association for Independent Living Centres describes the philosophy of ILRCs:

> The Independent Living (IL) approach recognizes the rights of citizens with disabilities to take control of their lives by examining choices, making decisions and even taking risks. The logic behind Independent Living is that people with disabilities are the experts in knowing what their needs are and are able to find solutions to problems surrounding disability issues. The Independent Living philosophy recognizes that people with disabilities have the right to run their own lives, make their own decisions, make their own mistakes and be an active participant in their community (http://www.cailc.ca).

The Independent Living philosophy has three aspects:

1. An approach that empowers consumers to make choices necessary to control their community and personal resources;

2. A set of organizational values or principles: consumer control, cross-disability, community based and full participation. Consumer control means that ILRCs are governed and controlled by persons with disabilities. At least 51 percent of the members of each board of directors must have a disability, and must have a balance of people with and without a disability. Cross-disability means that ILRCs are responsive to persons with all types of disabilities, including mobility,

Source: Statistics Canada. 2001. *Participation and Activity Limitation Survey.* Excludes Yukon, Northwest Territories, and Nunavut. "Developmental" data should be used with caution.

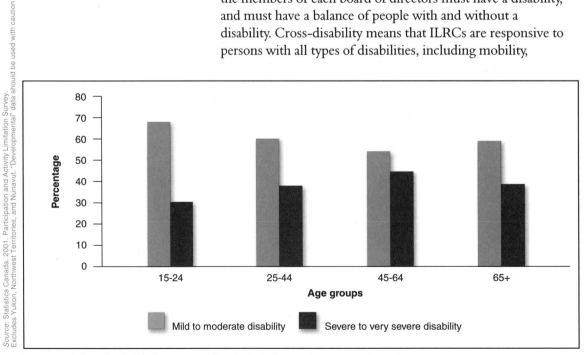

Figure 13.4: Severity of disability among adults with disabilities aged 15 years and over, by age groups.

sensory, cognitive, emotional, psychiatric and so forth. The concept of being community based implies that ILRCs are non-profit organizations committed to the development of programs and resources that complement rather than duplicate existing community resources. The IL philosophy believes that persons with disabilities are citizens with the right to participate in the community life and growth; and

3. An alternative model of program delivery. This alternative program model is one that has been created by and for persons with disabilities.

The Canadian Independent Living model consists of four core programs: information and referral, peer support, empowerment skills development, and research and demonstration. Although each community will have different needs and resources, in general all have these core programs.

1. *Information and Referral*: The Information and Referral program responds to requests from consumers. The Centre attempts to locate the information required or may refer the consumer to another community agency or ILRC program.

2. *Peer Support*: Peer support is consumers talking with and supporting other consumers.

3. *Independent Living/Empowerment Skills Development*: Through appropriate seminars, support and advice, the IL/Empowerment Skills Development program helps disabled people develop the skills that will allow them to advocate for themselves.

4 *Research and Demonstration*: The Research and Demonstration program researches the needs within the community and then promotes the development of services to meet those needs.

In 1997, CAILC undertook a study of the effects of the Independent Living Resource Centres and found that ILRCs succeed, in large part, not simply because they provide an opportunity to learn skills, access information, or receive support, but because they do so in a way that is consistent with the Independent Living philosophy.

The Association concluded that improvement in the quality of life for people with disabilities requires skill development as well as the removal of environmental, social and economic barriers. Individual empowerment was found to be a key benefit. It was particularly important in fostering competency in a variety of community living skills, as well as resulting in increased confidence and self-esteem. Finally, the Association found that individuals involved with some of the programs of the ILRC have knowledge of more programs than they are involved with, and highly value the programs with which they are directly involved and/or see as benefitting others (CAILC 1997).

Independent living means being able to function in one's community.

Health Canada.

Conclusion

The rehabilitation services are the primary area of social work with persons with disabilities. These services include hospitals, rehabilitation centres, group homes, chronic care facilities as well as educational institutions. Social workers are also employed by provincial and federal governments and by a variety of charitable organizations, both in the provision of direct services and in the development of social policies. For those involved in direct practice, work centres on counselling and helping with support services, including assisting with access to resources.

Since the 1970s, there has been a shift away from a narrow medical approach of disability to more of a sociopolitical model in which persons with disabilities are accepted as equal citizens. In line with the newer approach to disability, increasingly social workers are involved in campaigning on behalf of persons with disabilities, as advocates for social and political change. The Independent Living Movement has been a key organization in the promotion of human rights for persons with disabilities. Their successful philosophy is one that promotes self-direction, self-determination and full participation in the life of communities. This shift is to be welcomed and points the way towards significant advances in services and programs and a better life for persons with disabilities across Canada.

Chapter 13 Review
Social Work with Persons with Disabilities

Discussion Questions

1. Give some of the basic statistics that capture the extent of disability within the Canadian population.

2. What are important highlights in the history of disability in Canada?

3. What are the differences between a "social model of disability" and a "pathology model of disability"?

4. What is "ableism" and what might be some causes of ableism?

5. What are important issues that a social worker should consider when working with the family of a person with disabilities?

6. Briefly trace the origins of the Independent Living Movement and describe its main objectives.

Websites

Disability WebLinks
http://www.disabilityweblinks.ca

This site has been specifically developed for persons with disabilities and the site design, layout and technical features reflect the requirements identified by members of the community and internationally accepted guidelines for accessibility. Human Resources Development Canada is managing the site under the direction of the Federal/Provincial/Territorial Ministers responsible for Social Services.

Council of Canadians with Disabilities
http://www.ccdonline.ca

The Council of Canadians with Disabilities advocates at the federal level to improve the lives of men and women with disabilities in Canada by eliminating inequality and discrimination. Members include national, regional and local advocacy organizations that are controlled by persons with disabilities.

Disabled Women's Network Ontario
http://dawn.thot.net

DAWN Ontario is a progressive, volunteer-driven, feminist organization dedicated to the advancement of equality of rights of women with disabilities.

Canadian Association of Independent Living Centres (CAILC)l
http://www.cailc.ca

The Canadian Association of Independent Living Centres (CAILC) is a national umbrella organization that consists of local autonomous Independent Living Resource Centres (ILRCs). Their website contains a wealth of information about the topic, including a virtual library.

Key Terms

- Participation Activities Limitation Survey (PALS)
- Disability
- Disability rate
- Persons with disabilities
- Disability rights movement
- Personal tragedy theory of disability
- Social oppression theory of disability
- Stigma
- Ableism
- Publicly funded disability programs
- Privately funded disability programs
- Family systems theory
- Independent Living Movement (ILM)

Children from low-income families bathe in the Pacific Ocean across from Panama City. According to UNICEF, more than 50 percent of Panamanian children live below the poverty line; overall, 200 million children in poverty across Latin America.

14

International Social Work Practice

Helping People Help Themselves

The term "international social work" has a variety of meanings. It can refer to the examination and comparison of the social welfare systems in different countries (comparative social welfare). It can also denote work within international organizations, such as governmental or voluntary organizations, that carry out social planning, social development and welfare programs abroad. Finally, of course, international social work can simply refer to day-to-day social work with individuals, groups and communities in a country other than one's own.

The history of international social work is a distinguished one. Since the early days of Jane Addams, the profession's first Nobel Prize winner, social workers have been actively involved within various national and international forums. Social workers have also been and remain involved with the resettling of refugees and other persons displaced by war, operating emergency relief services for victims of natural and human-made disasters, advocating on behalf of disadvantaged and vulnerable populations, organizing groups of oppressed people into effective political entities and otherwise extending various programs of assistance to populations in need. In all these areas, they play an indispensable and often unacknowledged role, sometimes working in very difficult conditions.

This chapter focuses on the work of social workers in "Southern," "developing" or "Third World" countries. In particular, it examines the core problems of social and economic development in these underdeveloped countries in the modern context of economic globalization. Since those involved in social work at the international level tend to be heavily involved in local community development and human rights work, much of the chapter focuses on these areas.

Before going on, however, it is important to note that the work that social workers do abroad can be very dangerous at times. Not infrequently, their lives are at risk and their devotion goes well beyond the call of duty. This is a further testimony of the dedication of those individuals who are drawn into the social work profession today, and especially those involved in social work in the developing countries of the Third World.

Practising social work abroad has always been an important part of what Canadian social workers do. In pursuing the ideals of human rights and sustainable development and in defending oppressed groups, social workers practise in a wide range of governmental, religious and community organizations worldwide. Today, of course, this occurs in the context of the rapid globalization of social and economic life.

Children in a refugee camp in Kukes, Albania.

IN THE WORLD TODAY...

- 1.23 billion people live in absolute poverty
- 100 million are homeless
- 14 million go hungry every day
- 14 million children under five will die this year
- 900 million are without education

Source: CAFOD Fact Sheet on Poverty at: http://www.cafod.org.uk/povertyfs.htm

The Global Economy and Poverty

Any discussion of international social work must begin by acknowledging the enormous economic disadvantages faced by countries in the developing world. The *Progress on Nations* report published annually by the United Nations Children's Fund (UNICEF 2000) shows the brutal social and economic disparities between countries. The following are some of the highlights:

- Among the 192 nations of the world, per capita GNP is as low as $80 and as high as $45,360 a year.
- The under-five mortality rate varies from four to 320 deaths per 1,000 live births.
- The maternal death rate ranges from zero to 1,800 deaths per 100,000 live births.
- The primary school enrolment rate varies from 24 percent to 100 percent of young people.

The World Health Organization (WHO) estimates that malnutrition is associated with over half of all child deaths that occurred in developing countries. Of the nearly 11 million children under five who die each year in developing countries, mainly from preventable causes, the deaths of over 6 million, or 55 percent, are either directly or indirectly attributable to malnutrition. Poverty, of course, is one of the main causes of malnutrition and early death.

• The North-South Divide

The economic world divides, broadly speaking, along North-South lines (the so-called **North-South divide**), with the countries of the First World awash in relative affluence and those of the **Third World** in abject poverty. The countries of the South have 75 percent of the world's people, but only:

- fifteen percent of the world's energy consumption;
- seventeen percent of the world's GNP;
- thirty percent of the world's food grains;
- eighteen percent of the world's export earnings;
- eleven percent of the world's education spending;
- nine percent of the world's health expenditure;
- five percent of the world's science and technology;
- eight percent of the world's industry.

About one-third, or 1.2 billion people, live on an income of less than $1 a day (State of the World's Population 2004). Furthermore, according to the UN Human Development Report of 2004, about 7.8 million people worldwide live on less than $2 per day. Recognizing that there is an overwhelming need to eliminate such severe disadvantages is a prerequisite to effective international social work.

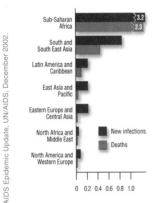

AIDS Epidemic Update, UN/AIDS, December 2002.

Figure 14.1: The global AIDS epidemic, 2003 (millions).

Clearly, the most pressing concern in poor countries is social and economic development. Economic development is a prerequisite if the people of these countries are to overcome the crushing poverty that many face daily. Unfortunately, for the economies of many rich countries, the developing nations serve mainly as a source of raw materials and cheap labour. Indeed, many would argue that, in relation to the industrialized nations, many countries in the Third World are not so much "developing" as "underdeveloping." In general, the development plans of the International Monetary Fund and World Bank have not led to economic prosperity. What has transpired under the banners of "globalization" and "development" appears to be more a continuing enslavement than economic liberation. (For more on globalization, see Chapter 2, page 43.)

In such desperate circumstances, dedicated social workers in these countries quickly realize that opportunities for bringing about effective social change, even on a local scale, are limited. For this reason, international social workers and political activists are increasingly advocating a new approach to development based on adherence to complementary guiding principles.

Two of these principles are:

(1) the promotion and protection of human rights, and

(2) ensuring sustainable development.

A great deal of useful international social work has taken place in pursuit of these key objectives, which are discussed below.

GLOBAL SUMMARY OF THE HIV/AIDS EPIDEMIC

Number of people living with HIV/AIDS

Adults	38.6 million
Women	19.2 million
Children under 15	3.2 million

People newly infected with HIV in 2002

Adults	5 million
Women	2 million
Children under 15	800,000

AIDS deaths in 2002

Adults	2.5 million
Women	1.2 million
Children under 15	610,000

Source: AIDS Epidemic Update, UN/AIDS, December 2002.

• **Did you know...**

Among the 73 countries for which there is data (representing about 80 percent of the world's people), 48 have seen inequality increase since the 1950s, 16 have experienced no change and only nine — with just 4 percent of the world's people — have seen a fall.

• **Did you know...**

Every year about 11 million children die of preventable causes, often for want of simple and easily provided improvements in nutrition, sanitation, maternal health and education. That is 21 children per minute.

• **Did you know...**

At the end of 2000, more than 12 million people were refugees, 6 million were internally displaced and nearly 4 million were returning refugees and asylum seekers —in all, this represented an increase of 50 percent from 1990.

• **Did you know...**

Seven rich countries hold 48 percent of the voting power at the IMF and 46 percent at the World Bank.

• **Did you know...**

The worst plague in human history is AIDS: Its death toll surpasses that of the bubonic plague in Europe during the Middle Ages. By the end of 2000, almost 22 million people had died from AIDS, 13 million children had lost their mother or both parents and more than 40 million were living with HIV/AIDS — 90 percent of them in developing countries, 75 percent of them in Sub-Saharan Africa.

• **Did you know...**

International development aid from rich countries is only $65 per person living in those countries.

Source: Human Development Report, 2004.

The Promotion and Protection of Human Rights

The idea of **human rights** is based on an acknowledgment that individuals possess certain inalienable political and civil rights. The notion that there is a duty to protect the rights of all people has become a recognized part of our human heritage. The recognition of universal human rights was consolidated in the 1948 Universal Declaration of Human Rights by the General Assembly of the United Nations, to which all the major countries of the world are signatories.

• Three Types of Rights

It is useful to distinguish between three types (or "generations") of human rights.

- • **Negative rights.** The first type, called *negative rights*, represents civil and political rights as set forth in Articles 2 to 21 of the Universal Declaration of Human Rights. These rights ensure protection of basic rights such as freedom from torture, false imprisonment or summary execution.

- • **Positive rights.** The second type represents *positive rights* or economic, social and cultural rights as detailed in Articles 22 to 27 of the Declaration. These rights are aimed at ensuring justice, freedom from want and participation in society.

Table 14.1: The Traditional "Three Generations" of Human Rights

	First generation	**Second Generation**	**Third Generation**
Type	Civil and Political Rights	Economic, Social and Cultural Rights	Collective Rights
Origin	Liberalism	Socialism, Social Democracy	Collectivism, Communitarianism
Examples	Right to vote	Right to education	Environmental rights: right to clean air, water
	Right to run for office	Right to housing	Right to enjoy nature
	Equality before the law	Right to employment	Right to benefit from development
	Freedom of expression	Right to health	Right to belong to a strong, cohesive society
	Freedom of assembly	Right to income security	
	Right to a fair and prompt trial	Right to earn an income	
	Freedom from torture and abuse	Freedom to spend money as one chooses	
	Freedom from arbitrary arrest	Choice of partner	
	Freedom from discrimination	Right to raise a family	
	Right to legal representation	Right to safe working conditions	
	Freedom of association	Freedom of cultural expression	
	Freedom of movement	Right to land	
	Freedom from slavery	Right to property	
		Children's rights	

- **Collective rights.** The third type encompasses the *collective rights* contained in Article 28, which states that "everyone is entitled to a social and international order in which the rights and freedoms set forth in this Declaration can be fully realized."

The levels move from a defensive stance (against the violation of basic rights), to an affirmation of the right to meet material needs and participate in society, to an understanding of collective rights and the equitable participation in the production and distribution of resources. Historically, the social work profession has tended to focus on meeting needs, rather than affirming rights, but social workers have increasingly moved in the direction of affirming and fostering all three levels of rights.

The basic legal instruments concerning human rights are:

- Charter of the United Nations (1945) available on-line at: http://www.un.org

- Universal Declaration of Human Rights (1948) available on-line at: http://www.un.org/Overview/rights.html

- The Covenants on Human Rights (1966)
  (a) International Covenant on Civil and Political Rights
  (b) International Covenant on Economic, Social and Cultural Rights

- International Convention on the Elimination of All Forms of Racial Discrimination (1965)

- Convention on the Elimination of All Forms of Discrimination Against Women (1979)

- Convention Against Torture and Other Cruel, Inhuman and Degrading Treatment or Punishment (1984)

- Convention on the Rights of the Child (1989)

- International Convention on the Protection of the Rights of All Migrant Workers and Members of Their Families (1990)

• International Policy on Human Rights

The **International Policy on Human Rights** (see Appendix D) adopted by the International Federation of Social Work (IFSW) affirms that all social workers have a special responsibility to advance the cause of human rights throughout the world. In its preamble, it states: "The history of human rights is that of the struggle against exploitation of one person by another. It is based on the recognition of basic rights founded on the concept of the inherent dignity and worth of every individual."

The policy asserts that human rights are a common standard and guide for the work of all professional social workers. It points out that social workers not only need to respect human rights, but also to work to oppose and eliminate all violations of human rights.

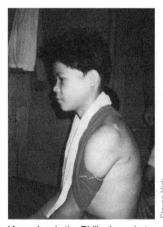

Young boy in the Philippines shot by the Marcos military in 1995.

Steven Hick.

SOCIAL DEVELOPMENT

Those interested in learning more about the social development approach to international social work can visit the International Council on Social Welfare website at http://www.icsw.org

Explore the social development link and examine the publications and government and organizations links. The publications section contains numerous articles that provide an overview of the situation of children, poverty, employment, health, old age and human development.

Ensuring Sustainable Development

An important principle of international social work is that of sustainable development. The most frequently quoted definition of sustainable development is from the report *Our Common Future* (also known as the Brundtland Report): "Sustainable development is development that meets the needs of the present without compromising the ability of future generations to meet their own needs" (World Commission on Environment and Development 1987, 43).

Sustainable development is not a new idea, of course — Aboriginal cultures have emphasized the need for a holistic approach or harmony between the environment, society and economy. What is new is the reaffirmation of these ideas within the context of global capitalism and an information-based society.

• Sustainable Social Progress

As an important extension to this concept, the International Council on Social Welfare (ICSW) advocates what it calls sustainable social progress, which goes beyond ecological and environmental concerns. The members of ICSW believe that, in order to promote sustainable social progress, social workers should support cooperation to strengthen governance and social standards internationally. International sustainable development, in this broader sense, includes all of the activities that international social workers carry out to enhance the participation of people in making decisions for themselves, combatting poverty, promoting women's health and advancing the cause of peace.

Sustainable development (or sustainable social progress) is a central organizing principle for international social workers. Its application involves three basic operating premises:

- *Equity and justice for all:* upholding the rights of the poor and disadvantaged within and between nations, and the rights of future generations.

- *Long-term view:* advancing the view that all claims on the earth's resources today have implications for future generations.

- *Structural understanding of the broader society:* taking into account the many interconnections between individuals, communities, the economy and the environment.

The concept is an important one for international social work practitioners and others involved in international development work. The idea challenges us to think beyond the here-and-now and look to the wider implications of our actions. In essence, it is a call to action — a call to do things differently and to realize that our actions have ripple effects throughout our interdependent world.

CP PHOTO/AP-Dario Lopez-Mills.

The World Summit on Sustainable Development (South Africa, 2002).

The Human Development Report

The **Human Development Report (HDR)** is an independent report that is released in June or July of each year. It is commissioned by the United Nations Development Programme (UNDP) and is the product of a team of leading scholars, practitioners and members of the Human Development Report Office. The HDR was first launched in 1990 with the goal of putting people back at the centre of the development process in terms of economic debate, policy and advocacy. It goes beyond income to assess the level of people's long-term well-being, emphasizing that the goals of development are choices and freedoms.

Since the first Report in 1990, four composite indices for human development have been developed by the HDR team — the Human Development Index, the Gender-related Development Index, the Gender Empowerment Measure, and the Human Poverty Index. In addition to releasing new indicators for the previous year, each Report also focuses on a highly topical theme, providing path-breaking analysis and policy recommendations. The Human Development Report Office also issues frequent global, national and regional reports on important topics of the day. The Reports' messages — and the tools to implement them — have been embraced by people around the world, evidenced by the publication of national human development reports at the national level in more than 120 countries.

• The Human Development Index

While the concept of human development is much broader than any single index can measure, the HDR's principal human development indicator, the **Human Development Index (HDI)**, offers a powerful alternative to income used alone as a measure of human well-being. The HDI focuses on three basic dimensions of development: (1) a long and healthy life, as measured by life expectancy at birth; (2) knowledge, as measured by the adult literacy rate and the combined gross enrolment ratio for primary, secondary and tertiary schools; and (3) a decent standard of living, as measured by GDP per capita in purchasing power parity (PPP) US dollars. The HDI was created to re-emphasize that people and their capabilities should be the ultimate criteria for assessing the development of a country, not economic growth. The index is constructed using indicators that are currently available and is based on a methodology that is simple and transparent.

The HDI itself does not claim to be comprehensive — for example, it does not include important aspects of human development, notably the ability to participate in political decisions. Likewise, it does not capture gender disparity and human deprivation, which are measured in other HDR indices (Gender-related Development Index, and the human Poverty Index). Nevertheless, the HDI is a powerful starting point for understanding, and advocating for, human development.

WHAT IS "HUMAN DEVELOPMENT"?

"Human development is about much more than the rise or fall of national incomes. It is about creating an environment in which people can develop their full potential and lead productive, creative lives in accord with their needs and interests.

"People are the real wealth of nations. Development is thus about expanding the choices people have to lead lives that they value. And it is thus about much more than economic growth, which is only a means — if a very important one — of enlarging people's choices."

Source: Human Development Reports, United Nations Development Program.

For more information on the HDR, its global, national and regional reports and the various development indexes, go to: http://hdr.undp.org

International Social Work Practice Models

Within international social work practice, three broad approaches or models can be identified. They are obviously not mutually exclusive; one might pursue more than one approach.

• Social Welfare Model

The more conventional **social welfare model** of international social work is largely based on Keynesian economics and American economist W.W. Rostow's "stages of industrialization" theory. Rostow's theory postulates that all societies go through five stages on the road to becoming a developed country: (1) traditional society, (2) long growth preconditions, (3) short period "take-off," (4) a rapid drive to maturity, and (5) the era of mass consumption (Rostow 1960). Using this approach, the primary goal is to create the basic welfare conditions required to help move countries through the necessary stages of development. The main concern is with the satisfaction of basic social and material needs of people (e.g., minimal standards of living, access to at least basic health, education and other essential social services).

• New World Order Model

What might be called the **new world order model** of international social work has its origins in the idea that the current world order is not a very democratic one but rather one controlled by a relatively small number of wealthy countries. Rather than being concerned with incremental change, those who follow this approach are concerned with bringing about widespread change in institutional arrangements that govern relationships between nations and, within nations, between groups of people. They focus on: (1) the active participation of all relevant sectors in the transformation process, (2) world peace and war prevention, (3) the alleviation of human suffering in the world, (4) the creation of effective systems of social protection and social service provision, (5) increased social and political justice, and (6) the protection and enhancement of the natural environment.

• Social Development Model

A third approach, which may be referred to as the **social development model**, falls somewhere between the above two approaches and has its origins in the community development field. Social workers who use this approach to international work seek primarily to address the immediate causes of human degradation, powerlessness and social inequality, and to guide collective action towards the elimination of all forms of oppression, injustice and violence. They are concerned with the fuller participation of people at all levels of the political and economic systems and with fostering social, political and economic systems that are more humane, inclusive and participatory.

TEP Photo Archives.

Solving basic health needs is key to social and economic development.

Respect for Cultural Diversity

Working in another country obviously involves being a practitioner in another cultural context. How does one prepare oneself for such work? How does one ensure that one is "culturally competent"?

In social work literature, the term **cultural competence** emphasizes the need for social workers to gain an understanding of the worldview or cultural frame of reference of the client. Thus, workers must make an effort to understand the history, language and background characteristics of the cultural groups with which they are working. However, practitioners working abroad also need to be careful to avoid what may amount to stereotypes based on a limited knowledge about another culture. For example, it would be inappropriate to work in China without considering the cultural differences among the various ethnic groups within the Chinese population. In addition, social workers must take their knowledge of the "other" culture and combine it with an analysis of how their own cultural outlook may influence their own social work interventions.

In other words, they need deep respect for the unique social conditions and cultural context within which they are working. Without such an appreciation, they will be less effective at assessing the problems at hand. Below are some common myths about development and cultural diversity that one should keep in mind.

DEBUNKING DIVERSITY MYTHS

• **MYTH 1:** People's ethnic identities compete with their attachment to the state, so there is a trade-off between recognizing diversity and unifying the state.

Fact: Countries do not have to choose between national unity and cultural diversity. Individuals can and do have multiple, complementary identities — ethnicity, language, religion and race, as well as citizenship. Identity is not a zero-sum game. There is no inevitable need to choose between state unity and recognition of cultural differences.

• **MYTH 2:** Some cultures are more thrifty or entrepreneurial than others, and some cultures have democratic values that others lack; so there is a trade-off between accommodating some cultures and promoting development and democracy.

Fact: There is no evidence of a relationship between culture and economic progress or democracy. In explaining economic growth rates, state policy, geography and the burden of disease are found to be highly relevant factors. But religious indicators — whether a society is Hindu, Muslim, or Christian, for example — are found to be statistically insignificant. Similarly, the commonly voiced view in the West that Islam is incompatible with democracy is belied by the fact that most of the world's Muslims live in societies now under democratic rule.

• **MYTH 3:** Ethnic groups are prone to violent conflict with each other in clashes of values, so there is a trade-off between respecting diversity and sustaining peace.

Fact: Empirical evidence suggests that cultural differences and clashes over values are rarely the root cause of violent conflict.

• **MYTH 4:** Multi-ethnic countries are less able to progress economically, so there is a trade-off between diversity and development.

Fact: There is no evidence that cultural diversity slows development. Malaysia, the tenth-fastest growing economy during 1970–1990, is an example of a culturally diverse country with economic success. Its population is 62 percent Malay, 30 percent Chinese and 8 percent Indian.

Source: Human Development Report, 2004.

What Do International Social Workers Do?

Social work, as a helping profession, is especially concerned with the problems and rights of the disadvantaged. In working towards these ends, international social workers can be found undertaking a wide range of activities in a variety of national, international and overseas organizations. These organizations include: (1) international intergovernmental organizations, (2) non-governmental organizations, (3) churches and other humanitarian organizations, and (4) community organizations. These are discussed below.

• International Intergovernmental Organizations

Many social workers are active in various **international intergovernmental organizations (IGOs)**, of which the United Nations (UN) is best known. Formed at the end of World War II, the UN seeks to develop a framework of international law that will be followed by all nation states around the world. Social workers function in a variety of roles in any of its 12 specialized agencies, which include the UN Development Program, UNICEF, World Health Organization, International Labour Office and the UN High Commissioner for Refugees. (For general information and links to its various agencies, go to http://www.un.org, the UN's main website.)

Within this arena, social workers participate as analysts and as direct practitioners in applying and monitoring the assistance and protection provided by UN declarations and conventions. Social workers also frequently work in a front-line capacity, providing refugee resettlement services, counselling children traumatized by war, distributing humanitarian assistance during disasters or war, or monitoring human rights abuses.

In Kosovo, for example, UNICEF provided life-saving assistance for children and women, and social workers were involved in distributing hygiene kits for babies, blankets, water purification tablets and basic medical supplies. They were also a part of trauma teams, along with medical professionals and psychologists, and participated in the long-term relief plans that emphasized support for educational systems and community organizations.

• Non-Governmental Organizations

Social workers are also to be found working in the multitude of **non-governmental organizations (NGOs)** around the world. NGOs are international organizations, but they are not directly linked to governments. This allows such organizations more freedom to take up important issues and bring about effective change. NGOs tend to be small dynamic groups that work on a variety of issues related to their particular political or philosophical stances.

Author at UN food aid supply in Kosovo.

Students of social work may find it helpful to do volunteer work for NGOs to build experience and make contacts for future work. Many NGOs have entry-level positions for new social workers without extensive experience. Non-government organizations such as Crossroads International, Canada World Youth and World University Service Canada provide excellent opportunities for social workers to gain international experience.

Social workers working with NGOs frequently find themselves directly participating in peace building and conflict resolution. For example, in the central Caucasus region — Georgia, Armenia and Azerbaijan — social workers are using art therapy to help children heal from the trauma of war and to build peace between the various groups torn by inter-ethnic conflict since the late 1980s. The projects encourage the children to express their thoughts and feelings through coloured pictures and paintings. Children from all ethnic groups attend the projects, and it is hoped that links will be established between communities.

CP PHOTO/AP-Manish Swarup.

Infants sit in a Community Health Education and Service (CHES) home in Madras in southern India. CHES is a non-governmental organization primarily working for women and children infected with the HIV virus.

• Churches and Other Organizations

Churches and other religious groups and organizations have an extensive variety of **overseas humanitarian programs**, and they frequently employ the services of social workers. These groups tend to operate in the poorer countries of Africa, Asia and Latin America. Nowadays, few churches use their programs primarily as a way to get new recruits (although some still do). For example, the United Church has excellent preparation and support throughout the world and does not send workers overseas unless requested by partner organizations.

As well as church and religious organizations, there are large international grant foundations that employ social workers as consultants, field representatives and country directors for programs that the foundation supports. The Canadian government also maintains offices in many countries that provide services to visiting Canadians and to local people. These services frequently involve social workers. Other federal government departments, such as the Department of Foreign Affairs and International Trade (http://www.dfait-maeci.gc.ca), the Canadian International Development Agency (CIDA; http://www.acdi-cida.gc.ca) and the International Development Research Centre (IDRC; http://www.idrc.ca), hire social workers to help with their work. The Canadian International Development Agency (CIDA) is the federal agency charged with planning and implementing most of Canada's development cooperation program in order to reduce poverty and to contribute to a more secure, equitable and prosperous world.

Working directly for government agencies of other countries is another option for social workers seeking international experience. These agencies are not necessarily international in focus, but certainly can be considered as part of an international social work career. Generally, however, one must have extensive language skills and direct contacts within the country in order to obtain such a position.

• International Community Work

A common type of social work activity in developing countries is **international community work**. Social workers work with communities by assisting with problem solving and with planning effective social services. They use community work to organize people to bring about major social change between nations, within nations and between groups of people. They work with communities to achieve the fullest participation of community members in transforming various aspects of their lives.

The ultimate goal of community work is the empowerment or fostering of the "sense in people that they have the ability and right to influence their environment" (Lee 1999, 43). Empowering people means that they can create and take action on their own behalf to meet their physical, spiritual and psychological needs and participate directly in the

A CIDA-supported community development initiative.

change process. To be able to act on their own behalf, however, people must see themselves as citizens, with the right and ability to express their opinions and to acquire resources. Reaching these objectives requires a genuine sense of community: "it is important for the members to have a positive sense of themselves as a distinct group" (ibid., 31). On the basis of community, new organizations can be built or improved upon and change can be effected.

The Canadian International Development Agency (CIDA), for example, is sponsoring a community-organizing project in Pakistan in which social workers play a key role. The goals of the $4.96–million project are to encourage more of Pakistan's rural poor to become involved in the process of developing their community, as well as to motivate and strengthen community-based organizations and female development organizations, and to encourage other groups to help get their community members involved in addressing development needs. Through this project, about 360 community organizations are being helped to undertake community development.

Local initiatives strengthen communities. These Filipino workers are protesting the displacement of local industries by large global corporations.

The Internet and International Social Work

As in all other areas of life, information and communication technology, of which the Internet is a major part, is having a significant impact on international social work. The Internet is not only enabling economic globalization, it is also enabling the connection of people and communities for the promotion of social justice and peace. It is being used for electronic advocacy, human rights protection and community building.

• Electronic Advocacy

Electronic advocacy might be the best way to conceptualize the importance of informational technology to social work. **Electronic advocacy** refers to the process of using communication and information technologies to disseminate information and to mobilize support from a large constituency to influence decision-making processes or to support efforts at policy change. It may include the use of telephone, fax, television, radio, e-mail, websites, on-line discussion groups, network newsgroups and other modes of communication technologies. These kinds of tools will become increasingly important to social workers in the years to come.

The Internet is also providing new and different ways for people in dispersed communities to connect and advocate for their own rights or the rights of others. In these new communities, sometimes called "on-line communities" or "virtual communities," people meet, discuss and share information via electronic means. This technology allows social workers to join and connect with people who would have been unreachable in the non-digital era, and familiarity with the Internet is becoming part of the skill set of international social workers.

Increasingly, the Internet has also become a tool for the promotion and protection of human rights. Human rights abuses, by their nature, often necessitate urgent action, and the Internet provides the obvious tool for disseminating immediate information.

• The Digital Divide

It is important to bear in mind that most of the world's peoples do not have access to this technology — a problem sometimes referred to as the **digital divide**. This is an important social justice issue in its own right. Studies show that access to the Internet follows general patterns of social inequality: Men have more access than women; higher income more than lower income; young more than old; well educated more than less educated. As information and scientific knowledge become increasingly important for economic and social development, addressing the problems associated with unequal access to information technology becomes especially important in the context of international social work.

Steven Hick.

"Digital divide": The developing world is far behind in technology.

The Internet, electronic advocacy and virtual communities are already important ingredients of modern social change strategies around the world. As the capabilities and capacity of the Internet increase, new uses and applications for social work will emerge. Intranets will enable organizations to streamline work procedures; virtual office environments will allow international NGOs to work together more effectively; video conferencing will emerge as a key tool for communication. During the Kosovo crisis, for example, the Internet was used to facilitate communication and collaboration within and between social workers in various NGOs.

The recent announcement by the Massachusetts Institute of Technology that all of its research material will be available free on-line over the coming years may foreshadow other important developments in this area. The implications of something as simple as this for a poverty-stricken world, where access to scholarly books and research publications is still a major source of educational disadvantage, would be remarkable. If MIT and other institutions hold to their promises, the world could be much richer.

REFLECTIONS FROM A RETURNED VOLUNTEER

Former Canadian Crossroads International volunteer Giovanna Panzera remembers what it felt like to come home:

My experience in Ecuador had been a series of firsts — my first time living and working in a developing country; my first time being away from home for such a long period of time; my first time dealing with a new language and culture as a complete stranger. It was an intense period of learning and adapting.

But, to a certain extent, this was to be expected. After all, how can you live in a completely different culture for five months and not experience some type of transformation? You are seeing things you never saw before. You are living in a way that is very different from what you are used to. You are living by another set of societal norms, which can contradict your own in fundamental ways. You have to learn to adapt, usually quite quickly, if you want to successfully integrate into the community in which you are placed.

After five months of getting used to my new environment, the time had come to leave. And even before my feet had left Ecuadorian soil, I was already anticipating a bumpy ride back to the life I had left behind.

Like most volunteer-sending organizations, CCI had done an excellent job of preparing me for the culture shock I would inevitably experience in Ecuador. All of that training proved useful, not in necessarily averting the shock, but in helping me to be ready for it (and giving me the tools to deal with the symptoms of fear, sadness, anger and isolation that ensued).

Human interaction is often sacrificed in our attempt to get as much done as quickly as possible — in Ecuador I learned to slow down and appreciate the moment, and it was a very valuable lesson.

What I was less prepared for — although I had heard other returned volunteers talk about it — were the feelings of isolation and uneasiness that I would experience upon returning to my native soil. This "reverse culture shock," as it is termed, seemed illogical to me before I left. How could you become "uncomfortable" with a culture that was your own? But, as my journal reflects, while I was anxious to return to the "norms" of my community, they seemed at odds with the new perspective I had gained overseas.

Source: http://www.citizens4change.org/personal_story4.htm

Participatory Action Research

Social workers overseas have widely and successfully employed a technique known as participatory research or **participatory action research (PAR)**. Participatory action research has provided social workers with a useful set of techniques with which to effect social change. PAR is an approach to knowledge generation that views research as the means by which collective actions against the causes of injustice, exploitation, violence and environmental degradation can occur.

Social workers using PAR in their overseas community work usually combine three types of activity: investigation, education and action. The objectives are attained through collective processes involving the participation of people who are directly affected by a program or service. People in the community therefore play a large part in all activities, since those involved in a program on a day-to-day basis, or those who are affected by a particular policy, usually know a great deal about it and should become the centre or beginning point of the social work process.

The notion of power equalization is important to social workers using PAR. Collective inquiry transfers control of knowledge as people move from being mere objects to acting as subjects in their own development process. Empowerment in the context of overseas community work involves giving control over the decision-making process to the members of the community. In CIDA's Southern Africa AIDS Training Program, for example, local organizations are given support in their efforts to serve those most vulnerable to HIV/AIDS. This includes setting up anti-AIDS clubs in schools, visiting orphans, working to keep families together and assisting families with food, counselling and education. To be successful, local people must have decision-making power in the conception of the program and in its operations.

To take another example, War Child, in conjunction with Street Symphony and The Dandelion Trust in Ethiopia, is working on projects aimed at providing practical aid as well as some fun and greater self-respect to street children. Street Symphony runs drama and dance projects that allow the street children to participate in performances for officials and dignitaries as well as the general public. While being trained as dancers, the children are fed, clothed and provided with a safe home. They learn to express themselves through drama and dance while also raising awareness of their plight through the performances.

• AH-HAH! Method: Working with Communities

The so-called **AH-HAH! method**, presented in *AH-HAH! A New Approach to Popular Education* (GATT-Fly 1983), was developed in Canada and is frequently used by Canadian social workers in overseas settings. The name refers to the exclamation of "Ah-hah!" emitted by a person at the moment clarity or understanding dawns.

Steven Hick.

Canadian social workers apply the AH-HAH! method in Kosovo.

The aim is to enable participants to piece together their individual experiences in a way that clarifies their understanding of political and socioeconomic systems. It closely follows the principles of Paulo Freire (1970), a Brazilian educator whose work has had a profound impact on education and the struggle for rational development.

People know the world as they see it, and through this knowledge are able to intervene to transform their situations. The AH-HAH! method involves, in part, the idea of drawing a picture that represents the experiences of the group. In the process, an image of the economic and social system begins to emerge, leading to a discussion of government, legal systems, ownership of businesses, the military and so forth.

Problem-posing education of this kind regards dialogue and critical thinking as indispensable to learning. This contrasts with a "banking" perspective towards education, in which participants are treated as empty vessels that must be filled with knowledge and information. The method is highly participatory and transformative, and involves concrete action as its objective.

CP PHOTO/AP–Saurabh Das.

Delegate stands among the 6,000 statues made by deprived South African communities at the World Summit on Sustainable Development in 2002. The statues represent the voices of people struggling to defend their lives, communities and environment.

Conclusion

International social work is increasingly being recognized as an important area of social work practice. This is due, in part, to the identification of economic globalization as a factor in world poverty and a recognition that our local concerns are connected to global ones. This "internationalization of social problems" implies that social workers increasingly need to be knowledgeable and skilled in international social work theory and practice. Accordingly, social workers need to acquire new technology skills so as to enhance their ability to work and think locally and globally.

Social workers who do international work do so through an entire network of government and quasi-government agencies. The most prominent of these agencies are those associated with the United Nations and its various bodies, and those agencies associated with voluntary international aid agencies, such as the ones organized by various religious organizations. A great deal of useful work is being done through these organizations around the world to alleviate suffering and promote economic growth. However, the scope of the problems facing the poor nations of the world is enormous and the potential risks are often great.

Chapter 14 Review
International Social Work Practice

Discussion Questions

1. What are a few of the indicators of global economic and social inequality?

2. Define the two key principles that underlie international social work.

3. Define and distinguish the three levels of human rights. Why is it important for social workers to affirm and work towards all three levels?

4. What are the three approaches to international social work practice?

5. Describe the various agencies that employ social workers abroad.

6. How is the Internet changing the way that social workers network and advocate for human rights?

7. What is it about the AH-HAH! method of working in communities that has made it so successful in international social work?

Websites

• New Internationalist
http://www.newint.org

This monthly print magazine is available on-line. It provides a clearly written and concise overview of the important global issues of concern to social workers. It is an excellent resource to kick-start an essay on international issues.

• United Nations Development Programme (UNDP)
http://www.undp.org

At the UN Millennium Summit, world leaders pledged to cut poverty in half by 2015. UNDP is charged with helping to make this happen. Their website contains comprehensive related links, publications and various UNDP speeches and reports. Their publications section has numerous complete books on-line, including their annual Overcoming Human Poverty Report at http://www.undp.org/povertyreport.

• Heritage Canada, Human Rights Program
http://www.pch.gc.ca/ddp-hrd

This comprehensive website has all the basic information about human rights in Canada and internationally. It contains most of the official UN human rights covenants and an excellent overview of how the international human rights system works.

Key Terms

• **North-South divide**

• **Third World**

• **Human rights**

• **Negative rights**

• **Positive rights**

• **Collective rights**

• **International Policy on Human Rights**

• **Sustainable development**

• **Sustainable social progress**

• **Human Development Report (HDR)**

• **Human Development Index (HDI)**

• **Social welfare model of international social work**

• **New world order model of international social work**

• **Social development model of international social work**

• **Cultural competence**

• **Intergovernmental organizations (IGOs)**

• **Non-governmental organizations (NGOs)**

• **Overseas humanitarian programs**

• **International community work**

• **Electronic advocacy**

• **Digital divide**

• **Participatory action research (PAR)**

• **AH-HAH! method**

CASW National Scope of Practice Statement

Approved by CASW Board, March 2000

Preamble

Social work developed as a 20th century profession out of its voluntary philan-thropy and social reform roots. These roots are deeply linked to ancient values and concepts of charity, equality and compassion toward others in times of need. The profession's contemporary roots are particularly connected to social welfare developments in the 19th century. These developments included reform movements to change negative societal attitudes toward people in need; charity organization societies to help individuals and families; settlement houses to improve living conditions at the neighbourhood level; and rising feminist advocacy for human rights, social justice and gender equality. The pro-fession of social work is uniquely founded on altruistic values respecting the inherent dignity of every individual and the obligation of societal systems to provide equitable structural resources for all their members.

Social work's primary concern is the social well-being of all people equally valued with the importance of their physical, mental and spiritual well-being. Social work pioneers were among the first to address the significance of deeply connected relationships that constitute the social context of people's lives. Out of this rich heritage social work is recognized for its familiar "person-in-envi-ronment" perspective, which characterizes the unique relationship-centred focus of the profession. Parallel advances in other fields now provide significant support for the ongoing advancement of social work as a relationship-centred profession with a repertoire of person- and environment-oriented methods of practice.

The purpose of the National Scope of Practice Statement (NSPS) is to foster a growing understanding of the social work profession. The NSPS is a reference for social workers, CASW member associations, students in social work, those served by social workers and the community at large to inform the public and promote an accountable, effective profession. The statement is prepared as a consultation document. It can be used in part or whole to assist in meeting the information needs of diverse audiences, including legislators and those served by social workers, who may require or prefer a plain language statement that briefly and concisely describes the scope of social work (Appendix 3).

Scope of Social Work

"Social well-being," "person-in-environment" and "social functioning" are key concepts in understanding the scope of social work. The World Health

Organization (WHO) recognizes social well-being as an integral component of a person's overall state of health, complementary to but different from physical, mental and spiritual well-being. The scope of social work has several defining elements.

Practice Domain

Social work's person-in-environment perspective describes the area or domain in which social workers conduct their practice. Person refers to developmental and social functioning abilities in the context of environmental influences. The concept of environment in social work includes factors in society that enhance or impede the development of individual social well-being. In particular, these factors include their natural support networks and the formal structures in their communities, which together are shaped by a variety of societal norms and expectations in the form of influential attitudes, beliefs, customs, policies and laws. Social functioning refers to the way people perform their social roles and to the way societies provide structural supports to help them perform their roles.

The person-in-environment domain gives social work a common organizing framework and a holistic context for its mission and vision. The global vision of social work is a world consistently working toward social justice and well-being for all citizens. The central mission is to have social workers engaged in activities that will improve social well-being structures and enhance individual, family and community social functioning at local, national and international levels.

The primary focus of social work practice is on the relationship networks between individuals, their natural support resources, the formal structures in their communities, and the societal norms and expectations that shape these relationships. This relationship-centred focus is a distinguishing feature of the profession.

Practice Preparation

In Canada, the profession of social work constitutes a community of post-secondary educated social workers. They are guided in their work by international ethical principles (Appendix 4); a national code of ethics (Appendix 5); provincial statutes governing registration, regulations and standards of practice; common curriculum requirements in schools of social work; and an expanding repertoire of evidence-based methods of practice. Social work includes generalist and specialist prepared practitioners who are well grounded in the knowledge, skills and ethical foundations of social work. Social workers are equally committed to the use of knowledge from the humanities and sciences to advance the development of common human rights, equitable social justice, and sufficient structural supports for individual, family and community social well-being in all human societies. To this end, social workers are expected to be sensitive to the value of cultural and ethnic diversity and strive to end discrimination, oppression, poverty, and other forms of social injustice.

Like other professions in Canada, accredited baccalaureate education is considered the first professional practice degree, preparing social workers to practice as generalists. Preparation for specialized practice and research advances in social work is provided at graduate (master's) and post-graduate (Ph.D.) levels. In some provinces, the social work community includes practitioners with diplomas from community colleges. Community college education generally provides diploma graduates with approved transfer credit opportunities to continue their social work education at the baccalaureate level.

Practitioners

Social workers are expected to have a comprehensive understanding of the complex nature of their own person-in-environment systems. They are prepared to rise above personal biases and preferences to advance the social well-being of others through their practice of social work. Practitioners are instructed to constantly monitor and evaluate personal and professional influences that bear on the scientific and intuitive ways they use themselves as social change agents in practice situations. At the professional level, they are expected to perform a variety of professional roles, integrate the relevant codes of professional conduct that apply to their practice activities and adhere at all times to explicit standard of care tenets.

Practice Methods

Social work's practice methods are rooted in the early adoption of a clearly stated study, diagnosis and treatment process to systematize practice in a person-in-environment context. Implementation of the practice process was initially done through a variety of fields of practice, including child welfare, family services, medical social work, psychiatric social work and school social work, and several method specialties, including social casework, social group work and community organization.

Contemporary practice methods are based on a systematic process of problem solving which empowers individuals, families, groups and communities to identify and use their own problem solving skills in order to improve their life situations, and requires social workers to simultaneously address broader social issues which affect people's ability to obtain needed resources. The practice method is facilitated through the application of social work values, ethical principles and practice skills to accomplish the core functions of social work.

- helping people obtain basic human need services;
- counselling and psychotherapy with individuals, families and groups;
- helping communities/groups provide or improve social and health services; and
- participating in relevant legislative and social policy processes.

Practice methods in social work are those commonly used by qualified social workers (Appendix 1) or identified as restricted activities limited to social workers with specific qualifications (Appendix 2). Social work practice activities used to accomplish the core functions include direct practice with clients, community organizing, advocacy, social and political action, policy development and implementation, education, and research and evaluation.

Future direction

Social work's original scope of practice was broadly defined by its pioneering and value-based person-in-environment perspective, which shifted to a narrower scope defined by practice methods and the influence of scientific methods of intervention. As the profession moves into the 21st century social work's practice will continue to be influenced by the scientific method but the sphere of influence is broadening again to include new advances being made in the humanities and sciences. The profession's distinguishing focus on relationship networks between people in their social environment contexts will continue to be a valued aspect of its scope of practice and increasingly a focus borrowed by other helping professions.

APPENDIX I

The following list is an example of practice methods commonly used by social workers. It is not presented as an exhaustive list or as an exclusive list that only social workers can practice.

Case management	Psychosocial therapy	Community resource coordination
Child protection assessments	Psychotherapy	Developmental social welfare
Client-centred therapy	Social casework	Grassroots mobilization/locality development
Clinical social work	Social group work	Program evaluation
Crisis management	Client advocacy	Neighbourhood and community organizing
Discharge planning	Network facilitation	Political and social action
Family and marital therapy	Network skills training	Social planning
Family mediation	Structural social work	Social policy analysis and development
Group therapy	Class action social work	Structural change

APPENDIX 2
Restricted Practice Activities

Restricted practice activities are practice methods defined to be exclusive to or restricted to a particular profession or specialty section of a profession. In social work, these activities are usually specified in provincial statutes or regulations governing the practice of social work. The specification of restricted practice activities may vary from province to province. The following social work activities are the most likely to be included as restricted practice methods: clinical social work, psychotherapy, child welfare and protection services and family mediation services.

APPENDIX 3
Brief Scope of Practice Statements

The following statements provide examples of what might be a brief and concise scope of practice statement that meets the requirements of a legislative body and/or the needs of the general public.

Social work is the application of social work knowledge, values, focus and practice methods in a person-in-environment context to improve social well-being structures in society and enhance individual, family and community social functioning at local, national and international levels.

Social work is the application of social work knowledge, values, focus and practice methods in a person-in-environment context to accomplish the core functions of social work:

- helping people obtain basic human need services;
- counselling and psychotherapy with individuals, families and groups;
- helping communities/groups provide or improve social and health services; and
- participating in relevant legislative and social policy processes.

APPENDIX 4
IFSW Declaration of Ethical Principles of Social Work

Social workers serve the development of human beings through adherence to the following basic principles:

Every human being has a unique value, which justifies moral consideration for that person.

Each individual has the right to self-fulfilment to the extent that it does not encroach upon the same right of others, and has an obligation to contribute to the well-being of society.

Each society, regardless of its form, should function to provide the maximum benefits for all of its members.

Social workers have a commitment to principles of social justice.

Social workers have the responsibility to devote objective and disciplined knowledge and skill to aid individuals, groups, communities, and societies in their development and resolution of personal-societal conflicts and their consequences.

Social workers are expected to provide the best possible assistance to anybody seeking their help and advice, without unfair discrimination on the basis of gender, age, disability, colour, social class, race, religion, language, political beliefs, or sexual orientation.

Social workers respect the basic human rights of individuals and groups as expressed in the United Nations Universal Declaration of Human Rights and other international conventions derived from that Declaration.

Social workers pay regard to the principles of privacy, confidentiality, and responsible use of information in their professional work. Social workers respect justified confidentiality even when their country's legislation is in conflict with this demand.

Social workers are expected to work in full collaboration with their clients, working for the best interests of the clients but paying due regard to the interests of others involved. Clients are encouraged to participate as much as possible, and should be informed of the risks and likely benefits of proposed courses of action.

Social workers generally expect clients to take responsibility, in collaboration with them, for determining courses of action affecting their lives. Compulsion which might be necessary to solve one party's problems at the expense of the interests of others involved should only take place after careful explicit evaluation of the claims of the conflicting parties. Social workers should minimize the use of legal compulsion.

Social work is inconsistent with direct or indirect support of individuals, groups, political forces or power-structures suppressing their fellow human beings by employing terrorism, torture or similar brutal means.

APPENDIX 5
CASW Code of Ethics Obligations

A social worker shall carry out his/her professional duties and obligations with integrity and objectivity.

A social worker shall have and maintain competence in the provision of social work service to a client.

A social worker shall not exploit the relationship with a client for personal benefit, gain or gratification.

A social worker shall maintain the best interest of the client as the primary professional obligation.

A social worker shall protect the confidentiality of all information acquired from the client or others regarding the client and the client's family during the professional relationship unless:

- a) the client authorizes in writing the release of specified information, or
- b) the information is released under the authority or statute or an order of a court of competent jurisdiction.

A social worker who engages in another profession, occupation, affiliation or calling shall not allow these outside interests to affect the social work relationship with the client.

A social worker in private practice shall not conduct the business of provision of social work services for a fee in a manner that discredits the profession or diminishes the public's trust in the profession.

A social worker shall advocate for workplace conditions and policies that are consistent with the code.

A social worker shall promote excellence in the social work profession.

A social worker shall advocate change:

- a) in the best interest of the client,
- b) for the overall benefit of society, the environment and the global community.

References

Capra, Fritjof (1996). *The Web of Life: A New Scientific Understanding of Living Systems.* New York: Anchor Books.

Greene, Roberta and Watkins, Marie (Eds.) (1998). *Serving Diverse Constituencies: Applying the Ecological Perspective.* New York: Aldine de Gruyter.

Karls, James & Wandrei, Karen (Eds.) (1994). *Person-in-Environment System: The PIE Classification System for Social Functioning Problems.* Washington, DC: NASW Press.

Kemp, Susan, Whittaker, James & Tracy, Elizabeth (1997). *Person-Environment Practice: The Social Ecology of Interpersonal Helping.* New York: Aldine de Gruyter.

Pincus, Allen & Minahan, Anne (1973). *Social Work Practice: Model and Method.* Itasca, IL: F.E. Peacock.

Sheafor, Brad, Horejsi, Charles, & Horejsi, Gloria (1994). *Techniques and Guidelines for Social Work Practice* (3rd Ed.). Boston: Allyn and Bacon.

APPENDIX B

CASW Code of Ethics

Canadian Association of Social Workers
January 1, 1994

[*This Social Work Code of Ethics, adopted by the Board of Directors of the Canadian Association of Social Workers (CASW) is effective on January 1, 1994 and replaces the CASW Code of Ethics (1983). The Code is reprinted here with the permission of CASW. The copyright in the document has been registered with Consumer and Corporate Affairs Canada, registration No. 427837.*]

DEFINITIONS

In this Code,

Best Interest of Client

means

(a) that the wishes, desires, motivations, and plans of the client are taken by the social worker as the primary consideration in any intervention plan developed by the social worker subject to change only when the client's plans are documented to be unrealistic, unreasonable or potentially harmful to self or others or otherwise determined inappropriate when considered in relation to a mandated requirement,

(b) that all actions and interventions of the social worker are taken subject to the reasonable belief that the client will benefit from the action, and

(c) that the social worker will consider the client as an individual, a member of a family unit, a member of a community, a person with a distinct ancestry or culture and will consider those factors in any decision affecting the client.

Client[1]

means

(a) a person, family, group of persons, incorporated body, association or community on whose behalf a social worker provides or agrees to provide a service

    (I) on request or with agreement[2] of the person, family, group of persons, incorporated body, associations or community, or

    (ii) as a result of a legislated responsibility, or

(b) a judge of a court of competent jurisdiction who orders the social worker to provide to the Court an assessment.[3]

Conduct Unbecoming

means behaviour or conduct that does not meet standards of care requirements and is therefore subject to discipline.[4]

Malpractice and Negligence

means behaviour that is included as "conduct unbecoming" and relates to social work practice behaviour within the parameters of the professional relationship that falls below the standard of practice and results in or aggravates an injury to a client. Without limiting the generality of the above,[5] it includes behaviour which results in assault, deceit, fraudulent misrepresentations, defamation of character, breach of contract, violation of human rights, malicious prosecution, false imprisonment or criminal conviction.

Practice of Social Work

includes the assessment, remediation and prevention of social problems, and the enhancement of social functioning of individuals, families, groups and communities by means of

  (a) the provision of direct counselling services within an established relationship between a social worker and client;

  (b) the development, promotion and delivery of human service programs, including that done in collaboration with other professionals;

  (c) the development and promotion of social policies aimed at improving social conditions and equality; and[6]

  (d) any other activities approved by CASW.[7]

Social Worker

means a person who is duly registered to practice social work in a province or territory or where mandatory registration does not exist, a person practising social work who voluntarily agrees to be subject to this Code.

Standard of Practice

means the standard of care ordinarily expected of a competent social worker. It means that the public is assured that a social worker has the training, the skill and the diligence to provide them with professional social work services.

~~~

PREAMBLE

Philosophy

The profession of social work is founded on humanitarian and egalitarian ideals. Social workers believe in the intrinsic worth and dignity of every human being and are committed to the values of acceptance, self-determination and respect of individuality. They believe in the obligation of all people, individually and collectively, to provide resources, services and opportunities for the overall benefit of humanity. The culture of individuals, families, groups, communities and nations has to be respected without prejudice.[8]

Social workers are dedicated to the welfare and self-realization of human beings; to the development and disciplined use of scientific knowledge regarding human and societal behaviours; to the development of resources to meet individual, group, national and international needs and aspirations; and to the achievement of social justice for all.

Professional Practice Conflicts

If a conflict arises in professional practice, the standards declared in this Code take precedence. Conflicts of interest may occur because of demands from the general public, workplace, organizations or clients. In all cases, if the ethical duties and obligations or ethical responsibilities of this Code would be compromised, the social worker must act in a manner consistent with this Code.

Nature of this Code

The first seven statements in this code establish ethical duties and obligations. These statements provide the basis of a social worker's relationship with a client and are based on the values of social work. A breach of any of these statements forms the basis of a disciplinary action. The remaining three statements are characterized as ethical responsibilities and are to be seen as being different from the ethical duties and obligations. These ethical responsibilities are not likely to form the basis of any disciplinary action if breached. However these sections may form the basis of inquiry. These ethical responsibilities may be used in conjunction with breaches of other sections of this code and may form the basis of necessary background information in any action for discipline. Of equal importance, these ethical responsibilities are desirable goals to be achieved by the social work profession which by its nature is driven by an adherence to the values that form the basis of these desirable ethical behaviours.

~~~

SOCIAL WORK CODE OF ETHICS

Ethical Duties and Obligations

1. A social worker shall maintain the best interest of the client as the primary professional obligation.

2. A social worker shall carry out her or his professional duties and obligations with integrity and objectivity.

3. A social worker shall have and maintain competence in the provision of a social work service to a client.

4. A social worker shall not exploit the relationship with a client for personal benefit, gain or gratification.

5. A social worker shall protect the confidentiality of all information acquired from the client or others regarding the client and the client's family during the professional relationship unless

(a) the client authorizes in writing the release of specified information,

(b) the information is released under the authority of a statute or an order of a court of competent jurisdiction, or

(c) otherwise authorized by this Code.

6. A social worker who engages in another profession, occupation, affiliation or calling shall not allow these outside interests to affect the social work relationship with the client.

7. A social worker in private practice shall not conduct the business of provision of social work services for a fee in a manner that discredits the profession or diminishes the public's trust in the profession.

Ethical Responsibilities

8. A social worker shall advocate for workplace conditions and policies that are consistent with the Code.

9. A social worker shall promote excellence in the social work profession.

10. A social worker shall advocate change

(a) in the best interest of the client, and

(b) for the overall benefit of society, the environment and the global community.

Chapter 1. Primary Professional Obligation

1. A social worker shall maintain the best interest of the client as the primary professional obligation.

1.1 The social worker is to be guided primarily by this obligation. Any action which is substantially inconsistent with this obligation is an unethical action.

1.2 A social worker in the practice of social work shall not discriminate against any person on the basis of race, ethnic background, language, religion, marital status, sex, sexual orientation, age, abilities, socio-economic status, political affiliation or national ancestry.[9]

1.3 A social worker shall inform a client of the client's right to consult another professional at any time during the provision of social work services.

1.4 A social worker shall immediately inform the client of any factor, condition[10] or pressure that affects the social worker's ability to perform an acceptable level of service.

1.5 A social worker shall not become involved in a client's personal affairs that are not relevant to the service being provided.

1.6 A social worker shall not state an opinion, judgment or use a clinical diagnosis unless there is a documented assessment, observation or diagnosis to support the opinion, judgment or diagnosis.

1.7 Where possible, a social worker shall provide or secure social work services in the language chosen by the client.

Chapter 2. Integrity and Objectivity

2. A social worker shall carry out his or her professional duties and obligations with integrity and objectivity.[11]

2.1 The social worker shall identify and describe education, training, experience, professional affiliations, competence, and nature of service in an honest and accurate manner.

2.2 The social worker shall explain to the client her or his education, experience, training, competence, nature of service and action at the request of the client.

2.3 A social worker shall cite an educational degree only after it has been received from the institution.

2.4 A social worker shall not claim formal social work education in an area of expertise or training solely by attending a lecture, demonstration, conference, panel discussion, workshop, seminar or other similar teaching presentation.[12]

2.5 The social worker shall not make a false, misleading or exaggerated claim of efficacy regarding past or anticipated achievement with respect to clients.

2.6 The social worker shall distinguish between actions and statements made as a private citizen and actions and statements made as a social worker.[13]

Chapter 3. Competence in the Provision of Social Work Services

3. A social worker shall have and maintain competence in the provision of a social work service to a client.

3.1 The social worker shall not undertake a social work service unless the social worker has the competence to provide the service or the social worker can reasonably acquire the necessary competence without undue delay, risk or expense to the client.

3.2 Where a social worker cannot reasonably acquire the necessary competence in the provision of a service to a client, the social worker shall decline to provide the service to the client, advising the client of the reason and ensuring that the client is referred to another professional person if the client agrees to the referral.

3.3 The social worker, with the agreement of the client, may obtain advice from other professionals in the provision of service to a client.

3.4 A social worker shall maintain an acceptable level of health and well-being in order to provide a competent level of service to a client.[14]

3.5 Where a social worker has a physical or mental health problem, disability or illness that affects the ability of the social worker to provide competent service or that would threaten the health or well-being of the client, the social worker shall discontinue the provision of social work service to a client

(a) advising the client of the reason and,[15]

(b) ensuring that the client is referred to another professional person if the client agrees to the referral.

3.6 The social worker shall have, maintain and endeavor periodically to update an acceptable level of knowledge and skills to meet the standards of practice of the profession.

Chapter 4. Limit on Professional Relationship

4. A social worker shall not exploit the relationship with a client for personal benefit, gain or gratification.

4.1 The social worker shall respect the client and act so that the dignity, individuality and rights of the person are protected.

4.2 The social worker shall assess and consider a client's motivation and physical and mental capacity in arranging for the provision of an appropriate service.

4.3 The social worker shall not have a sexual relationship with a client.

4.4 The social worker shall not have a business relationship with a client, borrow money from a client, or loan money to a client. [16]

4.5 The social worker shall not have a sexual relationship with a social work student assigned to the social worker.

4.6 The social worker shall not sexually harass any person.

Chapter 5. Confidential Information

5. A social worker shall protect the confidentiality[17] of all information acquired from the client or others regarding the client and the client's family during the professional relationship[18] unless

   (a) the client authorizes in writing the release of specified information,[19]

   (b) the information is released under the authority of a statute or an order of a court of relevant jurisdiction, or

   (c) otherwise authorized under this Code.

5.1 The requirement of confidentiality also applies to social workers who work as

   (a) supervisors,

   (b) managers,

   (c) educators, or

   (d) administrators.

5.2 A social worker who works as a supervisor, manager or administrator shall establish policies and practices that protect the confidentiality of client information.

5.3 The social worker may disclose confidential information to other persons in the workplace who, by virtue of their responsibilities, have an identified need to know as determined by the social worker.

5.4 Clients shall be the initial or primary source of information about themselves and their problems unless the client is incapable or unwilling to give information or when corroborative reporting is required.

5.5 The social worker has the obligation to ensure that the client understands what is being asked, why and to what purpose the information will be used, and to understand the confidentiality policies and practices of the workplace setting.

5.6 Where information is required by law, the social worker shall explain to the client the consequences of refusing to provide the requested information.

5.7 Where information is required from other sources, the social worker

   (a) shall explain the requirement to the client, and

   (b) shall attempt to involve the client in selecting the sources to be used.

5.8 The social worker shall take reasonable care to safeguard the client's personal papers or property if the social worker agrees to keep the property at the request of the client.

Recording Information

5.9 The social worker shall maintain only one master file on each client.[20]

5.10 The social worker shall record all relevant information, and keep all relevant documents in the file.

5.11 The social worker shall not record in a client's file any characterization that is not based on clinical assessment or fact.

Accessibility of Records

5.12 The social worker who contracts for the delivery of social work services with a client is responsible to the client for maintaining the client record.

5.13 The social worker who is employed by a social agency that delivers social work services to clients is responsible

   (a) to the client for the maintaining of a client record, and

   (b) to the agency to maintain the records to facilitate the objectives of the agency.

5.14 A social worker is obligated to follow the provision of a statute that allows access to records by clients.

5.15 The social worker shall respect the client's right of access to a client record subject to the social worker's right to refuse access for just and reasonable cause.

5.16 Where a social worker refuses a client the right to access a file or part of a file, the social worker shall advise the client of the right to request a review of the decision in accordance with the relevant statute, workplace policy or other relevant procedure.

Disclosure

5.17 The social worker shall not disclose the identity of persons who have sought a social work service or disclose sources of information about clients unless compelled legally to do so.[21]

5.18 The obligation to maintain confidentiality continues indefinitely after the social worker has ceased contact with the client.

5.19 The social worker shall avoid unnecessary conversation regarding clients.

5.20 The social worker may divulge confidential information with consent of the client, preferably expressed in writing, where this is essential to a plan of care or treatment.

5.21 The social worker shall transfer information to another agency or individual, only with the informed consent of the client or guardian of the client and then only with the reasonable assurance that the receiving agency provides the same guarantee of confidentiality and respect for the right of privileged communication as provided by the sending agency.

5.22 The social worker shall explain to the client the disclosure of information requirements of the law or of the agency before the commencement of the provision of social work services.

5.23 The social worker in practice with groups and communities shall notify the participants of the likelihood that aspects of their private lives may be revealed in the course of their work together, and therefore require a commitment from each member to respect the privileged and confidential nature of the communication between and among members of the client group.

5.24 Subject to section 5.26, the social worker shall not disclose information acquired from one client to a member of the client's family without the informed consent of the client who provided the information.

5.25 A social worker shall disclose information acquired from one client to a member of the client's family where

(a) the information involves a threat of harm to self or others,[22]

(b) the information was acquired from a child of tender years and the social worker determines that its disclosure is in the best interests of the child.[23]

5.26 A social worker shall disclose information acquired from a client to a person or a police officer where the information involves a threat of harm to that person.

5.27 A social worker may release confidential information as part of a discipline hearing of a social worker as directed by the tribunal or disciplinary body.

5.28 When disclosure is required by order of a court, the social worker shall not divulge more information than is reasonably required and shall where possible notify the client of this requirement.

5.29 The social worker shall not use confidential information for the purpose of teaching, public education or research except with the informed consent of the client.

5.30 The social worker may use non-identifying information for the purpose of teaching, public education or research.

Retention and Disposition of Information

5.31 Where the social worker's documentation is stored in a place or computer maintained and operated by an employer, the social worker shall advocate for the responsible retention and disposition of information contained in the file.

Chapter 6. Outside Interest

6. A social worker who engages in another profession, occupation, affiliation or calling shall not allow these outside interests to affect the social work relationship with the client.

6.1 A social worker shall declare to the client any outside interests that would affect the social work relationship with the client.

6.2 A social worker shall not allow an outside interest:

(a) to affect the social worker's ability to practice social work;

(b) to present to the client or to the community that the social worker's ability to practice social work is affected; or

(c) to bring the profession of social work into disrepute.[24]

Chapter 7. Limit on Private Practice

7. A social worker in private practice shall not conduct the business of provision of social work services for a fee in a manner that discredits the profession or diminishes the public's trust in the profession.

7.1 A social worker shall not use the social work relationship within an agency to obtain clients for his or her private practice.

7.2 Subject to section 7.3, a social worker who enters into a contract for service with a client

(a) shall disclose at the outset of the relationship, the fee schedule for the social work services,

(b) shall not charge a fee that is greater than that agreed to and disclosed to the client, and

(c) shall not charge for hours of service other than the reasonable hours of client services, research, consultation and administrative work directly connected to the case.

7.3 A social worker in private practice may charge differential fees for services except where an increased fee is charged based on race, ethnic background, language, religion, marital status, sex, sexual orientation, age, abilities, socio-economic status, political affiliation or national ancestry.

7.4 A social worker in private practice shall maintain adequate malpractice, defamation and liability insurance.

7.5 A social worker in private practice may charge a rate of interest on delinquent accounts as is allowed by law.[25]

7.6 Notwithstanding section 5.17 a social worker in private practice may pursue civil remedies to ensure payment for services to a client where the social worker has advised the client of this possibility at the outset of the social work service.

Chapter 8. Ethical Responsibilities to the Workplace

8. A social worker shall advocate for workplace conditions and policies that are consistent with the Code.

8.1 Where the responsibilities to an employer are in conflict with the social worker's obligations to the client, the social worker shall document the issue in writing and shall bring the situation to the attention of the employer.

8.2 Where a serious ethical conflict continues to exist after the issue has been brought to the attention of the employer, the social worker shall bring the issue to the attention of the Association or regulatory body.[26]

8.3 A social worker shall follow the principles in the Code when dealing with

(a) a social worker under the supervision of the social worker,

(b) an employee under the supervision of the social worker, and

(c) a social work student under the supervision of the social worker.

Chapter 9. Ethical Responsibilities to the Profession

9. A social worker shall promote excellence in the social work profession.

9.1 A social worker shall report to the appropriate association or regulatory body any breach of this Code by another social worker which adversely affects or harms a client or prevents the effective delivery of a social service.

9.2 A social worker shall report to the association or regulatory body any unqualified or unlicenced person who is practising social work.

9.3 A social worker shall not intervene in the professional relationship of a social worker and client unless requested to do so by the client and unless convinced that the best interests and well-being of the client require such intervention.

9.4 Where a conflict arises between a social worker and other professionals, the social worker shall attempt to resolve the professional differences in ways that uphold the principles of this Code and the honour of the social work profession.

9.5 A social worker engaged in research shall ensure that the involvement of clients in the research is a result of informed consent.

Chapter 10. Ethical Responsibilities for Social Change

10. A social worker shall advocate change

(a) in the best interest of the client, and

(b) for the overall benefit of society, the environment and the global community.

10.1 A social worker shall identify, document and advocate for the elimination of discrimination.

10.2 A social worker shall advocate for the equal distribution of resources to all persons.

10.3 A social worker shall advocate for the equal access of all persons to resources, services and opportunities.

10.4 A social worker shall advocate for a clean and healthy environment and shall advocate the development of environmental strategies consistent with social work principles.

10.5 A social worker shall provide reasonable professional services in a state of emergency.

10.6 A social worker shall promote social justice.

Notes

[1] A client ceases to be a client 2 years after the termination of a social work service. It is advisable for this termination to be clearly documented on the case file.

[2] This sub-paragraph identifies two situations where a person may be considered a voluntary client. The person who requests a social work service is clearly a voluntary client. A person also may originally be receiving services as a result of the actions of a court or other legally mandated entity. This person may receive a service beyond that originally mandated and therefore be able to terminate voluntarily that aspect of the service. A situation where a person is referred by another professional or family member clearly falls into this "voluntary service" relationship when that person agrees with the service to be provided. This type of social work relationship is clearly distinguishable from the relationship in sub-paragraph (ii) where the social worker does not seek or have agreement for the service to be provided.

[3] In this situation, the social worker is providing an assessment, information or a professional opinion to a judge of competent jurisdiction to assist the judge in making a ruling or determination. In this situation, the relationship is with the judge and the person on whom the information, assessment or opinion is provided is not the client. The social worker still has some professional obligations towards that person, for example: competence and dignity.

[4] In reaching a decision in *Re Matthews and Board of Directors of Physiotherapy* (1986) 54 O.R. (2d) 375, Saunders J. makes three important statements regarding standards of practice and by implication Code of Ethics:

(I) Standards of practice are inherent characteristics of any profession.

(ii) Standards of practice may be written or unwritten.

(iii) Some conduct is clearly regarded as misconduct and need not be written down whereas other conduct may be the subject of dispute within a profession.

[5] The importance of the collective opinion of the profession in establishing and ultimately modifying the Code of Ethics was established in a 1884 case involving the medical profession. Lord Esher, M.R. stated:

"If it is shown that a medical man, in the pursuit of his profession, has done something with regard to it which would be reasonably regarded as disgraceful or dishonourable by his professional brethren of good repute and competency," then it is open to the General Medical Council to say that he has been guilty of "infamous conduct in a professional respect."

[6] This definition except paragraph (d) has been taken from An Act to Incorporate the New Brunswick Association of Social Workers, chapter 78 of the Statutes of New Brunswick, 1988, section 2.

[7] The procedure for adding activities under this paragraph will be established as a bylaw by the CASW Board of Directors.

[8] Taken from: Teaching and Learning about Human Rights; A Manual for Schools of Social Work and the Social Work Profession; U.N. Centre for Human Rights,

Co-operation with International Federation of Social Workers and International Association of Schools of Social Workers, United Nations, New York, 1992.

9. This obligation goes beyond grounds of discrimination stated in most Human Rights Legislation and therefore there is a greater professional obligation than that stated in provincial legislation.

10. The term condition means a physical, mental or psychological condition. There is an implied obligation that the social worker shall actively seek diagnosis and treatment for any signs or warnings of a condition. A disclosure under this section may be of a general nature. See also 3.4.

11. The term objectivity is taken from the Québec Code of Professional Conduct. See Division 2: Integrity and Objectivity (6.0 Québec) November 5, 1979 Vol. 2 No. 30. The term objectivity is stated in the following: 3.02.01. A social worker must discharge his professional duties with integrity and objectivity.

12. The provincial associations may regulate the areas of expertise to be stated or advertised by a social worker. This will vary in each province according to its enabling legislation. Where there is not sufficient legislative base for this regulation, the claim of an expertise without sufficient training may form the basis of a determination of unprofessional conduct.

13. Even with a distinction made under this section, a social worker's private actions or statements may be of such a nature that the social worker cannot avoid the responsibilities under this Code. See also 6.2 (c).

14. This section should be considered in relation to section 1.4 and involves proper maintenance prevention and treatment of any type of risk to the health or well-being of the social worker.

15. It is not necessary in all circumstances to explain specifically the nature of the problem.

16. Where a social worker does keep money or assets belonging to a client, the social worker should hold this money or asset in a trust account or hold the money or asset in conjunction with an additional professional person.

17. Confidentiality means that information received or observed about a client by a social worker will be held in confidence and disclosed only when the social worker is properly authorized or obligated legally or professionally to do so. This also means that professionally acquired information may be treated as privileged communication and ordinarily only the client has the right to waive privilege.

Privileged communication means statements made within a protected relationship (i.e. husband-wife, professional-client) which the law protects against disclosure. The extent of the privilege is governed by law and not by this Code.

Maintaining confidentiality of privileged communication means that information about clients does not have to be transmitted in any oral, written or recorded form. Such information, for example, does not have to be disclosed to a supervisor, written into a workplace record, stored in a computer or microfilm data base, held on an audio or videotape or discussed orally. The right of privileged communication is respected by the social worker in the practice of social work notwithstanding that this right is not ordinarily granted in law.

The disclosure of confidential information in social work practice involves the obligation to share information professionally with others in the workplace of the social worker as part of a reasonable service to the client. Social workers recognize the need to obtain permission from clients before releasing information about them to sources outside their workplace; and to inform clients at the outset of their relationship that some information acquired may be shared with the officers and personnel of the agency who maintain the case record and who have a reasonable need for the information in the performance of their duties.

18. The social worker's relationship with a client can be characterized as a fiduciary relationship.

In *Fiduciary Duties in Canada* by Ellis, fiduciary duty is described as follows: ... where one party has placed its "trust and confidence" in another and the latter has accepted — expressly or by operation of law — to act in a manner consistent with the reposing of such "trust and confidence," a fiduciary relationship has been established.

[19.] The "obligation of secrecy" was discussed by the Supreme Court of Canada in *Halls* v. *Mitchell*, (1928) S.C.R. 125, an action brought by a disabled CNR worker against a company doctor who had disclosed the employee's medical history, to the latter's detriment. Mr. Justice Duff reviewed the duty of confidentiality:

> We are not required, for the purposes of this appeal, to attempt to state with any sort of precision the limits of the obligation of secrecy which rests upon the medical practitioner in relation to the professional secrets acquired by him in the course of his practice. Nobody would dispute that a secret so acquired is the secret of the patient, and, normally, is under his control, and not under that of the doctor. Prima facie, the patient has the right to require that the secret shall not be divulged; and that right is absolute, unless there is some paramount reason which overrides it.

Thus the right of secrecy/confidentiality rests squarely with the patient; the Court carefully provided that there is an "ownership" extant in the confidentiality of the personal information. Duff J. continued by allowing for "paramount" criteria which vitiates from the right:

> Some reasons may arise, no doubt, from the existence of facts which bring into play overpowering considerations connected with public justice; and there may be cases in which reasons connected with the safety of individuals or of the public, physical or moral, would be sufficiently cogent to supersede or qualify the obligations prima facie imposed by the confidential relation.

Duff J. continued:

> The general duty of medical men to observe secrecy, in relation to information acquired by them confidentially from their patients is subject, no doubt, to some exceptions, which have no operation in the case of solicitors; but the grounds of the legal, social or moral imperatives affecting physicians and surgeons, touching the inviolability of professional confidences, are not, any more than those affecting legal advisers, based exclusively upon the relations between the parties as individuals.

[20.] The master file refers to all relevant documents pertaining to the client consisting of such information as demographics, case recordings, court documents, assessments, correspondence, treatment plans, bills, etc. This information is often collected through various means including electronic and computer-driven sources. However the client master file exists as one unit, inclusive of all information pertaining to the client, despite the various sources of the recording process. The description and ownership of the master file is most often defined by workplace standards or policies. The client's master file should be prepared keeping in mind that it may have to be revealed to the client or disclosed in legal proceedings.

[21.] A social worker may be compelled to reveal information under the section when directly ordered by the court to do so. Before disclosing the information, the social worker shall advise the court of the professional obligations that exist under this section of the Code and where reasonably possible inform the client.

[22.] The case of *Tarasaff* v. *The Regents of the University of California et al.* (1976), 551 p.2d 334 (Cal. Supreme Court) focused on the obligation of a psychiatrist to maintain the confidentiality of his patients' statements in their discussions. In that case the patient told the psychiatrist that the patient had an intention to kill a certain woman. When the patient actually did kill this woman, her parents brought suit alleging that the psychiatrist owed a duty to tell the woman of the danger to her.

It was held that the psychiatrist did have a duty to tell the woman of the threat. The court recognized that the psychiatrist owed a duty to the patient to keep in confidence the statements the patient made in therapy sessions, but held there was also a duty to care to anyone whom the psychiatrist knew might be endangered by the patient. At a certain point the obligation of confidentiality would be overridden by the obligation to this third person. The psychiatrist's knowledge itself gave rise to a duty of care. What conduct would be sufficient to fulfil the duty to this third person would depend on the circumstances, but it might be necessary to give a warning that would reveal what the patient had said about the third party. The court in this case held that the psychiatrist had a duty to warn the woman about the patient's stated intention to kill her, and having failed to warn her the psychiatrist was liable in negligence. Moreover, the court stated that the principle of this duty of care belonged not just to a psychiatrist but also to a psychologist performing therapy. it would follow that the principle would also apply to social workers performing therapy.

[23.] For the purpose of this Code, a child of tender years shall usually be determined to be a child under the age of seven years subject to a determination by a social worker considering the child's social, physical, intellectual, emotional or psychological development.

[24.] This section brings the social worker's outside interest and personal actions in line with the professional duties and obligations as set out in this Code.

[25.] This rate shall be stated on all invoices or bills sent to the client.

[26.] In this situation the professional obligations outweigh any obligations to a workplace.

©1994 Canadian Association of Social Workers. Ottawa

APPENDIX C
Ethics in Social Work

Statement of Principles

Approved at the General Meeting of the International Federation of Social Workers and the International Association of Schools of Social Work, Adelaide, Australia, October 2004

1. Preface

Ethical awareness is a fundamental part of the professional practice of social workers. Their ability and commitment to act ethically is an essential aspect of the quality of the service offered to those who use social work services.

The purpose of IASSW and IFSW's work on ethics is to promote ethical debate and reflection in the member organisations, among the providers of social work in member countries, as well as in the schools of social work and among social work students. Some ethical challenges and problems facing social workers are specific to particular countries; others are common. By staying at the level of general principles, the joint IASSW and IFSW statement aims to encourage social workers across the world to reflect on the challenges and dilemmas that face them and make ethically informed decisions about how to act in each particular case. Some of these problem areas include:

- The fact that the loyalty of social workers is often in the middle of conflicting interests;
- The fact that social workers function as both helpers and controllers;
- The conflicts between the duty of social workers to protect the interests of the people with whom they work and societal demands for efficiency and utility;
- The fact that resources in society are limited.

This document takes as its starting point the definition of social work adopted separately by the IFSW and IASSW at their respective General Meeting in Montreal, Canada in July 2000 and then agreed as a joint one in Copenhagen in May 2001 (section 2). This definition stresses principles of human rights and social justice. The next section (3) makes reference to the various declarations and conventions on human rights that are relevant to social work, followed by a statement of general ethical principles under the two broad headings of human rights and dignity and social justice (section 4). The final section introduces some basic guidance on ethical conduct in social work, which it is expected will be elaborated by the ethical guidance and in various codes and guidelines of the member organisations of IFSW and IASSW.

2. Definition of Social Work

The social work profession promotes social change, problem solving in human relationships and the empowerment and liberation of people to enhance well-being. Utilising theories of human behaviour and social systems, social work intervenes at the points where people interact with their environments. Principles of human rights and social justice are fundamental to social work.

3. International conventions

International human rights declarations and conventions form common standards of achievement, and recognise rights that are accepted by the global community. Documents particularly relevant to social work practice and action are:

- Universal Declaration of Human Rights
- The International Covenant on Civil and Political Rights
- The International Covenant on Economic Social and Cultural Rights
- The Convention on the Elimination of all Forms of Racial Discrimination
- The Convention on the Elimination of All Forms of Discrimination against Women
- The Convention on the Rights of the Child
- Indigenous and Tribal Peoples Convention (ILO convention 169)

4. Principles

4.1. Human Rights and Human Dignity

Social work is based on respect for the inherent worth and dignity of all people, and the rights that follow from this. Social workers should uphold and defend each person's physical, psychological, emotional and spiritual integrity and well-being. This means:

(1) Respecting the right to self-determination - Social workers should respect and promote people's right to make their own choices and decisions, irrespective of their values and life choices, provided this does not threaten the rights and legitimate interests of others.

(2) Promoting the right to participation - Social workers should promote the full involvement and participation of people using their services in ways that enable them to be empowered in all aspects of decisions and actions affecting their lives.

(3) Treating each person as a whole - Social workers should be concerned with the whole person, within the family, community and societal and natural environments, and should seek to recognise all aspects of a person's life.

(4) Identifying and developing strengths – Social workers should focus on the strengths of all individuals, groups and communities and thus promote their empowerment.

4.2. Social justice

Social workers have a responsibility to promote social justice, in relation to society generally, and in relation to the people with whom they work. This means:

(1) Challenging negative discrimination[1] — Social workers have a responsibility to challenge negative discrimination on the basis of characteristics such as ability, age, culture, gender or sex, marital status, socio-economic status, political opinions, skin colour, racial or other physical characteristics, sexual orientation, or spiritual beliefs.

(2) Recognising diversity — Social workers should recognise and respect the ethnic and cultural diversity of societies in which they practice, taking account of individual, family, group and community differences.

(3) Distributing resources equitably — Social workers should ensure that resources at their disposal are distributed fairly, according to need.

(4) Challenging unjust policies and practices — Social workers have a duty to bring to the attention of their employers, policy makers, politicians and the general public situations where resources are inadequate or where distribution of resources, policies and practices are oppressive, unfair or harmful.

(5) Working in solidarity — Social workers have an obligation to challenge social conditions that contribute to social exclusion, stigmatisation or subjugation, and to work towards an inclusive society.

5. Professional conduct

It is the responsibility of the national organisations in membership of IFSW and IASSW to develop and regularly update their own codes of ethics or ethical guidelines, to be consistent with the IFSW/ IASSW statement. It is also the national organisation's responsibility to inform social workers and schools of social work about these codes or guidelines.

Social workers should act in accordance with the ethical code or guidelines current in their country. These will generally include more detailed guidance in ethical practice specific to the national context. The following general guidelines on professional conduct apply:

(1) Social workers are expected to develop and maintain the required skills and competence to do their job.

(2) Social workers should not allow their skills to be used for inhumane purposes, such as torture or terrorism.

(3) Social workers should act with integrity. This includes not abusing the relationship of trust with the people using their services, recognising the boundaries between personal and professional life, and not abusing their position for personal benefit or gain.

(4) Social workers should act in relation to the people using their services with compassion, empathy and care.

(5) Social workers should not subordinate the needs or interests of people who use their services to their own needs or interests.

(6) Social workers have a duty to take necessary steps to care for themselves professionally and personally in the workplace and in society, in order to ensure that they are able to provide appropriate services.

(7) Social workers should maintain confidentiality regarding information about people who use their services. Exceptions to this may only be justified on the basis of a greater ethical requirement (such as the preservation of life).

(8) Social workers need to acknowledge that they are accountable for their actions to the users of their services, the people they work with, their colleagues, their employers, the professional association and to the law, and that these accountabilities may conflict.

(9) Social workers should be willing to collaborate with the schools of social work inorder to support social work students to get practical training of good quality and up to date practical knowledge.

(10) Social workers should foster and engage in ethical debate with their colleagues and employers and take responsibility for making ethically informed decisions.

(11) Social workers should be prepared to state the reasons for their decisions based on ethical considerations, and be accountable for their choices and actions.

(12) Social workers should work to create conditions in employing agencies and in their countries where the principles of this statement and those of their own national code (if applicable) are discussed, evaluated and upheld.

The document "Ethics in Social Work, Statement of Principles" was approved at the General Meetings of the International Federation of Social Workers and the International Association of Schools of Social Work in Adelaide, Australia, October 2004.

[1] In some countries the term "discrimination" would be used instead of "negative discrimination". The word negative is used here because in some countries the term "positive discrimination" is also used. Positive discrimination is also known as "affirmative action". Positive discrimination or affirmative action means positive steps taken to redress the effects of historical discrimination against the groups named in clause 4.2.1 above.

APPENDIX D

International Policy on Human Rights

**Approved at the IFSW General Meeting,
Hong Kong, July 21–23, 1996**

Background

History of Human Rights

The history of human rights is that of the struggle against exploitation of one person by another. It is based on the recognition of basic rights founded on the concept of the inherent dignity and worth of every individual.

The recognition was consolidated in the Universal Declaration of Human Rights by the General Assembly of the United Nations. Its preamble asserted "recognition of the inherent dignity and of the equal and inalienable rights of all members of the human family is the foundation of freedom, justice and peace in the world."

The Basic Instruments concerning Human Rights are:

1. Charter of the United Nations (1945)

2. Universal Declaration of Human Rights (1948)

3. The Covenants on Human Rights (1966)

    a) International Covenant on Civil and Political Rights

    b) International Covenant on Economic, Social and Cultural Rights

4. International Convention on the Elimination of All Forms of Racial Discrimination (1965)

5. Convention on the Elimination of All Forms of Discrimination Against Women (1979)

6. Convention Against Torture and other Cruel, Inhuman and Degrading Treatment or Punishment (1984)

7. Convention on the Rights of the Child (1989)

8. International Convention on the Protection of the Rights of all Migrant Workers and Members of their Families (1990)

These global instruments are reinforced by:

1. The European Convention on Human Rights (1950)

2. The American Convention on Human Rights (1969)

3. The African Charter on Human Rights and Peoples Rights (1981)

The Covenants and Conventions are supported by United Nations Declarations:

a) The Rights of Mentally Retarded Persons (1971)

b) The Protection of Women and Children in Armed Conflicts (1974)

c) The Elimination of All Forms of Religious Intolerance (1981)

d) The Right to Development (1986)

Violations of Human Rights

Despite these agreements, gross and subtle violations of human rights are perpetrated every day against thousands of people. The phenomenon of the "disappeared," the torture of political prisoners, summary killings and arbitrary arrests, the increasing use of the death penalty, the extortion of confessions by physical and mental abuse, the manipulation of and the intellectual, emotional and moral pressures imposed on individuals in an attempt to condition their personalities, the detention of prisoners without trial, the economic exploitation of adults and children, displacement of populations due to internal conflicts — these and other violations are all too evident throughout the world. The victims of human rights abuses continue to suffer for many years as a result of their experience.

Many factors contribute to the violations of human rights. The collapse of totalitarian regimes in Eastern Europe did not bring an end to the human rights abuses. The resurgence of nationalism, xenophobia and anti-Semitism in countries with established democracies, as well as in the former Eastern bloc, posed new challenges to the United Nations. In Africa, the rise of tribalism undermined the integrity of nations and led to widespread abuse of the most basic rights to life. In more than one region of the world, there has been a disturbing re-emergence of genocide in situations of armed conflict.

Social Work Principles

Human Rights condenses into two words the struggle for dignity and fundamental freedoms which allow the full development of human potential. Civil and political rights have to be accompanied by economic, social and cultural rights.

Social workers serve human development through adherence to the following basic principles:

I) Every human being has a unique value, which justifies moral consideration for that person.

ii) Each individual has the right to self-fulfilment to the extent that it does not encroach upon the same right of others, and has an obligation to contribute to the well-being of society.

iii) Each society, regardless of its form, should function to provide the maximum benefit for all of its members.

iv) Social workers have a commitment to principles of social justice.

v) Social workers have the responsibility to devote objective and disciplined knowledge and skill to work with individuals, groups, communities, and societies in their development and resolution of personal-societal conflicts and their consequences.

vi) Social workers are expected to provide the best possible assistance without unfair discrimination on the basis of both gender, age, disability, race, colour, language, religious or political beliefs, property, sexual orientation, status or social class.

vii) Social workers respect the basic human rights of individuals and groups as expressed in the United Nations Universal Declaration of Human Rights and other international conventions derived from that Declaration.

viii) Social workers pay regard to the principles of privacy, confidentiality and responsible use of information in their professional work. Social workers respect justified confidentiality even when their country's legislation is in conflict with this demand.

ix) Social workers are expected to work with their clients, working for the best interests of the clients but paying due regard to the interests of others involved. Clients are encouraged to participate as much as possible, and should be informed of the risks and likely benefits of proposed courses of action.

x) Social workers generally expect clients to take responsibility for determining courses of action affecting their lives. Compulsion which might be necessary to solve one party's problems at the expense of the interests of others involved should take place after careful explicit evaluation of the claims of the conflicting parties. Social workers should minimise the use of legal compulsion.

xi) Social workers make ethically justified decisions, and stand by them, paying due regard to The Ethics of Social Work — Principles and Standards adopted by the International Federation of Social Workers.

These principles, drawn from the experience of social workers in carrying out their responsibility to help people with individual and social problems, place a special responsibility on the social work profession to advance the cause of human rights throughout the world.

Role of Social Workers

Social workers deal with common human needs. They work to prevent or alleviate individual, group and community problems, and to improve the quality of life for all people. In doing so, they seek to uphold the rights of the individuals or groups with whom they are working.

The value base of social work with its emphasis on the unique worth of each individual has much in common with human rights theory. Social workers frequently operate in situations of conflict, and are required by their national codes of Ethics and in the international Ethical Principles and Standards to demonstrate respect for all regardless of their previous conduct. Their experience of the impact of social conditions on the capacity of individuals and communities to resolve difficulties means that they recognise that the full realisation of civil and political rights is inseparable from the enjoyment of economic, social and cultural rights. Policies of economic and social development have, therefore, a crucial part to play in securing the extension of human rights.

As a result of their particular role and responsibility in society, social workers are often the conscience of the community. Therefore, the value system, training and experience of social workers requires that they take professional responsibility for promoting human rights. Social workers need to work with other professions and non-governmental organisations in action on human rights issues. As advocates for change, they are often in the forefront of movements for change and thus are themselves subject to repression and abuse. The IFSW Human Rights Commission was established in 1988 to support social workers under threat for pursuing their professional responsibilities.

Policy Statement

Human rights are those fundamental entitlements that are considered to be necessary for developing each personality to the fullest. Violations of human rights are any arbitrary and selective actions that interfere with the full exercise of these fundamental entitlements.

The social work profession, through historical and empirical evidence, is convinced that the achievement of human rights for all people is a fundamental prerequisite for a caring world and the survival of the human race. It is only through the recognition and implementation of the basic concept of the inherent dignity and worth of each person that a secure and stable world can be achieved. Consequently, social workers believe that the attainment of basic human rights requires positive action by individuals, communities, nations and international groups, as well as a clear duty not to inhibit those rights.

The social work profession accepts its share of responsibility for working to oppose and eliminate all violations of human rights. Social workers must exercise this responsibility in their practice with individuals, groups and communities, in their roles as agency or organisational representatives and as citizens of a nation and the world.

IFSW, representing the social work profession internationally, proclaims the following human rights as a common standard and guide for the work of all professional social workers:

Life

The value of life is central to human rights work. Social workers have not only to resist violations of human rights which threaten or diminish the quality of life, but also actively to promote life enhancing and nurturing activities.

Physical and psychological well-being is an important aspect of the quality of life. The deterioration of the environment and the non-existence or curtailment of health programs threaten life.

Social workers assert the right of individuals and communities to have protection from preventable disease and disability.

Freedom and Liberty

All human beings are born free. The fundamental freedoms include the right to liberty, to freedom from slavery, to freedom from arbitrary arrest, torture, cruel inhuman or degrading treatment, and freedom of thought and speech.

Next to life itself, freedom and liberty are the most precious human values asserting the worth of human existence.

Equality and Non-Discrimination

The fundamental principle of equality is closely linked to principles of justice. Every person regardless of birth, gender, age, disability, race, colour, language, religious or political beliefs, property, sexual orientation, status or social class has a right to equal treatment and protection under the law.

Social workers have to ensure equal access to public services and social welfare provision in accordance with the resources of national and local governments, and have a particular responsibility to combat discrimination of any kind in their own practice.

Justice

Every person has a right to protection against arbitrary arrest or interference with privacy, and to equal protection under the law. Where laws have been violated, every person has a right to a prompt and fair trial by an objective judicial authority. Those convicted are entitled to humane treatment whose purpose is to secure the reform and social readaptation of the individual.

The impartial operation of the law is a crucial safeguard for the citizen in the administration of justice. Social justice, however, requires more than a legal system untainted by interference by the executive. It requires the satisfaction of basic human needs and the equitable distribution of resources. It requires universal access to health care and education, thus enabling the achievement of human potential. It underpins concepts of social development. In the pursuit of social justice workers may have to face conflict with powerful elite groups in any given society.

Solidarity

Every person whose fundamental freedoms are infringed has a right to support from fellow citizens. The concept of solidarity recognises the fraternity ideal of the French Revolution, and the importance of mutual support. Social workers give expression to this through the Human Rights Commission in relation to social workers whose political freedoms are infringed. In their daily practice they express solidarity with the poor and oppressed. Poverty, hunger, and homelessness are violations of human rights. Social workers stand with the disadvantaged in campaigning for social justice.

Social Responsibility

Social responsibility is the recognition that each of us has a responsibility to family, to community, to nation and to the world community to contribute personal talents, energy and commitment to the advancement of human rights. Those with intellectual and physical resources should utilise them to assist those less well equipped. Social work's engagement with the disadvantaged is a reflection of that responsibility. No person or collective body has the right to engage in any activity, including propaganda, to incite war, hostility, hatred, bigotry or violence, contrary to the institution and maintenance of human rights.

Peace and Non-Violence

Peace is more than the absence of organised conflict. It is the goal of achieving harmony with self and with others. Social workers are committed to the pursuit of non-violence. Their experience in conflict resolution teaches that mediation and arbitration are effective instruments to overcome seemingly irreconcilable differences. Non-violence does not mean passivity in the face of injustice. Social workers will resist and exercise non-violent pressure for change, but will not engage in acts of violence in the course of their professional activity. Social workers devote their energies to constructive efforts to achieve social justice.

The Environment

Humankind has trusteeship responsibility for the care of the planet. Environmental degradation poses a threat to life itself in some areas, and to the quality of life in many countries. False development models based on industrialisation, the unequal distribution of resources, excessive consumerism and ignorance of the pernicious consequences of pollution have all contributed to this global plight. Social workers need to work with community groups in tackling the consequences of environmental decline and destruction.

Key Terms

Ableism — Discrimination and prejudice towards people with disabilities. Ableism supports the belief that people without disabilities are superior to people with disabilities.

Aboriginal approach to social work — The development of an Aboriginal approach to social work practice should be consistent with four key principles. These principles are: (1) the recognition of a distinct Aboriginal worldview; (2) the development of Aboriginal consciousness regarding the impact of colonialism; (3) an emphasis on the importance of cultural knowledge and traditions; and (4) the use of the concept of Aboriginal empowerment.

Aboriginal empowerment — In the context of social work, Aboriginal empowerment emphasizes the participation of community members in promoting self-determination and social change.

Aboriginal peoples — Individuals who have Native origins. It is a term commonly used to refer to Indians, Inuit and Métis in Canada. Aboriginal peoples have their own names for themselves in their respective languages, some of which are: Anishnaabe, Inuit, Innu, Nuu-chah-nulth, and Métis.

Aboriginal political activism — A surge of Aboriginal political activism, beginning in the 1970s, has led to the development of several national organizations representing and uniting distinct constituent groups. Among these are: (1) the Assembly of First Nations, which represents status Indians who reside on reserves across Canada; (2) the Inuit Tapirisat of Canada, representing Canada's Inuit population; (3) the Métis National Council; (4) the Congress of Aboriginal Peoples, representing off-reserve Aboriginal peoples; and (5) the Native Women's Association of Canada.

Aboriginal self-government — Quite simply, this concept expresses the desire of Aboriginal peoples to control their destiny. It precludes accountability to the provincial and federal governments in favour of accountability and responsibility to the Aboriginal peoples by their own Aboriginal leaders. Self-government is concerned with sovereignty in relation to the Canadian state — within it or outside it, depending on one's view.

Aboriginal worldview — While Aboriginal peoples do not have one common philosophy or worldview, one can draw upon the fundamental differences between Western Euro-Canadian and Aboriginal worldviews. For example, the concept of the circle captured in the Medicine Wheel illustrates the notion of balance prevalent in Aboriginal societies, in contrast to the typically linear models of cause and effect common in some Western societies.

Accessibility — One of five principles of medicare in Canada. This means that there must be a wide range of services, accessible services and a reduction or elimination of user fees. Each province is required to provide health care with reasonable access, both financially and geographically. This applies to ward care in a hospital, free choice of a physician, reasonable compensation to physicians and adequate payments to hospitals.

Activity theory — An early, prominent theory within social work practice with the elderly that maintained that a presumed decrease in the life satisfaction of seniors can be mitigated through increased personal and social activities.

Acute pain — Temporary pain that may be severe initially but declines over time.

Addiction — Addiction can be defined as a compulsive need for, or persistent use of, a substance known to be harmful.

Ageism — This term refers to prejudice and discrimination that is based on age. Ageism can be defined as any attitude, action or institutional structure that subordinates or oppresses a person or group on the basis of age. Ageism can be thought of as a universal experience as dominant culture in North America celebrates youth and devalues the worth of individuals as they age.

AH-HAH! method — An approach to popular education that aims to help people see how local problems are influenced by larger societal-level structures. It refers to the experience people have when they understand clearly something they previously knew only in a partial or confused way.

Ambiguity of social work — This refers to the dilemmas faced by social workers in the social work relationship. While social workers are helpers, they are also expected to enforce rules and regulations in the helping relationship with the client.

Anger-control theory — This theory focuses on the idea that men must be held accountable for their violent behaviour and learn to deal with and control their tempers, showing their feelings in more appropriate ways.

Anti-racism analysis tool — This tool is an effective means in which to apply an anti-racist approach to social work practice. Anti-racism emphasizes placing personal difficulties and life situations within larger social contexts. While not ignoring the individual problems and individual responsibilities, the anti-racism tool encourages the social worker to view the individual and the problem within the broader historical and contemporary context.

Anti-racist social work — Racism is the subordination of one group by another using arbitrary physical features such as skin colour. It can occur at the individual, institutional or societal levels in the form of attitudes, beliefs, policies or procedures. Anti-racist social work is an approach to practice that aggressively combats racism on all three levels.

Assessment and planning — The process of developing an understanding of the presented problem and a plan of action. It will include different elements and emphasis depending on the perspective or approach of the social worker.

Assimilationist policies — The policies of the federal government towards Aboriginal people that attempted to deny and destroy Aboriginal life, culture and society in favour of integrating Canada's First Nations into the mainstream. These policies were pursued vigorously and viciously in the residential schools.

Best interests approach — The "best interests" approach to child protection emphasizes the protection and well-being of the child, whereas the "least restrictive" approach emphasizes the least disruptive course of action that will leave the child with his or her family, if at all possible.

Biological determinism — The belief that every aspect of peoples' personalities, behaviours and attitudes is determined by genes. This theory minimizes and discounts the role of environmental factors within human development. In regards to sexuality, this theory explains sexual behaviours and preferences in terms of biology and thereby focuses on the organic causes of non-conventional sexual identities and behaviours.

Biological essentialism in sexual attraction — This approach assumes the origin of all sexual attraction and behaviour is innate and predetermined; a component of the person's biological endowment. It asserts that people are born homosexual, and professional treatment is required to ensure that people do not act upon "deviant" sexual drives and desires.

"Burnout" — The term burnout refers to the anxiety resulting from increased workplace pressure and increased workloads. This type of stress occurs among social workers and others who are faced with increasing responsibility and less and less control over how the work is to be completed

Campaign 2000 — A national anti-poverty coalition that attempted to hold the Canadian federal government accountable for its 1989 pledge to eliminate child poverty by the year 2000. This coalition released a report documenting the failure of the federal government to achieve this goal.

Canada Assistance Plan — Federal legislation, passed in 1966 and considered by many as a keystone of the Canadian welfare state. The legislation required the federal government to fund half the cost of social programs undertaken by the provinces.

Canada Health and Social Transfer (CHST) — Federal legislation that combines federal funding for health, post-secondary education and welfare, and transfers a designated amount of money based on population size to each province rather than transferring a percentage of actual costs. It replaced both the Canada Assistance Plan (CAP) and Established Program Financing (EPF).

Canada Health Transfer (CHT) — A federal block transfer payment that is made to each province and territory in order to assist the provinces and territories in paying for health care. The CHT comprises both a cash transfer and a tax transfer that are allocated on a per capita basis in order to equalize support provided to provinces and territories independent of population size. It is the responsibility of the provinces and territories to allocate this health care funding to their provincial/territorial health care priorities.

Canada Social Transfer (CST) — A federal block transfer payment that is made to each Canadian province and territory in order to assist the provinces and territories in paying for education, social assistance and social services. The CST comprises both a cash transfer and a tax transfer that are allocated on a per capita basis in order to equalize support provided to provinces and territories independent of population size.

Canadian Association of Schools of Social Work (CASSW) — A voluntary, national charitable association of university faculties, schools and departments offering professional education in social work at the undergraduate, graduate and post-graduate levels. Established in 1967, CASSW is the successor to the National Committee of Schools of Social Work, which, since 1948, had been the forum for programs offering professional education in social work.

Canadian Association of Social Workers (CASW) — Founded in 1926 to promote the profession of social work in Canada, to monitor employment conditions and to establish standards of practice within the profession. As a federation of the 10 provincial and one territorial social work organizations, the Canadian Association of Social Workers (CASW) provides a national leadership role in strengthening and advancing the social work profession in Canada.

Canadian Mental Health Association — The Canadian Mental Health Association (CMHA) exists to promote the mental health of Canadians through the provision of direct service to individuals with mental health issues by staff, including social workers, and volunteers. CMHA has branches in major cities throughout all provinces and territories and each operates on principles of empowerment, peer and family support, autonomy, citizenship and inclusion.

Casework — In social work, "casework" refers to using systematic methods of investigation, assessment and decision making.

Charity Organization Society — Social welfare agencies established in the latter part of the 1800s that used a "scientific charity" approach to studying the needs of individuals and families. The society was formed in London, England, in the 1860s by upper-class and professional men and women because of "urban chaos" and the indiscriminate giving of relief by uncontrolled charities. It differentiated between the deserving and undeserving poor, believing that indiscriminate material relief would cause pauperism.

Charter of Rights and Freedoms — The Canadian Constitution was patriated in 1982; that is, it was brought under Canadian control. The first section of the *Constitution Act*, the *Charter of Rights and Freedoms*, describes the fundamental individual and group rights of citizens, including freedom of religion, voting rights and equality rights. The government of Quebec did not endorse the act on the grounds that it failed to recognize Quebec's distinctness.

Child abuse — The physical, psychological, social, emotional or sexual maltreatment of a child whereby the survival, safety, self-esteem, growth and development of the person are endangered.

Chronic pain — Lingering pain which varies in intensity. Chronic pain can exist for a few months or can last for many years.

Code of Ethics — A profession's set of standards concerning the ethical behavior of its members. All members are expected to be guided by this code in their professional activities. The CASW has a code of ethics, which is a set of principles to guide a social worker as he or she deals with issues arising in the workplace.

Collective rights — Rights as set forth in Articles 22–27 of the Universal Declaration of Human Rights ensuring equitable participation by everyone in society in the production and distribution of wealth and resources.

Colonialism — Political domination of one nation over another that is institutionalized in direct political administration by the colonial power, control of all economic relationships and a systematic attempt to transform the culture of the subject nation.

"Coming out" — "Coming out," the political act and strategy of gay and lesbian liberation of the 1970s, is generally regarded as an important psycho-social developmental process for many people. It is also recognized that the decision to openly identify oneself as gay or lesbian is entirely up to the individual.

Community access centre — A community resource centre in which citizens can access a variety of services in one centralized location that are delivered by a service delivery team following a service plan.

Community health centres — In the 1970s, the federal government recommended the establishment of community health centres (CHCs) with the intention of providing primary care, health promotion and prevention services using salaried primary health care professionals. Studies have found that CHCs provide better primary care, decrease the costs of patient care and decrease hospitalization rates.

Community work — A social work method practised with communities. It involves six steps: entry, data collection and analysis, goal setting, action planning, action taking and termination.

Confidentiality — The use of client records raises concerns about the confidentiality of sensitive information: What constitutes the ethical disclosure of information about a client? A social worker is obligated to follow the guidelines of the agency or organization employing them and obey legislation and association policy. The CASW *Code of Ethics* stipulates, at length, the requirements for collecting, recording, storing and access of client records.

Consciousness-raising groups — The process by which an individual or members of a group become aware of and understand that other people share with them common experiences, that others too are restricted and damaged by certain practices, patterns of relations, beliefs, stereotypes, myths, expectations and social structures. It is the process by which people begin to understand the relationships between their own biographies, other people's biographies, history and the social infrastructure.

Continuity theory — A contemporary theory that maintains that the continuity of a person's lifestyle should be preserved as he or she progresses through the life cycle. It is believed that old age is a continuation of a person's past and that seniors should continue the roles and activities of their middle years in order to maintain life satisfaction.

Contracting out — The practice of hiring private for-profit companies to implement specified public social welfare activities and deliver certain services in return for payment from public funds.

Cost containment — Medical care costs in Canada have been rising steadily because of the ageing of the Canadian population, the emphasis on curative and high technology medicine, the increasing demand for hospital services and for expensive equipment and the increasing fees of medical personnel. Cost containment has become an area of major concern.

Court order — A directive from a child welfare court. Court order options include the placement of the child with some other person subject to the agency's provision, child welfare agency wardship, Crown wardship or consecutive child welfare agency wardship and supervision order.

Cultural competence — This model means that workers develop the ability to acknowledge different perceptions and experiences and incorporate these into practice applications. In other words, the worker must take this knowledge of the "other" culture and combine it with an analysis of how his or her own culture affects social work interventions.

Culture — The generally shared knowledge, beliefs and values of members of society. Culture is conveyed from generation to generation through the process of socialization.

Cycle-of-violence theory — This theory seeks to explain what happens in individual relationships that causes violence against women in a three-step process: tension-building, acute battering and honeymoon period.

Demogrants — These are universal flat-rate payments made to individuals or households solely on the basis of demographic characteristics, such as number of children or age, rather than on the basis of proven need, as in the case of minimum income programs, or as in contributions in the case of social insurance.

Deserving poor — This refers to those who are deemed to be deserving of relief. This is a concept that historically underpinned charity relief and continues to influence income security provision today.

Diagnostic approach — In the diagnostic approach, the emphasis is on understanding the condition of the individual by reference to causal events in his or her early life. This approach requires a skilled worker who can diagnose the problem and establish and carry out a plan for treatment.

Digital divide — Most of the world's peoples do not have access to computers, the Internet and advanced communications technology. This problem is sometimes referred to as the "digital divide."

Direct social work — This involves working directly with people as individuals, in families or households and communities in a direct face-to-face way (i.e., in a counselling role).

Disability — Any restriction or lack (resulting from an impairment) of ability to perform an activity in the manner or within the range considered normal for a human being.

Disability organizations — Organizations that provide services to disabled people. For examples, see Chapter 12 on Social Work with Persons with Disabilities.

Disability rate — The total number of persons who reported activity limitations, which is then expressed as a percentage of the population.

Disability rights movement — The rise of disability rights organizations in Canada is rooted in the rise of the consumer movement, the civil rights movement, the peace movement, the gay rights movement and the women's movement of the late 1960s and the early 1970s. Disability rights activists attempted to redefine their social status. Rather than be labelled "defective or handicapped," they argued that they should be seen as members of a minority group.

Discrimination — The unequal treatment of individuals on the basis of their personal characteristics, which may include age, sex, sexual orientation, ethnic or physical identity.

Disengagement theory — An early, prominent theory within social practice with the elderly that maintained that withdrawing from activities and social life is a natural part of the ageing process and that this withdrawal acts to assist seniors to adjust to ageing. This theory is in opposition to activity theory.

Disk list system — One gross example of the nature of state intervention in Inuit lives was the disk list system. As bureaucrats would not formally acknowledge the Inuktitut names for individuals, the disk list system assigned a numbered disk to each Inuk in order to identify them.

Duty to report — Not only child protection workers have a responsibility to report suspected instances of child abuse or neglect. Every member of society has a responsibility to report child abuse or neglect when there are reasonable grounds for believing a child may be in need of protection. People in professions that bring them into contact with children have a particular responsibility to ensure that young people are safe.

Early education and development — This refers to federal, publicly-funded programs for children. Each country regulates its own system of early education and development and countries vary widely in their provision of these services for families.

Ecological/Systems theory perspective — This approach evolved from attempts by social workers to address issues in a way that goes beyond diagnosing individual problems by looking only at the individual factors. Practitioners recognized that it is also important to examine elements such as the family, community and institutions in society. Whereas those formulating a structural approach looked to critical theory, power theory and political economy theory, those developing the ecological/systems approach adopted "systems theory." Systems theory focuses on the systems in the person's immediate environment that may be causing the individual's problem.

Economic globalization — The growing integration and expansion of global markets for goods, services and finances. Economic globalization is the latest expression of market liberalism and the latest stage in the development of advanced capitalist economies. Economic globalization includes free trade and investment, international trade expansion, the development of powerful transnational corporations and the use of agreements between nations and international bodies. Because of a lack of restraining national legislation, economic globalization enables multinational corporations to pursue their agendas of successful markets and inexpensive labour.

Elder abuse — The abuse and neglect of seniors by those in a position of trust, power or responsibility for their care. Elder abuse and neglect may occur within homes or institutional care settings and in either case, is often hidden and silenced.

Electronic advocacy — The process of using communication and information technologies to disseminate information and mobilize support from a large constituency to help influence decision-making processes.

Emotional abuse — Emotional attacks or omissions that cause, or could cause, serious emotional injury. This could include behaviour of parents or guardians who persistently do not take an interest in their child, for example, by not talking to or hugging their child, or by being chronically emotionally unavailable to their child. This could also include repeated threats, confinement, repeated exposure to violence, ongoing humiliation and ridicule and fundamental attacks on a child's sense of self.

Employment equity — All Canadian provinces and the federal government have equal employment opportunity legislation in place, usually as part of their human rights codes. This legislation prohibits discrimination on the basis of race, age, religion, nationality and sex. Employment equity legislation, designed to help women's employment and promotion opportunities, was not introduced in Canada until the 1980s.

Empowerment — The sense that people can create and take action on their own behalf to meet their physical, spiritual and psychological needs.

Equal employment and employment equity — Within Canada, citizens are protected by equal opportunity legislation which prohibits discrimination on the basis of race, age, religion, nationality, ability and sex. The prohibition of discrimination on the basis of sex was generally added during the 1960s and 1970s, however, employment equity legislation was not introduced until the 1980s. Although research into the impact of employment equity legislation is limited, small improvements in occupational advancement for socially marginalized communities have been detected.

Equal-pay policies — During the 1950s and 1960s, every Canadian province enacted legislation requiring equal pay for similar or substantially similar work. During the 1970s both Quebec and the federal government introduced pay equity legislation that required equal pay for work of equal value (allowing comparisons between occupations). In the 1980s, most other jurisdictions followed suit, at least with respect to public sector employment.

Ethical dilemmas — In the course of their work, social workers are inevitably confronted with situations in which the policy and regulations of the agency conflict with what they, as experienced social workers, see as being in the best interests of their client. As well, the standards and ethics of the profession may be inconsistent with an agency's procedures and practices.

Balancing one's beliefs, professional standards and agency rules can be difficult.

Ethnicity — *Ethnicity*, from a Greek word meaning "people," refers to a group of people who share a common heritage, identity or origin. Isajiw defines an ethnic group as "an involuntary, community-type group of persons who share the same distinct culture or who are descendants of those who have shared a distinct culture and who identify with their ancestors, or their culture or group" (Isajiw 1999).

Ethnocentrism — An attitude that one's own culture, society or group is inherently superior to all others. Ethnocentrism means an inability to appreciate others whose culture may include a different racial group, ethnic group, religion, morality, language, political system, economic system and so on. It also means an inability to see a common humanity and human condition facing all women and men in all cultures and societies beneath the surface variations in social and cultural traditions.

Evaluation/termination — The final step in the social work process, in which the client and the social worker have worked together to assist the client to achieve a resolution to the original problem.

Extra-billing — Extra-billing is an extra charge levied by the physician beyond the negotiated or scheduled rates set by the provinces.

Facilitating programs — Many changes, other than directly labour-related legislation, have been introduced to help put women on an equal footing with men in the Canadian labour market. Among other things, these include changes in divorce laws, policies against sexual harassment at work, expanded maternity leave provisions, policies to protect part-time and temporary workers and policies designed to ensure women have equal access to higher education.

Family or household groups — In Statistics Canada's 2001 Census, a Census family was defined as a married couple with or without children, or a couple living common-law (can be of opposite or same sex) with or without children, or a lone parent living with one or more children. This excludes persons living in collective households. The Vanier Institute of the Family defines family as any combination of two or more persons who are bound together over time by ties of mutual consent, birth and/or adoption or placement and who, together, assume responsibilities for variant combinations of some of the following: physical maintenance and care of group members; addition of new members through procreation or adoption; socialization of children; social control of members; production, consumption, distribution of goods and services, and affective nurturance — love

Family systems theory — The belief that all families are social systems. Families are perceived as interrelated networks in which an impact on one component has significant consequences for all others in the system. As such, family members influence the actions of other members and a change in one family member will affect other members.

Federalism — A system of government in which sovereignty is divided between a central government and several provincial or state governments.

Feminist social work practice — Many of the principles of feminist social work are similar to those of social work practice in general, such as the empowerment of the individual and examining society through a critical lens, egalitarian client-therapist relations and working at both the individual and social levels, although to varying degrees. As with other approaches to social work, feminist social work practice seeks to understand a client's situation by acquiring knowledge of the client's history, family and social relations and cultural context. However, in analyzing individual problems and working out effective interventions, the feminist approach gives greater emphasis to the harmful role of patriarchal relations within the family and within wider society.

Feminist theory — There are different definitions of feminism and numerous formulations and debates in feminist theory. There is, however, a common core theory asserting that sex-role stereotypes and social structures perpetuate women's subordination.

Feminization of poverty — The number of women in poverty is increasing faster than that of men.

Five Principles of Medicare — Principles derived from the *Canada Health Act* (1984) that affirm the philosophy of the universal health care system within Canada. These principles include public administration, comprehensiveness, universality, portability and accessibility. In order for each province and territory to receive federally funded medicare, each has to meet these stated five principles.

Food banks and feeding programs — With cutbacks in many income security programs, Canadians are increasingly resorting to food banks and feeding programs in order to survive.

Freudian thought — Freudian thought played an increasingly important role in social work in the 1920s. Social work shifted from a concern with the societal context to a concern with a person's psychological make-up as the source of problems.

Functional approach — Attitude theories that emphasize that people develop and change their attitudes based on the degree to which they satisfy different psychological needs. To change an attitude, one must understand the underlying function that the attitude serves.

Gender — Issues of sex and gender are often conflated (or seen as the same) when, in fact, they refer to quite different aspects of our identities. Sex (usually man or woman) is what doctors attribute to babies based largely on the size of their genitalia. In fact, sex is determined by genetics, chromosomes and hormones, which can combine to create an indeterminate number of sexes. Gender has two components, first gender identity, which is the sense we have of ourselves as male, female or transgendered; and secondly our gender role, which is our adherence to cultural norms of femininity and masculinity.

Gender diversity — This refers to the dynamic boundaries around gender identity. Many individuals who identify as transsexuals, transvestites, drag-queens and cross-dressers, identify with gender roles outside the traditional binary of male and female.

Gender Equality — The belief that women and men should live in an environment that affords them equal opportunities to realize full human rights in order to contribute to national, political, economic, social and cultural development and to benefit from the results of that development. In order to achieve this goal, gender equity programs provide measures to compensate women for previously suffered historical and social disadvantages.

General Social Survey (GSS) — An American survey instrument which collects data on demographic characteristics and general attitudes of American citizens. In 1999, the GSS determined that 7 percent of seniors experience some form of emotional or financial abuse by a family member.

Generalist approach — A theoretical approach that analyzes problems from a variety of different perspectives. This approach goes beyond diagnosing individual problems by acknowledging and exploring factors that exist outside of the individual. This approach emphasizes problem-solving within micro, mezzo and macro levels and social workers adopting this approach typically use systems theory while fulfilling a variety of different roles within their work with clients. Generalist social workers use problem-solving in combination with systems theory to both assess a client's situation and to develop and implement interventions that establish the social functioning of individuals, families, groups, communities or organizations.

Geographic community — A geographic community is as defined by a specific neighbourhood, city district or local ward, with specific geographical boundaries.

Gerontology — A multidisciplinary field of study that concentrates on the biological, psychological, sociological, health and economic aspects of the aging process and the differential effects of these aspects on individuals as they progress through the life cycle.

Global social welfare — In this new era of globalization, the traditional concerns of social welfare practitioners in addressing the immediate needs of their clients will need to be broadened to include a concern with the issue of global human rights. Global social welfare refers to concern for justice, social regulation, social provision and redistribution between nations.

Globalization — See "economic globalization."

Great Depression — The largest downturn or economic depression in the economy in Canada took place in 1930s. It was characterized by deflation, which occurs when prices for goods and services decrease.

Group work — A social work method practised with groups of individuals. This method includes five steps: intake, assessment and case plan, group composition, intervention and termination.

Hall Report — A report completed by the Royal Commission on Health Care, chaired by Justice Emmett Hall in 1964, that highlighted the fact that millions of Canadians did not have medical coverage. This report recommended that a comprehensive, publicly administered universal health service plan be implemented and in 1968, the *Medical Care Act* was passed.

Harm-reduction approach — Increasingly, social workers in addiction treatment programs are taking a harm-reduction approach instead of an abstinence approach to treatment. The harm-reduction approach seeks to minimize or reduce the adverse consequences of drug use.

Hate crimes — When people are the targets of violence solely because of who they are, or who they are thought to be, they are the victims of hate crimes. The most common targets of hate-motivated crime are Black people, Jewish people and gay people.

Healing lodges — Lodges that provide residential treatment or both treatment and lodging for people who become overwhelmed by social, emotional and spiritual problems. Approximately 50 treatment facilities currently provide Aboriginal residential healing. The Nechi Institute and Poundmaker's Lodge in Alberta are examples, providing healing and lodging for people dealing with addictions.

Health gap — Despite the availability of public health care across the country, there is a serious health gap between the rich and the poor in Canada. The rich are healthier than the middle class, who are in turn healthier than the poor. The well educated are healthier than the less educated, the employed are healthier than the unemployed and so on.

Heterosexual privilege — The comfort and power accorded to people who are in, or are expected to be in, a relationship with a person of a different sex and who conform to dominant gender norms. Heterosexual privilege allows someone to escape the social risks, dangers and costs associated with not conforming to conventional gender norms.

Heterosexism — Heterosexism describes beliefs and actions that denigrate and stigmatize any non-heterosexual form of behavior, identity, relationship, or community.

Holistic approach to healing — This means that the whole of the person and the situation is examined and acted upon.

Holistic approach to health care — The holistic approach to health care involves taking into account not only the physical aspects of health, which have commonly been addressed by physicians, but also the social, cultural, mental and spiritual aspects of the person.

Home care — Health care service delivery that is provided in one's home as opposed to within hospitals and other health-care settings. Home care programs provide a wide range of services including health promotion, curative medicine, end-of-life care, rehabilitation, support and maintenance, social adaptation, integration and caregiver support. Home care programs are provided to a variety of individuals and are often complemented by community-based services that can provide additional care and supports.

Homophobia, biphobia and transphobia — These are terms that are used to describe an individual's and/or society's fear and hatred of gay men, lesbians, bisexuals and transgendered persons.

Human Development Index (HDI) — The indicator of human development used within the Human Development Report (HDR). This index involves other dimensions besides income in measuring human well-being. It was created to re-emphasize that people and their capabilities should be the ultimate criteria for assessing the development of a country.

Human Development Report (HDR) — An independent report commissioned by the United Nations Development Programme that assesses the level of long-term well-being of people within developing nations. The purpose of the HDR is to ensure the inclusion and participation of people in these nations within economic debate, policy and advocacy is supported. The HDR emphasizes the goals of development to be choices and freedoms for citizens.

Human rights — Those rights that are inherent in our nature and without which we cannot live as human beings, based on the recognition of individual political and civil rights and collective cultural, social and economic rights.

Human rights commissions — All federal and provincial jurisdictions have legislated rights protection law and have created rights commissions to implement such policy. National human rights legislation in Canada began with the passage of the Canadian Bill of Rights in 1960. Later in that decade other provinces enacted similar legislation, and by 1975, all provinces in Canada had human rights codes.

Human rights legislation — National human rights legislation in Canada began with the passage of the Canadian Bill of Rights in 1960. Later in that decade other provinces enacted similar legislation, and by 1975, all provinces in Canada had human rights codes. The constitutional division of powers determines whether a rights violation complaint is heard at the federal or provincial levels. Grounds of discrimination vary slightly depending on the jurisdiction.

Ideology — A system of beliefs and values that explains society and prescribes the role of government.

Immigration policy — Ethnic and race relations in Canada have been heavily influenced by immigration policy. Prior to 1967, "Nationality" was one of the criteria used to qualify for admission to Canada, and Canadian immigration policy was undoubtedly Eurocentric. In 1967, new legislation introduced a point system, whereby prospective immigrants had to qualify based on such criteria as education, work experience, language fluency and age.

Income security — Income support in the form of demogrants, social insurance, Social Assistance, and income supplementation that can be unconditional or based on an income or needs test, or negative income tax.

Income supplementation — Programs that, as the name suggests, supplement income that is obtained elsewhere whether through paid employment or through other income security programs. These programs are not intended to be the primary source of income. Family Allowance (which was also a universal demogrant) and the National Child Benefit are examples of income supplementation programs.

Independent Living Movement (ILM) — The Independent Living Movement has been a key player in the struggle to achieve human rights legislation for people with disabilities. Originating in the United States during the early 1970s and introduced to Canada in 1979, the Movement has become a dominant force in disability rights activity in Canada. In addition to promoting disability rights, the ILM promotes the social oppression theory of disability.

Indian Act of 1876 — Legislation that provides the Government of Canada with the legal framework of authority over Indians and lands reserved for Indians, as stated in the *Constitution Act, 1867*. The main purpose of the Act is to control and regulate Indian lives. An "Indian" is a person who is registered or entitled to be registered in the Indian Register (a centralized record).

Indian Agent — The *Indian Act* was, and still is, a piece of social legislation of very broad scope, which regulates and controls virtually every aspect of Native life. The so-called Indian Agent administered the Act in Aboriginal communities. These agents were to displace traditional Aboriginal leaders so as to institute a new way of living consistent with the intentions of the government. The Indian Agents had extraordinary administrative and discretionary powers. In order to ensure this, Clause 25 of the Act established the government's guardianship over Native lands.

"Indian problem" — With the colonization of what would become known as Canada, the land's original inhabitants became known as "the Indian problem," and impediments to "civilization." Colonial representatives and, later, government officials devised various schemes to address the "Indian problem", including land-cession treaties and assimilation policies.

Indirect social work — Social work of benefit to those in need, but the work is often with organizations that advocate, research, plan and implement social service and income security programs. Most often those who do indirect social work will be working with government, social service agencies or what are called advocacy or research groups, and organizations whose purpose is to advocate for and with people in need.

In-home services — In-home services are provided to help a household or family members live together harmoniously in a secure and safe environment. The main categories of in-home services include family counselling services, parenting supports, child protection, in-home child care, homemaker services and family educational services.

Institutional abuse — Abuse that occurs in health and extended care facilities for Seniors and other vulnerable populations. Institutional abuse is defined as any act or omission directed at a resident that causes the person harm, or wrongfully deprives that person of his or her independence.

Institutional view of social welfare — A view that emphasizes the preventive role of social welfare in modern industrial societies and sees the welfare of the individual as the responsibility of the social collective. The market will not, and cannot, meet the needs and aspirations of all people and, therefore, the optimal distribution of welfare can only be achieved by an acknowledgment that there is a significant role for a publicly funded and organized system of programs and institutions.

Intake — Intake is usually the first step taken by a worker when a client seeks help. Intake is a process whereby a request for service is made by or for a person, and it is then determined whether and what kind of service is to be provided. The social worker attempts to gather initial information from the client in order to determine what assistance is needed, and whether the agency and worker is the appropriate provider.

Integrated Service Delivery (ISD) — A comprehensive model of service delivery in which social and health services are coordinated in order to meet the diverse needs of individuals or families. This model is both client-focused and team-based and enables people to access different services from a variety of service-providers within one centralized location.

Intergovernmental organizations (IGOs) — International organizations that consider worldwide issues and relations between nations. Social workers are active in various international intergovernmental organizations (IGOs). The United Nations is the best known of these IGOs. Formed as World War II came to an end, the UN seeks to develop a framework of international law that will be followed by all nation states around the world.

International Association of Schools of Social Work (IASSW) is an association of educators and institutions involved in social work education worldwide. It helps to promote social work education, facilitate mutual exchanges and represent social work educators at the international level.

International community work — A common social work activity in developing countries is international community work. Social workers use community work to organize people to bring about major social change between nations, within nations, and between groups of people. They work through communities to achieve the fullest participation of people in transforming different aspects of their lives.

International Federation of Social Workers (IFSW) — The International Federation of Social Workers is a successor to the International Permanent Secretariat of Social Workers, which was founded in Paris in 1928. In 1950, the International Federation of

Social Workers was created, with the goal of becoming an international organization of professional social workers. Today the IFSW represents over half a million social workers in 55 different counties. The IFSW seeks to promote social work as a profession, link social workers from around the world and promote the participation of social workers in social policy and planning.

Intersexuals — Intersexuals are individuals whose external sex (genitalia) are indederminant, people who appear to be males but are medically/biologically females, people with female physical attributes who are medically/biologically males as well as those of us having the external appearance of both sexes and the DNA chromosome karyotypes of both sexes.

Intervention — An "action" step in which a client provides the social worker with information and shares whatever progress has been made in attempting to resolve the problem.

Involuntary clients — Those who accept social work services because of a legal mandate, such as prisoners on parole or children in care.

Keynesian — Describes an economic theory, named after British economist John Maynard Keynes, which holds that economic efficiency and equity are compatible. Social spending helps economic recovery, enhances productivity and keeps the labour market flexible. Also called demand-side economics: If people are employed, they will spend money, the demand for products will increase, and the economy will improve.

Kinsey Report — A report published in 1948 by scientist Alfred Kinsey that documented men's sexual habits and behaviours. This report, entitled *Sexual Behaviour in the Human Male*, demonstrated that people's sexual behaviours combined both normal and so-called perverse behaviours.

Land-cession treaties — The desire by the government to obtain land held by Aboriginal peoples for the settlement of non-Aboriginal people was a primary goal for much of the policy directed towards Native peoples. Reserves were seen as a way to move Aboriginal people into agriculturally-based communities, both to assimilate them and also to free up vast tracks of land for non-Aboriginal settlement. Further to this end, numerous treaties were signed between Native groups and colonial officials between 1670 and 1923. It is these land treaties (in many cases, the lack of them) that are currently in dispute across the country today.

Learning theory — The main idea in this theory is that violence is a behaviour learned in childhood. Boys learn that it is okay to be violent, and girls learn that it is okay to be on the receiving end of violence — that is what relationships are about. This theory holds that all children are socialized to accept violence in our society and that this, coupled with the different roles that boys and girls are socialized into, supports and perpetuates abuse. Children who witness violence in the home are much more likely, than children who don't, to become abusers or be abused.

"Least restrictive approach" — The "least restrictive" approach to child protection emphasizes the least disruptive course of action that will leave the child with his or her family, if at all possible.

LGBTQ — The acronym for "lesbians, gay men, bisexuals, transgendered persons and people who identify as queer."

Life course theory — This theory suggests that individuals progress through a variety of distinct stages over the course of their lives. Each stage has particular benefits, limitations and characteristics and stages are not perceived as more or less satisfactory then another. Further, this theory maintains that within each life stage, various distinct pathways are selected by individuals as they progress through life.

Low Income Cut-offs (LICOs) — According to Statistics Canada, those who spend more than 55 percent of their earnings on basic needs are living under the LICO. A household that spends 20 percent more than the average household spends on food, clothing and shelter is below the LICO or in "straightened circumstances." Although LICO is not put forth as an official poverty line, many analysts, including the United Nations, treat it as such. For example, the 2000 LICO for a family of four in a medium-sized city of 100,000–500,000 is $29,356. Some have called it a "relative necessities" approach.

Low Income Measure (LIM) — A relative measure of poverty that measures low-income rates as one-half of the median income of a particular country. The LIM is often used around the world to compare international rates of child poverty and is calculated based on information obtained by Statistics Canada.

Macro social work — This refers to indirect social work practice. Macro social work practice is directed towards transforming social structures and social systems so that they better serve and support all people.

Macro-level theory — Social work practice theory that concentrates on social structures, social processes and systems and the effects of these on the experiences of people throughout society. Within this theoretical paradigm, the abilities of people to overcome the influences of existing social structures and systems on their lives is limited.

Market Basket Measure (MBM) — A relative measure of poverty proposed by Human Resources

Development Canada (HRDC). The MBM is calculated by taking the amount of income needed by a particular household in order to meet its basic needs as determined by pre-existing community norms. By defining income needs, as opposed to terms of bare subsistence, this index progresses beyond an absolute measure of poverty and reflects changes in the cost of consumption rather than changes in income.

Maternal feminists — This term generally refers to the notion that it is because of a woman's special roles as mother and homemaker that she has an obligation and a right to participate in the public sphere. Although they brought women into public life and social work, the early maternal feminists now tend to be viewed as being quite conservative, insofar as they supported more traditional conceptions of the family in which women were expected to stay in the home.

Medical model of disability — The view that behavioral and emotional problems are analogous to physical diseases.

Medical social work practice — One of the chief settings for medical social work practice is the hospital. Almost every hospital in Canada has social workers in its departments, including in emergency services, oncology, pediatrics, surgery, intensive care, rehabilitation, gerontology and orthopaedics.

Medicare — Government-funded health insurance within Canada's health care system. This health insurance is delivered both publicly by hospitals and privately by physicians. This health care funding is available to all Canadian provinces and territories on the condition that they meet the five principles of medicare.

Membership community — A membership community is defined by a sense of belonging to a specific group; for example, the gay and lesbian community, the Black community, the Native community and so on.

Mental illness — A general term referring to psychological, emotional or behavioral disorders, as well to the view that these disorders are diseases of the mind.

"Micro," "mezzo" and "macro" social work — These are categories for describing different kinds of social work intervention. "Micro social work" refers to direct practice with individuals. "Mezzo social work" is social work with groups and communities. "Macro social work" involves working with organizations or communities to improve or change laws or policies in general society.

Minimum income — Social Assistance is a minimum income program. It provide the bare minimum needed to survive.

Model of community development — The nature of community work differs depending on the perspective informing one's practice. A useful approach is Rothman's model of community development, which allows one to see the differences between the various forms of community development discussed and debated in Canada today.

Monetarists — An economic theory that asserts, among other things, that social spending stimulates inflation, undermines labour market flexibility and productivity and distorts the work-leisure trade-off.

Multiculturalism — In 1971, Canada became the first country to adopt multiculturalism as an official policy. The policy was aimed at a greater integration of Canadian society by providing diverse ethnic minority groups with a sense of belonging to Canada.

Negative Rights — Civil and political rights as set forth in Articles 2–21 of the Universal Declaration of Human Rights. These rights ensure the protection of basic human rights.

Neglect — Sustained deprivation of food, clothing, hygiene, shelter and other needed care so as to cause, or potentially cause, physical, emotional, developmental or psychological harm.

New world order model (of international social work — This approach has its origins in the idea that the present world order is not very democratic at all, but is controlled by a relatively small number of wealthy countries that manipulate the international system to their own advantage. Those who practice with this approach in mind are oriented more towards a fundamental rebuilding of the global cultural, social, political and economic structures.

Non-governmental organizations (NGOs) — NGOs are international organizations not directly linked to governments, allowing them more freedom in taking up important issues and bringing about effective change. NGOs tend to be small dynamic groups that work on a variety of issues depending on their particular political or philosophical stances.

North-South divide — The economic world divides, broadly speaking, along North-South lines, the so-called North-South divide, with the countries of the First World awash in relative affluence and those of the Third World, in abject poverty.

Out-of-home services — Out-of-home services are implemented when the home situation becomes unsuitable for the upbringing of a child. These services include foster care, adoption, day care centres, community supports (e.g., the Community Action Program for Children and Aboriginal Head Start), group homes, institutional care, parenting self-help and empowerment groups and family housing assistance.

Overseas humanitarian programs — Churches and other religious groups and organizations have perhaps the most extensive variety of overseas humanitarian programs and frequently employ the services of social workers. These groups tend to operate in the poorer countries of Africa, Asia and Latin America.

Palliative care — Health care that is provided to individuals who are living with a terminal illness. Palliative care is typically provided when the illness is at an advanced stage and its purpose is to provide relief, comfort and to maintain the highest possible quality of life for as long as the person is still alive.

Participation Activities Limitation Survey (PALS) — A report conducted by the Canadian federal government in 2001 which detailed the prevalence of disabilities, the various supports that exist for persons with disabilities and the employment profile of persons with disabilities, as well as their incomes and extent of their participation within society.

Participatory action research (PAR) — A type of community work that refers to a process of research comprised of education, investigation and action directed at changing the structures that promote inequality and the structures that produce knowledge that perpetuates the current power structures.

Patriarchy — Patriarchy literally means the "rule by the father" but, in a broader sense, it has come to mean the domination of society by men. Men are still the major stakeholders in Canadian society, men continue to be represented in higher numbers in positions of authority and male interests continue to take precedence over those of females.

Person with disabilities — The term describes a person whose physical or mental condition limits his or her ability to perform certain functions. Terms such as *cripple, defective, abnormal, handicapped, physically challenged* or *mentally challenged* have been applied to people who are disabled. The most acceptable terms are those that put the person first and not the disability: *people with disabilities, person with disability, person with intellectual disability* and so on. *Disabled person* is now also generally acceptable usage.

Personal tragedy theory of disability — The view that a disability condition is an unfortunate life event where some form of professional or medical assistance is required.

Person-in-the-environment — A key aspect of effective social work practice is to go beyond "internal" (psychological) factors and examine the relationship between individuals and their environment. This person-in-the-environment approach is partly what distinguishes social work practice from other helping professions. These "environments" extend beyond the immediate family and include interactions with friends, neighbourhoods, schools, religious groups, laws and legislation, other agencies or organizations, places of employment and the economic system.

Persons with disabilities — This phrase is widely endorsed as the most appropriate term to be used when referring to individuals who have a disability. "People first" activists support this phrase as disability is only one of the many facets of an individual. However, many disability rights activists and advocates have challenged this conceptualization of disability and argue that this phrase should be replaced by "disabled person", a phrase which does not minimize or de-politicize disability.

Phases in long-term care — This refers to distinct phases in care within long-term care settings which include: pre-admission, admission, residency and discharge/transfer/death.

Physical abuse — Physical assaults such as hitting, kicking, biting, throwing, burning or poisoning that cause, or could cause, physical injury as well as behaviours or omissions that cause, or could cause, physical injury.

Political economy — The economic outlook that believes that the operation of economic markets is tied to private concentrations of ownership of the productive enterprise and is essentially exploitative. Social spending is a right fought for by the working class. Some within this approach believe that social spending serves to prop up and justify the economic system. This is called the accumulation and legitimating functions of the welfare state.

Political rights model of disability — A theory of disability primarily concerned with broader social and political change. It contends that a comprehensive understanding of disability can only occur through examination of a social oppression theory of disability, along with the already predominant personal tragedy theory of disability.

Poor relief — The early English legislation, the Poor Law, required local parishes to provide relief to the deserving poor (those who were elderly, ill or disabled). Parishes were administrative districts organized by the Church of England. Each had a local council that was responsible for assistance to the poor, known as poor relief.

Positive rights — Economic, social and cultural rights as set forth in Articles 22–27 of the Universal Declaration of Human Rights. These rights ensure justice, freedom and social participation.

Poverty gap — Poverty rates do not show whether poor people are living in abject poverty or merely a few dollars below the poverty line. To determine this, we need to measure the poverty gap or how much additional income would be required to raise an individual or household above the LICO.

Power theory — A feminist-based theory explaining that wife abuse is a societal problem that occurs because of the power imbalance between men and women, specifically because of the dominance of men and men's roles. Wife abuse continues because there has been historical acceptance of abuse and of men's right to control women, even by force.

Prejudice — An adverse opinion that "pre-judges" entire groups based on incomplete and inaccurate information.

Pre-payment health plans — From 1880 to the 1950s, there were a variety of pre-payment health plans in place across Canada, sponsored by local governments, industries and volunteer agencies. These voluntary insurance plans did not cover all medical services, and they were available only to those who could afford to pay the premiums.

Preventive medicine — Provincial governments have begun to practice preventive medicine, using policies designed to anticipate and reduce the likelihood of illness or its worsening.

Private charities — The pre-industrial phase of the development of social work includes the period from the formation of Canada up to the 1890s. Private charities developed during this time, offering material relief and lessons in moral ethics. Many were explicitly associated with religious organizations, and it was religiously motivated individuals working through these organizations who became the early social workers.

Private welfare — Social welfare programs funded by voluntary charitable contributions of individuals and private organizations, by fees people pay for the services they receive, or which are provided by funds spent by corporations to provide social welfare services for their employees.

Privately funded disability programs — Privately funded disability programs include programs that are provided through private insurance plans or through long-term disability plans as part of job benefits. These private income security programs are based on the amount of funding that the recipient has contributed directly to the plan, or funding which has been contributed to the plan on behalf of the recipient.

Privatization — The use of the private sector to provide social welfare services, often in addition to or instead of existing public services. .

Problem-solving techniques — An approach to social work that breaks down every problem into component parts and develops objectives that must be met in order to solve the overall problem.

Professional associations — Today, most Canadian social workers are members of professional associations. The associations represent social workers in issues pertaining to the development of the profession, the education of its members and in discussions of social issues and social policy.

Personal Security Index — An index developed by the Canadian Council on Social Development in order to measure annual changes in the security of Canadians within areas of economy and finances, health, and physical safety. The PSI measures changes in both empirical data and in people's perceptions of their personal security.

Public sector unions — Today most Canadian social workers are members of public sector unions. Indeed, they were part of the wider unionization of the public sector during the 1960s and 1970s, when, for the first time, public sector employees were permitted to join a union. The unions represent their members in the areas of pay or working conditions. The professional association and the union complement each other and both have mandates to act as voices for those they represent.

Public welfare — Public welfare refers to the provision of welfare services at the three levels of government: the federal or national government, the provincial and territorial governments and the regional and municipal governments.

Publicly funded disability programs — Publicly funded disability programs are programs covered by federal, provincial and municipal legislation. These programs include the Canada Pension Plan-Disability Pension (a federal program), and various provincial disability support programs.

Queer activism — Efforts and actions towards social change by LGBTQ communities. Queer activism is significantly more confrontational than the 1990s' gay and lesbian movement and demands dramatic changes to ways sexual diversity is perceived within society.

Queer theory — Within this theory, sexuality is understood and explained through the social construction of categories of normative and deviant sexual behaviour. Queer theory maintains that all sexual behaviours, sexual identities and sexual categories are social constructs with social meaning and as such, legislative changes within the current capitalist democracy will not result in fundamental social change and liberation for LGBTQ people.

Race — Race is an arbitrary classification of human beings based on skin colour and other superficial physical characteristics. This classification, conceived in Europe in the colonial period, placed the populations of the world in a hierarchical order with white Europeans superior to all others. Modern biologists do not recognize "race" as a meaningful scientific category and recent human genome research is conclusive on this point.

Racism — Individual and institutionalized beliefs and practices that advocate that some "races" are inferior to others. The belief that one's racial group is somehow superior to other groups leads, with the aid of stereotypes, to discrimination and prejudice.

Reclaiming Aboriginal culture — A principle of Aboriginal social work that goes beyond regaining language, religion and folkways in emphasizing an awareness of and reflection on common aspects of culture and identity. By examining Aboriginal history, culture and traditions and by dispelling conventional views of Aboriginal reality flowing from colonialism, Aboriginal people can begin to see the structural causes of individual problems.

Relative poverty — A definition of poverty that looks at income in comparison to the income of other Canadians.

Residential school system — This school system was used to remove Native children from Native homes and communities and to restrict their culture and language. It separated children from their families and communities for up to years at a time. The purpose was to fulfill the assimilation policies of the federal government. Large numbers of Native children experienced emotional, physical and sexual abuse.

Residual view of social welfare — This view asserts that governments should play only a limited role in the distribution of social welfare. The state should step in only when normal sources of support fail and the individual is unable to help himself or herself.

Risk assessment — In the area of child abuse, risk assessment refers to an educated prediction regarding the likelihood that a child will be maltreated based on a careful examination of pertinent data.

Role theory — This theory maintains that people define roles for themselves and that they will adopt these roles. As applied to seniors, this theory attempts to understand the adjustment of ageing people to new roles that they adopt throughout the ageing process.

Rothman's model of community development — A useful approach to conceptualizing community development is a typology developed by Rothman, involving three components: locality development, social planning and social action. To these should be added a fourth: participatory action research.

Royal Commission on Aboriginal Peoples — The Final Report of 1996 brought together six years of research and public consultation on First Nations issues. This is the most extensive research to date and provides the basis for significant strides forward. Among the many issues discussed, the Report examines the need for Aboriginal people to heal from the consequences of domination, displacement and assimilation. The foundation for a renewed relationship, according to the Report, involves recognition of Aboriginal nations as political entities.

Scientific philanthropy — An historical approach that contributed to the rise of social work with the idea that charities should become organized in order to deal more systematically with the problem of poverty. It emerged from ideals of social reform and social progress, which were increasingly influenced by scientific methods and approaches.

"The Scoop" — "The Scoop" refers to the massive removal of Aboriginal children from their families and communities and their placement in non-Aboriginal foster and adoptive homes. This primarily took place in the 1960s.

Scrip system — The situation of the Métis in the late nineteenth and early twentieth centuries was unique. The Métis in western Canada could seek to become status Indians by aligning themselves to certain treaty areas or they could "take scrip." The scrip system entitled the bearer of a scrip certificate to either land or money; in exchange, the person who took scrip gave up all further claims to land.

Selective programs — Target benefits aimed at those determined to be in need or eligible based on a means test (sometimes called an income test) or a needs test.

Self-help community — A self-help community consists of non-professional persons with similar problems or difficulties (e.g., those living with addiction, disability or unemployment, or coping with illness or the death of a loved one), who provide mutual support and exchange information.

Self-help or peer groups — The acquiring of information or the solving of one's problems, without the direct intervention of professionals or experts, through joining or forming a group comprised of others who have the same problem.

Settlement houses — A movement that began in the late 1800s, in which the middle and upper classes lived with the poor and advocated for better social and working conditions. The purpose was to bring the educated middle class and even the charitable upper class or gentry to live among the urban poor in working class neighbourhoods.

Sexism — Similar to the dynamics of racism. Males are believed to be superior to females, and when this belief is put into action, females are treated as objects, the last to be hired, first to be fired, and paid less for equal work.

Sexology — The systematic study of human sexual behaviour. Sexology developed out of the efforts of early scientists to understand, categorize, and document sexual relations and sexual attraction.

Sexual abuse — Any sexual exploitation of a child whether consented to or not. It includes touching of a sexual nature or any behaviour of a sexual nature towards a child.

Sexual assault — Any form of unwanted sexual activity that is forced upon another person without obtaining that person's consent. Sexual assault includes a wide range of physical and non-physical sexual acts that are all defined as crimes under the Criminal Code.

Sexual harassment — Any behaviour, comment, gesture or contact of a sexual nature in which someone is treated as a sexual object. The primary legal difference between sexual assault and sexual harassment is that sexual assault crimes are prosecuted under the Criminal Code and sexual harassment is prosecuted under civil law.

Sexual orientation — Sexual orientation is defined by more than the identity of the person with whom we have sex or want to have sex. Relatively few people are exclusively homosexual or heterosexual. Instead, it is an emotional, romantic, sexual or affectional attraction to another person. It is not dependent upon a person's gender identity, which is our sense of ourselves as being male, female or transgendered, or our ability or willingness to adhere to cultural norms of masculine or feminine (gender roles).

Social change mandate — The social change mandate of social work means working in solidarity with those who are disadvantaged or excluded from society so as to eliminate the barriers, inequities and injustices that exist in society.

Social constructionism (in relation to sexual attraction) — In this approach sociocultural experience is given primacy in the construction of a homosexual identity and role. Social constructionism gave rise to perspectives of "choice" and "lifestyles," challenging the innate deterministic understanding of sexual orientation as advanced by essentialism.

Social development model of international social work — Social workers who hold to this approach seek primarily to address the immediate causes of human degradation, powerlessness and social inequality and to guide collective action towards the elimination of all forms of oppression, injustice and violence. They are concerned with the fuller participation of people at all levels of the political and economic systems of their countries and with fostering social, political and economic systems that are more humane, inclusive and participatory.

Social gospel movement — A movement that began in the 1880s and was directed towards a more socially oriented church among the Anglican, Methodist, Presbyterian and Congregationalist churches. It advocated for improved living and working conditions and basic social justice.

Social insurance — A type of income security program in which participants make regular payments into a fund from which they receive benefits if the risk covered by the insurance occurs. These programs follow the insurance principle of shared risk. Many contribute with the understanding that not all will necessarily need to access the benefits of the program.

Social isolation — A lack of satisfying and rewarding relationships within one's immediate social environments. Social isolation is distinct from social loneliness.

Social loneliness — The satisfaction, or lack thereof, that one experiences in relation to the quantity and quality of existing relationships with others within his or her social environments. Social loneliness is distinct from social isolation.

Social oppression theory of disability — In contrast to the personal tragedy theory of disability, the social oppression theory of disability argues that the problems faced by people with disabilities are not the result of physical impairments alone, but are the result of the social and political inequality that exists between disabled people and people without diabilities.

Social policies — The rules and regulations, the laws and other administrative directives, that set the framework for state social welfare activity.

Social programs — A detailed outline of state activity that follows and implements a specific social welfare policy. A social program outlines the funds to be spent and the purposes for which they will be spent.

Social safety net — This refers to the network of laws, policies and programs currently in place around the country through which the Canadian state creates opportunities for individuals experiencing difficulties in their lives and helps them get back on their feet. In countries where the social safety net is weak or non-existent, there is little or no protection of this kind and individuals are often left to fend for themselves.

Social security — This is sometimes used as a substitute for the term *social welfare* or *income security*. It is generally an American term, but has been also used by Canadian governments. For example, *Social Security in Canada*, published in 1994 by the federal government, uses the term to refer to both income security and social services, but the term *social welfare* is more widely accepted.

Social services — Non-monetary personal or community services provided by the state and non-profit organizations for members of the community, such as day care, housing, crisis intervention, and support groups for women experiencing abuse.

Social survey research — Towards the end of the nineteenth century, social survey research was beginning to be used to highlight the extent of poverty and inequality in Canadian cities. Early studies by social researcher and reformers, such as J.J. Kelso in Toronto and J.S. Woodsworth in Winnipeg, contributed to an understanding of poverty and what to do about it. Royal Commissions also contributed to increased awareness and a growing interest in social service and social work.

Social Union Agreement of 1999 — The Social Union Agreement of 1999 between the Government of Canada and the provinces and territories is the umbrella under which governments will concentrate their efforts to renew and modernize Canadian social policy. So far, several social welfare initiatives have been established under this framework: the National Child Benefit, the national children's agenda for child care, and services for persons with disabilities.

Social welfare — This refers to how people, communities and institutions in a society take action to provide certain minimum standards and certain opportunities. It is generally about helping people face contingencies. Social welfare comprises a range of institutions and involves the provision of programs of income security and social services.

Social welfare model of international social work — The more conventional social welfare model of international work is based on the notion that basic social welfare services should be developed in all countries to meet basic human needs. Social workers following this model of international practice are mainly concerned with the satisfaction of basic social and material needs of people (e.g., minimal standards of living, access to at least basic health, education, and other essential social services).

Social work practice — Work, consisting of a series or process of interventionist actions, that is of benefit to those in need, especially work undertaken by trained staff. It may consist of social work with individuals, group work or community work. Social work is an action-oriented field in which individual and social change play key parts.

Social work with individuals — Social work with individuals is directed towards helping individuals using counselling and other one-on-one methods.

Social worker roles — In performing their day-to-day work, a social worker is expected to be knowledgeable and skillful in a variety of roles. The role that is selected and applied should ideally be the role that is most effective with a particular client in particular circumstances.

Stages of group development — For successful group work intervention, it is important to know how to identify the stages of group development. The intervention tasks for group work will be quite different depending on the type of group (e.g., self-help or treatment), but the stages of group development will often be the same for each type of group. By identifying the group's stage of development, workers can better help the group meet its needs and goals.

Stereotype — A set of beliefs or perceptions of groups of people, or ideas held by a number of people, often not based on fact.

Stigma — A social judgement upon people that are perceived as undesirable. People who are stigmatized are often discriminated against and typically have low social status. People with disabilities are a stigmatized population, although there is nothing inherent in disability that should lead to the development of social belief systems wherein biological difference is linked to biological inferiority.

Stonewall Rebellion — A series of riots instigated by the gay and lesbian communities in response to a police raid on a Greenwich Village gay bar. This is thought of as the unification of the then current gay and lesbian political movements, as it represented the first significant collective uprising by these communities against state oppression. In addition, it marked the beginning of a much more public, large-scale movement for gay and lesbian rights.

Structural social work — An approach to social work practice that integrates critical theory and political analysis into work with clients. This approach has its roots in radical social work but offers a direct practice application of this perspective that leads to social change. Although there is not one universal definition of this approach, workers using the approach acknowledge broader social structures that shape an individual's problems and focus on the root causes of a client's problems in conjunction with the client's presenting personal issues or behaviour.

Suffragette movement — The suffragette movement campaigned for the right for all women to vote. The following are the years in which women's suffrage was obtained in a variety of countries: New Zealand (1893); Australia (1902); Finland (1906); Norway (1913); Denmark (1915); the Netherlands and the Soviet Union (1917); Canada and Luxembourg (1918); Austria, Czechoslovakia (now the Czech Republic and Slovakia), Germany, Poland and Sweden (1919); Belgium (partial, 1919; full, 1948); Ecuador (1929); South Africa (1930); Brazil and Uruguay (1932); Turkey and Cuba (1934); France (1944); Italy and Japan (1946); China and Argentina (1947); South Korea and Israel (1948); Chile, India and Indonesia (1949). Switzerland granted the franchise to women in 1971. Women in the US won the right to vote when the 19th Amendment was passed in 1920. Some states had passed laws prior to 1920 giving women the right to vote, and some women had won election to public office before the 19th Amendment became law. Women in England did not win full voting rights until 1928, however.

Sustainable development — Development that meets the needs of the present without compromising the ability of future generations to meet their own needs.

Sustainable social progress — An extension of the notion of sustainable development that goes beyond ecological and environmental concerns. The members of ICSW believe that, in order to promote sustainable social progress, social workers should support cooperation to strengthen governance and social standards internationally.

Systemic discrimination — The operating policies, structures and functions of an ongoing system of normative patterns that serve to subjugate, oppress and force the dependence of individuals or groups. This involves establishing and sanctioning unequal rights, goals and priorities and sanctioning inequality in status as well as access to goods and services.

Task groups — This term is used to signify any group in which the major purpose is neither intrinsically nor immediately linked to the needs of the members of the group. In task groups, the overriding purpose is to accomplish a mandate and complete the work for which the group was convened.

Therapy groups — Therapy groups consist of individuals who do not share a household together or have any kind of relationship with one another outside the group setting. They are people seeking individual assistance.

Third World — The Third World includes the developing countries of Central and South America, Africa, and Asia. (The First World refers to the Western capitalist countries of America and Western Europe. The Second World refers to the former Soviet Union countries.)

Transition houses — Transition houses are homes set up to respond to the needs of abused women and their children. Because of their success, the number of transition houses or shelters is growing.

Transgender — Transgender is inclusive of people identify as bigender, gender benders, gender outlaws, cross-dressers, drag queens, drag-kings, transvestites and transsexuals. Some intersexuals also identify as transgender. Some transgendered persons understand their experience in dimorphic absolutes (i.e. a man trapped in a female body), while others inhabit a more ambiguous zone "between" the sexes.

Transsexuals — Transsexuals are people whose gender identity is at odds with their physical sex. Psychiatry still considers transsexualism a mental illness that requires treatment. Some transsexuals undergo gender re-assignment surgery in order to have their anatomy coincide with their gender. Others use hormones to shape their body. Not everyone who identifies as transsexual uses medical interventions to change their physical appearance.

Treatment groups — Treatment groups gather for the purpose of meeting the therapeutic objectives of the group members. Individuals work as a group to address problems that they experience personally. The three types of treatment groups are family or household groups, therapy groups and self-help or peer groups.

Two-tier health system — A two-tiered health system refers to one in which those who can pay the extra fee or who work for employers who have extended health benefits are more privileged than others.

Undeserving poor — Poor people designated as undeserving were not seen as being of good moral character or only temporarily out of luck through no fault of their own. This is an historical concept that arose with the early Poor Laws, but it still informs income security today.

Unemployment rate — The percentage of individuals who are actively looking for work and are able to work but do not have a job (i.e., the number of unemployed individuals, divided by the total number of people 15 years of age and older who have a job or are actively looking for work expressed as a percentage).

Universal Child Care Program — This model aims to provide high-quality, affordable, regulated childhood education and care to all families. A universal childcare program is most notably demonstrated in Quebec where accessible childcare is provided to many families.

Universal Programs — Social welfare programs that are equally available to all citizens within a specific category such as age, disability etc. These program benefits are equally accessible and available to all persons regardless of need or financial situation.

Universal public health care — Canadians have not always had ready access to quality health care. Prior to the late 1940s, access to health care was based solely on one's ability to pay. Universal public health care for everyone in Canada took over five decades to evolve.

User fees — A small extra fee above the scale charged directly to the patient for hospital and physician services.

Virtual community work — Today, the Internet makes it possible for community workers and activists to expand their networks by identifying and contacting people in other communities who have similar interests and concerns. This could be loosely referred to as a kind of virtual community work.

Visible minorities — Within the Canadian context, this term (widely used in government statistics) refers to individuals who can be visibly identified and perceived as belonging to a racial group other than those of European origin. For this reason, it is a somewhat contentious term.

Voluntary clients — People who have chosen to seek the services of a social worker.

Welfare state — A system whereby the state ostensibly undertakes to protect the health and well-being of its citizens, especially those in financial need.

Workfare — Work for a specific minimum number of work units (measured in hours or output) in a job that is designated or approved by the welfare authority to qualify for the basic welfare benefit.

Youth Criminal Justice Act (YCJA) — An Act implemented in 2003 whose purpose was to emphasize the rehabilitation and re-entry of young offenders into society. The YCJA sought to develop clear principles by which the Youth Criminal Justice System can accomplish their goals of crime prevention, appropriate punishment, rehabilitation, and re-integration of offending youths back into society.

References

Ad Hoc Federal-Provincial-Territorial Working Group Reviewing Spousal Abuse Policies and Legislation. 2003. *Spousal Abuse Policies and Legislation: Final Report*. Available on-line at: http://www.justice.gc.ca/en/ps/fm/reports/spousal.html.

Addams, Jane. 1961. *Twenty Years at Hull House*. New York: Signet Books.

Adema, W. 1999. *Net Social Expenditure, Organization for Economic Co-operation and Development. Labour Market and Social Policy*. Occasional Papers No. 39 (August). Available on-line at: http://www.olis.oecd.org/OLIS/1999DOC.NSF.

Alberta. 1999–2000. *Annual Report*. Alberta: Children's Services.

Albrecht, Dennise, and Patrick Lapointe. 1995. "Community Health Centres in Canada: In a Land of Opportunities and Threats." Paper presented to the International Conference on Community Health Centres, December 3–6.

Alexander, Lincoln. 2001. Speech to the Canadian Race Relations Foundation's Award of Excellence Symposium, Vancouver. March 2. Available on-line at: http://www.crr.ca.

Allen, Richard. 1971. *The Social Passion: Religion and Social Reform in Canada, 1914–1928*. Toronto: University of Toronto Press.

Angus, Douglas E., and Pran Manga. 1990. *Co-op/Consumer Sponsored Health Care Delivery Effectiveness*. Ottawa: Canadian Co-operative Association.

Appleby, G. and Anastas, J. 1998. *Not Just a Passing Phase: Social Work with Gay, Lesbian and Bisexual People*. New York: Columbia University Press.

Armitage, A. 1970. *The First University Degree in Social Work*. Ottawa: Canadian Association for Education in Social Service.

Armitage, Andrew. 1993. "Family and Child Welfare in First Nation Communities." In Brian Wharf, ed., *Rethinking Child Welfare in Canada*. Toronto: McClelland and Stewart Limited.

Armstrong, Pat. 1997. "Privatized Care," in Pat Armstrong et al., eds., *Medical Alert*. Toronto: Garamond Press.

Asch, Adrienne. 1999. "Prenatal Diagnosis and Selective Abortion: A Challenge to Practice and Policy." *American Journal of Public Health*. Vol. 89, pp. 1649–1657.

Asch, Adrienne. 2001. "Disability, Bioethics, and Human Rights." In Gary L. Albrecht, Katherine D. Seelman and Michael Bury, *Handbook of Disability Studies*. Thousand Oaks, California: Sage Publications. pp. 297–326.

Assembly of First Nations. 1994. *Breaking the Silence: An Interpretive Study of Residential School Impact and Healing as Illustrated by the Stories of First Nations Individuals*. Ottawa: Assembly of First Nations.

Assembly of First Nations. 1999. *First Nations Health Priorities 2001–2002*. Ottawa: Assembly of First Nations.

Assembly of First Nations. 2000. *First Nations Health Priorities 2001–2002*. Ottawa: Assembly of First Nations.

Baird, V. 2001. *The No-Nonsense Guide to Sexual Diversity*. Toronto: Between the Lines Press.

B.C. Ministry of Community, Aboriginal and Women's Services. "A Minute of Silence." Available on-line at: http://www.mcaws.gov.bc.ca/womens_services/a-minute_20of_20silence/weq_print.htm.

Barnes, Colin. 2003. *Disability*. Cambridge, England: Polity Press, pp. 42–64.

Blyth, J.A. 1972. *The Canadian Social Inheritance*. Toronto: The Copp Clark Publishing Company.

Boldt, Menno. 1993. *Surviving as Indians: The Challenge of Self-Government*. Toronto: University of Toronto Press.

Bowe, Frank. 1978. *Handicapping America: Barriers to Disable People*. Harper and Row, New York, NY.

British Columbia Ministry for Children and Families. 1998–99. *Annual Report*.

Campaign 2000. 2001. *Child Poverty in Canada: Report Card 2000*. Toronto: Campaign 2000. Available on-line at: http://www.campaign2000.ca.

Campaign 2000. 2004. *One Million Too Many: Report on Child Poverty in Canada*. Available on-line at: http://www.campaign2000.ca/rc/.

Canadian Association of Chiefs of Police. 1996. *Hate Crimes in Canada: In Your Back Yard*. Ottawa: Canadian Association of Chiefs of Police.

Canadian Association of Elizabeth Fry Societies. 2003. *Elizabeth Fry Week – Fact Sheet*. Available on-line at: http://www.elizabethfry.ca/eweek03/factsht.htm#prison.

Canadian Association of Schools of Social Work. 2001. *In Critical Demand: Social Work in Canada, Final Report*. Ottawa. Available on-line at: http://www.socialworkincanada.org.

Canadian Association of Social Workers. 1994. *Code of Ethics*. Ottawa: CASW.

Canadian Centre for Policy Alternatives. March 2000. *CCPA Monitor*. Available on-line at: http://www.policyalternatives.ca/publications/articles/article225.html.

Canadian Centre on Substance Abuse. 1999. *Canadian Profile: Alcohol, Tobacco and Other Drugs.* Ottawa: Canadian Centre on Substance Abuse and the Centre for Addiction and Mental Health.

Canadian Health Coalition. 2000. *Health Alert: Newsletter 2000.* Ottawa. Available on-line at: http://www.healthcoalition.ca.

Canadian Health Coalition. 2001. *Home Care: What We Have and What We Need.* Prepared by Colleen Fuller. Ottawa. Available on-line at: http://www.healthcoalition.ca/factsheets/ HomeCare_May22_2001.pdf.

Canadian Home Care Association. 2002. *Portraits of Home Care: A Picture of Progress and Innovation.* Ottawa: Canadian Home Care Association.

Canadian Institute for Health Information. 1999. *National Trauma Registry 1999 Report Hospital Injury Admissions 1997/98.* Ottawa.

Canadian Medical Association. 1993. *Submission to the Royal Commission on Aboriginal Peoples.* Ottawa: Canadian Medical Association.

Canadian Psychiatric Association. 1996. *Mental Illness and Work.* Ottawa.

Canadian Race Relations Foundation. 2000. *Unequal Access: A Canadian Profile of Racial Differences in Education, Employment and Income.* Available on-line at: http://www.crr.ca/Load.do?section=26&subSection=38&id=3 21&type=2.

Carniol, B. 2000. *Case Critical: Challenging Social Services in Canada.* Toronto: Between the Lines.

Carol Thomas. 1999. "Disability and the Feminist Perspectives: The Personal and Political." In *Female Forms: Experiencing and Understanding Disability.* Buckingham: Open University Press.

Carrigan, Owen. 1998. *Juvenile Delinquency in Canada: A History.* Concord: Irwin Publishing.

Catholic Agency for Overseas Development. 2001. *Fact Sheet on Poverty.* Available on-line at: http://www.cafod.org.uk.

Center for Health Program Studies. 1998. *For Our Patients, Not for Profits: A Call to Action, Chartbook and Slideshow.* The Center for Health Program Studies, Harvard Medical School/The Cambridge Hospital.

Chappell, N. 2001. "Canadian Social Policy and Ageing." For the Canada-Japan Social Policy Research Project, Asia Pacific Foundation of Canada, Vancouver, presented in Osaka, Japan.

Chappell, R. 2001. *Social Welfare in Canadian Society,* 2nd ed. Toronto: Thomson Nelson.

Chartrand, Paul. 1991. "Terms of Division: The Problems of Outside-Naming for Aboriginal People in Canada." *Journal of Indigenous Studies.* Vol. 2, No. 2, pp. 1–22.

Child Welfare League of Canada. 1995. *The Young Offenders Act, Its Implementation and Related Services: A Child Welfare Perspective.* Ottawa: CWLC.

Child Welfare League of Canada. 2003. *A Summary of Current Issues and Trends with Recommendations for Future Research.* Child Welfare League of Canada.

Clarke, Juanne. 1990. *Health, Illness and Medicine in Canada.* Toronto: McClelland and Stewart Inc.

Coll, B.D. 1973. *Perspectives in Public Welfare: A History.* Washington: U.S. Government Printing Office.

Connel, R.W. 2003. "The Big Picture: Masculinities in Recent World History." In Jeffrey Weeks, Janet Holland and Matthew Waites, eds., *Sexualities and Society: A Reader.* Cambridge: Polity Press.

Cook, R. 1985. *The Regenerators: Social Criticism in Late Victorian English Canada.* Toronto: University of Toronto Press.

Copp, T. 1974. *The Anatomy of Poverty: The Condition of the Working Class in Montreal, 1897–1929.* Toronto: McClelland and Stewart Limited.

Cumming, M.M. 1985. *An Historical Review of Medical Insurance Legislation in Canada and the Effects of Dominant Ideology.* Unpublished Master's Thesis, Carleton University School of Social Work, Ottawa.

Dauvergne, Mia. 2003. "Family violence against seniors," *Canadian Social Trends.* Spring. Statistics Canada, Catalogue No. 11–008.

Davis, Allen F. 1967. *Spearheads for Reform: The Social Settlements and the Progressive Movement, 1890–1914.* New York: Oxford University Press.

Dominelli, L. 1988. *Anti-Racist Social Work: A Challenge for White Practitioners and Educators.* London: Macmillan Education Ltd.

Dominelli, L. 2004. *Social Work: Theory and Practice for a Changing Profession.* Cambridge: Polity Press.

Dorais, M. 2004. *Dead Boys Can't Dance: Sexual Orientation, Masculinity and Suicide.* Montreal: McGill-Queens University Press.

Elder, Glen H., Jr. and Monica Kirkpatrick Johnson. 2002. "The Life Course and Aging Challenges: Lessons and New Directions." In Richard A. Settersten, Jr., ed., *Invitation to the Life Course: Towards New Understandings of Later Life.* Amityville, NY: Baywood, pp. 49–81.

Ellison, K. 1992. Presentation to RCAP (28 October). Aboriginal Women's Council of Saskatchewan. Saskatoon, SK.

Estes, R.J. 1992. *Internationalizing Social Work Education: A Guide to Resources for a New Century.* Philadelphia: University of Pennsylvania.

Evans, Robert G. 1998. "Health Care Reform: Who's Selling the Market, and Why?" *Journal of Public Health Medicine.* Vol. 19, No.1, pp 45–49.

Eyolfson, C. 1992. Presentation to RCAP (30 October). Strong Earth Woman Lodge, Fort Alexander, Manitoba.

Fausto-Sterling, A. 2000. *Sexing the Body, Gender Politics and the Construction of Sexuality.* New York: Basic Books.

Federal, Provincial, and Territorial Advisory Committee on Population Health. 1996. *Report on the Health of Canadians.* Ottawa.

Federal, Provincial, and Territorial Advisory Committee on Population Health. 1999. *Toward a Healthy Future: Second Report on the Health of Canadians.* Ottawa. Available on-line at: http://hc-sc.gc.ca.

Federal-Provincial-Territorial Ministers Responsible for the Status of Women. 2002. *Assessing Violence Against Women: A Statistical Profile.* Ottawa: Status of Women Canada.

Feinberg, L. 1996. *Transgender Warriors: Making History from Joan of Arc to Dennis Rodman*. Boston: Beacon Press.

Ferns, H., and B. Ostry. 1976. *The Age of Mackenzie King*. Toronto: Lorimer Books.

Foucault, M. 1978. *The History of Sexuality, Volume One: An Introduction*. New York: Vintage.

Fournier, S., and E. Crey. 1998. *Stolen from Our Embrace*. Vancouver: Douglas & McIntyre Ltd.

Freiden, Lex. 1983. *Independent Living in the United States and Other Countries*. Handicaps Monthly, 54B61.

Freire, P. 1984. *Pedagogy of the Oppressed*. New York: Herder and Herder.

Friendly, M. Beach, J. and Turano M. 2002. *Early Childhood Education and Care in Canada*. Toronto: Childcare Resource and Research Unit. University of Toronto.

GATT-Fly. 1983. *Ah-Hah! A New Approach to Popular Education*. Toronto: Between the Lines.

Gibbins R., and J. Rick Ponting. 1986. "Historical Overview and Background." In J. Rick Ponting, ed., *Arduous Journey: Canadian Indians and Decolonialization*. Toronto: McClelland and Stewart.

Girard, Philip. 1987. "From Subversion to Liberation: Homosexual and the Immigration Act 1952–1977". *Canadian Journal of Law and Society* 24(2): pp. 1–27.

Goldstein, H. 1973. *Social Work Practice: A Unitary Approach*. Columbia University of South Carolina Press.

Guest, D. 1999. *The Emergence of Social Security in Canada,* 3rd ed. Vancouver: University of British Columbia Press.

Gunderson, Morley. 1998. *Women and the Canadian Labour Market: Transitions Towards the Future*. Ottawa/Toronto: Statistics Canada/ITP Nelson.

Hall, D. 1992. Ikwe Widdjiitiwin. Presentation to RCAP (23 April). Winnipeg, Manitoba.

Hanes, Roy. 1995. "Linking Mental Defect to Physical Disability: The Case of Crippled Children in Ontario, 1890–1940." *Journal of Developmental Disability* 4 (1) Nov.

Hay, D. 1997. "Campaign 2000: Child and Family Poverty in Canada." In J. Pulkingham and G. Ternowetsky, eds., *Child and Family Policies: Struggles, Strategies and Options*. Halifax: Fernwood Publishing.

Health Canada. 1997. *National Health Expenditures in Canada, 1975–1996: Fact Sheets*. Ottawa: Health Canada.

Health Canada. 1998. *HIV and AIDS in Canada: Surveillance Report to December 31, 1997*. Ottawa: Health Canada, Division of HIV/AIDS Surveillance.

Health Canada. 2001. *Hope to Cope with Alzheimer's*. Ottawa: Health Canada. Available on-line at: http://www.hc-gc.ca/english/feature/magazine/2001_01/alzheimer.htm

Health Canada. 2004. *HIV and AIDS in Canada: Surveillance Report to June 30 2004*. Ottawa: Health Canada, Division of HIV/AIDS Surveillance.

Healtada. 2000. *Canada's Health Care System*. Available at: http://www.hc-sc.gc.ca.

Henry, Frances. 1994. *The Caribbean Diaspora in Toronto: Learning to Live with Racism*. Toronto: University of Toronto Press.

Hunter, S. and J. Hicherson. 2003. *Affirmative Practice: Understanding and Working with Lesbian, Gay, Bisexual and Transgender Persons*. Washington: NASW Press.

Ife, Jim. 2004. "Human Rights Beyond the 'Three Generations.'" Presented at the Centre for Human Rights Education, Curtin University of Technology, Activating Human Rights and Diversity Conference, Byron Bay, NSW, July 2003.

Indian and Northern Affairs Canada and Tungavik. 1993. *Agreement Between the Inuit of the Nunavut Settlement Area and Her Majesty the Queen in Right of Canada*. Ottawa: Indian and Northern Affairs Canada.

Indian and Northern Affairs Canada. 2001. *Basic Departmental Data 2001*, Catalogue No. R12–7/2000E.

Institute of Indigenous Government. 1996. *The Final Report of the Royal Commission on Aboriginal People*. Hull: Canada Communications Group-Publishing.

Isajiw, Wsevolod W. 1999. *Understanding Diversity: Ethnicity and Race in the Canadian Context*. Toronto: Thompson Educational Publishing.

John Howard Society of Alberta. 1999. "The Harsh Reality of the Young Offenders Act." Alberta. Available on-line at: http://www.johnhoward.ab.ca/PUB/C9.htm.

Johnson, O. 2004. *The Sexual Spectrum: Exploring Human Diversity*. Vancouver: Raincoast Books.

Katz, Jonathan Ned. 1995. *The Invention of Heterosexuality*. New York: Penguin Group.

Kelly, Karen. 1995. "Projection of Visible Minority Groups, 1991–2016." *Canadian Social Trends*. (Summer).

Kessler, S. 1998. *Lessons from the Intersexed*. New Brunswick, NJ: Rutgers University Press.

Kiju Kawi, Shirley. 1994. *I Am First Nations*. Chester Basin: Mulda'qati Books.

Kinsman, G. 1996. *The Regulation of Desire: Homo and Hetero Sexualities*. Montreal: Black Rose Books.

Kinsman, G. 2003a. "National Security as Moral Regulation: Making the Normal" and Kinsman, G. 2003b. "Queerness is Not in Our Genes: Biological Determinism Versus Social Liberation." In Deborah Brock, ed., *Making Normal: Social Regulation in Canada*. Scarborough: Thomson Nelson Learning.

Kristen D. Tower. 1997. "Consumer-Centered Social Work Practice: Restoring Client Self-Determination." *Social Work*. Vol. 39, No. 7, March, pp. 191–197.

Land, Helen. 1995. "Feminist Clinical Social Work in the Twenty-first Century." In Nan Van Den Bergh, ed., *Feminist Practice in the 21st Century*. New York: NASW Press.

League for Human Rights of B'nai Brith. 2000. *Annual Audit of Anti-Semitic Incidents*. Downsview, Ontario: B'nai Brith Canada.

League for Human Rights of B'nai Brith. 2003. *Annual Audit of Anti-Semitic Incidents*. Downsview, Ontario: B'nai Brith Canada.

Lee, B. 1999. *Pragmatics of Community Organization*. Mississauga: Common Act Press.

Lee, K. 1999. "Measuring Poverty among Canada's Aboriginal People." *Insight*. Vol. 23, No. 2. Ottawa: Canadian Council on Social Development.

Leiby, J. 1978. *A History of Social Welfare and Social Work in the United States*. New York: Columbia University Press.

Lindsay, Colin. 1999. *A Portrait of Seniors in Canada*, 3rd ed. Ottawa: Statistics Canada.

Lindsay, Colin and Marcia Almey. 2004. *A Quarter Century of Change: Young Women in Canada in the 1970s and Today*. Status of Women Canada and Statistics Canada.

Litwak, E. 1960. "Geographic Mobility and Extended Family Cohesion." *American Sociological Review*. Vol. 25, pp. 385–394.

Livneh, Hanoch. 1984. "On the Origins of Negative Attitudes Toward People with Disabilities." *Rehabilitation Literature*. pp. 338–347.

Lyons, W. 1995. *Coping and Helping with Alzheimer's Disease*. Ottawa: National Advisory Council on Aging.

Mackelprang, Romel W. and Richard O. Salsgiver. 1999. "Models of Professional Practice" and "Guidelines for Practice for People with Disabilities." In *Disability: A Diversity Model Approach in Human Service Practice*. Pacific Grove, California: Brooks/Cole Publishing Co., pp. 228–251.

Manitoba. 1991. *Report of the Aboriginal Justice Inquiry of Manitoba, Volume I: The Justice System and Aboriginal People*. Winnipeg: Province of Manitoba.

Marshak, Laura, Milton Seligman and Fran Prezant. 1999. "Families Coping with Disability: Foundational and Conceptual Issues" and "Therapeutic Interventions for Families Coping with Disability." *Disability and the Family Life Cycle*. New York: Basic Books.

Miller, J.R. 1989. *Skyscrapers Hide the Heavens: A History of Indian-White Relations in Canada*, rev. ed. Toronto: University of Toronto Press.

Morrissette V., B. McKenzie, and L. Morrissette. 1993. "Towards an Aboriginal Model of Social Work Practice: Cultural Knowledge and Traditional Practices." *Canadian Social Work Review*. Vol. 10, No. 1 (Winter), pp. 91–108.

Moscovitch, Allan, and Andrew Webster. 1995. "Aboriginal Social Assistance Expenditures." In Susan Philips, ed., *How Ottawa Spends 1995–96: Mid-Life Crisis*. Ottawa: Carleton University Press.

Murray, C.J.L., and A.D. Lopez. 1996. *The Global Burden of Disease*. Cambridge: Harvard University Press.

NASW. 1981. *Standards for Social Work Services in Long-Term Care Facilities*. NASW Press.

National Advisory Council on Aging. 2001. "Beware of Fraud." *Expression*. Vol. 14, No. 2, Spring 2001, p. 3.

National Advisory Council on Aging. 2001. *Seniors in Canada: A Report Card*. Ottawa: National Advisory Council on Aging.

National Advisory Council on Aging. 2003. *Seniors in Canada: Interim Report Card*. Ottawa: National Advisory Council on Aging.

National Advisory Council on Aging. 2004. *Hidden Harm: The Abuse of Seniors*. Ottawa: Advisory Council on Aging.

National Clearinghouse on Family Violence. 2001. *Family Violence in Canada: Facts*. Ottawa: Health Canada.

National Council of Welfare. 1990a. *Health Care Report*. Ottawa: National Council of Welfare.

National Council of Welfare. 1990b. *Achieving Health for All*. Ottawa: National Council of Welfare.

National Council of Welfare. 1999. *Poverty Profile 1997*. Ottawa: National Council of Welfare.

National Council of Welfare. 1999. *Poverty Profile 1999*. Ottawa: National Council of Welfare.

National Population Health Survey (NPHS). 1998–99. Data analyses performed for NACA by the Canadian Council on Social Development (CCSD).

Nova Scotia Department of Community Services. 1993. *Advisory Committee Report on Children and Family Services Act*. December 9.

Nova Scotia Department of Family Services. 1990. *Children and Family Services Act*.

O'Brien, C. 1999. "Contested Territory: Sexualities and Social Work." In Adrienne Chambon, Allan Irving and Laura Epstein, eds., *Reading Foucault for Social Work*. New York: Columbia University Press.

Oliver, Michael. 1996. "The Social Model of Disability" in *Understanding Disability: From Theory to Practice*. London: St. Martin's Press.

Oliver, Michael. 1990. "Disability Definitions: The Politics of Meaning." In *The Politics of Disablement*. London, England: MacMillan Press.

Ontario Association of Children's Aid Societies. 2000. *OACAS Facts*. Available on-line at: http://www.oacas.org.

Ontario Ministry of Community and Social Services. 1999. *Annual Report*.

Ontario. 1995. *Final Report of the Commission on Systemic Racism in the Ontario Criminal Justice System*. Toronto: Queen's Printer for Ontario.

Philip, Margaret. 2001. "Children's Aid Staff Face Burnout." *The Globe and Mail*, February 20.

Picard, Andre. 2005. "Stop moaning about medicare." *Globe and Mail*, April 7.

Pitsula, James. 1979. "The Emergence of Social Work in Toronto." *Journal of Canadian Studies*. Vol. 14, No.1.

Podnieks, E., Pillemer, K., Nicholson, J.P., Shillington, T., and Frizzel, A. 1990. *National Survey on Abuse of the Elderly in Canada*. Toronto: Ryerson.

Purich, Donald. 1988. *The Métis*. Toronto: James Lorimer and Company, Publishers.

Rice, James, and Michael Prince. 2000. *Changing Politics of Canadian Social Policy*. Toronto: University of Toronto Press.

Roberts, J.V. 1995. *Disproportionate Harm: Hate Crime in Canada*. Ottawa: Department of Justice Canada.

Robinson, Paul. "Youth Court Statistics, 2002/03." *Juristat*. Vol. 24, No. 2. Catalogue No. 85–002–XPE. Ottawa: Statistics Canada.

Rodgers, K. 1994. "Wife Assault: The Findings of a National Survey." *Juristat*. Vol. 14, No. 9. Ottawa: Statistics Canada, Canadian Centre for Justice Statistics.

Rooke, Patricia, and R.L. Schnell. 1983. *Discarding the Asylum: From Child Welfare to the Welfare State in English Canada, 1800–1950*. Boston: University Press of America.

Rosario, V. (ed.) 1997. *Science and Homosexualities*. New York: Routledge.

Ross, David P., E.R. Shillington, and C. Lochhead. 1994. *The Canadian Fact Book on Poverty*. Ottawa: CCSD.

Ross, David P., Katherine Scott, and Peter Smith. 2000. *The Canadian Fact Book on Poverty*. Ottawa: CCSD.

Rostow, W.W. 1960. *The Stages of Economic Growth: A Non-Communist Manifesto*. Cambridge: Cambridge University Press.

Rothman, J. 1970. "Three Models of Community Organization Practice." In F. Cox et al., eds., *Strategies of Community Organization*. Illinois: Peacock Press, pp. 22–39.

Rounds, Kathleen, Marie Weir and Kathleen Kirk Bishop. 1994. "Practice with Culturally Diverse Families of Young Children with Disabilities." *Families in Society: The Journal of Contemporary Human Services*, pp. 3–15.

Royal Commission on Aboriginal Peoples. 1995. *Aboriginal Self-Government: Legal and Constitutional Issues*. Ottawa: Canada Communications Group Publishing.

Royal Commission on Aboriginal Peoples. 1996. *Perspectives and Realities*. Volume 4. Ottawa: Canada Communications Group Publishing.

Satzewich, V., (ed.) 1998. *Racism and Social Inequality in Canada: Concepts, Controversies and Strategies of Resistance*. Toronto: Thompson Educational Publishing.

Sauvé, Roger. 2002. *The Current State of Canadian Family Finances*. People Patterns Consulting.

Savoie, Josée. n.d. Violent Youth Crime. *Juristat*. Vol. 19, No. 13. Catalogue No. 85–002–XPE. Ottawa: Statistics Canada.

Schneider, M. 1997. *Pride and Prejudice: Working with Lesbian, Gay and Bisexual Youth*. Toronto: Central Toronto Youth Services.

Scott, Kimberly A. 1994. *Aboriginal Health and Social History: A Brief Canadian History*. Unpublished manuscript.

Shannon, Michael and Michael Kidd. 2001. "Projecting the Trend in Canadian Gender Wage Gap 2001–2031." *Canadian Public Policy*. Vol. XXVII, No. 4.

Shebib, B. 2004. Choices: Interviewing and Counselling Skills for Canadians. Toronto: Prentice Hall.

Sheppard, Bruce. 1997. *Deemed Unsuitable*. Toronto: Umbrella Press.

Siporin, M. 1975. *Introduction to Social Work Practice*. New York, N.Y.: Macmillan Publishing.

Smith, Derek G. 1993. "The Emergence of Eskimo Status: An Examination of the Eskimo Disk List System and the Social Consequences, 1925–1970." In Noel Dyck and James B. Waldram, eds., *Anthropology, Public Policy and Native Peoples in Canada*. Montreal. McGill-Queen's University Press.

Social Development Canada. 2004. *Advancing the Inclusion of Persons with Disabilities 2004*. Ottawa: Social Development Canada. Retrieved from http://www.sdc.gc.ca on Dec. 7, 2004.

Splane, Richard. 1965. "Review: The Role of Public Welfare in a Century of Social Welfare Development" (originally published in 1965). In Carl A. Meilicke and Janet A. Storch, Eds., *Perspectives on Canadian Health and Social Services Policy: History and Emerging Trends*. 1980. Ann Arbour, Michigan: Health Administration Press, pp. 38–49.

Statistics Canada. 2001. *Canadian Crime Statistics 2000*. Catalogue 85–205, Ottawa: Canadian Centre for Justice Statistics, Statistics Canada.

Statistics Canada and Canadian Institute for Health Information. 2002. "Leisure-time physical activity, by age group and sex, household population aged 12 and over, Canada 2000/01." *Health Indicators*. Available on-line at: http://www.statcan.ca/english/freepub/82–221–XIE/00502/tables/html/2165.htm.

Statistics Canada and Centre for Justice Statistics. 2000. *Incident-based Uniform Crime Reporting Survey*.

Statistics Canada. *Cansim Matrices 2198 and 2199*. Cat. No. 85–205–XIB.

Statistics Canada. 1999. *Low Income Cut-offs*. Cat. No. 13–551–X1B.

Statistics Canada. 2000. *Family Violence in Canada: A Statistical Profile*. Ottawa: Statistics Canada.

Statistics Canada. 2001. Participation and Activity Limitation Survey (PALS). Catalogue no. 89–577–XIE. Ottawa, ON.

Statistics Canada. 2004. "Hate Crime in Canada." *Juristat*. Vol. 24, No. 44.

Stebner, E. 1997. *The Women of Hull House: A Study in Spirituality, Vocation and Friendship*. New York: SUNY.

Stobert, Sussan and Cranswick, Kelly. 2003. "Looking after seniors: Who does what for whom?" *Canadian Social Trends*. Spring. Statistics Canada, Catalogue No.11–008.

Stone, D. 1984. *The Disabled State*. Temple University Press, Philadelphia, PA.

Struthers, James. 1991. "How Much is Enough? Creating a Social Minimum in Ontario, 1930–44." *The Canadian Historical Review*. Vol. 72, No. 1, p. 39.

Thompson, Neil. 1997. "Disability and Social Handicap." In *Anti-Discriminatory Practice*. London: St. Martin's Press.

Timpson, Joyce B. 1990. "Indian and Native Special Status in Ontario's Child Welfare Legislation: An Overview of the Social, Legal and Political Context." *Canadian Social Work Review*. Vol. 7, No. 1, pp. 49–68.

Tjepkema, Michael. 2004. *Alcohol and Illicit Drug Dependence*. Supplement to Health Reports. Statistics Canada.

Toseland, R., and Rivas, R. 1995. *An Introduction to Group Work Practice*, 2nd ed. Boston: Allyn & Bacon.

Townson, M. 2000. *A Report Card on Women and Poverty*. Ottawa: Canadian Centre for Policy Alternatives.

Trocmé, N. 1991. "Child Welfare Services." In Child, Youth and Family Policy Research Centre, *The State of the Child in Ontario*. Don Mills: Oxford University Press.

Trocmé, N., et al. 2001. *Canadian Incidence Study of Reported Child Abuse and Neglect: Final Report*. Ottawa, Ontario: Minister of Public Works and Government Services Canada.

Tully, P., and Mohl, C. 1995. "Older Residents of Health Care Institutions." *Health Reports*. Vol. 7, No. 3. Statistics Canada, Cat. No. 82–003, pp. 27–30.

Turner, F.J. 1999. *Social Work: A Canadian Perspective*. Scarborough: Prentice-Hall, Allyn & Bacon Canada.

UNAIDS/WHO. 1998. *Report on the Global HIV/AIDS Epidemic*. (June).

UNICEF. 1999. *Poverty across Industrialized Nations*. Innocenti Occasional Papers. Economic and Social Policy Series No. 71.

UNICEF. 2000. *Child Poverty in Rich Nations*. Innocenti Report Card. United Nations Children's Fund.

UNICEF. 2000. *The Progress of Nations 2002*. Available on-line at: http://www.unicef.org/publications/index_5628.html.

United Nations. 1993. The Standard Rules on the Equalization of Opportunities for Persons with Disabilities. Adopted by the United Nations General Assembly, forty-eighth session, resolution 48/96, annex, of 20 December.

United Nations. 1998. Report of the Committee on Economic , Social and Cultural Rights, Concluding Observations, Section 36.

Van Wormer, K., Wells, J. and Boes, Mary. 2000. *Social Work with Lesbians, Gays and Bisexuals: A Strengths Perspective*. Needham Heights: Allyn & Bacon.

Vayda, Eugene, and Raisa B. Deber. 1995. "The Canadian Health Care System: A Developmental Overview." In R.B. Blake and J. Keshen, eds., *Social Welfare Policy in Canada: Historical Readings*. Toronto: Copp Clark Ltd., pp. 311–325.

Varela, Rita A. 1983. "Changing Social Attitudes and Legislation Regarding Physically Disabled." In Crewe, Nancy M. and Zola, Irving Kenneth, *Independent Living for Physically Disabled People*. Jossey-Bass Publishers, San Francisco, CA.

Walker, J. 1997. *Race, Rights and the Law in the Supreme Court of Canada*. Kitchener: The Osgoode Society for Canadian Legal History and Wilfred Laurier University Press.

Waller, Irvin. 1989. *Current Trends in European Crime Prevention: Implications for Canada*. Ottawa: Supply and Services Canada.

Warner, Tom. 2002. *Never Going Back: A History of Queer Activism in Canada*. Toronto: University of Toronto Press.

Wendell, Susan. 1996. "The Social Construction of Disability." In *The Rejected Body: Feminist Philosophical Reflections on Disability*. New York: Routledge, pp. 35–57.

Whitton, Charlotte. 1943. *The Dawn of Ampler Life*. Toronto: Macmillan Company of Canada.

Whyte, Susan Reynolds and Benedicte Ingstad. 1995. "Disability and Culture: An Overview." In *Disability And Culture*. Berkeley, California: University of California Press, pp. 3–34.

Wilson, B., and C. Steinman. 2000. *HungerCount 2000*. Toronto: Canadian Association of Food Banks. Available on-line at: http://www.cafb-acba.ca/english/EducationandResearch-ResearchStudies.html.

Woodroofe, K. 1962. *From Charity to Social Work in England and the United States*. Toronto: University of Toronto Press.

World Commission on Environment and Development. 1987. *Our Common Future*. New York: Oxford University Press.

York, G. 1990. *The Dispossessed: Life and Death in Native Canada*. Toronto: Little, Brown & Company.

Younglai, Rachelle. "Canada's North and Health Care." CBC News Online. Available on-line at: http://www.cbc.ca/news/background/healthcare/cdn_north_healthcare.html.

Zola, Irving Kenneth. 1986. *The Independent Living Movement*. Jossey-Bass Publishers, San Francisco, CA.

Index